AF778405

Transitional Justice and Peacebuilding on the Ground

This book seeks to refine our understanding of transitional justice and peacebuilding, and long-term security and reintegration challenges after violent conflicts.

As recent events following political change during the so-called "Arab Spring" demonstrate, demands for accountability often follow or attend conflict and political transition. While traditionally much literature and many practitioners highlighted tensions between peacebuilding and justice, recent research and practice demonstrate a turn away from the supposed "peace vs justice" dilemma.

This volume examines the complex relationship between peacebuilding and transitional justice through the lenses of the increased emphasis on victim-centered approaches to justice and the widespread practices of disarmament, demobilization, and reintegration (DDR) of ex-combatants. While recent volumes have sought to address either DDR or victim-centered approaches to justice, none has sought to make connections between the two, much less to place them in the larger context of the increasing linkages between transitional justice and peacebuilding.

This book will be of great interest to students of transitional justice, peacebuilding, human rights, war and conflict studies, security studies, and IR.

Chandra Lekha Sriram is Professor in Law at the School of African and Oriental Studies (SOAS), University of London, UK.

Jemima García-Godos is Associate Professor, Department of Sociology and Human Geography, University of Oslo, Norway.

Johanna Herman is a Research Fellow, Centre on Human Rights in Conflict (CHRC), University of East London, UK.

Olga Martin-Ortega is a Senior Research Fellow, Centre on Human Rights in Conflict, University of East London, UK.

Law, Conflict and International Relations

Series Editors: Chandra Lekha Sriram, SOAS, Julie Mertus, American University, Karin Aggestam, University of Lund and Lorraine Elliott, Australian National University

This series will bring together cutting-edge, interdisciplinary scholarship on law, conflict, and international politics, encompassing the fields of international criminal law, international human rights law and international humanitarian law, and law relating to the use of force; conflict prevention and resolution, peacemaking, and peacebuilding; and resort to the use of force.

International Law, Politics and Inhumane Weapons
The effectiveness of global landmine regimes
Alan Bryden

Transitional Justice and Peacebuilding on the Ground
Victims and ex-combatants
Edited by Chandra Lekha Sriram, Jemima García-Godos, Johanna Herman and Olga Martin-Ortega

Transitional Justice and Peacebuilding on the Ground

Victims and ex-combatants

Edited by
Chandra Lekha Sriram, Jemima García-Godos, Johanna Herman and Olga Martin-Ortega

Routledge
Taylor & Francis Group
LONDON AND NEW YORK

First published 2013
by Routledge
2 Park Square, Milton Park, Abingdon, Oxon, OX14 4RN

Simultaneously published in the USA and Canada
by Routledge
711 Third Avenue, New York, NY 10017

Routledge is an imprint of the Taylor & Francis Group, an informa business

© 2013 selection and editorial material, Chandra Lekha Sriram, Jemima García-Godos, Johanna Herman and Olga Martin-Ortega; individual chapters, the contributors

The right of the editors to be identified as the authors of the editorial material, and of the authors for their individual chapters, has been asserted in accordance with sections 77 and 78 of the Copyright, Designs and Patents Act 1988.

All rights reserved. No part of this book may be reprinted or reproduced or utilised in any form or by any electronic, mechanical, or other means, now known or hereafter invented, including photocopying and recording, or in any information storage or retrieval system, without permission in writing from the publishers.

Trademark notice: Product or corporate names may be trademarks or registered trademarks, and are used only for identification and explanation without intent to infringe.

British Library Cataloguing in Publication Data
A catalogue record for this book is available from the British Library

Library of Congress Cataloging in Publication Data
Sriram, Chandra Lekha, 1971-
Transitional justice and peacebuilding on the ground : victims and ex-combatants / edited by Chandra Lekha Sriram, Jemima García-Godos, Johanna Herman and Olga Martin-Ortega.
p. cm. – (Law, conflict and international relations)
Includes bibliographical references and index.
1. Transitional justice. 2. Peace-building. 3. War victims – Legal status, laws, etc. 4. Veterans – Legal status, laws, etc. I. Title.
K5250.S65 2013
341.5'23 – dc23
2012016306

ISBN: 978-0-415-63759-6 (hbk)
ISBN: 978-0-203-08435-9 (ebk)

Typeset in Baskerville
by Taylor & Francis Books

MIX
Paper from responsible sources
FSC® C004839

Printed and bound in Great Britain by
TJ International Ltd, Padstow, Cornwall

"Is the pursuit of justice a necessary route to lasting peace in post-conflict settings? Do peace-building efforts routinely undermine durable justice? The editors explode this false dichotomy in their exciting new volume. Drawing on recent experiences from Colombia and Sierra Leone to Lebanon and Uganda they consider the trade-offs routinely confronted by traumatised societies at war's end. They show how activities often cast as oppositional, in particular restorative justice versus disarmament, demobilization and reintegration, are more closely aligned than assumed."

– *Dr. Robert Muggah, Small Arms Survey, Geneva, Switzerland*

"Through nuanced case studies guided by a fresh analytical framework, the book manages to convey both the local complexity faced by countries undergoing transition, as well as the common challenges and opportunities. It asks practical questions and provides much food for reflection for both academics and practitioners."

– *Hugo van der Merwe, Centre for the Study of Violence and Reconciliation (CSVR), Johannesburg, South Africa*

Contents

Contributors

Stephen Brown is Associate Professor of Political Science at the University of Ottawa, Canada. His main research interests are foreign aid, democratization, political violence, peacebuilding, and transitional justice, especially in relation to sub-Saharan Africa. He has published widely on various aspects of Kenyan politics. He maintains a website at <http://aix1.uottawa.ca/~brown>.

Par Engstrom (BA UCL, MSc London, DPhil Oxford) is Lecturer in Human Rights at the Human Rights Consortium, School of Advanced Study, University of London, UK. He is also co-chair of the London Transitional Justice Network. His current research interests focus on regional human rights institutions with a particular reference to the Inter-American human rights system, transitional justice, and the international relations of the Americas.

Jemima García-Godos (Dr.Polit. Human Geography, University of Oslo, Norway) is currently a researcher at the Norwegian Centre for Human Rights, University of Oslo and the Chr. Michelsen Institute, Norway. Her research on transitional justice focuses on victim reparations and Latin America. She has published in the *Journal of Latin American Studies*, *International Journal of Transitional Justice* and *Nordic Journal of Human Rights*.

Johanna Herman is Research Fellow at the Centre of Human Rights in Conflict at the University of East London, UK. Her research includes transitional justice, peacebuilding, human rights and the participation of victims at the Extraordinary Chambers in the Courts of Cambodia. She received her MA in International Affairs from Columbia University's (NY) School of International and Public Affairs.

Olga Martin-Ortega is Senior Research Fellow at the Centre on Human Rights in Conflict, University of East London, UK. Her research focuses on the peacebuilding, transitional justice and human rights responsibilities of multinational corporations. She is the author of *Empresas Multinacionales y Derechos Humanos en Derecho Internacional* (2008).

Rosemary Nagy is Associate Professor in Gender Equality and Social Justice at Nipissing University in North Bay, Canada. Her research in transitional justice examines the interactions between local and global processes and norms, including in South Africa, Rwanda, Uganda, and Canada. She is co-editor (with Melissa Williams and Jon Elster) of the forthcoming *Transitional Justice* volume of the Nomos Yearbook of the American Society for Political and Legal Philosophy.

Joanna R. Quinn is Associate Professor of Political Science, Director of the Centre for Transitional Justice and Post-Conflict Reconstruction, and Director of The Africa Institute at The University of Western Ontario, Canada. Her current research considers the utility of customary practices of justice in the acknowledgement of past crimes.

Rosalind Raddatz is a Trudeau Scholar completing her doctorate at the University of Ottawa, Canada. Her dissertation examines the relative influence of power and resource sharing, civil society, international intervention, and mediation in Sierra Leone and Liberia's negotiated peace agreements. Other research interests include mass violence/genocide, peacebuilding, institutional accountability, transitional justice, and post-conflict gender issues, primarily in sub-Saharan Africa.

Dustin Sharp is an Assistant Professor at the Kroc School of Peace Studies at the University of San Diego, CA. A graduate of Harvard Law School (MA), he formerly served as a researcher at Human Rights Watch, covering Francophone West Africa. His academic work focuses on the role of law in post-conflict reconstruction.

Chandra Lekha Sriram is Professor of Law at the University of London, School of Oriental and African Studies, UK. She has written extensively on conflict prevention, transitional justice, international criminal accountability, and peacemaking and peacebuilding. She is the author most recently of *Peace as Governance: Power-Sharing, Armed Groups, and Contemporary Peace Negotiations* (Palgrave, 2008).

Lars Waldorf is Senior Lecturer in International Human Rights Law at the Centre for Applied Human Rights, University of York, UK. He has co-edited three books: *Remaking Rwanda: State Building and Human Rights after Mass Violence* (University of Wisconsin Press, 2011); *Localizing Transitional Justice: Interventions and Priorities after Mass Violence* (Stanford University Press, CA, 2010) and *Disarming the Past: Transitional Justice and Ex-Combatants* (SSRC, 2009).

Acknowledgements

This book emerges from a project funded by the United States Institute of Peace (USIP), entitled "Transitional justice as peacebuilding?" (Grant 002–9F), a joint project involving the four co-editors Chandra Lekha Sriram (principal investigator), Jemima García-Godos (co-investigator), Johanna Herman and Olga Martin-Ortega (researchers). We were interested in exploring the potential role and limitations of transitional justice as an element of peacebuilding, and the present volume is the result of this joint intellectual effort.

The concept idea for the project was developed at the Norwegian Centre for Human Rights, University of Oslo in Norway, and the Centre on Human Rights in Conflict at the University of East London, United Kingdom. We thank both institutions for their support during the initial phases. Jemima García-Godos's research on Colombia, which is the basis of her chapter in this volume, was made possible with support from a post-doctoral research grant from the Research Council of Norway. Chandra Lekha Sriram's research in Lebanon, Olga Martin-Ortega's research in Bosnia, and Johanna Herman's research in Cambodia, which formed the foundation of their chapters in this volume, were supported as part of a larger EU Framework VII Grant, "A just and durable peace by piece," led by the University of Lund, Norway (no. 217488) (<www.justpeace.se>). Johanna Herman's research was also supported by the University of East London Promising Researcher grant. Olga Martin-Ortega also acknowledges the support of the British Academy Grant (SG100735), "The role of hybrid courts in the institutional and substantive development of international criminal justice," in the writing of her chapter. We would like to thank USIP for the research grant that allowed new field research to be undertaken in three sites (Colombia, Sierra Leone, and Liberia) and the organization of an authors' meeting in May 2011. We are grateful to our referees, Professors Michael Doyle and Simon Chesterman, for their support, and to the anonymous referees at USIP.

David Backer, our Program Officer at USIP, provided valuable feedback to our project. At the authors' meeting, we benefited greatly from thoughtful comments provided by Janet Adama Mohammed and Elizabeth Drew of Conciliation Resources. Stephen Brown offered exceptional editorial advice on the "Introduction." Several of the papers also benefited from useful comments at the International

Studies Association annual conference in New Orleans in 2010 and the European Consortium for Political Research annual conference in Reykjavik, Iceland, in 2011. We also offer our sincere thanks to all of our interviewees and those who supported our individual field research.

Finally, we would like to offer our sincere gratitude to our editor Andrew Humphrys for his continuing support.

Abbreviations

CSO	civil society organization
DDR	disarmament, demobilization, and reintegration of ex-combatants
DDRR	disarmament, demobilization, rehabilitation, and reintegration of ex-combatants
DPA	Department of Political Affairs
DPKO	Department of Peacekeeping Operations
ECCC	Extraordinary Chambers in the Courts of Cambodia
GOU	Government of Uganda
ICC	International Criminal Court
ICTR	International Criminal Tribunal for Rwanda
ICTY	International Criminal Tribunal for the Former Yugoslavia
IDDRS	Integrated Disarmament, Demobilization and Reintegration Standards
IDP	internally displaced person
IHL	international humanitarian law
IHRL	international human rights law
IMF	International Monetary Fund
INGO	international non-governmental organization
NATO	North Atlantic Treaty Organization
NGO	non-governmental organization
OHCHR	Office of the High Commissioner for Human Rights
OHR	Office of the High Representative
OTP	Office of the Prosecutor
PB	peacebuilding
PBC	United Nations Peacebuilding Commission
PBF	Peacebuilding Fund
PBSO	Peacebuilding Support Office
RPF	Rwandan Patriotic Front
RtoP	Responsibility to Protect
SCSL	Special Court of Sierra Leone
SSR	security sector reform
STL	Special Tribunal for Lebanon
TJ	transitional justice

TRC	Truth and Reconciliation Commission
UN	United Nations
UNDP	United Nations Development Programme
UNHCR	United Nations High Commissioner for Refugees
UNSC	United Nations Security Council
WCC	War Crimes Chambers of the State Court of Bosnia and Herzegovina

1 Introduction

Jemima García-Godos and Chandra Lekha Sriram

Introduction and rationale

Traditionally, peacebuilding and transitional justice literatures and practice either have not engaged one another or have been in tension, or even opposition. This is in part because long-standing "peace versus justice" debates posit that transitional justice and peacebuilding are necessarily in tension: that states emerging from violent conflict would have to choose to pursue peace *or* justice, but not both. This putative dilemma has never been, in fact, the reality, and a notable number of peace processes and subsequent peacebuilding activities have included measures of transitional justice, if not always criminal accountability. Thus we ask: Can transitional justice be not a challenge to, but an instrument of, peacebuilding? A range of contemporary post-conflict processes suggest different ways in which transitional justice mechanisms may contribute as an impetus for peacemaking and as a facilitator of peace implementation.

In this book, we seek to distill the findings of a range of studies designed for this purpose, examining the interaction between two specific aspects of transitional justice and peacebuilding: the promotion of victim-centered approaches to justice and short-term disarmament, demobilization, and reintegration (DDR) of ex-combatant processes, and longer-term security challenges and social return and reintegration of ex-combatants. We focus on these specific aspects here, as they are often in tension with one another and increasingly involve programming that deals with overlapping activities and actors, without significant reflection or planning. The individual chapters address a number of recurring themes, including development and post-conflict priorities, decisions on timing and sequencing, and choices about whether to integrate DDR processes (or at least reintegration) more tightly with justice processes. The conclusion explores the findings of the volume in more detail and seeks to tease out policy implications. The aim of this introductory chapter is thus to set up the conceptual framework guiding our academic inquiry. We hope not only to contribute to the academic scholarship on transitional justice and peacebuilding, but also to inform practitioners seeking to refine their own work in this area.

Transitional justice and peacebuilding: ongoing debates

Much ink has been spilled on the purposes and content of both transitional justice and peacebuilding, and both concepts continue to evolve. Here, we do not take a stand on narrow vs broad conceptions of each, on critiques of practices such as "liberal peacebuilding," or on calls for greater emphasis on development in transitional justice. Nor do we engage in far wider debates in the related and extraordinarily diverse field of peace and conflict studies. Rather, we briefly outline what the theory and practice of transitional justice and peacebuilding generally entail, and how they interact.

Transitional justice

Transitional justice is a broad set of practices that emerged from efforts by countries in transition from authoritarianism and conflict to address past abuse. Today, these practices are carried out by a mixture of local actors, national governments, the UN and other international organizations, bilateral donors, and national and international non-governmental organizations (NGOs).[1] According to a 2004 UN report on transitional justice and rule of law, it:

> comprises the full range of processes and mechanisms associated with a society's attempts to come to terms with a legacy of large-scale past abuses, in order to ensure accountability, serve justice and achieve reconciliation. These may include both judicial and non-judicial mechanisms, with differing levels of international involvement (and none at all) and individual prosecutions, reparations, truth-seeking, institutional reform, vetting and dismissals, or a combination thereof.[2]

We focus on a specific subset of mechanisms which are often expected to address the needs and demands of victims, specifically prosecutions, reparations, commissions of inquiry, and traditional justice processes.

As we shall see, in many countries more than one mechanism is deployed, although often not in a coordinated way.[3] Increasingly, transitional justice processes are initiated alongside peacekeeping and peacebuilding operations, working in parallel to, and sometimes in tension with, a range of peacebuilding activities, including disarmament, demobilization, and reintegration of ex-combatants.[4] However, although they often operate simultaneously, transitional justice practices have a complex and contested relationship to peacemaking and peacebuilding.

Peacebuilding

Peacebuilding activities may be defined in a range of ways.[5] For the purposes of this volume, we rely on the approach of the UN system to peacebuilding, first defined in 1994 in *An Agenda for Peace* as the provision of assistance for institutional reforms in support of democratization, to reform security forces and rebuild and reform state institutions. These build on, and often emerge from, peacekeeping operations, which received increasingly wide mandates from the UN Security Council during the 1990s, to address not just immediate security needs but also the original causes of conflict and build a durable peace.[6] These expanded peacekeeping missions begat peacebuilding as a multidimensional, longer-term political endeavor. Yet the record of peacebuilding activities to date has been mixed.[7] As part of a series of efforts to improve peacebuilding activities, in 2005 the UN General Assembly established the Peacebuilding Commission.[8] Sierra Leone, one of the countries examined in this volume, was one of the first countries to host an integrated peacebuilding mission supported by the commission. While peacebuilding activities have expanded, and increasingly overlapped with transitional justice activities, scholars and practitioners have continued to debate the appropriate relationship between each, in particular questioning whether accountability and transitional justice processes might interfere with peacemaking and peacebuilding.

Does transitional justice impede peace?

Although transitional justice measures often operate on the same territory, they are not necessarily complementary to peacebuilding missions, and much of the early literature on peace and justice suggested that the former would impede the latter.[9] Transitional justice can in fact interact in positive or negative ways with efforts to create and sustain peace in the wake of violent conflict or repression.

Advocates of transitional justice generally, and particularly of criminal accountability, claim that it promotes peace and may deter future abuses.[10] Some also claim that dealing with the past is essential to longer-term peacebuilding and to stop cycles of violence and prevent revenge and retaliation.[11] A few further state that the failure to pursue accountability will undermine the rule of law and the legitimacy of the post-transition government.[12] Finally, many advocates of accountability argue—and this is critical for the current inquiry—that it is needed to address the demands and needs of victims.[13]

On the other hand, peacebuilders are often concerned that transitional justice processes might disrupt fragile peace agreements. They are particularly concerned that parties to peace agreements, former combatants who are frequently responsible for abuses, might abandon peace processes and become spoilers, should they become targets of transitional justice.[14] For this reason, many peace agreements have included amnesties, though developing international norms reject blanket amnesties for serious international crimes, and United Nations mediators are not permitted to support their inclusion in peace deals.[15] Still, power-sharing deals often insulate parties to conflict from accountability without the use of amnesties.[16] Further, DDR processes often include former combatants in new or reformed security forces, in tension with demands for accountability or vetting and exclusion from roles in government of those who have abused human rights.[17]

Thus, while transitional justice processes continue to pose challenges to peacebuilding, and there is as yet insufficient empirical evidence to demonstrate that it can play a positive role in peacebuilding, further research is critical to learn whether, and if so how, this might be. This is the case, not least because practitioners operate with the belief or hope that rule of law and transitional justice efforts do support peacebuilding through statebuilding, enhancing the legitimacy of key actors and institutions.[18] The issue is thus not *whether* accountability is possible in processes of peacemaking and peacebuilding, but whether and, if so, *how* greater integration between the two might be achieved. In short, we ask: What are the necessary conditions and the major obstacles to coordination between accountability and peacebuilding processes, or even to the integration of accountability into peacebuilding processes? In this book, researchers investigate ways in which victim-centered approaches to transitional justice interact with peacebuilding, and specifically with DDR processes that seek to ensure the reincorporation into society of former combatants, many of whom may also have perpetrated serious human rights abuses. In order to understand the interplay between these two aspects of transitional justice and peacebuilding, we turn to victim-centered justice and DDR in turn.

Victim-centered justice

Developments in transitional justice have shown that justice is not only about retribution and perpetrators, but also about truth, reparations, the victims of past abuse, and the concerns of affected communities and the wider society. In the past two decades, the needs of victims of human rights violations and the promotion and protection of victims' rights have gained increasing international attention, in the fields of both international practice and academic inquiry.[19] While victims' rights are usually associated with reparations, the term also involves several other aspects of victims' needs, such as retributive justice and the right to truth. Related terms, such as "victim-centered" approaches or "victim-oriented" perspectives, are increasingly found in the transitional justice literature, unfortunately with various degrees of reflection upon what actually constitutes victims' rights. In this book we use the term, "victim-centered justice," in an attempt to highlight the encompassing dimension of victims' rights with regard to different aspects of transitional justice.

What are victims' rights?

Victims' rights have emerged as a body of norms within the fields of international human rights law, international criminal law, and international humanitarian law, determining the treatment and entitlements that victims of human rights violations ought to have with regard to remedy and reparation. Two critical parallel processes or "tracks" have directly contributed to this development: (i) the UN's work on the *Basic Principles and Guidelines on the Right to Remedy and Reparation*;[20] and (ii) the International Criminal Court's (ICC) focus on victims.[21]

The United Nations General Assembly approved the *Basic Principles on the Right to Remedy and Reparation* in December 2005, after about 16 years in the drafting process. According to Shelton, the principles refer to three categories of obligations and rights.[22] First, general obligations emanating from international human rights law (IHRL) and international humanitarian law (IHL) to ensure and protect victims' right to access to justice and to provide substantive remedies. Second, the obligation to investigate and prosecute violations to IHL and IHRL that constitute international crimes. And third, rights of access to justice, the right to substantive reparations, and the right to access to information (read "truth") in the event of gross violations of IHL and IHRL. Common to all three categories is the right to access to justice, while the right to substantive remedies is common to the first and third categories.

In its Preamble, the *Basic Principles* document not only identifies the legal sources from which the principles derive, but also announces the international community's adoption of a "victim-oriented perspective" based on human solidarity and respect for the international legal principles of accountability, justice, and the rule of law. On these legal and moral grounds, the *Basic Principles* basically bring together existing standards of IHRL and IHL regarding victims of human rights violations and violations of IHL to establish a more comprehensive and detailed set of rights to which all victims are entitled. The *Basic Principles* establish what is to be understood as victims' rights: access to justice, reparations, and truth. Each element is addressed by the *Basic Principles*, although the section on reparations is developed in most detail. They list specific forms of reparation, including compensation, restitution, rehabilitation, satisfaction, and guarantee of non-repetition. The latter two also include elements referring to the right to truth and access to information, as well as institutional and legal reform to guarantee non-repetition of abuses.

The *Basic Principles* make explicit reference to the ICC Statute and the ICC's requirements concerning the treatment of victims of core international crimes, specifically the establishment of various forms of reparation, the creation in the ICC Statute of a trust fund for victims, and the protection and participation of victims during court proceedings. Indeed, the ICC's Statute and Rules of Procedure and Evidence both establish a series of rights for victims of crimes that fall under its jurisdiction.[23] One innovation in the Statute is the provision for the participation of victims during court proceedings and the possibility to present their views and observations before the court. Regarding reparations, the court has the power to order individuals to pay reparation to other individuals, and it has the option of granting individual or collective reparation. Reparations may include restitution, indemnification, and rehabilitation, and the court may order these to be paid through the Victims' Fund. The ICC has two special units to ensure victims' participation. While the Victims' Participation and Reparation Section provides public information on reparation proceedings and applications, the Office of Public Counsel for Victims provides legal support and assistance to the legal representatives of victims and to victims.

Restorative justice

In addition to the inclusion of victim participation in the Statute, the inclusion of a reparations regime demonstrates the introduction of "reparative justice thinking" into international criminal procedures.[24] There are nonetheless concerns about the ability of international tribunals such as the ICC to actually ensure the effective participation of victims and the protection of victims' rights.[25] We turn now to several elements of victim-centered approaches to justice, beginning with restorative justice.

Restorative justice is commonly associated with victims' rights and victim-oriented perspectives, as it acknowledges the suffering and needs of victims and attempts to restore the damage done. It assumes that physical, psychological, and social damage must be acknowledged and addressed in order to heal and reconcile. In order to understand the role and influence of restorative justice in present-day processes of transitional justice and peacebuilding, it may be useful to address the origins of restorative justice, which lie outside transitional justice practice.

The principles of restorative justice developed in modern Western societies in the late 1970s as an alternative to retributive justice, expressing a deep dissatisfaction with traditional criminal justice systems.[26] Restorative justice emphasizes the need to understand crime or harm done in terms of the social actors involved or affected: offenders/victimizers, victims, and communities. In order to restore the damage done, the interests and needs of all three should be addressed. Contact between offenders and victims is considered a necessary step to seek understanding and reconciliation between otherwise opposing parties.[27] These principles are at the basis of various mechanisms of conflict mediation and conflict resolution now well established in Western societies.[28] Similar but distinct mechanisms have also developed in countries in the South, often based on or incorporating elements from customary law or traditional practices of conflict resolution, as we will see below.

The introduction of restorative justice principles to the practice of transitional justice is perhaps not a surprising development, and potentially may support wider goals for sustainable peace. While restorative justice generally emphasizes the needs of victims, programmers have also been concerned with taking a restorative approach to the reintegration of offenders into society. Offenders are expected to take responsibility for the harm done, and the community to provide for the protection and support of victims, as well as the effective reintegration of offenders.[29] Restorative principles have been incorporated in the practices of specific transitional justice mechanisms. The participation of local communities is emphasized to secure a satisfactory reintegration of ex-combatants.

The interaction between victims and victimizers is becoming more widespread in both truth commissions and judicial processes, although with mixed results. In Rwanda, traditional local practices are put at work to settle accounts and restore social relations damaged by past atrocities, albeit not without controversy and difficulty.[30] In Colombia, interaction between victims and victimizers occurs under restrictive security measures. Direct visual contact is not allowed, but victims or their legal representatives—sitting in a separate room—can ask questions to the victimizer through a microphone, seeking information for the clarification of specific cases. The application of restorative justice principles in the realm of transitional justice must bear in mind the great differences existing between individual criminal offences (involving often a single offender and a single victim) and contexts where oppressive regimes or collective actors have committed massive human rights violations, often the result of complex situations where a number of factors, such as ethnicity, class, political allegiance, and religion, may combine to produce systems of oppression, violence, and abuse. Nonetheless, restorative processes that seek to promote reconciliation are not without risks: they have the potential to revictimize and stigmatize both victims and perpetrators. Victim-centered justice, however, builds on one of the most basic principles of restorative justice: the need to restore the dignity of victims on the victims' terms.[31] Retributive and restorative processes are ideally not in opposition or alternative to one another, but rather elements of a more coherent and sustainable approach to transitional justice and peacebuilding.[32]

While the rights formulated by the *Basic Principles* and the ICC Statute are grounded in international law, and influenced by principles of restorative justice, the practice of victims' rights is grounded in the everyday realities of victims and practitioners. As the country studies in this volume demonstrate, where transitional justice has been placed on the public agenda, so too have victims' rights. Victims' rights are often associated with the direct implementation of victim reparations programs; however, as we have seen earlier, victims' rights involve also access to justice and the right to truth. A focus on victim-centered justice can help us identify if and how specific transitional justice mechanisms incorporate a victim's perspective and take victims' needs into account. We thus examine the extent to which victims' needs, perceptions, and interests have been taken into account by policymakers in designing transitional justice mechanisms. Victim reparations programs have been a common response in the past 10–15 years, in an attempt to address the vulnerability of victims. In spite of the increased interest in victim reparations, such programs are still more the exception than the rule in transitional justice practice. Their design involves a number of political choices that governments in post-conflict or post-authoritarian contexts often find difficult or may be unable to make, due to economic or political constraints.

Why is it important to address victims' needs, beyond moral and ethical considerations? There is also a political rationale. Compared to the more visible and short-term effects and benefits of, for example, the demobilization of former combatants, the societal benefits of addressing the needs of victims are less apparent, in terms of both physical, visible effects and political impact. However, addressing victims' needs constitutes a central aspect of peacebuilding because, by so doing, governments and societies actively support ongoing processes of political transformation. Addressing the needs of victims enhances the legitimacy of political transitions in the eyes of victims. Various forms of remedy and reparations, in particular, demonstrate to victims that the state and society at large recognize their suffering and vulnerability. Addressing victims' needs can help to signal their social inclusion or reinclusion into societies in which their rights have been violated. According to De Greiff, victim reparations can "be seen as a method to achieve one of the aims of a just state, namely, inclusiveness, in the sense that all citizens are equal participants in a common political project."[33]

In the wake of violent conflict, the formal justice system may be compromised or destroyed and international justice may be limited or unavailable; in such cases communities, the state, or international actors may promote the use of so-called traditional justice practices, a loose term used to refer to a range of largely non-state conflict resolution and justice mechanisms. Such practices vary widely across communities and countries, involving cleansing and forgiveness rituals, reconciliation ceremonies, or retributive measures. The use of such measures is not uncontroversial, given that traditional justice processes did not historically address serious large-scale crimes and often are modified to address them, as Nagy discusses in relation to *gacaca* in Rwanda in this volume.

Traditional justice processes may as noted involve retribution, but are also often restorative, and thus appeal to those who seek to both address the needs of victims and pursue reconciliation among victims, perpetrators, and communities.[34] In some countries, such as Sierra Leone and Uganda, they have been utilized to promote the reintegration of former combatants into communities, particularly children and adolescents. Advocates of traditional justice often argue that such processes are more local and legitimate, and better designed to promote reconciliation than retributive justice.[35]

However, as several of the chapters in this volume explore, the use of such processes to address serious international crimes has significant pitfalls, particularly when they are simultaneously expected to promote reintegration of former combatants who may be perpetrators and to promote reconciliation. In many cases, traditional processes may be used coercively or abusively, or be inconsistent with international human rights standards.[36] There is therefore reason for caution regarding their utility in supporting victims.

Peacebuilding

Peacebuilding processes involve an ever-increasing range of activities, both political and technical. These include the rebuilding of state institutions, including rule of law, DDR, and security sector reform, to list those most likely to overlap with efforts at pursuing transitional justice. It is conducted by a wide range of actors, including the UN and other multilateral organizations, bilateral donors, and national and international NGOs. Some analysts criticize contemporary peacebuilding processes, arguing that they are shaped by Western liberal paradigms emphasizing democratization and market liberalization, and that they fail to take sufficient account of local needs and demands. These criticisms are not the primary focus of the chapters here, although they have facilitated new discussions about the roles of local actors in peace and justice.[37] We focus on DDR, while recognizing that peacebuilding activities have a wider scope.

Why focus on DDR and reintegration?

This book focuses specifically on the relationship of DDR processes and the longer-term reintegration of former combatants with victim-centered justice. It does so both because DDR is essential to stabilizing security and limiting the risks of return to violence and because it has the potential to be in tension with victim-centered approaches to justice, as efforts to promote reintegration necessarily involve engagement with victims and affected communities. DDR has become a central part of international peacekeeping and peacebuilding operations, but its success depends on political will of all participants, including that of former combatants themselves.[38] While numerous DDR processes have been reasonably successful in disarmament and demobilization of former combatants, reintegration—as many chapters in this volume illustrate—is far more challenging.[39]

What does DDR entail? Most DDR programs involve combatants from state and non-state armed groups and proceed in several stages. The UN Integrated DDR Standards articulate the stages as follows.[40] First, disarmament involves the collection, documentation, and disposal of small arms, ammunition, explosives, and light and heavy weapons from former combatants and civilians. Second, demobilization entails the discharge of combatants from armed groups, often with their placement in cantonments or other assembly areas. Ex-combatants are given reinsertion support during demobilization, before reintegration. This may involve material assistance, including food and shelter, financial assistance, and technical training and education to enable them to transition to gainful employment. Finally, reintegration seeks to return ex-combatants to civilian status and provide them with viable employment. It also aims to place them in their own former communities or other communities, if return is not feasible, and thus relies on the willingness of communities to accept their return. As these are communities that may have been directly affected by abuses committed by former combatants, longer-term social reintegration often proves challenging.

The financial and material support, including training provided to former combatants at the demobilization and cantonment stage, as well as reintegration support, often in the form of cash payouts, may appear to victims or affected communities to unfairly benefit one group. Local communities may view these processes as compensation to those who perpetrated violence and abuses, while victims often receive no form of reparation, or are provided with reparations far later. Some reintegration may be eased with community consultation and incentives.

Regardless, DDR processes necessarily interact with transitional justice processes, by either comparison of benefits given to possible perpetrators and identified victims, or the participation of ex-combatants in transitional justice processes including truth commissions, trials, and traditional justice mechanisms. This is particularly the case as the practice of DDR has expanded in frequency and activities.[41] DDR has an inevitable effect on accountability for past violations because ex-combatants from one or more parties are likely to be highly resistant to any accountability processes, and thus transitional justice efforts may be blocked by amnesties already enshrined in peace agreements. Leaders and their cadres are less likely to cede arms and canton fighters if they fear arrest. At the same time, the presence of large numbers of individuals responsible for abuses either in positions of power, or simply mixing with the rest of the population, may generate resentment and the risk of backlash, and is clearly in tension with calls for more victim-centered justice.

However, just as former combatants will demand a degree of impunity, victims and human rights advocates will demand accountability. Peace agreements may provide for a range of accountability (or non-accountability) mechanisms including vetting, or exclusion from certain official functions of those responsible for serious abuses, prosecution, truth commissions, reparations, and amnesty. Given the common objections of armed factions to accountability, it may be necessary to seek a compromise that balances demands for justice with the need for DDR, bearing in mind that the UN *Draft Set of Principles to Combat Impunity* reject blanket amnesties and amnesties for the most serious international crimes (such as genocide, war crimes, and crimes against humanity) and that international prosecution of such crimes is not subject to a statute of limitations.

DDR processes also operate alongside, and sometimes seek to utilize, non-state justice and conflict resolution mechanisms, often without recognizing that they may have an impact on these processes. They also rely openly or less so on these processes to aid "reintegration," but without any critical reflection. Thus, for example, returning fighters may take part in community or "traditional" cleansing or reconciliation ceremonies, as with some former members of the Lord's Resistance Army in Northern Uganda through the Acholi *mato oput* traditional justice or conflict resolution practices. While such processes may ease reintegration, it is worth recalling not only that traditional practices are not designed to cope with ordinary killing, much less mass atrocities, but also that the practices themselves may be inconsistent with international human rights standards. There are no formal guidelines for assessing which non-state practices of justice merit support, or to determine how they should interface with DDR processes. Because traditional systems are frequently utilized in post-conflict situations, practitioners need a greater understanding of how they engage communities, victims, and perpetrators.

Cross-cutting issues

While this volume focuses on the interplay between transitional justice and peacebuilding as expressed through the promotion of victim-centered justice and DDR practices, a number of cross-cutting issues run through most of the chapters, discussions of which may contribute to broader debates in transitional justice practice.[42] The issues are: development and priorities in post-conflict societies, timing and sequencing, and coordination/integration between transitional justice and peacebuilding programming. These are raised in very different contexts across many of the chapters, although some are more salient in particular countries than others. In the conclusion, we seek to identify the key opportunities and risks related to these cross-cutting issues and to identify implications for practitioners.

Development and priorities in post-conflict societies

The challenges of socio-economic development are common to most transitional societies, creating constraints on the pursuit of transitional justice. The primary problem is funding: Amid a sea of demands for basic social services, public infrastructure, and the (re-)establishment of public institutions, how to legitimate public spending for the prosecution of perpetrators or a truth commission? However, the relation between transitional justice and development goes beyond funding, ultimately referring to what could be considered the overall objective of transitional societies—peacebuilding. Ongoing debates on the links between transitional justice and development emphasize the need for awareness of the national and local contexts where accountability mechanisms are to be applied, in order to tune transitional justice goals to national development objectives and policies.[43] Some advocates argue that sustainable peace needs to address structural inequalities, calling for the inclusion of distributive justice goals as an integral part of transitional justice.[44] While transitional justice and the goals of distributive justice can indeed be complementary, the mechanisms available to transitional justice, with their focus on addressing past violations, are generally insufficient or inappropriate to address structural inequalities.[45]

There is also an ongoing debate on the appropriateness of development projects as a form of collective reparations. For transitional societies with limited financial resources and large numbers of victims, collective reparation programs that provide goods and services—such as schools, small roads, community houses, start-up materials, and capital for community enterprises—are attractive alternatives to individual compensation schemes. However, human rights organizations in particular are keen to point out that such services are the duty of states in any situation, and do not capture or consider the restorative aspect of victim reparations. The position taken by victims' organizations on this issue varies greatly in different contexts. Empirically based research on the relation between collective reparation and development will contribute to illuminate this debate and, preferably, from a victim-centered perspective.

Timing and sequencing

There is no one-size-fits-all solution to the question of timing and sequencing, whether of peacebuilding or transitional justice generally; advocates continue to argue about the priority which one must take over the other.[46] Yet, frequently, justice measures are initiated, or reinitiated, well after the commission of the original crimes or after political transition, as has been the case in Argentina, Cambodia, Bosnia, and Lebanon.[47] In general, immediate security and stabilization concerns, and the dictates of peace agreements, mean that DDR processes specifically are initiated early, at the start of transition and peacebuilding, while victim-oriented processes, whether criminal accountability or reparations, are significantly delayed. This may appear to be preferential treatment for ex-combatants who may also be perpetrators of abuses, and be resented in particular by victims and their advocates. However, in the absence of closer integration between DDR processes and victim-oriented processes, the time lag may be inevitable.

Policy and programming: coordination or integration?

This leads to an important question: Should DDR be more tightly integrated with transitional justice processes, including victim-centered approaches to justice? As we have discussed, DDR processes not only take place earlier than transitional justice in most countries, but also tend to engage successfully in disarmament and demobilization more frequently than in reintegration. In Colombia, DDR, truth-telling, retributive justice, and reparations have been linked to a degree, albeit not by evident design. In Sierra Leone and Northern Uganda, traditional justice processes have been touted as a means to return some former combatants and engage victims and communities. Yet, as the chapters on processes in these countries illustrate, tighter integration of processes may have a down side. In this volume, Lars Waldorf suggests that it is not the solution, but rather that transitional justice processes be left to take on elements of integration, while leaving peacebuilding processes with the earlier stages of disarmament and demobilization. The balance of evidence in the chapters suggests that coordination is preferable to tighter integration, although civil society actors interviewed in Sierra Leone frequently expressed a preference for the latter.

About this book

Methodology and research approach

This volume presents a number of thematic, cross-cutting chapters, followed by a series of country case study chapters. The thematic chapters address UN peacebuilding and transitional justice policy, the specific challenges of DDR, legal pluralism and the role of traditional justice, and the challenges of pursuing justice in ongoing conflicts, where peacebuilding remains a challenge. The country chapters present structured, focused case comparisons of a range of experiences from Africa, Asia, Latin America, and Europe. With a clear recognition that each country has its own particular history, political culture, conflict dynamics, and accountability processes, we seek to identify common challenges, themes, and approaches taken by these countries.[48] The country chapter authors were instructed to engage specifically with the broader literatures on peacebuilding and transitional justice, and to consider in their own studies the role or demands of victim-centered approaches to justice, and the place—if any—of DDR processes and longer-term questions of social reintegration. The way in which the country chapters engage with the two processes varies because of the significant differences amongst country experiences. In some instances, countries engaged relatively little with transitional justice, while in others very little with peacebuilding, and in a few countries transitional justice processes were embedded in peacebuilding processes.

Structure

The volume proceeds in two parts. First, four chapters explore critical themes that arise across the volume, including the role of the UN Peacebuilding Commission, the challenges of pursuing justice in ongoing conflicts, the specific challenges of pursuing DDR and transitional justice, and legal pluralism and traditional justice. Second, eight country-specific chapters consider the challenges of peacebuilding and transitional justice, with a focus on victim-centered approaches to justice and DDR, and longer-term reintegration, allowing for comparative analysis of enduring challenges and possible opportunities.

We considered clustering chapters by the primacy of national, international, or hybrid processes and institutions. However, we found that too many countries experience several of these to draw meaningful distinctions. We also considered dividing countries between those that experienced "standard" peacebuilding or transitional justice processes vs those that did not, but found again that, while there were some evident outliers, such as Lebanon, Colombia, and Kenya, which have not truly experienced either, other countries were sufficiently atypical that the distinction did not further meaningful comparative analysis. We decided ultimately to present country experiences in loosely chronological order (based on the original transition or conflict termination point) and elaborate on lessons learned in the conclusion of this volume.

Thematic chapters

Dustin Sharp's chapter discusses ways in which the UN Peacebuilding Commission might play a stronger role in developing more integrated approaches to DDR and transitional justice. Despite the challenges, he finds that current policy approaches to reintegration need improvement. Specifically, Sharp examines how local practices in justice and reconciliation could be an area where the commission plays an important role in sharing experience, while relying and using its expertise to tailor initiatives to the particular context. He argues that, while overlap between DDR and transitional justice may well pose risks, there are also significant opportunities for better integrated policies and outcomes.

Par Engstrom's chapter discusses the challenges of pursuing transitional justice in the midst of ongoing conflict. He discusses the ways in which transitional justice is increasingly part of conflict resolution and peacebuilding efforts, and considers the role of judicial activities in the midst of conflicts. He observes several challenges. First, the increased use of judicial processes in conflict settings has helped to provoke calls for proof of the impact of transitional justice, which is often hard to produce. Second, the internationalization of transitional justice activities poses a challenge to local actors and their role in the processes. Third, narrow legal and judicial approaches to transitional justice may not be well suited to address complex social/political problems and may indeed obscure their political nature.

Lars Waldorf's chapter on integrating DDR and transitional justice focuses on reintegration as the main area of overlap between the two fields. He examines whether the best way forward should be integration or coordination, and looks at specific transitional justice mechanisms: amnesties, prosecutions, truth commissions, local justice, reparations, vetting and screening, and how they can influence the social reintegration of ex-combatants and peacebuilding. He suggests that a more realistic approach would be the coordination of disarmament and demobilization and transitional justice in the short term, with longer-term reintegration left to other actors, rather than DDR programmers.

Rosemary Nagy discusses the pluralization of transitional justice in a number of dimensions: first, the diversification of measures beyond those that are internationally driven to those that are locally driven and second, the operation of justice in locales with both formal and informal or traditional justice sectors. She discusses in particular the complex ways in which traditional justice interacts with internationally driven justice, in particular highlighting concerns that this interaction may serve negatively to consolidate state power at the expense of justice, reconciliation, and durable peace.

Country chapters

The chapter by Johanna Herman examines the relationship between peacebuilding and transitional justice in Cambodia, focusing in particular on the work of the Extraordinary Chambers in the Courts of Cambodia (ECCC). Cambodia's experience demonstrates the need for a pragmatic approach, as Herman describes it, to advance and link transitional justice and peacebuilding efforts. Such an approach can help actors to seize the few opportunities available as they come, as has been the case with victim participation in the ECCC, one of the most notable innovations of the tribunal.

The chapter by Chandra Lekha Sriram urges us to reflect on what constitutes peacemaking and peacebuilding, what constitutes a transitional justice mechanism, and what does not. Focusing on the Special Tribunal for Lebanon (STL), she considers the establishment and workings of the tribunal in a context of limited peacebuilding (if it can be so termed) and even more limited accountability, questioning the prospects of the STL to encourage domestically driven efforts to address a broad legacy of past violations during the civil war and the Syrian occupation. While she sees little relevance of the STL for wider accountability in Lebanon for significant abuses committed during and after the conflict, she suggests that there is a limited opportunity created by its presence for human rights advocates and victims' groups to make accountability part of public discourse. This is, however, limited by official policies of silence and the continued political dominance of former combatant groups.

Olga Martin-Ortega explores the interactions between peacebuilding and transitional justice in the reconstruction process in Bosnia and Herzegovina. At a superficial level at least, peacebuilding has been successful, because the country has not reverted to violence and national institutions have been consolidated. However, a closer look at the processes and mechanisms implemented in Bosnia shows a more nuanced picture. She argues that failures in managing nationalistic structures and dealing with demobilization and security have undermined the capacities of the country to promote accountability. Prosecutions have, she argues, contributed to the process of peacebuilding and helped pave the way for consolidating formal rule of law. However, justice has been mainly driven by the international community and has not promoted complementary, locally driven processes, and the reliance on retributive measures has not contributed to wider goals of social reconciliation.

Chandra Lekha Sriram's discussion of peacebuilding and transitional justice in Sierra Leone demonstrates both the challenges of attempting to link victim-centered justice to reintegration of ex-combatants and the problems of pursuing victim-centered justice well after formal DDR concludes. Victims' groups and civil society have strongly criticized the long delay between the completion of the DDR program, seen by some as unfairly privileging possible perpetrators of abuses, and the initiation of the relatively small reparations program. Yet, at the same time, efforts at social reintegration of former combatants through traditional justice measures emphasizing the engagement of victims, perpetrators, and communities have their own pitfalls.

Rosalind Raddatz discusses peacebuilding and transitional justice in Liberia. She suggests that, against great odds, important strides have been made in both, but cautions against "great expectations." She outlines the shortcomings and criticisms of the Truth and Reconciliation Commission (TRC) and the turn to viewing traditional justice mechanisms as a more viable solution than formal prosecutions. She outlines, too, the initial challenges faced by DDR, and its general failure to deal sufficiently with women and girls who had played a role in fighting forces. The extensive reparations recommended by the TRC are unlikely to ever receive significant funding. In short, the numerous demands for justice, security, and recognition espoused by Liberians seem unlikely to be addressed.

In her chapter on Uganda, Joanna Quinn brings our attention to one of the cross-cutting themes addressed in this volume, the relation between transitional justice and development. While calls for greater coordination and integration between the two fields are made by donors and international organizations, the case of Uganda demonstrates how difficult it is to develop effective and meaningful policies and programs that not only bring both fields together but, most importantly, take into consideration the distinctive requirements of the fields, particularly with regard to the needs of the people they are supposed to serve. This chapter demonstrates that, in situations with limited government capacity and will, amid many demands from national and international actors, the mixing of several related agendas can be a poor way to address the various issues.

Jemima García-Godos considers the unusual situation in Colombia, with the application of typical transitional justice measures in the context of ongoing conflict and in the absence of a transition or a peace agreement. Yet, as she notes, the Justice and Peace Law, and the attendant institutional structures that have grown up around the demobilization processes in Colombia, have linked demobilization and the rights of victims. The process has developed its own dynamic and, most importantly, it has contributed to the legitimation of victims' rights. While the process in Colombia faces many challenges and is far from a success, it illustrates one mode in which DDR and victims' rights may be linked, as well as possible limitations.

Stephen Brown assesses the contributions of the National Dialogue and Reconciliation process to transitional justice and peacebuilding in the Kenyan context—and the relationship between justice and peace. He argues that it is difficult to apply to Kenya traditional debates on the trade-offs between or complementarity of transitional justice and peacebuilding because there has not been a meaningful break with the past: suspected high-level perpetrators of large-scale violence have not been prosecuted and, in fact, several remain in positions of power. He suggests that the experience of Kenya serves as a cautionary tale for other countries, including on the dangers of adopting transitional justice mechanisms in the absence of a significant transition; the risk of entrenched elites sabotaging domestic justice mechanisms; the need for disarmament even in violent situations that fall short of civil war; and the vulnerability of victims.

The chapters in this book seek to explore relatively uncharted territory within the burgeoning fields of transitional justice and peacebuilding. Spanning decades and continents, the studies in this volume examine the interaction, and in some cases increased intertwining, of victim-centered approaches to justice and DDR programs. They document the challenges of pursuing both simultaneously, but also the pitfalls of failure to pursue justice, demobilization, and reintegration. As discussed in the conclusion, the lessons are complex, and in many cases potentially contradictory; there is much more research to be done. We hope, however, that the chapters that follow offer a contribution to important academic and policy debates.

Notes

1 Neil J. Kritz, ed., *Transitional Justice: How emerging democracies reckon with former regimes* (Washington, DC: United States Institute of Peace Press, 1995); Martha Minow, *Between Vengeance and Forgiveness: Facing history after genocide and mass violence* (Boston: Beacon Press, 1998); Chandra Lekha Sriram, *Confronting Past Human Rights Violations: Justice versus peace in times of transition* (London: Frank Cass, 2004); Sriram, *Globalizing Justice for Mass Atrocities: A revolution in accountability* (London: Routledge, 2005); Rama Mani, *Beyond Retribution: Seeking justice in the shadows of war* (Cambridge: Polity Press, 2002); and Ruti G. Teitel, *Transitional Justice* (New York: Oxford University Press, 2000).

2 Report of the UN Secretary-General, *The Rule of Law and Transitional Justice in Conflict and Post-conflict Societies* (2004) para. 8.

3 Naomi Roht-Arriaza, "The new landscape of transitional justice," in Naomi Roht-Arriaza and Javier Mariezcurrena, eds, *Transitional Justice in the Twenty-First Century* (New York: Cambridge University Press, 2006), pp. 1–16.

4 This is emphasized in the most recent UN report on the subject. See *The Rule of Law and Transitional Justice in Conflict and Post-conflict Societies*, Report of the Secretary-General, UN Doc. S/2011/634 (12 October 2011), paras 11–12.
5 Oliver Richmond, *The Transformation of Peace* (London: Palgrave, 2005); Roger MacGinty, *International Peacebuilding and Local Resistance: Hybrid forms of peace* (London: Palgrave, 2011).
6 *An Agenda for Peace, Preventive Diplomacy, Peacemaking and Peace-keeping* (17 June 1992) UN Doc. A/47/277 – S/24111, para. 61.
7 Elizabeth M. Cousens and Chetan Kumar, *Peacebuilding as Politics* (London: Lynne Rienner, 2001) p. 15; Chandra Lekha Sriram and Karin Wermester, eds, *From Promise to Practice: Strengthening UN capacities for the prevention of violent conflict* (Boulder, CO: Lynne Rienner, 2003); Stephen John Stedman, Elizabeth Cousens, and Donald Rothchild, *Ending Civil Wars: The implementation of peace agreements* (Boulder, CO: Lynne Rienner, 2001).
8 GA Res. 60/180, UN GAOR, 60th Sess. UN Doc. A/Res/60/180 (30 December 2005) and UN SC Res. 1645, UN Doc. S/Res/1645 (20 December 2005).
9 Sriram, *Confronting Past Human Rights Violations*, op. cit.; Wendy Lambourne, "Transitional justice and peacebuilding after mass violence," *International Journal of Transitional Justice*, vol. 3 (2009), pp. 28–48; Chandra Lekha Sriram, "Transitional justice and the liberal peace," in Edward Newman, Roland Paris, and Oliver P. Richmond, eds, *New Perspectives on Liberal Peacebuilding* (Tokyo: United Nations University Press, 2009), pp. 112–30; Gerhard Thallinger, "The UN Peacebuilding Commission and transitional justice," *German Law Journal*, vol. 8 (2007), pp. 681–710, <*www.germanlawjournal.com/index.php?pageID=11&artID=844*>.
10 Luc Huyse, "Amnesty, truth or prosecution," in Luc Reychler and Thania Paffenholz, eds, *Peace-building, A Field Guide* (Boulder: Lynne Rienner, 2001).
11 *The Rule of Law and Transitional Justice in Conflict and Post-conflict Societies* (2004), op. cit., para. 2.
12 Huyse, "Amnesty, truth or prosecution," op. cit., p. 325.
13 Priscilla B. Hayner, *Unspeakable Truths: Confronting state terror and atrocity* (New York: Routledge, 2001), p. 28.
14 Chandra Lekha Sriram and Youssef Mahmoud, "Bringing security back in," in Thomas Biersteker, Peter Spiro, Chandra Lekha Sriram, and Veronica Raffo, *International Law and International Relations: Bridging theory and practice* (London: Routledge, 2006), p. 223.
15 *Set of Principles to Combat Impunity* (latest update) at UN Doc. E/CN.4/2005/102/Add.1 (8 February 2005).
16 Stef Vandeginste and Chandra Lekha Sriram, "Power-sharing and transitional justice: A clash of paradigms?" *Global Governance*, vol. 17, no. 4 (October 2011); Ellen Lutz, "Transitional justice: Lessons learned and the road ahead," in Roht-Arriaza and Mariezcurrena, eds, *Transitional Justice in the Twenty-first Century*, p. 330.
17 Vandeginste and Sriram, "Power-sharing and transitional justice," op. cit.; Chandra Lekha Sriram and Johanna Herman, "DDR and transitional justice: Bridging the divide?" *Conflict, Security, and Development*, vol. 9, no. 4 (December 2009), pp. 455–74.
18 Report of the UN Secretary-General, *The Rule of Law and Transitional Justice in Conflict and Post-conflict Situations* (2011), paras 16–17.
19 Koen De Feyter *et al.*, eds, *Out of the Ashes: Reparation for victims of gross and systematic human rights violations* (Antwerp and Oxford: Intersentia, 2005); Pablo De Greiff, ed., *The Handbook of Reparations* (Cambridge: Cambridge University Press, 2006).
20 United Nations General Assembly Resolution 147, UN GA, 60th Session, UN Doc. A/RES/60/147 (2005), *Basic Principles and Guidelines on the Right to a Remedy and Reparation for Victims of Gross Violations of International Human Rights Law and Serious Violations of International Humanitarian Law.* To be referred to as the *Basic Principles*.
21 For a more detailed discussion of each of these tracks, see Jemima García-Godos, "Victim reparations in transitional justice: What is at stake and why," *Nordic Journal of*

Human Rights, vol. 26 (2008), pp. 111–30. Developments in international law supporting this trend include also jurisprudence and court sentences, such as the influential *Velásquez-Rodríguez v Honduras* decision by the Inter-American Court of Human Rights in 1988, which identified a "right to truth." See: <*www.corteidh.or.cr/docs/casos/articulos/seriec_04_ing.pdf*>.

22 Dinah Shelton, "The United Nations Draft Principles on Reparations for Human Rights Violations: Context and content," in Koen De Feyter *et al.*, eds, *Out of the Ashes*, op. cit., p. 20.

23 García-Godos, "Victim reparations," op. cit., p. 116.

24 Conor McCarthy, "Reparations under the Rome Statute of the International Criminal Court and reparative justice theory," *International Journal of Transitional Justice*, vol. 3 (2009), pp. 250–71. McCarthy uses the term "reparative justice" to refer to what is commonly known in the literature as "restorative justice." For a discussion of 'reparative justice' as a concept that emphasizes the "the principle of reparation, as the origin and core of the need for justice in times of violent and brutalizing transition," see Rama Mani, "Reparations as a component of transitional justice: Pursuing 'reparative justice' in the aftermath of violent conflict," in Koen De Feyter *et al.*, eds, *Out of the Ashes*, op. cit., pp. 53–82.

25 Elisabeth Baumgartner, "Aspects of victim participation in the proceedings of the International Criminal Court," *International Review of the Red Cross*, vol. 90 (2008), issue 870, pp. 409–40; Mina Rauschenbach and Damien Scalia, "Victims and international criminal justice: A vexed question?," *International Review of the Red Cross*, vol. 90 (2008), issue 870, pp. 441–59; Ralph Henham, "Some reflections on the role of victims in the international criminal trial process," *International Review of Victimology*, vol. 11 (2004), pp. 201–24.

26 Ronald L. Cohen, "Provocations of restorative justice," *Social Justice Research*, vol. 14 (2001), pp. 209–32.

27 Pamela Blume Leonard, "An introduction to restorative justice," in Elisabeth Beck *et al.*, eds, *Social Work and Restorative Justice. Skills for dialogue, peacemaking and reconciliation* (Oxford: Oxford University Press, 2011), pp. 31–63. For foundational works of restorative justice, see Nils Christie, "Conflict as property," *British Journal of Criminology*, vol. 17 (1977), pp. 1–15; John Braithwaite, *Crime, Shame, and Reintegration* (Cambridge: Cambridge University Press, 1989).

28 For this understanding and practice of restorative justice, see <*www.restorativejustice.org*> for the USA-based Restorative Justice Online network and <*www.euforumrj.org*> for the European Forum for Restorative Justice. Both sites last accessed 31 October 2011.

29 Blume Leonard, "Introduction to restorative justice," op. cit., p. 48.

30 See generally Scott Straus and Lars Waldorf, eds, *Remaking Rwanda: State building and human rights after mass violence* (Madison: University of Wisconsin Press, 2011).

31 This does not mean that the risk of re-traumatizing victims is not present in restorative justice, although restorative justice professionals are possibly more aware of this problem.

32 Lambourne, "Transitional justice and peacebuilding," op. cit.

33 Pablo De Greiff, "Justice and reparations," in Pablo De Greiff, ed., *The Handbook of Reparations*, pp. 451–77, 464. To be clear, we do not assume that victims' interests and demands are homogeneous.

34 Mark A. Drumbl, *Atrocity, Punishment, and International Law* (Cambridge: Cambridge University Press, 2007), pp. 94–97.

35 Stovel and Valiñas, "Restorative justice after mass violence," p. 31. Some argue that reintegrative shaming is effective in more "traditional" communitarian societies. See Braithwaite, *Crime, Shame, and Reintegration*, op. cit.

36 Chandra Lekha Sriram, "(Re)building the rule of law in Sierra Leone," in Chandra Lekha Sriram, Olga Martin-Ortega, and Johanna Herman, eds, *Peacebuilding and Rule of Law in Africa: Just peace?* (London: Routledge, 2011).

37 Roland Paris, *At War's End: Building peace after civil conflict* (Cambridge: Cambridge University Press, 2004); Richmond, *The Transformation of Peace*; Roger MacGinty, *International Peacebuilding and Local Resistance: Hybrid forms of peace* (London: Palgrave 2011).

38 *Report of the Secretary General on Disarmament, Demobilization and Reintegration*, UN Doc. A/60/75 (2 March 2006), para. 9b.
39 See, e.g., the chapters by Sriram and Waldorf in this volume.
40 *United Nations Integrated Disarmament, Demobilization, and Reintegration Standards* (2006 and as periodically expanded and updated), available at <*www.unddr.org/iddrs/framework.php*>.
41 Robert Muggah, "Innovations in disarmament, demobilization and reintegration policy and research: Reflections on the last decade," *NUPI Working Paper 774* (Norwegian Institute of International Affairs, 2010), available at *http://english.nupi.no/Publications/Working-Papers/2010/Innovations-in-disarmament-demobilization-and-reintegration-policy-and-research.*
42 We discuss these issues further in the conclusion to this volume.
43 Roger Duthie, "Toward a development-sensitive approach to transitional justice," *International Journal of Transitional Justice*, vol. 2 (2008), pp. 292–309.
44 Distributive justice is understood here as a form of justice that takes into consideration the socio-economic and political forms of distribution and access to power and resources in any given society. Roger Duthie, ibid.; Lambourne, "Transitional justice and peacebuilding," op. cit., p. 28; Chris Huggings, "Linking broad constellations of ideas: Transitional justice, land tenure reform, and development," in Pablo De Greiff and Roger Duthie, eds, *Transitional Justice and Development: Making connections* (New York: Social Science Research Council, 2009).
45 Pablo De Greiff, "Articulating the links between transitional justice and development: justice and social integration," in De Greiff and Duthie, eds, *Transitional Justice and Development*, pp. 28–75; Knut Andreas O. Lid and Jemima García-Godos, "Land restitution in the Colombian transitional justice process," *Nordic Journal of Human Rights*, vol. 28 (2010), pp. 262–88.
46 This is discussed in Quinn's chapter in this volume.
47 The situation in Lebanon is of course unique in that accountability measures do not pertain to international human rights law or international humanitarian law violations. See chapters by Sriram on Lebanon, Martin-Ortega on Bosnia, and Herman on Cambodia in this volume; see also Chandra Lekha Sriram, Olga Martin-Ortega, and Johanna Herman, "Justice delayed? Internationalised criminal tribunals and peacebuilding in Lebanon, Bosnia and Cambodia," *Conflict, Security, and Development*, vol. 11, no. 3 (July 2011), pp. 335–56.
48 Alexander L. George, "Case studies and theory development: The method of structured, focused comparison," in P. G. Lauren, ed., *Diplomacy: New approaches in history, theory, and policy* (New York: Free Press, 1979), pp. 43–68.

Part I

Critical themes

2 Bridging the gap: The United Nations Peacebuilding Commission and the challenges of integrating DDR and transitional justice

Dustin Sharp

Introduction

While peacebuilding is a long-term and complex endeavor, a cacophony of actors and agendas, together with a persistent tendency to focus on short-term needs at the expense of long-term priorities, stymie efforts to build lasting peace. Complex problems call for innovative and integrated interventions. The staples of post-conflict peacebuilding—including: disarmament, demobilization, and reintegration (DDR); security sector reform (SSR); rule-of-law initiatives; and transitional justice mechanisms ranging from prosecutions to truth commissions—are meant to serve overlapping constituencies and common purposes. In practice, however, such initiatives have often operated on separate tracks, leading to redundancy, avoidable tensions, and lost opportunities.

This chapter focuses on the special challenges that arise out of the need to develop more integrated approaches to DDR and transitional justice and argues that the United Nations Peacebuilding Commission (PBC) must play a stronger role in bringing together this and other pieces of the post-conflict puzzle. Even though the possibility of tension between transitional justice mechanisms and DDR programs cannot be eliminated, careful attention to areas of overlap should be part of innovative and integrated approaches to post-conflict peacebuilding going forward in order to advance common goals. The gains of such an approach would be modest, but worthwhile.

This chapter begins by describing the rationale behind the creation of the PBC and outlining its general functions and responsibilities. After exploring transitional justice and DDR in the UN system more generally, I discuss the particular challenges that the PBC faces in attempting to craft integrated approaches to both areas. Finally, I argue that one means of implementing a more integrated approach to DDR and transitional justice could be through the use of local justice and reconciliation practices, examining the particular example of Burundi. While such practices are no panacea, they could help to bridge an important peacebuilding gap.

Closing a "key institutional gap"[1]

The gap between the needs of communities recovering from conflict and the ability of the international community to tailor a coordinated response may contribute to a relapse into conflict. Understanding and confronting this gap has been part of a difficult learning curve that began with the rapidly escalating United Nations (UN) involvement in post-conflict efforts in the early 1990s with the end of the Cold War and accompanying deadlock in the United Nations Security Council.

As the Security Council became increasingly willing to intervene in conflict and post-conflict environments, traditional peacekeeping actions—in which neutrality, consent, and minimum force were considered paramount—soon gave way to complex and multidimensional initiatives. The broadening of mandates and obligations of peacekeeping missions to include significant elements of peacebuilding was not met with a corresponding evolution of the UN's institutional doctrine or structure, leading to redundant and *ad hoc* efforts, and a lack of coordination.[2] With involvement in increasingly complex post-conflict initiatives seemingly inevitable, the need for a better institutional framework to address past failings and future challenges became clear.

The United Nations Peacebuilding Commission (PBC) was created in 2005 and tasked with playing a critical role in bringing together pieces of the post-conflict puzzle. Together with the Human Rights Council, the PBC was one of the most significant initiatives to come out of the 2005 World Summit.[3] In recognition of the challenges facing peacebuilding activities, both the United Nations Security Council and General Assembly emphasized the need for a "coordinated, coherent, and integrated approach to post-conflict peacebuilding and reconciliation," and gave the PBC a mandate to advise on and propose integrated strategies.[4] In addition, the PBC is further tasked with helping to marshal resources for peacebuilding programs, thereby bridging the gap between short-term deficits and the need for longer-term strategies in the post-conflict context, and otherwise keeping the spotlight on challenges and country situations that could be all too easily forgotten.

"Peacebuilding" as a term was not defined as part of the PBC's creation, but has continued to develop along with emerging policy and practice. Though there are wide-ranging definitions of the word "peacebuilding," according to a working definition adopted by the UN Secretary-General's policy committee in 2007, it "involves a range of measures targeted to reduce the risk of lapsing or relapsing into conflict, to strengthen national capacities at all levels for conflict management, and to lay the foundations for sustainable peace and development."[5] The UN is quick to emphasize that such measures "should comprise a carefully prioritized, sequenced, and therefore relatively narrow set of activities aimed at achieving the above objectives."[6] Even while emphasizing the importance of "national ownership" of peacebuilding initiatives, it is hard to overlook the fact that the principles of non-interference and non-engagement with internal governance have long been abandoned in practice.[7] The shift over time from first to successive generations of peacekeeping, with increasing incorporation of elements of peacebuilding, culminating in the creation of the PBC, would appear to represent a growing institutional commitment to the idea of building "positive peace," rather than simply maintaining "negative peace," to use Galtung's famous terms.[8]

This commitment is further reflected in the other components of the UN's new "peacebuilding architecture": first, a Peacebuilding Support Office (PBSO), which acts as a secretariat to the PBC, and serves the UN Secretary-General in coordinating United Nations agencies in their peacebuilding efforts; and second, a Peacebuilding Fund (PBF), administered by the PBSO, intended to address immediate peacebuilding needs in countries emerging from conflict and thereby fill a critical gap in post-conflict project financing. Taken together, the PBC's innovative structure and mandate are designed to allow it to bring together the pillars of the United Nations—peace and security, development, and human rights—into an integrated approach to peacebuilding.

The PBC in its first five years

Since its creation, the PBC has focused its attention on relatively small countries that might otherwise be ignored by the international community. In its first year, the PBC added two countries to its agenda, Burundi and Sierra Leone, and its efforts in both countries have since been centered on the elaboration and monitoring of strategic frameworks for peacebuilding, which are intended to bring together governments and partners, both national and international, around a shared set of peacebuilding objectives.[9] In this, much of the PBC's value added has been political, in terms of its ability to convene key stakeholders, increase available donor funding, and help set a "big-picture" agenda. Subsequent countries to come to the PBC's agenda, at the individual country's request, include Guinea Bissau, the Central African Republic, and Liberia.

While the PBC's function as convening body and think tank are important, actual implementation of peacebuilding programs at the United Nations, including implementation of any of the strategic peacebuilding frameworks elaborated by the PBC, is the work of many UN agencies, ranging from the Department of Political Affairs (DPA) and the Department of Peacekeeping Operations (DPKO) to the United Nations Development Programme (UNDP), the Office of the High Commissioner for Human Rights (OHCHR), and the Office of the United Nations High Commissioner for Refugees (UNHCR). Thus, while the PBC may work to help set a larger agenda for peacebuilding in a given country, the complex work of day-to-day implementation falls to a host of institutions, greatly complicating the task of integration and coordination in practice. The coordination, direction, and implementation of the vast majority of on-the-ground peacekeeping missions across the world is done by DPKO, and many such missions have significant peacebuilding components.

It should also be noted that, although the UN is often the major player, the larger post-conflict peacebuilding picture is far more complicated than those UN agencies most directly associated with peacekeeping and peacebuilding, and includes the international financial institutions (IFIs) such as the World Bank; key bilateral donors, such as the USA, the European Union, and Japan; national governments; civil society actors; and various local constituencies. Indeed, the ultimate success of the strategic frameworks for peacebuilding elaborated by the PBC will depend on all of these actors, both inside and outside of the United Nations system. Post-conflict peacebuilding is a pot with many cooks, using many different recipes at the same time, a fact which presents significant challenges for any institution tasked with coordination and integration. The PBC's task of getting these varied actors to "work from the same page" is also complicated by the stovepiping, territorialism, and overlapping mandates of many of the agencies within the UN system, to say nothing of the bureaucracies of major institutions outside of the UN.

A UN high-level five-year review of the PBC's work has emphasized that the modalities and intensity of engagement for individual countries can and should vary based on the needs of each country, and it appears that stand-alone integrated peacebuilding strategy documents may be merged with other high-level planning documents such as the Poverty Reduction Strategy Paper (PRSP) in order to avoid imposing an unnecessarily cumbersome planning process on fragile states.[10] It remains to be seen whether this evolving practice will diminish the focus and value added of planning documents with an exclusive focus on peacebuilding priorities. The same review stressed the need for greater "national ownership" of the peacebuilding process, a leitmotif in most PBC documents. Given that the PBC is not an implementing agency, and much of its work takes place far from the countries that fall on its agenda, emphasis on the concept of national ownership seems sensible in principle, even if ill-defined in practice.

Some five years after its creation, the PBC is still working to find its optimal strategic niche and value-added role. No one can object to the need to develop better-coordinated approaches to post-conflict peacebuilding. Moving beyond that truism, however, to make integration a reality presents a number of challenges, requiring the PBC to manage historic tensions and step over discursive, disciplinary, and institutional boundaries. Coordination and integration must also be done without unnecessary duplication of efforts, no easy task given the tangle of UN and non-UN actors already focused on various aspects of post-conflict peacebuilding. Complicating the task still further, as an advisory body, the PBC has no direct authority over the actors it hopes to coordinate and inspire to more integrated action and cannot impose strategies upon a country.

Outside the UN, many of those evaluating the PBC's performance thus far have been united in the view that the PBC has allowed itself to play a rather limited role in its first five years, far short of the aspirations and visions of 2005, and that a higher degree of assertiveness and leadership is now required.[11] When it comes to bringing together relevant actors, and developing best practices and integrated strategies, all of which are listed among the "main purposes" of the PBC, one area where the PBC could potentially play a stronger role is in developing synergies between DDR and transitional justice, two different staples of post-conflict peacebuilding.[12] Both areas serve as an example of the kind of work that the PBC could be doing in helping to avoid a "separate-tracks" approach to peacebuilding going forward, and also serve to illustrate some of the challenges.

Peacebuilding, transitional justice, and the quest for accountability

While the range of factors that shape the risk of lapsing or relapsing into conflict is clearly very broad, "chief among the challenges of contemporary peacebuilding is that of addressing demands for some form of accountability, often termed transitional justice."[13] Many of the practices associated with the modern field of transitional justice have deep historical roots. Nevertheless, transitional justice as a domain of policy, practice, and academic study largely emerged in the 1990s with the wave of transitions in both Eastern Europe and Latin America that followed in the wake of the end of the Cold War.[14] It encompasses the diverse ways in which societies attempt to grapple with a legacy of widespread human rights abuses as part of their transition to more democratic and less authoritarian forms of government.[15]

Transitional justice is at once backward looking, insofar as it is preoccupied with abuses committed by various factions prior to the transition or conflict, and forward looking, insofar as it attempts to prevent recurrence and lay the groundwork for long-term positive peace. The most iconic mechanisms associated with transitional justice are undoubtedly prosecutions and truth commissions. Beyond this, however, the field has broadened a great deal since the early 1990s to include a range of mechanisms and practices designed to encourage reconciliation and differing forms of accountability. Thus, fostering community-level dialogue between former perpetrators and survivors of human rights abuses, and the construction of public memorials to preserve memory of the conflict, are today as much a part of transitional justice as a prosecution before a war crimes tribunal.

The quest for accountability within local governments and security forces is often the lynchpin of a host of reform initiatives, including SSR, and judicial and other rule-of-law reform measures. Failure to address accountability deficits within the security and judicial sector can impede progress with respect to both development and security, and ultimately weaken the legitimacy and efficacy of reform initiatives, giving the appearance of sanctioning prior conduct.[16] The principle of accountability—that a government will have to answer for its actions before its own people—underlies the most basic principles of democracy and good governance. By contrast, "[n]o sector is spared the ramifications and effects of corruption and impunity."[17] Corrupt judges, abusive police services, and impunity leading to lack of faith in the legal and security system all threaten the prospects of success for peacebuilding initiatives.[18]

Transitional justice is tightly linked with this reform of formerly abusive state institutions. Elements of SSR, including vetting and dismissals of rights abusers from their posts, judicial reform, and other rule-of-law initiatives could arguably be considered to fall under the rubric of transitional justice.[19] Many of these reforms and processes are, of course, not solely concerned with accountability, even though they ultimately remain closely linked.[20] It could be difficult, for example, to pursue broader accountability and institutional reform initiatives in the absence of stabilization, which often entails some initial success in DDR and SSR reform. By the same token, DDR and SSR cannot be successful in isolation, but are linked to numerous other elements of the recovery process, including broader governance and accountability reforms. In these ways, the accountability that can be achieved through various transitional justice mechanisms is hard to separate from broader institutional reform efforts that often form the backbone of post-conflict peacebuilding initiatives. As one example, possible overlap between transitional justice and the implementation of DDR in Burundi will be explored later on in this chapter.

Transitional justice and the United Nations system

Though many transitional justice initiatives are nationally created, owned, and implemented, the United Nations system as a whole is a deep repository of accumulated transitional justice experience. The first international war crimes tribunals since Nuremburg, the international criminal tribunals for the former Yugoslavia (ICTY) and Rwanda (ICTR), were created by the Security Council. In Sierra Leone, East Timor, Cambodia, Bosnia, and Lebanon the UN created hybrid international tribunals that were adapted to the country context. Today, the UN agency with the lead responsibility for transitional justice issues is the Office of the High Commissioner for Human Rights, having supported transitional justice programs in some 20 countries.[21] In a smaller way, the Bureau of Crisis Prevention and Recovery (BCPR) at UNDP also works to support transitional justice efforts by national actors by facilitating dialogue and developing capacities.

For its part, the PBC does not have an explicit mandate to engage in the work of transitional justice. It must be noted, however, that the mandate it has been given to "propose integrated strategies for post-conflict peacebuilding and recovery," coupled with the Security Council's emphasis on the need for "reconciliation with a view to achieving sustainable peace," is very broad.[22] As previously discussed, the current working definition of the term "peacebuilding" does little to narrow the field of possibilities.[23] What can be said, however, is that transitional justice and peacebuilding are both open-ended concepts with substantial overlap "contrived in order to achieve a common purpose": long-term positive peace.[24] Both seek to rebuild social trust and social capital, and attempt to address problems of governance, accountability, and the need for institutional reform. The PBC cannot be expected to do everything, and one must be wary of overreach. That said, given the mainstreaming of human rights throughout programming across UN agencies, and high-level UN commitments to justice and accountability, it would be a strained reading of the PBC's mandate that excluded transitional justice and other accountability-related initiatives as a subset of the PBC's peacebuilding work.

Indeed, in practice the PBC has already confirmed the relevance of transitional justice to its work in Burundi, one of the first two countries added to its agenda. In Burundi, the PBC identified a lack of accountability for human rights abuses as a cause of the conflict, and continued impunity as a factor contributing to potential relapse into conflict.[25] With this in mind, support for transitional justice initiatives forms one of the pillars in Burundi's strategic framework for peacebuilding today.[26] In practice, however, the transitional justice mechanisms themselves, which are supposed to include both a truth and reconciliation commission and a tribunal, have been greatly delayed.[27] Despite the broad public support for truth and justice mechanisms reflected in "national consultations" on transitional justice conducted in 2009, the Burundi government's commitment to implementation appears weak, possibly owing to the integration of a number of former rights abusers into government.[28] In the near term, retributive justice therefore appears unlikely, though transitional justice mechanisms built around concepts of restorative justice may prove more feasible.

Beyond the specific example of Burundi, the question remains, just what the exact modalities of the PBC's engagement with transitional justice mechanisms should be. Particularly once transitional justice mechanisms have been identified as a priority by the PBC in a given country, the question of how those mechanisms should relate to and be coordinated with other priorities is also raised. One such area is that of DDR, which, together with transitional justice, forms one of the pillars of the strategic framework in Burundi.

DDR and the United Nations system

DDR programs have become a staple of post-conflict programming, with some 34 DDR programs created between 1994 and 2005.[29] The UN defines DDR as a:

> process that contributes to security and stability in a post-conflict recovery context by removing weapons from the hands of combatants, taking the combatants out of military structures and helping them to integrate socially and economically into society by finding civilian livelihoods.[30]

In addition to the last seven peacekeeping operations established by the UN Security Council, which have all included DDR in their mandate,[31] the UN is also supporting DDR programs in many countries where there is not a UN peacekeeping operation.[32] UN support for DDR programs may come from the DPKO, the UNDP, or a combination of UN entities.

With a historic focus on short-term security and trading guns for cash, many DDR programs have been criticized for their "narrow focus and short-term approach."[33] Over time, the disappointing results of many DDR programs, particularly when it comes to the reintegration component, have led the UN to stress the need for a more "integrated" approach.[34] This culminated in the 2006 launch of the Integrated Disarmament, Demobilization and Reintegration Standards (IDDRS), a policy guide that sets forth best practices for DDR programming and the various ways in which it can and should be linked with other post-conflict programmatic areas, including transitional justice.[35]

Transitional justice and DDR; tensions and overlap

Bringing together the pillars of the United Nations—peace and security, development, and human rights—into an integrated approach to peacebuilding is a task fraught with both difficulty and exciting potential. This is especially true in programmatic areas that share some overlap and common purpose, but which also have the potential to conflict with each other. DDR and transitional justice are two such areas. In the post-conflict context, there is often a tension between the needs of stability and security on the one hand, and the exigencies of accountability and human rights on the other. When any institution, including the PBC, starts to grapple as a policy matter with the intersection of DDR and transitional justice, it too must confront these tensions.

Historically, DDR has not been thought of as an element of transitional justice, and there have been few formal institutional linkages between DDR programs and transitional justice mechanisms in practice.[36] The lack of coordination has at times resulted in lost opportunities. For example, it has been reported that some former combatants in Sierra Leone feared that the national commission for DDR was sharing their photographs with the Truth and Reconciliation Commission and the Special Court for Sierra Leone. Better coordination, in this instance, might have resulted not in sharing the type of information feared by the former combatants, but in anticipating the confusion at an earlier stage and working to quell such misinformation at multiple levels.[37] Improved coordination between DDR and transitional justice programs might result in new opportunities, an idea that will be explored in more depth later on in this chapter.

Part of the reason for the disconnect between the two realms is that transitional justice and DDR are seen to serve different constituencies for different purposes. If transitional justice practices, such as truth-telling and prosecutions, serve the needs of "victims," DDR serves those of "perpetrators."[38] If transitional justice mechanisms focus on the needs of justice, accountability, and the rule of law, DDR serves the needs of military and short-term security objectives.[39] However, despite the potential to work at cross-purposes, DDR programs and transitional justice mechanisms share a number of common goals. According to one UN definition, the aims of transitional justice include ensuring accountability, serving justice, achieving reconciliation, and the prevention of human rights violations in the future.[40] The IDDRS similarly underscore the centrality of DDR programs to preventing renewed violence, encouraging trust and confidence, and reconciliation.[41] The importance of furthering the shared aims of trust-building, prevention of renewed violence, and reconciliation, and of simultaneously managing potential tensions, underscores the need for better coordination.

In practice, the tangled web of victim and perpetrator in post-conflict societies presents enormous peacebuilding challenges. Treating these groups as discrete categories or constituencies to be served by entirely separate processes, or the "separate tracks" approach, can prove to be problematic for both DDR and transitional justice programs. For example, provision of reinsertion and reintegration benefits to former combatants, when victims in the same community receive nothing, could lead to the impression that combatants are being rewarded for bad behavior, and potentially hinder reintegration.[42] In a similar way, fear of truth-telling and other transitional justice processes on the part of ex-combatants, fueled in part by the perception that these are victim-only affairs, might hinder reconciliation. The reality is that both groups, victim and perpetrator, must live together in the aftermath of conflict. Going forward, addressing the needs of both constituencies in a more integrated way might be accomplished through better coordination between DDR and transitional justice programs.

The IDDRS is without doubt a large step forward in building on best practices from previous programs and making integrated approaches to DDR a reality. At the same time, the permissive modalities it establishes for coordination with transitional justice programs do not go far beyond the case-by-case coordination that could have existed prior to its publication. For example, the IDDRS indicates that any necessary coordination can take place between OHCHR representatives and DDR practitioners or between human rights officers who work as part of the UN peacekeeping missions and DDR initiatives. While these are important channels of communication, and the establishment of working-level "focal points" for both DDR and transitional justice within different agencies would be a positive step, it should also be noted that OHCHR may not always be involved in transitional justice processes around the world where the UN nevertheless finds itself working. Individual human rights officers working in peacekeeping missions may find themselves overwhelmed with ordinary reporting duties or lack the big picture perspective or expertise to help devise integrated strategies. Thus, the need for day-to-day coordination at an operational level is essential, but avoiding the tensions between DDR programs and transitional justice initiatives and exploiting synergies arising out of common goals will also require high-level planning and forethought. The "symphony conductor" for such a process is a role that could in many instances be played by the PBC, at least for those countries on its agenda.

The challenge of the PBC: towards a more integrated approach

Although individual states and some institutions might choose to continue to view DDR through a primarily military and security lens, the PBC does not have this luxury. The UN has wide-ranging commitments to human rights and accountability, and has mainstreamed rights-based approaches throughout much of its programming. Peacekeeping operations have been increasingly mandated to promote and protect human rights and to help build the rule of law. The IDDRS has established the importance of more integrated approaches to DDR, including better coordination with transitional justice processes. Taken together with the PBC's core mandate to develop and propose integrated solutions to peacebuilding challenges, bridging the gap between DDR and transitional justice programs is a challenge that the PBC must face.

Exactly how the PBC should go about bridging the gap between DDR programs and transitional justice initiatives remains an open question. One serious challenge for the PBC in this regard is that, because there have historically been no linkages between DDR programs and transitional justice mechanisms, there are few if any best practices when it comes to better coordination. The PBC might also face resistance in some quarters from DDR practitioners who argue that linkages with transitional justice mechanisms go beyond the scope of DDR, resulting in a danger of dilution and overreach.[43] One might argue that it is hard enough to do DDR well, even with a narrowly focused program, and anything more risks becoming unmanageable. In partial response, it might be said that DDR programs have failed in the past in part because they were narrowly construed and they too easily traded off the quantifiable "deliverables" of guns collected and cash dispersed against the more vexing and long-term goal of reintegration.[44] Given past failures in this regard, there is likely much to be gained from new approaches. It should also be noted that one further challenge to better coordination is that DDR programs are often carried out in the immediate aftermath of conflict, whereas transitional justice programs often take years to be initiated. If this lack of synchronicity occasionally alleviates some sequencing challenges, such as the likelihood of prosecutions taking place concurrently with disarmament, it may also result in missed opportunities, such as the chance to better dovetail the reconciliation components of transitional justice programs with DDR reintegration efforts, as discussed in more detail below. Finally, it is worth recalling that the PBC does not work from a blank slate, as the parameters for potential peacebuilding activities are often shaped in part by the peace settlement itself, including power-sharing arrangements and some of the modalities of DDR.

The development of more integrated approaches to the various pillars of peacebuilding, including DDR and transitional justice, would not require wholesale reinvention of the respective fields, nor is integration a fetish to be pursued for its own sake. It is not a question of turning DDR into an arm of the transitional justice enterprise, or removing the focus on accountability and victim empowerment from transitional justice. Rather, the development of more integrated approaches to DDR and transitional justice through better coordination would likely involve incremental strategic shifts in planning and praxis to better serve the common goals of both fields.

At a policy level, focus on the goals common to both DDR and transitional justice might involve several shifts. First, a more integrated approach to both fields would involve greater emphasis on the often forgotten "R" of DDR, reintegration, "the weakest link in the DDR chain."[45] There is much room for improvement over previous efforts. For example, a 2007 study on DDR in Sierra

Leone concluded that combatants who did not participate in DDR were reintegrated as successfully as those who did.[46]

One of the most powerful means of furthering reintegration of perpetrators may be through reconciliation activities at the community level. To this end, practices associated with transitional justice could be an important component.[47] For example, truth-telling on the part of both victims and perpetrators has been an important component of reconciliation efforts in many countries. While fear of prosecution is often thought to limit willingness to participate in DDR programs, in practice most prosecutions after mass atrocity are limited to the biggest perpetrators. With proper sensitization of key constituencies, this may have the effect of satisfying the victims' need to see justice done, while making it clear that most combatants were not among the worst offenders and can be reconciled to their community.[48] In sum, it can be argued that, in order to accomplish the goals of DDR, the "R" for reintegration must also stand for greater emphasis on reconciliation.[49] This in turn implies that the security and stability that come with proper reintegration of ex-combatants are not merely a function of disarmament and jobs as suggested by the current UN definition,[50] but disarmament, jobs, and reconciliation, which cannot be separated from broader justice initiatives.

In tandem with greater emphasis on reintegration and reconciliation, a more integrated approach to both fields would involve a shift from emphasis on a single constituency, be it perpetrator or victim, to one that takes greater account of multiple constituencies and blurred constituencies (such as those who have been both perpetrator and victim), and their need to live together in the aftermath of conflict. As is increasingly recognized, to achieve success, DDR programs must focus not just on combatants, but also on the communities where they are to resettle.[51] In a similar way, transitional justice initiatives such as truth commissions cannot serve all of their intended purposes without fuller participation of perpetrators.

Beyond emphasis on reintegration, a more integrated approach to both fields would likely involve greater focus on human-rights-vetting to ensure that abusive former combatants are not simply channeled into reconstituted security services, hampering reconciliation efforts and the credibility of reforms. Linking DDR to larger security sector reform in this way would serve the common goal of both DDR and transitional justice to prevent recurrence of violence. Finally, a more integrated approach to both fields would suggest a greater incorporation of human rights sensibilities into the design of DDR programs from the outset. Such a justice-oriented approach to DDR would perhaps more instinctually look to gender concerns in the DDR process, which has historically been a blind spot in many DDR programs, with many women associated with fighting forces unnecessarily excluded from the process.[52]

Given that the PCB is an intergovernmental advisory body that is in some ways remote from the realities of day-to-day operations, its ability to ensure that DDR and transitional justice initiatives are implemented in ways that exploit complementaries is in a sense compromised from the outset. At the same time, because the PBC stands to some extent "above the fray" of individual implementing agencies and institutions, it has the ability to help set a larger agenda, including by mobilizing funding, which could help to increase the chances of better coordination on the ground. At the most basic level, articulating some of the policy shifts discussed above within a country's strategic framework for peacebuilding would be one way of promoting a more integrated approach.

The mantra of "national ownership" and the turn to the local

One of the most intriguing ways in which the common goals of trust-building, prevention of renewed violence, and reconciliation might be served is by drawing upon local justice and reconciliation practices in both DDR and transitional justice programs.[53] Such approaches have featured among the package of transitional justice initiatives implemented in a number of countries, including Rwanda, East Timor, Mozambique, Sierra Leone, and Uganda, and can combine elements of punishment, truth-telling, and reparations. Though practices vary widely, there is often also an emphasis on reconciliation, ritual, and restoring harmony to the community as a whole, concepts often associated with restorative justice. In Sierra Leone, for example, the non-governmental organization Fambul Tok ("Family Talk" in the local Krio language) has taken elements of truth and reconciliation commission practice and brought them down to the village level. As part of this process, communities spend months engaged in dialogue and truth-telling sessions, bringing former perpetrators and their victims together face to face. At the conclusion of these dialogues, the village as a whole performs a reconciliation ceremony based on rituals of its own choosing. In Mozambique, many former combatants were reintegrated into their villages through the use of ceremonies that included elements of ritual cleansing, confession, and reparation.[54] In East Timor, the Community Reconciliation Process (CRP) combined elements of local justice, arbitration, and mediation in bringing perpetrators and former combatants into dialogue with their estranged communities. Sessions involved truth-telling and could result in some form of punishment such as community service and fines as a condition of reacceptance by the community.[55]

The incorporation of local practices into reintegration and reconciliation efforts presents a number of potential benefits, including familiarity and perceived legitimacy in the eyes of local populations, and relative accessibility and affordability. At the same time, drafting such highly context-specific practices into the service of national and international processes is an extremely complex issue. The incorporation of local justice practice and custom varies widely in terms of their association with the state and the formal justice system. As noted, the legitimacy of such practices and acceptance as genuine custom are often critical to their success. To take one example of the difficulties this can present, in Rwanda, the local dispute-settlement practice of *gacaca* has been modified and adopted at a national level to address justice and reconciliation issues that followed in the wake of the 1994 genocide. Many have noted that *gacaca* is now being used to address problems of a kind and scale for which it was not traditionally used, and has been implemented in ways that, while they serve the interests of the Kagame government, may not fully serve the needs of community justice and reconciliation.[56] As the Rwanda example shows, putatively local practices may therefore be subject to capture by and become subservient to larger political currents.[57]

At times, local justice practices can also be difficult to square with international principles because of low standards of evidence, insufficient protections for the rights of the accused, punishments that violate international human rights norms, or provisions that discriminate, particularly against women.[58] There is also the risk that some victims may feel, or be, compelled to publicly forgive as part of such rituals, just as some perpetrators may feel, or be, compelled to confess.[59] Given the challenges involved, integration of local practices into DDR and transitional justice programming in order to further reintegration and reconciliation in ways that maintain legitimacy in the eyes of community stakeholders, while at the same time addressing potential concerns of national and international policy makers, is a very delicate balancing act.

Local justice and reconciliation practices may therefore have much potential in both the DDR and transitional justice arenas, and especially as relates to the strongest areas of overlap between the two, reintegration and reconciliation, but they are no panacea. They need to be subjected to the same exacting scrutiny as other programmatic possibilities in the fields of DDR and transitional justice.[60] Nevertheless, as the PBC works to bring stakeholders together and propose integrated approaches to DDR and transitional justice, it can play an important role in reminding all players of the possibility of building upon such practices and sharing experiences in this regard from other countries, both positive and negative. One might note in this respect that, at the highest policy levels, the UN has already embraced the notion that "due regard must be given to indigenous and informal traditions for administering justice or settling disputes," even while it has also expressed reservations as to their compatibility with international human rights standards.[61] Although what such "due regard" might entail has not yet been fully clarified at the level of UN practice and field operations, this could be one area where the PBC might help to develop a set of best practices out of the real-world scenarios on which it is focused. Beyond these local practices, the PBC can also rely on considerable expertise in more mainstream forms of transitional justice and DDR within the UN system and channel this knowledge to propose a tightly tailored package of initiatives in the individual country context.[62] The end result could be a better reflection of each country's historical experience with the implementation of context-specific mechanisms.

To take one example of what this might look like in practice, one can look to the DDR work that has been done in Burundi. Though the demobilization process is completed, like many DDR programs around the world, socio-economic integration has been identified as a key ongoing challenge.[63] Failure with respect to reintegration is not without costs. During periods of the PBC's involvement, crime and impunity have remained high in Burundi, in part as a result of "deviant soldiers" and poorly reintegrated former combatants.[64] The PBC has recently committed itself as one of four "entry points" for its future engagement to support implementation of transitional justice initiatives in Burundi.[65] Though it may be too late to dovetail transitional justice and DDR from the outset, careful attention to the policy shifts discussed above and the potential use of local custom to foster community-level reconciliation might be one way to further reintegration of former combatants on the back end. Greater integration of the "local" with respect to both DDR and transitional justice in Burundi could also be one way of putting some weight behind the idea of "national ownership," a virtual mantra in many PBC documents.

At the same time, the case of Burundi illustrates one of the complexities inherent in the notion of "national ownership." In particular, what should the PBC do when elements of its strategic framework for peacebuilding no longer have the full support of the national government, as appears to be the case with transitional justice in Burundi, even while there is general support among ordinary citizens for truth and justice mechanisms?[66] In such instances, how does one determine whether a peacebuilding framework is "nationally owned," and what balance should the PBC attempt to strike between viable and independent transitional justice mechanisms and the likely realities of pushing a national government to implement initiatives that it may not fully support? Given the apparent lack of political will on the part of the government to engage in aspects of retributive justice at present, victim-centered restorative justice approaches, based at least in part on local ritual, may be one of the only options available in the near term. Such dilemmas offer no easy answers, and one should not be overly sanguine about the ability of any international institution, including the PBC, to thread the needle that might stitch together victim's rights, international standards, local traditions and ownership, and political reality. These challenges may ultimately demonstrate the continued relevance to peacebuilding of local NGOs and community groups and their own innovative attempts to fill the gaps arising out of the limits and politics of intergovernmental organizations and national governments.

Conclusions

The PBC was created in large part in order to develop more coherent and coordinated responses to the serious challenges faced by fragile states in the post-conflict context. Integration, of course, is not an end in and of itself, but must be pursued only insofar as common goals are advanced, tensions mitigated, and duplication of effort avoided. Transitional justice mechanisms and DDR programs share a number of common goals, including trust-building, prevention of renewed violence, and reconciliation. Even though the possibility for tensions between them cannot be entirely eliminated, careful attention to sequencing and coordination can help minimize frictions. The UN has in recent years taken strides in recognizing the need for both fields to speak to each other in ways that better serve to lay the foundations for long-term peace. While it has clearly expressed the need for greater linkages between the two, there are as yet few examples in practice to draw from, and existing mechanisms for coordination may be insufficient for many circumstances.

It is too early to say how well the PBC will fare in practice as symphony conductor in attempting to ensure that these two pillars of post-conflict peacebuilding do not operate on entirely separate tracks, as has most often been the case in the past. We do know, however, that, in assessing the PBC's work thus far, its marks for coordination in general have been rather low.[67] The PBC needs to take a stronger leadership role in crafting and proposing creative and integrated solutions to the world's most vexing peacebuilding challenges. In this, while much of the coordination and funding may be international, much of the wisdom and best practices will be local. The challenge for the PBC is to help chart a course consistent with international human rights standards, but in tune with the cultural, political, and socio-economic realities of individual post-conflict states. Going forward, developing better coordinated approaches to DDR and transitional justice that advance the common goals of each would be one way for the PBC to begin to live up to the aspirations and vision behind its creation.

Notes

1 A More Secure World: Our Shared Responsibility; Report of the Secretary General's High-level Panel on Threats, Challenges, and Change, UN Doc A/59/565 (2 December 2004), para. 261, available at <*www.un.org/secureworld*>, accessed 7 June 2011.

2 Liliana Lyra Jubilut, "Towards a New Jus Post Bellum: The United Nations Peacebuilding Commission and the Improvement of Post-Conflict Efforts and Accountability," *Minnesota Journal of International Law*, vol. 9 (2011), p. 31.

3 See generally 2005 World Summit Outcome, UN Doc. A/RES/60/L.1 (16 September 2005), available at <*www.un.org/summit2005/documents.html*>, accessed 7 June 2011.

4 United Nations General Assembly Resolution 60/180, UN Doc. A/RES/60/180 (30 December 2005); United Nations Security Council Resolution 1645, UN Doc. S/RES/1645 (20 December 2005).

5 Quoted in Erin McCandless, "Lessons from Liberia: Integrated Approaches to Peacebuilding in Transitional Settings," Occasional Paper 160, Institute for Security Studies (2008), p. 2.

6 Ibid.

7 See Chandra Lekha Sriram, Olga Martin-Ortega, and Johanna Herman, "Promoting the Rule of Law, From Liberal to Institutional Peacebuilding," in Chandra Lekha Sriram, Olga Martin-Ortega, and Johanna Herman (eds), *Peacebuilding and Rule of Law in Africa* (New York: Routledge, 2010), p. 9.

8 Johan Galtung, "Violence, Peace and Peace Research," *Journal of Peace Research*, vol. 6, no. 3 (1969), pp. 167–91.

9 Strategic Framework for Peacebuilding in Burundi, UN Doc. PBC/1/BDI/4 (22 June 2007), p. 1, available at <*www.un.org/peace/peacebuilding/pbc-countrymtgs.shtml*>, accessed 7 June 2011.

10 Review of the United Nations Peacebuilding Architecture, UN Doc. A/64/868-S/2010/393 (21 July 2010), para. 51, available at <*www.un.org/peace/peacebuilding/review.shtml*>, accessed 7 June 2011.

11 See, e.g., Rob Jenkins, "Re-engineering the UN Peacebuilding Architecture," Working Paper, The Future of the Peacebuilding Architecture Project, Center for International Policy Studies, University of Ottowa (2010).

12 United Nations Security Council Resolution 1645, op. cit., para. 2.

13 Chandra Lekha Sriram, Olga Martin-Ortega, and Johanna Herman, "Evaluating and Comparing Strategies of Peacebuilding and Transitional Justice," JAD-PbP Working Paper Series No. 1 (May 2009), p. 5.

14 See generally, Neil Kritz, *Transitional Justice: How Emerging Democracies Reckon with Former Regimes, Volume I. General Considerations* (Washington: United States Institute of Peace, 1995).

15 According to a landmark UN report, transitional justice "comprises the full range of processes and mechanisms associated with a society's attempts to come to terms with a legacy of large-scale past abuses, in order to ensure accountability, serve justice and achieve reconciliation. These may include both judicial and non-judicial mechanisms, with differing levels of international involvement (or none at all) and individual prosecutions, reparations, truth-seeking, institutional reform, vetting and dismissals, or a combination thereof." Report of the Secretary-General: The Rule of Law and Transitional Justice in Post-conflict Societies, UN Doc. S/2004/616 (23 August 2004), para. 8, available at <*www.un.org/Docs/sc/sgrep04.html*>, accessed 7 June 2011.

16 Liliana Lyra Jubilut, "Towards a New Jus Post Bellum: The United Nations Peacebuilding Commission and the Improvement of Post-Conflict Efforts and Accountability," *Minnesota Journal of International Law*, vol. 9 (2011), p. 27.

17 Adedeji Ebo, "Security Sector Reform as An Instrument of Sub-Regional Transformation in West Africa," in Alan Bryden and Heiner Hanggi (eds), *Reform and Reconstruction of the Security Sector* (Munster: DCAF/LIT Verlag, 2004), p. 19.

18 Ibid.

19 For a review of both tensions and overlap between transitional justice, SSR, and judicial reform, see Alexander Mayer-Rieckh and Roger Duthie, "Enhancing Justice and Development Through Justice-Sensitive Security Sector Reform," in Pablo de Greiff and Roger Duthie (eds), *Transitional Justice and Development: Making Connections* (New York: Social Science Research Council, 2009), p. 214; Muna B. Ndulo and Roger Duthie, "The Role of Judicial Reform in Development and Transitional Justice," in Pablo de Greiff and Roger Duthie (eds), *Transitional Justice and Development: Making Connections* (New York: Social Science Research Council, 2009), p. 250.

20 Sriram *et al.*, "Evaluating and Comparing Strategies of Peacebuilding and Transitional Justice," op. cit., p. 13.

21 Message by Ms. Navanethem Pillay at the Special Summit of the African Union (22 October 2009), available at <*www.unhchr.ch/huricane/huricane.nsf/0/110E705F1034E048C1257657005814CE?opendocument*>, accessed 7 June 2011.

22 United Nations Security Council Resolution 1645, op. cit., preamble and para. 2(b).

23 Peacebuilding "involves a range of measures targeted to reduce the risk of lapsing or relapsing into conflict, to strengthen national capacities at all levels for conflict management, and to lay the foundations for sustainable peace and development." Quoted in McCandless, "Lessons from Liberia," op. cit., p. 2.

24 Gerhard Thallinger, "The UN Peacebuilding Commission and Transitional Justice," *German Law Journal*, vol. 8, no. 7 (2007), p. 696.

25 Strategic Framework for Peacebuilding in Burundi, op. cit., paras 30–31.

26 Ibid., para. 16.

27 IRIN News, "Burundi: Delays in Justice Mechanisms 'Fuel Impunity'" (3 December 2010).

28 For a more detailed analysis of the possible reasons behind the delay, see Human Rights Watch, "Seductions of 'Sequencing'" (18 March 2011), available at <*www.hrw.org/en/news/2011/03/18/seductions-sequencing#&_;Toc288230733*>, accessed 11 July 2011.

29 Lars Waldorf, "Linking DDR and Transitional Justice," in Ana Cutter Patel, Pablo de Greiff, and Lars Waldorf (eds), *Disarming the Past, Transitional Justice and Ex-Combatants*, (New York: International Center for Transitional Justice, 2009), p. 18.

30 United Nations Department of Peacekeeping Operations (DPKO), *Integrated Disarmament, Demobilization and Reintegration Standards (IDDRS)* (New York: DPKO, 2006), sec. 1.2.

31 These are the United Nations Assistance Mission in Sierra Leone (UNAMSIL, 1999), the United Nations Mission in the Democratic Republic of Congo (MONUC, 1999), the United Nations Mission in Liberia (UNMIL, 2003), the United Nations Mission in

Côte d'Ivoire (UNOCI, 2004), the United Nations Stabilization Mission in Haiti (MINUSTAH, 2004), the United Nations Operation in Burundi (UNOB, 2004), and the United Nations Mission in the Sudan (UNMIS, 2005).

32 These include: Aceh (Indonesia), Afghanistan, the Central African Republic, Republic of Congo, Niger, Somalia, and Uganda.

33 United Nations Development Programme, *Practice Note: Disarmament, Demobilization and Reintegration of Ex-Combatants* (New York: UNDP, 2005), p. 18.

34 Disarmament, Demobilization and Reintegration: Report of the Secretary-General, UN Doc. A/60/705 (2 March 2006), p. 3.

35 United Nations Department of Peacekeeping Operations (DPKO), *Integrated Disarmament, Demobilization and Reintegration Standards (IDDRS)*, op. cit.

36 Waldorf, "Linking DDR and Transitional Justice," op. cit., p. 16.

37 The full impact of this lack of coordination is hard to evaluate. In the end, the majority of ex-combatants in Sierra Leone remained willing to participate in TRC activities despite any misgivings. It remains unclear, however, how many more might have participated if such misinformation had been corrected at an earlier stage. Lars Waldorf, "Ex-Combatants and Truth Commissions," in Ana Cutter Patel, Pablo de Greiff, and Lars Waldorf (eds), *Disarming the Past, Transitional Justice and Ex-Combatants*, (New York: International Center for Transitional Justice, 2009), p. 115.

38 The victim/perpetrator distinction can be problematic in several respects, particularly in the context of DDR, where many former combatants are both perpetrator and victim at the same time. Nevertheless, the categories are used in this chapter as they continue to have relevance to analysis of policy and programming for both DDR and transitional justice, so long as they are not understood with undue rigidity.

39 Kimberly Theidon, "Transitional Subjects: The Disarmament, Demobilization, and Reintegration of Former Combatants in Columbia," *The International Journal of Transitional Justice*, vol. 1 (2007), p. 67.

40 Report of the Secretary-General: The Rule of Law and Transitional Justice in Conflict and Post-Conflict Societies, op. cit., p. 4.

41 United Nations Department of Peacekeeping Operations (DPKO), *Integrated Disarmament, Demobilization and Reintegration Standards (IDDRS)*, op. cit., sec. 2.10.

42 The concrete impact of any such resentment on reintegration has been disputed, and may vary from country to country. For a fuller discussion, see the chapter by Waldorf in this volume.

43 Lars Waldorf, "Linking DDR and Transitional Justice," op. cit., p. 18.

44 Michael Knight and Alpaslan Ozerdem, "Guns, Camps, and Cash: Disarmament, Demobilization and Reinsertion of Former Combatants in Transitions from War to Peace," *Journal of Peace Research*, vol. 41, no. 4 (2004), p. 499.

45 Sami Faltas, "DDR without Camps: The Need for Decentralized Approaches: Topical Chapter of the Conversion Survey" (Bonn International Center for Conversion, 2005), p. 2, available at <*www.sweden.gov.se/content/1/c6/06/54/02/5d16fcf2.pdf*>, accessed 7 June 2011.

46 Macartan Humphreys and Jeremy M. Weinstein, "Demobilization and Reintegration," *Journal of Conflict Resolution*, vol. 51, no. 4 (August 2007), p. 549.

47 Stockholm Initiative on DDR (March 2006), Article 55, available at <*www.sweden.gov.se/sb/d/4890*>, accessed 7 June 2011.

48 In Sierra Leone, for example, the Special Court's outreach efforts included activities targeting ex-combatants to explain the meaning of the phrase "those who bear the greatest responsibility" for crimes within its mandate. The intent was to dispel rumors that the court intended to indict every fighter. Mohamed Gibril Sesay and Mohamed Suma, "Transitional Justice and DDR: the Case of Sierra Leone," International Center for Transitional Justice (June 2009), pp. 18–19.

49 Kimberly Theidon, "Transitional Subjects," op. cit., p. 90.

50 "Reintegration is the process by which ex-combatants ... gain sustainable employment and income. Reintegration is essentially a social and economic process with an open time-frame, primarily taking place in communities at the local level. It is part of the general development of a country ... and often necessitates long-term external assistance." DPKO, *IDDRS*, sec. 4.30.

51 Nat J. Colletta and Robert Muggah, "Context Matters: Interim Stabilization and Second Generation Approaches to Security Promotion," *Conflict, Security & Development*, vol. 9 (2009), p. 444.

52 Tsjeard Bouta, "Gender and Disarmament, Demobilization and Reintegration, Building Blocs for Dutch Policy" (The Hague: Netherlands Institute of International Relations "Clingendael," 2005), p. 8.

53 These practices are sometimes referred to as "traditional practices." Some scholars object to the use of the word "traditional" both because it can be read to suggest that practices are static, rather than dynamic, and because it can also have pejorative implications. In this chapter, I have chosen to use the word "local" to avoid these suggestions, and yet to try to distinguish these practices from those more often associated with formal, "modern," or Westernized legal systems.

54 Roger Duthie, "Local Justice and Reintegration Processes as Complements to Transitional Justice and DDR," in Ana Cutter Patel, Pablo de Greiff, and Lars Waldorf (eds), *Disarming the Past, Transitional Justice and Ex-Combatants* (New York: International Center for Transitional Justice, 2009), p. 233.

55 See generally Patrick Burgess, "A New Approach to Restorative Justice—East Timor's Community Reconciliation Process," in Naomi Roht-Arriaza and Javier Mariezcurrena (eds), *Transitional Justice in the 21st Century* (Cambridge: Cambridge University Press, 2006).

56 For example, crimes committed by the Rwandan Patriotic Front, the Tutsi-led military force that stopped the genocide, are excluded from the *gacaca* process. See Christopher Le Mon, "Rwanda's Troubled Gacaca Courts, Human Rights Brief," vol. 14, no. 2, p. 16, Winter 2007, available at <*www.wcl.american.edu/hrbrief/14/2lemon.pdf*>.

57 In this, local practices are not unlike more formal legal systems, though the checks and balances in both systems are likely to be different, and highly variable from state to state.

58 Roger Duthie, "Local Justice and Reintegration Processes as Complements to Transitional Justice and DDR," op. cit., pp. 243–45.

59 See the chapter by Nagy in this volume.

60 Johanna Herman, "Reintegration, Justice and Reconciliation in the Great Lakes Region: Lessons from the Multi-Country Demobilization and Reintegration Program" (paper prepared for the Annual Convention of the International Studies Association, San Francisco, CA (March 26–29, 2008), pp. 2–3.

61 Report of the Secretary-General: The Rule of Law and Transitional Justice in Post-conflict Societies, para. 36. Similarly, the *IDDRS* provides that "[re]integration programmes for ex-combatants should ... support the establishment of local conflict-resolution mechanisms," while also providing that "any connection to locally based processes must respect international human rights norms." DPKO, *IDDRS*, sec. 2.30 and 4.30.

62 Gerhard Thallinger, "The UN Peacebuilding Commission and Transitional Justice," p. 699.

63 Review of Progress in the Implementation of the Strategic Framework for Peacebuilding in Burundi, para. 21.

64 Ibid.

65 Report of the Peacebuilding Commission on its Fourth Session, UN Doc. A/65/701-S/2011/41 (28 January 2011), para. 34, available at <*www.un.org/peace/peace building/docsandres.shtml*>, accessed 7 June 2011.

66 Human Rights Watch, "Seductions of 'Sequencing,'" op. cit.

67 Review of the United Nations Peacebuilding Architecture, op. cit., paras 57–59.

3 Transitional justice and ongoing conflict

Par Engstrom

Introduction

The field of transitional justice (TJ) emerged out of attempts to give theoretical meaning to *ad hoc* accountability policies adopted as part of broader processes of political democratization in Latin America and Eastern Europe. From these beginnings TJ has dramatically expanded in scope and ambition. The hugely increased normative ambitions of TJ are nowhere more apparent than in practices of judicial intervention in situations of ongoing conflict. Such interventions have brought the field of TJ into much closer contact with the related, but distinct, fields of conflict resolution and peacemaking (or peacebuilding). Peacebuilders have also dramatically expanded their policy objectives beyond the cessation of armed conflict to include the establishment of a sustainable peace, the neutralization of the incentives for a return to conflict, and the realization of a variety of accountability and rule of law strategies. This chapter accounts for the expanding normative ambitions of the field of TJ and evaluates the implications for TJ of its involvement in ongoing conflicts. It also suggests some tentative ways for TJ to recast its engagement with ongoing conflicts.

The chapter is divided into three parts. The first examines the ways in which TJ is increasingly embedded in conflict resolution and peacebuilding efforts and evaluates the relatively recent trend towards judicial intervention in ongoing conflicts. It examines two main underlying trends that drive these developments: the intractability of contemporary armed conflict, and the dramatic development of the "global accountability regime" and the associated expansion of the rights of victims. It also briefly assesses the normative and operational overlaps inherent in the ambitious agenda of "liberal peacebuilding."

The second part analyzes three particularly significant aspects of judicial interventions in ongoing conflict. First, the move towards judicial interventions in ongoing conflict is anchored in a consequentialist logic that has generated increasingly strident demands for empirical evidence of TJ claims. Yet, in part because of the complex and indeterminate causal pathways of such claims, robust empirical evidence is still lacking. Second, the internationalization of transitional justice has created significant tensions between international and local agency. Yet, the problematic effects of international judicial pressures are also exacerbated by local institutional fragility and by attempts to implement TJ in highly inhospitable conditions, including in the absence of any discernible political transition. Third, the dominance of legal and judicial approaches to TJ has tended to privilege retributive forms of justice in ways that often are not conducive to conflict resolution or political and societal reconciliation. But the judicialization of TJ also runs the risk of obfuscating politics in ways that almost invariably benefit elite interests.

The final part of the chapter attempts to move beyond the current theoretical and policy impasse by outlining a proposal for a (possible) way forward that emphasizes the complexity inherent in the field of TJ. It also provides brief reflections on the contours of a prudent, incremental, and politically attuned strategy of TJ engagement with ongoing conflict.

I. The expansion of transitional justice

The trend towards judicial intervention in ongoing conflicts is relatively recent.[1] In the modern period, TJ developed as a field of theory and practice concerned with questions of truth, justice, and reconciliation in the context of political regime change: from military regimes to electoral democracy in South America; following the fall of communist regimes in Eastern Europe; and at the end of civil war in Central America. From these beginnings TJ has dramatically expanded both in terms of geographical coverage and in terms of normative ambitions. The hugely increased normative ambitions of TJ are nowhere more apparent than in practices of judicial intervention in situations of ongoing conflict. The intervention of the International Criminal Court (ICC) in Libya is but the most recent reflection of the emergence of the ICC as a key actor on the contested terrain of conflict resolution. As a result, there has been a discernible shift from the pursuit of accountability strategies after the cessation of armed hostilities on the one hand, and in the aftermath of political transitions on the other, to attempts to achieve accountability for atrocities even before a political settlement of armed conflict has been reached.

The practice of international judicial interventions in ongoing conflicts can be traced back to the beginning of the 1990s and the establishment of the International Criminal Tribunal for the former Yugoslavia (ICTY). The United Nations Security Council (UNSC) resolution that established the ICTY was adopted in the midst of ongoing conflict in Bosnia and before the start of peace negotiations at Dayton. Yet, the ICTY issued only few indictments during the armed conflict itself and cases only came to trial after the end of the war. Instead, the first significant attempt to pursue justice during ongoing conflict came with the indictment of Slobodan Milosevic during the NATO bombing of Kosovo. But, the pursuit of justice during ongoing conflict has become increasingly contentious since the adoption of the Rome Statute and the creation of the ICC. The ICC's temporal jurisdiction that limits potential prosecution to crimes committed after 1 July 2002 has pushed the Court and the ICC Prosecutor towards engaging with ongoing conflicts.[2] The increasing number of ICC indictments and investigations in recent years has led to the close involvement of international criminal justice in ongoing conflicts in Uganda, the Democratic Republic of the Congo, Sudan, Kenya, Colombia, and, most recently, Libya.

1. Contemporary conflict and transitional justice

The creation of the ICC represents a dramatic shift in the global accountability regime. While under the "Nuremberg model" the militarily victorious parties used their power to pursue justice after the cessation of conflict, under the "Rome model" interventions are undertaken by third-party judicial actors. As a consequence of this shift, judicial interventions are initiated not following military victories, but rather during ongoing conflict. Two main underlying trends underpin and drive these developments: the intractability of contemporary armed conflict; and the dramatic expansion of the international legal architecture.

Character of contemporary armed conflict

There has been a discernible shift from the industrialized total warfare of the first half of the twentieth century, to contemporary forms of low-intensity conflict in conditions of state breakdown. Interstate warfare, as part of foreign policy and with distinct lines between state, army, and society, has lost much of its institutional character. Wars have in this sense become more irregular, a trend further accentuated by the privatization of much contemporary warfare.[3] This can especially be seen in the division between civilians and soldiers. In contemporary warfare, uniforms are not always used, in part because of the increased use of irregular and paramilitary forces. Whilst most war fatalities in the early twentieth century were military personnel, at the turn of the century most war fatalities were civilian.[4]

For some, the underlying problem is the legitimacy of the state, and problematic or "weak" statehood as a legacy of the post-colonial era.[5] As long as major interstate war remains unlikely,[6] and legitimation problems of weak states continue, such conflicts are likely to persist. This is further exacerbated by the ethnic dimensions of contemporary conflicts, which have inscribed these conflicts with, as Shaw has noted, a genocidal impulse.[7] This is not to deny that identity in terms of distinguishing between "us" and "them" has always been important, especially since the advent of nationalism in the nineteenth century. Concerns surrounding identity are always present in any political community, and not only in the context of the breakdown of political legitimacy.

Nonetheless, these general patterns of contemporary conflict all have implications for attempts to resolve conflict, but also, crucially, questions of how to ensure accountability for atrocity crimes.[8] The centrality of ethnic identity and the specific organization of armed groups in conflict matter fundamentally both for the efforts to end hostilities and for accountability. In particular, the blurred lines between "war" and "peace" in much contemporary conflict have led to attempts to implement TJ policies in institutionally and politically very fragile and unstable situations, before any discernible transition (from "war" to "peace") has taken place.[9]

Development of the international legal architecture

There are two key dimensions to the development of the international legal architecture governing accountability efforts in the context of ongoing conflict. The first is related to the greatly increased normative ambitions inherent in the development of international human rights institutions in recent decades. The UN has assumed a prominent peacebuilding role, incorporating human rights protection into its operations as guiding principles. The more overtly coercive dimensions of human rights enforcement have emerged front and center in contemporary debates on the appropriate response of the international community to massive human rights violations. Movement towards politically legitimating humanitarian intervention based on collective action—including the use of force—is embodied in the principle of "Responsibility to Protect" or RtoP, and associated efforts to redefine threats to international peace and security that have pushed human rights compliance onto the agenda of the UNSC. This development reflects both the broadening of interpretations of threats to international peace and security, including mass atrocities, and the increased acceptability of the use of force for a broad range of policy objectives and associated beliefs in the utility of military power.

One remarkable feature of the normative development of international human rights in recent decades is the emergence of individual accountability as a guiding principle for TJ. This should be seen against the broader global trend, uneven as it may be, toward the criminal prosecution of those responsible for grave human rights violations. As a result, international criminal justice—with the ICC as its central institution—has emerged as a form of global governance, with specific underlying principles, values and norms, in the process reshaping human rights politics and institutions.[10] Liberal assumptions concerning the ability to individualize guilt, and the ability to deter violence absent the use of force, have become deeply embedded in the international criminal justice regime.[11]

In particular, the current development of international criminal law has tended to advance a rather narrow understanding of "accountability" that focuses on individual criminal accountability at the expense of broader alternative conceptions of accountability as conventionally enshrined in international human rights law (i.e. state, or public, accountability). Retributive approaches to justice have also gained a privileged position within the international criminal justice regime at the expense of restorative approaches, with "justice" primarily conceived of as "punishment" of transgressors. Moreover, the traditional distinctions between the different bodies of international law have become increasingly blurred, with the laws of war—regulating conduct in armed conflict—coming into a closer relationship with international human rights law on the one hand and international criminal law on the other.

Hence, overall, the expansion of the international legal architecture has created a much higher presumption against impunity and in favor of accountability than what existed one decade ago.[12] The UN Secretary-General has taken the view that UN-endorsed peace agreements can never grant amnesties for genocide, war crimes, crimes against humanity, or gross violations of human rights.[13] This presumption is also deeply embedded in the overarching objective of the Rome Statute, namely "to put an end to impunity for the perpetrators of [the most serious crimes of concern to the international community] and thus to contribute to the prevention of such crimes."[14]

The second dimension is related to the rise in "victim-centered" notions of justice. There has been a steady increase in provisions for victims' rights in recent years. This can be seen in the growth of reparations programs, in the creation of a victims' trust fund at the ICC, and in the adoption of UN guidance and principles pertaining to restorative justice.[15] The increased emphasis on victims' rights has brought criminal justice into a closer relationship with human rights in the field of TJ. The strengthening of victims' rights has also led to the incorporation of human rights into international criminal justice processes. The potential link between restorative and retributive forms of justice can most clearly be seen in the increasing trend in international criminal justice towards the recognition of the role of victims in these processes, especially in the design of reparation policies.

Clearly, expectations of victims for justice have increased, at least partly as a result of changes in international criminal law and the dramatic expansion of the TJ field. Nevertheless, giving privileged attention to victims' interests and demands also raises several complex issues. The participation of victims in TJ processes is often complicated, particularly since victims are not a homogeneous group, and the nature of abuses they have suffered may vary. In many cases, victims groups include relatives of those killed and/or disappeared, in some cases entire groups and communities of people have been victimized, and, in others, the primary group of victims are smaller groups of political activists. In some instances, individuals and groups who have suffered human rights violations may reject the term "victim" and prefer the term "survivor." There are also circumstances in which some "victims" were also "perpetrators" (e.g. child soldiers).

Yet, TJ processes are often driven by victims' groups. While victims' groups clearly have a legitimate role in shaping transitional institutions and processes that affect them directly, it is less clear to what extent their demands should be privileged when these collide with broader conceptions of the public interest, a category within which "peace," however understood, falls. Victims and affected communities may also demand types of justice and forms of punishment that may be unacceptable to those not directly affected and, in some circumstances, by external actors (such as the death penalty). The participation of victims raises therefore a host of intrinsically complex questions regarding definitions of what constitutes the "public interest," whose definition counts, and classical dilemmas in democratic theory between majoritarian interests on the one hand and individual rights and protections on the other.

2. Liberal peacebuilding and transitional justice: overlapping agendas and operational tensions

The practice of international judicial interventions in ongoing conflicts has brought the field of TJ into much closer contact with the related, but distinct, fields of conflict resolution and peacebuilding. The primary objective of peacemakers has traditionally been to secure a peace agreement that would ensure an end to the armed conflict. In recent decades, however, peacebuilders have dramatically expanded their policy objectives beyond the cessation of armed conflict to include the establishment of a sustainable peace, the neutralization of the incentives for a return to conflict, and the realization of a variety of accountability and rule of law strategies.[16] In the process, peacebuilding and human rights have also become an integral part of the agenda of the UNSC and the management of international peace and security more broadly. While traditionally based on principles of consent, neutrality and the limited use of force, the UNSC-mandated peacebuilding missions over the course of the last two decades have included election observation, provisional administration, and coercive rules of military engagement.

Hence, the expansion of both TJ and peacebuilding has created significant normative and operational overlaps between these traditionally distinct fields of theory and practice. There are indeed many shared features within the broader global context of enthusiasm for "liberal peacebuilding" that gained a certain momentum through the 1990s and into the 2000s. For some, TJ policies are closely associated with the rise of state-building.[17] For others justice plays a central role "in establishing the foundations for genuine and long-lasting peace."[18] Similarly, for former UN Secretary-General Kofi Annan, TJ and peacebuilding are based on mutually reinforcing imperatives: "Justice and peace are not contradictory forces. Rather, properly pursued, they promote and sustain one another. The question, then, can never be whether to pursue justice and accountability, but rather when and how."[19]

Yet, despite the partially overlapping development of TJ and peacebuilding, attempts to bring these fields together have generated significant tensions. Partly, this is due to the fact that not all components of liberal political practice can easily be reconciled and partly to institutional boundaries, professional trajectories, normative commitments, and policy preferences of these fields of theory and practice.[20] Demands for accountability have traditionally tended to be construed as obstacles to peace. Indeed, for the recently created UN Peacebuilding Commission (PBC), accountability is not a top priority. For the PBC, it seems, given the absence of TJ in its institutional mandate, accountability should, at best, be deferred until later in peacebuilding processes.

II. Judicial intervention in ongoing conflict

There has been a dramatic shift in the practice of TJ towards the pursuit of accountability, particularly through prosecutions, during ongoing conflict. This trend of (external) judicial interventions in the midst of conflict and the pursuit of TJ in the absence of an apparent transition can be explained by the combined effects of the developments examined in the previous section. However, from intervention in ongoing conflicts, a number of specific challenges have become particularly acute. First, international judicial interventions are underpinned and reinforced by the belief held by some proponents that the tool of indictments and the threat of prosecution can alter the prospects for achieving peace. Second, judicial interventions during conflict have exacerbated the internationalization of TJ in ways that risk undermining local accountability processes. Third, international judicial interventions have further strengthened the trend towards the increasing judicialization of TJ.

1. Rise of consequentialism and the empirical turn in transitional justice research

The shift in TJ debates over the course of the last two decades has been significant. For advocates such as Diane Orentlicher in the beginning of the 1990s the focus was on the legal status of a *duty* to prosecute.[21] Although TJ practitioners were indeed concerned with the potential impact of strategies adopted, particularly with regards to the potentially destabilizing effects of wide-ranging prosecutions on fragile transitional societies, both the policy and scholarly debate was overwhelmingly normative in character. This can be explained in large part by the fact that the TJ agenda was overwhelmingly driven by activists often with personal histories of suffering as opposed to the more professionalized cadre of actors who have subsequently been driving the policy agenda.

In recent years, however, with the practice of judicial interventions in ongoing conflicts, particularly through the ICC, combined with the rise of donors' "impact agenda," TJ advocates have increasingly justified their activities on the basis of utilitarian logics in general and the logic of deterrence in particular. Indeed, as Vinjamuri highlights, "recent arguments have emphasized the instrumental purposes of justice, essentially recasting justice as a tool of peacebuilding and encouraging proponents and critics alike to evaluate justice on the basis of its effects."[22] Hence, the decision to pursue justice during ongoing conflict has been justified primarily in terms of its capacity to alter the outcome of the conflict by enhancing the prospects for peace through judicial deterrence. For proponents, the deterrence effect of criminal punishment affects the cost-benefit calculations of potential perpetrators. Credible threats of punishment deter rights-violating behavior and encourage engagement with peace processes. Indicting abusive political leaders may also marginalize, delegitimize, and remove perpetrators and potential spoilers of peace processes.

Skeptics argue, however, that punishment for perpetrators of serious violations undermines efforts to bring violent conflict to an end and precludes the possibility of forgiveness, reconciliation, and other societal goals.[23] On this view, attempts to hold individuals to account may prevent possibilities of ending conflicts through negotiation and may provoke a backlash or intensification of political and societal divisions. The prospects of being held to account for violations leave potential spoilers with little choice than to undermine peace processes. Containing spoilers, not holding them to account, should, on this view, be the top priority of peace negotiators.

The turn towards empiricism

The shift from an emphasis on a putative duty to prosecute to a logic of consequences has shaped debates surrounding "deterrence effects" of international prosecutions in ongoing conflicts and prevention of future conflicts. Since the creation of the ICC the debate as to whether seeking justice for grave international crimes interferes with efforts to resolve armed conflict has undoubtedly intensified as the likelihood and credibility of prospects for prosecution have increased. In particular, the move towards judicial interventions in ongoing conflict, underpinned by a consequentialist logic, has led to demands for empirical support of TJ claims. However, the jury is still very much out when it comes to the empirical evidence to support claims regarding the impact of TJ (or lack thereof).[24] For example, several recent studies of the impact of TJ mechanisms on peace have failed to confirm the claim that the pursuit of international criminal justice leads to peace, or that justice initiatives are necessary for sustained peace.[25]

Undoubtedly, the causal pathways involved in these relationships are highly complex and indeterminate. Still, the lack of robust empirical evidence is clearly problematic for any claim based on the logic of consequences. By the same token, however, there is little evidence to suggest that the anticipated negative consequences of pushing for accountability actually materialize.[26] There is, in other words, not sufficient empirical evidence to conclude either that accountability strategies increase the risk of conflict or that they increase the likelihood of continuing conflict.

For some proponents of accountability, the absence of robust empirical evidence that shows that pushing for accountability undermines peace and leads to a deterioration of the human rights situation provides solid grounds for continued advocacy.[27] Yet, the absence of robust empirical evidence has forced accountability advocates towards the adoption of "faith-based" policy prescriptions.[28] After all, most TJ advocates often have neither the resources nor the training to conduct impact assessment exercises or to collect the necessary empirical evidence. There are also inherent difficulties in identifying and evaluating the many complex variables shaping TJ outcomes and a relative absence of long-term data sets that would allow for comparisons over time. But it is also the case, as argued by Clark and Palmer, that "[t]he field of TJ balances uneasily between analysis and advocacy … [and the] fervent certainty of much human rights advocacy has often hampered the tasks of impartial research and informed policymaking."[29]

2. Internationalization of transitional justice

The early TJ efforts of the 1980s, particularly in Latin America, were distinctly local in origins and primarily driven by local actors. But starting in the 1990s the

Nuremberg precedent was revived in the form of *ad hoc*, international tribunals. Yet, these tribunals were soon criticized for being far removed from the populations affected by the violations and for the lack of support from domestic judicial systems. Partly in response to these criticisms, on the one hand, hybrid courts combining national and international law were established and, on the other, a permanent international tribunal, the ICC, was eventually created. Yet, the internationalization of TJ activities, in combination with the coercive and highly politicized character of international judicial processes, has created significant tensions between international and local agency.

Global solutions to local problems

The considerable influence of international actors in the TJ field jeopardizes local ownership of and participation in TJ processes. As argued by Nagy in this volume, TJ as a field of practice and "normative inquiry" has become increasingly institutionalized within the broader structures of global governance over the course of the last decade in particular. True, as a partial corrective to this globalizing force, many practitioners have embraced localized, or "traditional," forms of TJ. Still, considerable tensions and legitimacy deficits exist in the gaps between international and local agency.

First, the influence of international generalist "expertise," funds, and emphasis on global models tends to shape TJ agendas in ways that often are to the detriment of domestic actors. International donors and consultants, although well-meaning, wield considerable influence in ways that risk the "crowding-out" of local actors. Second, as pointed out by Vinjamuri, "[s]ecuring international justice, securing peace, and devolving justice to national actors are likely to be incompatible goals, especially in states where institutions are weak and a high degree of instability persists."[30] Hence, decisions to judicially intervene in ongoing conflict are likely to be taken by outsiders and may therefore undermine local ownership of justice initiatives. Third, international interventions are often overly ambitious and their ultimate objectives are rarely explicit. This is partly because there is little agreement on what constitutes success, but also the expectations on what TJ processes can achieve are often inflated.

The coercive character of international justice

There is also the problem of the coercive and highly politicized character of international judicial processes. As the vast literature on "humanitarian intervention" repeatedly points out, politicization and selectivity are inherent in the practice of intervention by powerful states. This can be seen, for example, in the uneven character of international responses to some of the most recent high-profile humanitarian/human rights crisis and conflict situations: Syria (weak condemnation and piecemeal UN sanctions regime); Libya (forceful and immediate ICC/NATO intervention); and Sri Lanka (delayed investigations). Moreover, as recently highlighted in the initial response by the UNSC to the outbreak of civil war in Libya to refer the situation to the ICC, judicial interventions can also be aimed at replacing diplomacy and attempts at political solutions, hence reinforcing the trend towards judicialization.

Similarly, international judicial interventions are intimately linked to the development of conceptions of "human security" that underwrote practices of interventions in humanitarian crises by Western states following the end of the Cold War. Scholars of "securitization" highlight that the move towards linking human rights with the high politics of international security has a number of problematic implications, including privileging coercive force over political responses to crisis situations. Another problem is related to the potential of international (judicial) interventions to alter power balances and thereby the relative power of the warring parties. Such interventions are of course highly political and, as Vinjamuri points out, "the assumption that justice can be pursued neutrally during conflict is inconsistent with the claim that justice can independently affect the prospects for peace by marginalizing some actors and empowering others."[31] As seen in international judicial interventions in, for example, Libya, Sudan/Darfur, and Uganda, such interventions are not perceived as neutral or driven by legal considerations of selecting situations and cases to investigate in accordance with the Rome Statute. Critics of the ICC also argue that it selectively applies international criminal justice against less powerful states. This criticism is bolstered by the predominantly African focus of investigations initiated thus far by the ICC's Office of the Prosecutor (OTP).

Transitional justice in inhospitable conditions

The problematic effects of international judicial pressures are exacerbated by domestic institutional fragility. In conflict situations, local capacity to implement accountability strategies is particularly limited. The sheer number of perpetrators in societies afflicted by mass atrocity would overwhelm even a well-functioning judicial system.[32] Similarly, the delivery of TJ, particularly when administered in conjunction with peacebuilding programs such as demobilization, is institutionally very complex and burdensome.[33] Trial justice, for example, requires robust domestic justice institutions, which in most (post-)conflict societies are absent. In addition, the pursuit of TJ in weakly institutionalized environments is particularly subject to political manipulations.[34]

As a result, TJ, on its own and without broader institutional and political reforms, is unlikely to assist where it is needed the most. Attempts to implement TJ in inhospitable conditions, including the pursuit of justice initiatives in the absence of any discernible political transition, may mean reaching for the most difficult. TJ as a distinct field of theory and practice emerged in the context of political transition from, primarily, military rule to democratic governments in Latin America. Processes of TJ in Latin America are, however, likely to be quite different from those in countries that are moving from internal armed conflict, or are still engulfed in conflict, in Africa and in other parts of the world. The applicability of TJ findings in the region of Latin America (and in post-Soviet states) may be limited for a number of reasons including differences in patterns of state formation, colonization and decolonization, civil society activism, legal and judicial traditions, democratization, and socio-economic development. Indeed, for some, "there are grounds to suspect that TJ is best suited to states with relatively strong institutions and a certain minimum level of democracy."[35] This seems to echo the early modernization literature on democratization that viewed only countries that had attained a certain level of socio-economic development as "fit" for democracy. Nonetheless, such tensions are bound to intensify as the attention of international actors is currently undergoing a regional refocus towards the Middle East and the Arab world more broadly.

Challenges of legitimacy

International actors and institutions have carved out a central role for themselves when dealing with mass atrocities. As an increasing number of TJ institutions are established around the world, the agency of the specific actors involved is central to the pursuit of TJ. Yet, the question remains on what grounds external interventions, and particularly judicial interventions, are legitimate. Indeed, "who should be deciding on these processes, implementing them and ultimately benefiting from them are deeply contested issues."[36] Human rights activists and legal professionals often assert the authority of international legal norms and institutions on positivist grounds. This may not be altogether surprising given the extensive mobilization of resources around the values underpinning the international human rights and criminal justice regimes. Conventional understandings of the legitimacy of international legal norms either focus on the procedural fairness (due process guarantees) of criminal justice, or adopt legal positivist positions, accepting the authority of international law. For some, the legitimacy of international criminal justice ultimately rests on both its procedural fairness and its sources of authority (in terms of the relevant community that can/should be able to hold perpetrators to account).[37]

Regarding the latter, the crucial question is: accountable to whom? The common justification for international sanction for international crimes is that such abuses constitute an affront to humanity as a whole. For scholars such as Henham, however, "whatever measures are taken in the name of humanity to 'penalise' or 'punish' or 'deter' perpetrators of international crimes, these must draw moral support from both global and local constituencies."[38] This highlights the importance of context and agency in TJ processes. As argued by Clark and Palmer, "[w]ho implements transitional justice processes, what needs they respond to, and how particular interventions are ultimately understood by affected populations, are critical in determining the legitimacy and efficacy of transitional responses."[39] There are, however, also pragmatic reasons for why the particular histories, social norms, and cultural practices of affected communities must shape the development and implementation of TJ policies. For, without giving such considerations due attention, the legitimacy deficits of internationalized practices of TJ inevitably determine their impact.

3. Judicialization of transitional justice

Legal and judicial strategies have become dominant in the field of TJ. For proponents, the increase in international prosecutions, even in the context of ongoing conflict in recent years, demonstrates that law can prevail over politics, and that the criminal prosecution of abuses can assist in breaking the "wall of impunity."[40] For some, as outlined above, there is a strong consequentialist rationale for criminal prosecution as a way to reassert the legitimacy of the state, to strengthen the rule of law, and to promote political democratization.[41]

Yet, there are significant limits to what legal and judicial mechanisms can achieve in relation to TJ outcomes. In the first instance, there are the limits inherent in the recourse to judicial procedures and logics in addressing complex social and political problems: the challenges inherent in processes of judicialization per se. It remains crucial therefore to recognize the limits of what judicial approaches to accountability can achieve, especially through international courts and tribunals. In response to the complex objectives of contributing to conflict resolution, increasing political stability, combating impunity, and promoting reconciliation, any positive contributions of trial-based approaches to accountability are likely to remain modest.

Moreover, the specific character of the development of international criminal justice has privileged retributive forms of justice in ways that often are not conducive to conflict resolution or political and societal reconciliation. The international criminal justice system, as encapsulated by the ICC, aims primarily at the prosecution and punishment of individuals, and retribution and deterrence have been promoted as the primary objectives of punishment. The development of international criminal justice has taken place, however, at the expense of restorative approaches of justice and of broader notions of human rights accountability. Yet, despite the prevalence of claims of effectiveness of the international criminal justice regime in terms of deterrence, there is a dearth of empirical evidence documenting such claims. Also, especially in the context of large-scale organized political violence, there are inherent limitations in retributive approaches to criminal justice. As mentioned before, simply given the vast number of cases in such contexts, attempts to establish individual criminal responsibility tend ultimately to be unsatisfactory. To focus on a handful of cases may invite accusations of selectivity and further contribute to the politicization of the judicial system. Although the prosecution of individual cases may be symbolically very significant, criminal prosecutions are not likely to bring about political reconciliation.

The judicialization of TJ also risks obfuscating politics in ways that almost invariably benefit elite interests. Clearly, judicial interventions do not cancel out politics; they are both fundamentally driven by politics and, in turn, shape politics. In other words, Moreno Ocampo's aspiration that the ICC statute would result in a move "from a world based on power to one based on law,"[42] veers towards an attempt at depoliticization. As seen in Uganda, for example, the intervention of international tribunals can be manipulated by local elites for their own political ends. Hence, the potential for dislocation of politics that processes of judicialization entail may lead to elite capture and local power structures to condition the impact of TJ processes.

III. Recasting transitional justice and conflict resolution in an imperfect world

The final part of the chapter outlines some possible ways for TJ to recast its engagement with ongoing conflicts. In the first instance there is the need to recalibrate TJ strategies in the context of ongoing conflict in terms of: management of expectations; acknowledgement of the limits of the "transitional" paradigm when applied to ongoing conflicts; recognition that consensus is unlikely and probably undesirable; embracing of complexity and the blurred boundaries inherent in the field of TJ; and recognition that any gains made are prone to reversals.

1. Prudence, incrementalism and the constant potential for reversal

The theory and practice of TJ has its roots in the understanding that transitional contexts constitute disruptions of "politics as usual" that offer opportunities to recast justice and its foundations.[43] Yet, TJ issues are invariably complex. At the core of TJ debates is a set of moral and political dilemmas, which are not readily reduced to general theories. As with any morally fraught subject there are very rarely any straightforward solutions available. Consensus surrounding most issues relating to TJ remains elusive and, as with any morally thorny issue, probably undesirable.

There is still a need, nonetheless, to go beyond the binary debates that tend to dominate the field (peace vs justice, law vs politics, local vs international, etc.) and recognize the complexity and blurred boundaries inherent in the field of TJ. On the one hand the tensions between, say, peace and justice are likely to be less pronounced than what is often maintained. On the other, there are fertile grounds to explore useful ways forward beyond sterile dichotomies.[44] It is also important to better manage the expectations of what TJ mechanisms can realistically achieve. For many critics, the pursuit of TJ in the early stages of a political transition, or even in the absence of a transition, may be considered premature.[45] Indeed, it is crucial to recognize the limits of the "transitional" paradigm (as developed in the context of democratic transitions) when applied to ongoing conflicts. In particular, the paradigm may be misleading, as it implies that countries moving away from a difficult past will necessarily make the transition toward democracy and stability. Overburdening TJ mechanisms with excessive roles tends to give rise to inflated expectations of what TJ can deliver. In the context of ongoing conflict, rather than there being a rupture with the past, the legacies and challenges of the past are likely to fundamentally shape any future developments.

There is also the need to recognize that any normative progress with regards to TJ is prone to reversals. Consider the framework of Responsibility to Protect (RtoP) that increasingly underpins, both discursively and institutionally, attempts to intervene in ongoing conflicts. RtoP highlights the reality of constant renegotiations of state sovereignty in matters of human rights and the legitimate form and scope of international interventions in the domestic affairs of sovereign countries. It has shifted understandings of what sovereignty entails towards a less absolutist understanding of sovereignty over the course of the last decades. These trends also invoke understandings of sovereignty not as entitlement but as status, understandings of what it means to be a legitimate member of an international society, and the capacity to engage in increasingly complex transactions with other members of the system.[46]

However, if one accepts that normative understandings of the legitimate scope for intervention in conflict are prone to change, there will also be the potential for pushback, reversal, and stagnation. As Welsh observes, "[e]fforts to implement norms open up new areas of contestation for those sceptical of the norm's provisions, and can lead to either backsliding or differential interpretations of the norm's meaning."[47] What does this mean for the pursuit of accountability strategies by external actors during ongoing conflict? There may indeed be broad recognition of certain fundamental principles enshrined in the international criminal justice system and the associated concept of RtoP concerning state responsibility and intervention. But criticism from rising powers, such as Brazil, India, and China, suggests that these states are not yet willing to fully accept the compatibility between the principle of non-interference and international criminal justice. More generally, resistance to the more coercive efforts to enforce international criminal justice—in Libya and Sudan/Darfur for example—needs to be seen in the context of an uncertain future for the global human rights regime more broadly in light of the wider implications of the rise of non-Western states and shifting global power balances. As power shifts globally, therefore, competing understandings of sovereignty that emphasize sovereign equality may reassert themselves, challenging the demands and expectations of accountability advocates.

2. *Strategizing transitional justice*

Against this background of challenges, in the spirit of "strategizing" TJ, five points are highlighted in summary form:

First, any morally defensible strategy of TJ would include not only legal considerations, but also the inherently political context in which the strategy is developed and implemented. According to some, international judicial actors, and particularly the ICC Prosecutor, should openly admit the political nature of their activities, which would enable them to make more informed political decisions. Yet, most advocates of international criminal justice tend to maintain that their role is to operate autonomously from political influences. Clearly, justice actors and institutions are both affected by and effect politics. Judiciaries, whether domestic or international, do not operate in a political vacuum. They are often attuned to and generally accommodate political shifts. The law, however, and the interests and normative preferences of its practitioners, cannot be simply reduced to politics. Developments in international law fundamentally shape the normative environment in which political actors operate. More specifically, the force of legal norms does not merely manifest itself in the form of constraints. Legal norms also have important creative, generative and constitutive influences on political practice. For Finnemore and Toope, for example, international law is more than merely a matter of cases and courts, or formal treaty negotiation. It has a constructive dimension in which actors participating in law's construction "contribute to legitimacy and obligation, and to the continuum of legality from informal to more formal norms."[48] Law in this view draws attention to those rules, norms, and decision-making procedures of institutions that shape expectations, interests, and behavior.

Second, and building on this last point, by considering "the interests of justice" the complexities of sequencing and timing must be better understood. In the first instance, further research on the causal effects of TJ mechanisms, including indictments and amnesties, on the dynamics of ongoing conflict is required. Recent research findings suggest that the timing of TJ mechanisms matter, but it remains unclear exactly how and why this is the case.[49] Indeed, Article 53 of the Rome Statute provides that the ICC Prosecutor may desist from opening an investigation if it appears to him that this would be in the "interests of justice."[50] However, the Rome Statute gives little guidance on what criteria the OTP should apply to determine what these constitute. Beyond the obligation to consider the gravity of the crime and the interests of victims, the Rome Statute makes no reference to the interests of peace and security, for example. Still, the notion of the interests of justice suggests that there is a strong rationale to defer prosecutions, i.e. delay justice, in times of political instability.

A better understanding of the dynamics of time also includes a recognition that incentives and norms tend to change over time, and hence also what is both normatively desirable and politically/practically possible. Accountability measures are not likely to serve short-term interests of bringing violent conflict to an end. Accountability norms may very well complicate peace negotiations. TJ, therefore, is quite clearly a moving target. Political circumstances change as power balances shift, consequently altering the incentives facing relevant political actors. But more subtle changes also occur over time in the normative environment in which actors operate. In other words, what is both possible and desirable is prone to change over time. Hence, although accountability claims have a tendency to persist over time, timing is important, rendering what may seem as a morally desirable sequencing of TJ mechanisms difficult to implement.

Third, TJ strategies must be clearer on objectives. What objectives do and should TJ mechanisms accomplish and for whom? In terms of TJ policies, there are some hard questions that need to be addressed: what is it for, what social and political functions should the particular approach adopted fulfill, and what actors are—and should be—the beneficiaries? Does the specific mechanism actually deliver what it is set out to deliver; for example, does it bring the citizenry together (reconciliation) or in fact divide or further polarize the population between the beneficiaries and supporters of the *ancien régime* and its victims? Do trials not only combat impunity and establish accountability but also satisfy that powerful human instinct—revenge? Moreover, what are the institutional implications of court prosecutions for a judiciary that may already be under considerable institutional strain and political pressure? That is, do the policies on TJ strengthen or debilitate state institutions mandated to develop and implement these policies? A wide variety of mechanisms are now included in the TJ "toolkit"—investigations to establish the truth and identify perpetrators, reparations programs for the victims of human rights violations (financial and symbolical, in terms of memory sites), institutional measures to establish mechanisms to prevent recurrence of violations, and of course prosecutions and trials. However, the last few decades of accumulated TJ experience show that it is often not a simple matter of choosing between different TJ mechanisms.

Fourth, when engaging with ongoing conflicts, TJ advocates might consider a stronger focus on rights-abusing behavior in conflict rather than on the broader political dynamics of the conflict itself. Violent conflict is of course part of human history and is likely to remain so for the foreseeable future. Instead, advocates are better served by focusing on certain types of behavior in armed conflict—i.e. atrocity crimes—and to aim to hold perpetrators accountable for having committed grave crimes. That is, more focus should be given to the actual conduct of armed conflict rather than to the broader conflict per se. Too often this distinction is lost in both scholarly and policy debates. This is ultimately a principled (and modest) position that is not easily reduced to impact assessments. True, international criminal law targets the type of behavior (war crimes, crimes against humanity, genocide) that is the result of planning and systematic execution. Hence, it might not be easy to separate individual crimes from the broader conflict dynamics. Yet, making the case for accountability for perpetrators of grave human rights crimes does not have to lead advocates to exaggerated claims that TJ can end or prevent armed conflicts. It is therefore important to focus on abusive behavior in conflict, rather than merely participation in the conflict itself.

Finally, there is a strong normative case that some form of accountability ought to be part of efforts to end ongoing conflict and to build peace. Many TJ advocates argue that peace is not sustainable without some form of accountability. Although there is a lack of compelling evidence to support this claim, the key point to note here, however, is that accountability measures can take different forms. Article 53 of the Rome Statute, for example, highlights the question of whether prosecution is the only appropriate response to international crimes, or whether other mechanisms (such as amnesties and truth commissions) are acceptable alternatives. Non-retributive TJ mechanisms such as truth commissions and other alternative mechanisms also have potential accountability effects. Accountability measures may indeed complicate efforts to reach an end of armed conflict. But without any type of accountability measures as part of a peace settlement, serious doubts are likely to be cast on the character of the "peace" obtained. In particular, there is a need to expand the focus beyond individual criminal accountability. For example, the relative advantages of human rights mechanisms over criminal justice mechanisms in the context of post-conflict societies include: locating victims at the center; a demonstrated capacity to deal with a larger caseload; and a focus on state accountability, rather than individual accountability. From this perspective, redress goes beyond the individual case and highlights the needs of broader institutional and structural reforms.[51]

Amnesties, for instance, when appropriately designed, can constitute a legitimate form of accountability. It is generally recognized that international law obligates countries to prosecute genocide, crimes against humanity, and war crimes. Developments in international criminal law, in particular, have limited the ability of negotiators to trade off justice for a peace deal (e.g. in the form of blanket amnesties and explicit impunity deals). But, international law and norms also potentially provide common discursive grounds for the formulation of conflict resolution policies and appropriate TJ mechanisms. International law provides norms to enable the formulation of amnesty policies that could assist in efforts to end conflict while staying within its strictures: for example, with regards to certain types of conditional amnesties. The accumulated result of several decades of TJ practice is a broad set of duties of states, rights of victims and families, and obligations to provide reparations that limit the discretion of governments and mediators. Accountability constitutes therefore a key component of any efforts to achieve peace and eventual reconciliation and raises the possibility to promote accountability by other means than criminal prosecutions, such as truth commissions, lustration, reparations, etc. For Snyder and Vinjamuri, for example, properly designed and enforced amnesties have a better track record than trials and truth commissions of ending civil wars and encouraging human rights, democracy, and the rule of law (at least as measured by Freedom House and Polity IV). According to their study, trials only contribute to the ending of abuses when spoilers are weak and where domestic justice institutions are robust.[52]

Yet, certain measures are neither legitimate nor appropriate. This raises the question of what criteria should be used to evaluate legitimacy. At the minimum, accountability measures should be sensitive to local contexts and must be driven by and respond to local demands and needs. Therefore, to inform our understanding of what is possible, and even desirable, in societies engulfed in conflict it remains imperative to adequately and modestly recognize local political and historical particularities before using any general "lessons" to advance specific policy recommendations. An emphasis on local needs does not, however, exclude international efforts per se. On the contrary, this may demand such efforts in order to support local attempts to push accountability against entrenched interests. As argued by Seils and Wierda:

> [t]he existence of an external body with both the will and the means to achieve accountability means that negotiators are no longer hostage only to domestic realities. It may be that in some situations this will allow for greater

> clarity in persuading parties to conflicts that some degree of meaningful accountability in respect of serious crimes will have to form part of the solution.[53]

However, to really bring conflict to an end, root causes need to be addressed. This is beyond the will and capacity of outsiders and a very long-term process for which there are no quick policy fixes.

Conclusion

The normative expansion of the field of TJ is particularly evident in practices of judicial intervention in situations of ongoing conflict. The combined effect of an increasingly intrusive international legal architecture, the rise of victims' movements and their NGO support networks worldwide, and the intractability of contemporary armed conflict, has moved international judicial proceedings forward, with interventions taking place not after, but during, ongoing conflict. International judicial interventions are also spearheaded by practical constraints posed by the ICC's temporal limitation in investigating cases prior to July 2002. As a result, TJ has become an integral part of the political and legal context in which conflict resolution and peacebuilding strategies are formulated and implemented.

This chapter has highlighted a number of particularly pressing challenges that have become increasingly apparent in the cases of international judicial interventions in ongoing conflict to date, including: the dearth of robust empirical evidence to support the belief held by many advocates of judicial interventions that the tool of indictments and the threat of prosecution can alter the prospects for achieving peace; the risks of undermining local accountability processes inherent in international interventions, particularly in situations characterized by ongoing conflict and institutional fragility; and the privileged status of retributive forms of justice and the judicialization of TJ strategies at the expense of other potentially complementary strategies.

These challenges notwithstanding, the TJ field is undoubtedly continually evolving and the practice of judicial intervention in ongoing conflict is fairly recent. It may therefore be an opportune juncture to reflect on what prudent, incremental, and politically attuned strategies of TJ engagement with ongoing conflict may look like. This chapter has sought to outline some of the key dimensions that such an engagement might need to consider. Yet, whatever the merits of this approach to the complex issues that shape the pursuit of accountability strategies during ongoing conflict may be, the complexity inherent in the field of TJ means that consensus regarding foundational issues is unlikely and probably undesirable.

Notes

The author is grateful to Olga Martin-Ortega for helpful comments on earlier drafts and for coaxing the chapter from me. Chandra Lekha Sriram, Caroline Holmqvist-Jonsäter, and Thomas Pegram offered very constructive comments on a previous draft.

The participants at the authors' workshop at the School of Oriental and African Studies, University of London, provided the ideal intellectual environment for the discussion of many of the themes covered in this chapter. The author has also greatly benefitted from the discussions over the years with members of Oxford Transitional Justice Research (OTJR), particularly Phil Clark and Nicola Palmer, and the co-chairs of the London Transitional Justice Network, Chandra Lekha Sriram, Iavor Rangelov, and Leslie Vinjamuri. The usual caveats apply.

1 For analysis of justice trends, see Leslie Vinjamuri and Aaron P. Boesenecker, "Accountability and Peace Agreements: Mapping Trends from 1980 to 2006, *Centre for Humanitarian Dialogue Report*, September 2007.

2 When it comes to the scope of the ICC's prosecutions, Moreno Ocampo argues: "The ICC's mandate to select the most serious crimes committed after July 1, 2002, requires that we engage in judicial proceedings in relation to conflicts even before they have ended. Working in these circumstances can mean conducting investigations in situations where physical access is sometimes impossible or where there is a total collapse of functioning institutions. My Office has to pursue its justice mandate when there are negotiations for peace with the worst perpetrators or when the allegations are against the members of the government." Luis Moreno Ocampo, "Transitional Justice in Ongoing Conflicts," *International Journal of Transitional Justice*, vol. 1 (2007), p. 8.

3 On the role of private economic interest in such wars, see further: Kal Holsti, *The State, War, and the State of War* (Cambridge: Cambridge University Press, 1996), and Mary Kaldor, *New and Old Wars: Organized Violence in a Global Era* (Cambridge: Polity Press, 2002).

4 With regard to civilian casualties in contemporary armed conflict, figures in the range of 80–90 percent of civilian war victims are frequently cited. For a nuanced discussion of these figures and the inherent difficulties assessing civilian war casualties, see Adam Roberts, "Lives and Statistics: Are 90% of War Victims Civilians?" *Survival: Global Politics and Strategy*, vol. 52 (2010), pp. 115–36.

5 For Freedman: "the prototypical conflict now is a function of the weak state. States are weak because of the fragile nature of the civil society upon which they have been built, their undeveloped institutional structures, which are often unable to contain and channel political tensions, and their problems of poverty and economic adjustment. These weaknesses can lead to breakdowns of law and order, to secessionist movements, to outright civil war." Lawrence Freedman, *War* (Oxford: Oxford University Press, 1994), p. 359.

6 For an opposing perspective and for the likelihood of inter-state war, see John J. Mearsheimer, "The Gathering Storm: China's Challenge to US Power in Asia," *The Chinese Journal of International Politics*, vol. 3 (2010), pp. 381–96.

7 Martin Shaw, *War and Genocide* (Cambridge: Polity Press, 2003).

8 For an excellent analysis of post-Cold War narratives of conflict from the perspectives of primarily Anglo-American theorists, see Caroline Holmqvist-Jonsäter, *Policing Wars: A Twenty-First Century Discourse on War* (PhD dissertation, King's College London, 2010), Chapter 1.

9 Some studies show, for example, that about half of all countries that emerge from war lapse back into violence within five years. Paul Collier *et al.*, *Breaking the Conflict Trap: Civil War and Development Policy* (Washington: World Bank, 2003).

10 Paige Arthur, "How 'Transitions' Reshaped Human Rights: A Conceptual History of Transitional Justice," *Human Rights Quarterly*, vol. 31 (2009), pp. 321–67. On TJ as a form of global governance see, further, Rosemary Nagy's chapter in this volume.

11 Bruce Broomhall, *International Justice and the International Criminal Court: Between Sovereignty and the Rule of Law* (Oxford: Oxford University Press, 2004).

12 Paul Seils and Marieke Wierda, "The International Criminal Court and Conflict Mediation," *International Center for Transitional Justice Occasional Paper Series*, June 2005.

13 United Nations Secretary-General, *The Rule of Law and Transitional Justice in Conflict and Post-conflict Societies*, UN Doc. S/2004/616 (3 August 2004).
14 Rome Statute, preamble, available at <*http://untreaty.un.org/cod/icc/statute/99_corr/preamble.htm*>, accessed 12 October 2011.
15 See, further, Chandra Lekha Sriram's contribution to this volume.
16 For an excellent overview, see Richard J. Ponzio, *Democratic Peacebuilding: Aiding Afghanistan and Other Fragile States* (Oxford: Oxford University Press, 2011).
17 Gerhard Thallinger, "The UN Peacebuilding Commission and Transitional Justice," *German Law Journal*, Part I/II, 8 (2007), pp. 681–710, available at <*www.germanlawjournal.com/index.php?pageID=11&artID=843*>, accessed 12 October 2011. The literature on state-building is extensive; see, for example, Richard Caplan, *International Governance of War-Torn Territories: Rule and Reconstruction* (Oxford: Oxford University Press, 2005); Simon Chesterman, *You, The People: The United Nations, Transitional Administration, and State-Building* (Oxford: Oxford University Press, 2004); and Dominik Zaum, *The Sovereignty Paradox: The Norms and Politics of International Statebuilding* (Oxford: Oxford University Press, 2007).
18 M. Cherif Bassiouni, "Searching for Peace and Achieving Justice: The Need for Accountability," *Law and Contemporary Problems*, vol. 59 (1996), pp. 9–28.
19 United Nations Secretary-General, *The Rule of Law and Transitional Justice*, op. cit., para. 21.
20 On the limits of transitional justice vis-à-vis peacebuilding, see Wendy Lambourne, "Transitional Justice and Peacebuilding after Mass Violence," *International Journal of Transitional Justice*, vol. 3 (2009), pp. 28–48.
21 Diane Orentlicher, "Settling Accounts: The Duty to Prosecute Human Rights Violations of a Prior Regime," *Yale Law Journal*, vol. 100 (1991), pp. 2537–615. Orentlicher has subsequently partly revised her position by emphasizing the *scope* of the duty to prosecute. Diane Orentlicher, "'Settling Accounts' Revisited: Reconciling Global Norms with Local Agency," *International Journal of Transitional Justice*, vol. 1 (2007), pp. 10–22. See also Carlos Nino's reply to Orentlicher: Carlos Nino, "The Duty to Punish Past Abuses of Human Rights Put into Context: The Case of Argentina," *Yale Law Journal*, vol. 100 (1991), pp. 2619–40.
22 Leslie Vinjamuri, "Deterrence, Democracy, and the Pursuit of International Justice," *Ethics and International Affairs*, vol. 24 (2010), pp. 191–211.
23 Jack Snyder and Leslie Vinjamuri, "Trials and Errors: Principle and Pragmatism in Strategies of International Justice," *International Security*, vol. 28 (2003/04), pp. 5–44.
24 For an overview, see Oskar N. T. Thoms *et al.*, "State-level Effects of Transitional Justice: What Do We Know?" *International Journal of Transitional Justice*, vol. (2010), pp. 1–26.
25 See: Tove Grete Lie, Helga Malmin Binningsbo, and Scott Gates, "Post-Conflict Justice and Sustainable Peace," *Post-Conflict Transition Working Paper*, World Bank Policy Research Working Paper (April 2007); Eric Brahm, "Uncovering the Truth: Examining Truth Commission Success and Impact," *International Studies Perspectives*, vol. 8 (2007), pp. 16–35; Oskar N. T. Thoms, James Ron, and Roland Paris, "The Effects of Transitional Justice Mechanisms: A Summary of Empirical Research Findings and Implications for Analysts and Practitioners," *Centre for International Policy Studies Working Paper*, April 2008.
26 See, however, James Meernik, "Justice or Peace: How the International Criminal Tribunal Affects Societal Peace in Bosnia," *Journal of Peace Research*, vol. 42 (2005), pp. 271–90.
27 Payam Akhavan, "Are International Criminal Tribunals a Disincentive to Peace? Reconciling Judicial Romanticism with Political Realism," *Human Rights Quarterly*, vol. 31 (2009), pp. 624–54.
28 Thoms *et al.*, "State-level Effects," op. cit., p. 5.
29 Nicola Palmer, Phil Clark and Danielle Granville (eds.), *Critical Perspectives in Transitional Justice* (Antwerp: Intersentia, 2011).
30 Vinjamuri, "Deterrence," op. cit., p. 202.

31 Vinjamuri, "Deterrence," op. cit., p. 203.
32 In Liberia, as pointed out by Raddatz in her contribution to this volume, the capacity of the domestic legal system to try alleged perpetrators remains constrained.
33 As highlighted by García-Godos in this volume.
34 See, for example, Brown's chapter in this volume.
35 Thoms *et al.*, "State-level Effects," op. cit., p. 25.
36 Clark and Palmer, "Challenging," op. cit.
37 See, further, Roberto Gargarella, "Human Rights, International Courts and Deliberative Democracy," in Palmer, Clark and Granville (eds.), *Critical Perspectives*, op. cit.
38 Ralph Henham, "International Sentencing as a Force for Achieving Peace through Justice," in Oxford Transitional Justice Research (OTJR) (eds), *Critical Perspectives in Transitional Justice* (Antwerp: Intersentia, 2011).
39 Clark and Palmer, "Challenging," op. cit.
40 See, for example, Jo-Marie Burt, "Accountability after Atrocity in Peru: The Trial of Former President Alberto Fujimori in Comparative Perspective," in Palmer, Clark and Granville (eds.), *Critical Perspectives*, op. cit. See, more generally, Kathryn Sikkink, *The Justice Cascade: How Human Rights Prosecutions are Changing World Politics* (New York: W.W. Norton & Company, 2011).
41 See, generally, Juan Méndez, "Accountability for Past Abuses," *Human Rights Quarterly*, vol. 19 (1997), pp. 255–82.
42 Moreno Ocampo, "Transitional Justice in Ongoing Conflicts," op. cit. p. 8.
43 Ruti G. Teitel, *Transitional Justice* (Oxford: Oxford University Press, 2000).
44 Take the example of retributive and restorative forms of justice. Carolyn Hoyle argues that "[w]hile there is by no means consensus on the compatibility of restorative and retributive justice, it is clear that restorative justice (on the whole) does not necessarily reject all punitive measures associated with retributive justice and *vice versa*, and that there is more common ground between the two forms of justice than is often recognised." Carolyn Hoyle, "Can International Justice Be Restorative Justice? The role of Reparations," in Palmer, Clark and Granville (eds.), *Critical Perspectives*, op. cit.
45 See, for example, Snyder and Vinjamuri, "Trials and Errors," op. cit.
46 As Annan argued, "sovereignty implies responsibility, not just power." Kofi Annan, "Intervention," Ditchley Foundation Lecture XXXV, 1998, p. 2.
47 Jennifer Welsh, "Implementing 'The Responsibility to Protect': Where Expectations Meet Reality," *Ethics and International Affairs*, vol. 24 (2010).
48 Martha J. Finnemore and Stephen Toope, "Alternatives to 'Legalization': Richer Views of Law and Politics," *International Organization*, vol. 55 (2001), pp. 744–47.
49 Tricia D. Olsen, Leigh A. Payne, and Andrew G. Reiter, *Transitional Justice in Balance: Comparing Processes, Weighing Efficacy* (Washington: United States Institute of Peace, 2010).
50 Article 53(1)(c) of the Rome Statute expressly recognizes that a prosecutor must consider whether "taking into account the gravity of the crime and the interests of victims, there are nonetheless substantial reasons to believe that an investigation would not serve the interests of justice."
51 On this point, see further, Antoine Buyse, "Hybrid Human Rights Mechanisms in Post-conflict Transitions: The Experience of the Bosnian Human Rights Chamber" in Palmer, Clark and Granville (eds.) *Critical Perspectives*, op. cit.
52 Snyder and Vinjamuri, "Trials and Errors," op. cit.
53 Seils and Wierda, "The International Criminal Court and Conflict Mediation," op. cit.

4 Just peace? Integrating DDR and transitional justice

Lars Waldorf[1]

Introduction

Since 1989, there has been a remarkable proliferation of disarmament, demobilization, and reintegration (DDR) programs and transitional justice mechanisms in post-conflict states.[2] Yet, even as both became common features of "liberal peacebuilding,"[3] they continued operating along parallel tracks. This was hardly surprising given their differing objectives, beneficiaries, and constituencies. After all, DDR focuses on security and ex-combatants, while transitional justice emphasizes accountability and victims. In other words, DDR and transitional justice were seen to inhabit different sides of the "peace-versus-justice" debate.[4]

That began changing with the UN Secretary-General's 2004 report on transitional justice. There, Kofi Annan sought to shift the debate from peace *versus* justice to peace *and* justice:

> Justice and peace are not contradictory forces. Rather, properly pursued, they promote and sustain one another. The question, then, can never be whether to pursue justice and accountability, but rather when and how.[5]

Annan committed the UN to promote transitional justice and the rule of law throughout its peacebuilding programs.[6]

In 2006, the UN adopted an "integrated" approach to DDR that links security, human rights, and development. The resulting Integrated Disarmament, Demobilization and Reintegration Standards (IDDRS) recently added a module on the linkages between DDR and transitional justice. The module aims to promote "more systematic and improved coordination between DDR and transitional justice processes, so as to best support the successful transition from conflict to sustainable peace."[7]

This chapter explores how transitional justice may contribute to DDR's "ultimate aim": to "prevent a return to violent conflict, i.e. to make peace irreversible."[8] It begins with an overview of DDR. The chapter then looks at reintegration, as that is where transitional justice may be able to make a contribution. It next examines how specific transitional justice mechanisms—amnesties, trials, truth commissions, local justice, reparations, and vetting—may benefit DDR. Finally, it concludes by arguing that DDR would be better off leaving reintegration to transitional justice and other peacebuilding programs.

Disarmament, demobilization, and reintegration (DDR)

Overview

DDR has become a regular feature of negotiated peace agreements and peacekeeping missions since its first formal appearance in 1989.[9] DDR has been part of UN peacekeeping missions in countries such as Burundi, Cote d'Ivoire, Democratic Republic of Congo, Haiti, Liberia, and Sudan. The UN has also been involved with DDR even where it does not have a peacekeeping presence, such as Aceh (Indonesia), Afghanistan, Central African Republic, Somalia, and Uganda. The UN concluded that the "[d]emobilization of combatants is the single most important factor determining the success of peace operations."[10] In 2005, over 1.2 million ex-combatants (and their dependents) participated in DDR programs in 22 countries at a total cost of US $1.9 billion.[11]

DDR is designed to transform combatants into civilians and to ensure that they do not take up arms again (whether as combatants or bandits).[12] It has three constituent parts—disarmament, demobilization, and reintegration—which need not occur in any particular sequence.[13] Disarmament involves the collection, registration, storage, and often destruction of small arms and light weapons. It is "a highly symbolic act that signifies the ending of an individual's active role as a combatant."[14] Demobilization is more complicated as it encompasses both physical and psychological processes of transforming combatants into civilians.[15] It usually consists of two stages: (1) processing combatants in cantonment sites or temporary centers; and (2) providing a support package, commonly called reinsertion, which can last for up to a year.[16] Reintegration is the long-term process whereby ex-combatants become reintegrated into civilian society.[17]

During the disarmament and demobilization phases, combatants are screened to make sure that they are eligible for DDR and for program assistance.[18] While the eligibility criteria are usually laid out in peace accords or national legislation, DDR programs still face difficult choices when it comes to defining and identifying *bona fide* combatants, especially in the context of civil wars, where many combatants are irregulars, part-time, or coerced.[19] A program that is underinclusive risks instability by leaving behind a reserve pool of armed combatants, while an overinclusive program may be seen as unfair and corrupt.

Women and children pose particular challenges for DDR.[20] Early programs often restricted eligibility to those with ownership of, or expertise in, weapons.[21] Yet, many women and children who accompany fighting forces (and who provide support as porters, cooks, messengers, "war wives," etc.) are unarmed. Even those women who are armed combatants often have their weapons taken away and given to male non-combatants at the start of DDR processes "for personal financial or political gain."[22]

DDR programs have generally paid less attention to female combatants because they are seen as less of a security threat than male combatants.[23] In addition, many female combatants, especially girl soldiers, self-demobilize to avoid social stigma when they return or to avoid sexual violence in male-dominated demobilization camps.

Minimalist versus maximalist approaches

There is an ongoing policy debate over whether DDR should focus on short-term security (the minimalist approach) or on long-term development (the maximalist approach).[24] Until recently, most donors and practitioners shared a minimalist outlook: they treated DDR as a short-term technical exercise typified by counting weapons, establishing demobilization camps, and handing out reinsertion and reintegration packages—the "guns, camps, and cash" approach.[25] The emphasis was on individual ex-combatants rather than on war-affected communities.

The UN committed itself to a maximalist approach in 2006. The Secretary-General stressed the "vital" need to coordinate DDR "with the wider peace, recovery, and development frameworks."[26] He proposed an "integrated" UN approach which would ensure that DDR be: (1) "people-centered" (through the promotion of international human rights and humanitarian law); (2) "flexible enough to provide 'local solutions to local problems'"; and (3) nationally owned.[27] That same year, the UN launched the Integrated DDR Standards, which sees DDR as "a complex process, with political, military, security, humanitarian and socio-economic dimensions."[28]

The publication of the IDDRS did not resolve the policy debate between minimalists and maximalists. Instead, the integrated approach met with resistance inside the UN. "Integration inertia was provoked by challenges from above (e.g. normative disagreements and lack of higher-order political support) and from below (e.g. inter- and intra-agency tensions)."[29] The piloting of integrated DDR in Haiti and Sudan ran into trouble as the security-oriented Department of Peace Keeping Operations clashed with the development-oriented UNDP and children's charity, UNICEF.[30]

Scholar-practitioners joined the fray. Robert Muggah rightly observed that "DDR is becoming a kind of hamper into which many priorities—some of them not necessarily complementary—were added."[31] Kathleen Jennings was more critical, stating that DDR is "so broad in scope and aims as to undermine chances of effective implementation."[32] Indeed, integrated DDR is saddled with unrealizable goals.

Individual versus community reintegration

The minimalist-maximalist debate has played out largely in the context of reintegration, with minimalists arguing for an individual focus and maximalists arguing for a community focus. The reason that the debate centered on reintegration is twofold. First, disarmament and demobilization phases were always the short-term, security-driven aspects of DDR. Second, reintegration was something of a blank slate as it had been largely neglected by DDR programming.[33]

Reintegration has economic, social, and political dimensions. First, it aims to create sustainable livelihoods for ex-combatants.[34] Second, reintegration seeks to rebuild social capital and social cohesion.[35] Finally, it offers ex-combatants an opportunity to resolve political grievances through legitimate channels rather than through force of arms.[36]

DDR programs generally put most of their efforts into economic reintegration (which is more easily measured). That strategy is based on two seemingly faulty assumptions. The first is that many combatants and armed groups are economically motivated, when, in fact, their motivations are "heterogenous and differentiated."[37] The second assumption is that social and political reintegration will follow from economic reintegration, whereas these different facets of reintegration appear to be independent of one another.[38]

The key debate in the reintegration literature (which parallels the larger security-versus-development debate) is whether reintegration should narrowly target ex-combatants or provide broader support to war-affected groups and communities. The IDDRS tries to have it both ways. The IDDRS justifies preferential treatment for ex-combatants in the short term:

> Returning ex-combatants are potential "spoilers" of peace. This is why, while other war-affected groups, such as refugees and internally displaced persons (IDPs) may far outnumber them, ex-combatants will usually need focused, sustainable support if they are to succeed in making the transition from military to civilian life.[39]

Yet, as the IDDRS is quick to observe, this risks "turning [ex-combatants] into a privileged group within the community"[40]—something that is clearly not conducive to their longer-term reintegration.

The IDDRS proposes a twofold solution to this thorny problem. First, reintegration assistance "must be harmonized with the assistance given to other returnees to minimize competition and resentment."[41] Second, direct assistance to ex-combatants should be phased out over time and replaced with community-based reintegration (what the IDDRS equates with "sustainable reintegration").

There is a real danger, however, that DDR programs that pay increased attention to other returnees and communities run the risk of losing their focus, as well as the trust of ex-combatants. In addition, such programs can create confusion among beneficiaries—as happened with a DDR program in the Democratic Republic of Congo that provided short-term micro-finance to former combatants and medium-term grants to communities.[42] Furthermore, there is very little experience of DDR programs focusing on both combatants and communities.[43]

To resolve the tensions between the minimalist and maximalist conceptions of DDR, some scholars and practitioners have proposed "de-linking reintegration from DDR."[44] For example, James Pugel argues:

> One way of reducing the scope of DDR as currently conceived is by substituting "reintegration" with "reinsertion" in order to focus the programmes

away from long-term and open-ended commitments to short-term and fixed objectives. Reintegration could then emerge as a more deliberate intervention tool, or be superseded by mainstream development programmes entirely.[45]

In fact, it would make more sense if long-term reintegration, focused on both ex-combatants and their receiving communities, was handled by development actors rather than DDR. This approach is recommended by the World Bank in the final report on its seven-year and US$500 million DDR program in the Great Lakes region.[46]

Factors contributing to reintegration

The debate over individual versus community reintegration is stymied by a weak evidence base. There has been surprisingly little empirical research on reintegration.[47] The IDDRS recognizes that DDR programs have focused on short-term, quantitative outcomes rather than longer-term, qualitative impacts.[48] Anders Nilsson goes further: he bluntly criticizes reintegration as "a theoryless field" of untested assumptions, descriptive case studies, and lessons learned.[49] Still, it is worth looking at what is currently known about three factors thought to influence reintegration: participation in DDR programs, payments to ex-combatants, and combatants' wartime roles.

So far, there is little evidence that DDR programs actually promote successful reintegration.[50] Based on surveys with over 1,000 ex-combatants in Sierra Leone, Humphreys and Weinstein found no significant correlation between participation in DDR programs and reintegration.[51] They are quick to point out that lack of correlation does not mean that DDR had no positive impact. Still, Humphreys and Weinstein state that "the nonfindings should be seen as a wakeup call to advocates of these programs" to moderate their claims and devise better methodologies for measuring DDR's impact.[52] Peter Uvin found that DDR programs had marginal positive impacts in Burundi: ex-combatants who went through the program were more likely to be optimistic about the future.[53] Other scholars argue that DDR programs can have unintended negative consequences for the reintegration of ex-combatants. According to Jennings, these include "cementing divisions between ex-combatants and non-combatants; hardening group identity; buttressing harmful prewar authority structures … ; and contributing to participation in criminalized economies."[54] And in countries like Tajikistan, former fighters were successfully reintegrated without DDR programs.[55] In the end, then, it is not certain whether DDR programs positively affect reintegration.

The effect of reintegration payments to ex-combatants on their social reintegration is also unclear. Some studies have found that these payments did not create tensions between individual ex-combatants and their communities.[56] Based on his ethnographic study of several communities in Burundi, Peter Uvin concluded that "the jealousy problem is much less severe than is often thought."[57] On the other hand, Blattman and Annan found that distribution of financial aid to ex-combatants in Northern Uganda generated high levels of resentment among civilians.[58] Similarly, Peter Barron discovered that separate programs for ex-combatants and for victims in Aceh "has in cases hardened conflict-era group identities."[59]

By contrast, a factor that does appear to impact reintegration is an ex-combatant's wartime role.

Humphreys and Weinstein found that "[p]ast participation in an abusive military faction is the strongest predictor of difficulty in achieving social reintegration."[60] They also found that:

> the degree of abuse experienced by local communities during the war is powerfully related to the level of acceptance of ex-combatants. Consistent with stories told by some of our respondents about reintegration, their membership in a faction mattered not because of their personal characteristics, but because of the reputation of the group in the area where they lived.[61]

As will be discussed further below, these two findings suggest that transitional justice processes might aid the reintegration of such former combatants.[62]

DDR and transitional justice

Transitional justice

Like DDR, transitional justice has expanded rapidly. Initially associated with trials and truth commissions, it now "comprises the full range of processes and measures associated with a society's attempt to come to terms with a legacy of large-scale past abuses, in order to ensure accountability, serve justice and achieve reconciliation."[63] These processes now include memorialization, education, and local justice. There is also much greater effort to mix and match different mechanisms depending on the context.

Transitional justice has also been unmoored from its origins in the democratizing transitions of Eastern Europe and the Southern Cone. It can now be implemented before, during, after, and even without transitions. It can also take place before, during, and after violent conflict. Transitional justice has also expanded its remit from international crimes (e.g. genocide) and gross human rights abuses (e.g. disappearances) to violations of economic, social, and cultural rights.

There are ongoing policy debates over whether transitional justice should be minimalist or maximalist.[64] The minimalist approach focuses on short-term legalistic goals (e.g. strengthening the rule of law, expressivism) whereas the maximalist approach emphasizes long-term goals that are less easily measured (e.g. ending impunity, reconciliation). Over the past several years, the transitional justice "industry"—exemplified by the International Center for Transitional Justice and the *International Journal of Transitional Justice*—has embraced a maximalist approach that links transitional justice to development, migration, and DDR.

Linking DDR and transitional justice

Rationales

The IDDRS module sets out three, somewhat incompatible, arguments for linking DDR and transitional justice: legal, moral, and instrumental. The legal argument is that DDR programs must conform to international human rights norms, international humanitarian law, and international criminal law.[65] Hence, the IDDRS transitional justice module rules out the use of amnesties even though they can be effective tools for DDR.[66] It also restricts DDR from using local justice processes that discriminate against women and children[67]—despite the fact that "local justice addresses the (comparatively neglected) reintegration aspect of [DDR] programs more directly, quickly, and efficiently than other transitional justice measures."[68]

The second argument is that DDR and transitional justice have "long-term shared objectives of reconciliation and peace."[69] While acknowledging that reconciliation is "a difficult concept to define or measure," the IDDRS transitional justice module states that both DDR and transitional justice seek to build trust: between ex-combatants and society, and between victims and society.[70] This maximalist conception of transitional justice as trust-building is rooted in the influential work of Pablo de Greiff, ICTJ's research director.[71]

Finally, the instrumental argument is that transitional justice mechanisms may help the reintegration of former combatants. Unlike the previous two arguments, this one can be empirically tested. The IDDRS transitional justice module claims that transitional justice mechanisms:

> can increase the likelihood that DDR programmes will achieve their aims, by strengthening the legitimacy of the programme[s] from the perspective of the victims of violence and their communities, and contributing in this way to their willingness to accept returning ex-combatants.[72]

As Humphreys and Weinstein suggest, this is more likely to be the case where ex-combatants participated in abusive armed groups, particularly if they are reintegrating into a local community that suffered at the hands of their armed group.

Integration versus coordination

Once it is accepted that DDR and transitional justice should be linked, there is still the question of how that should happen. The IDDRS urges integrated planning between DDR actors and other peacebuilding actors. When the UN piloted integrated DDR in Haiti and Sudan, it went further, pushing for integrated implementation.[73] The poor results prompted a group of scholar-practitioners to recommend that "alternative approaches emphasizing coordination may be more effective than full-scale integration."[74] As one DDR donor told me: "If you want to design something that's manageable, don't be too holistic."[75]

Prominent transitional justice advocates differ over whether there should be integration or coordination. Kimberly Theidon argues that "successful reintegration requires ... fusing the processes and goals of DDR programs with transitional justice measures."[76] By contrast, Pablo de Greiff contends that "the more ambitious dimensions of reintegration should be carried out by means of *coordination with other programs* rather than being the responsibility and parts of the DDR program."[77] The IDDRS module on transitional justice adopts the latter approach, emphasizing coordination.[78] A different, and arguably more realistic, approach would see the coordination of DDR and transitional justice programs in the short term (when transitional justice programs pose the greatest risk to disarmament and demobilization), but leave longer-term reintegration to transitional justice, development, and other peacebuilding programs.

Sequencing

There are often real tensions between DDR and transitional justice and, more broadly, between security and accountability, in the short term. Whereas many ex-combatants (some of whom may have perpetrated international crimes) want amnesty, many victims want some form of justice or truth-telling. Furthermore, ex-combatants and victims compete for scarce resources from the state and international donors. Here, ex-combatants usually win out: of the 22 countries with DDR programs in 2005, not one had a reparations program for survivors.

Some of these tensions can be mitigated by coordination around sequencing. For the most part, there has been very little coordination to sequence DDR and transitional justice. This is largely because DDR programs usually start before transitional justice programs. The UN Secretary-General's Report on Peacebuilding stressed that "Getting the timing and sequencing right among priorities requires a delicate balance and difficult trade-offs within the framework of a coherent strategy."[79] It acknowledged that elections and security sector reform "if pursued too early after conflict, can undermine a fragile peace."[80] Similarly, specific transitional justice mechanisms (e.g. trials) could jeopardize peacebuilding if they happen too soon.[81] The IDDRS module on transitional justice makes some helpful suggestions about how to facilitate greater sequencing.[82] For example, it states that "Assistance offered to excombatants is less likely to foster resentment if reparations for victims are provided at a comparative level and within the same relative time period."[83]

Specific transitional justice mechanisms

I now want to briefly look at how six key transitional justice mechanisms—amnesties, trials, truth commissions, local justice, reparations, and vetting—might positively influence the social reintegration of ex-combatants, and thus the larger project of post-conflict peacebuilding.[84] These are in the nature of claims or hypotheses that will need to be tested empirically.

Amnesties

The short-term tensions between DDR and transitional justice are most apparent when it comes to amnesties for gross human rights abuses. Peace negotiators and DDR practitioners generally view amnesties as useful bargaining chips for getting potential spoilers to sign on to peace agreements and to disarm and demobilize their forces. By contrast, most human rights and transitional justice advocates argue that amnesties are morally unacceptable and (increasingly) legally impermissible. Since the 1999 Lome Peace Accord in Sierra Leone, the UN has taken a principled stance against amnesties for gross human rights abuses—especially for genocide, crimes against humanity, and war crimes.[85] The IDDRS has followed this approach: "while national amnesties may be agreed to, the UN system upholds the principles of international law, and cannot support processes that do not properly deal with serious violations of human rights and humanitarian law."[86] Similarly, the IDDRS module on transitional justice rejects the use of amnesties[87]—even though a serious case can be made for amnesties as a peacebuilding tool.[88]

Prosecutions

There is an understandable tendency to think of DDR and prosecutions as mutually exclusive: after all, many combatants will be less willing to disarm and demobilize if they fear being prosecuted for gross human rights abuses. Yet, the tension between DDR and prosecutions has been overstated. Eric Witte found "no evidence that prosecutions have seriously derailed DDR."[89] This is partly because most combatants or ex-combatants have little to fear in the way of prosecution. In certain contexts, DDR and prosecutions may even share a common aim in removing potential spoilers from the peace process. The clearest example of this is Colombia, where those who demobilize as part of plea bargains receive lighter sentences.[90]

Prosecutions may also help ex-combatants reintegrate in two ways. First, they may enable victims and communities to individualize guilt by differentiating between those combatants who perpetrated gross human rights abuses and those who did not. Second, prosecutions might reduce victim and community mistrust and resentment of ex-combatants by "providing communities with some assurance that those whom they are asked to admit back into their midst do not include the perpetrators of serious crimes under international law."[91]

Truth commissions

Truth commissions may aid the social reintegration of ex-combatants by giving them a forum where they can apologize to victims and communities, and explain their actions (including coerced participation).[92] For example, many ex-militia in Timor Leste sought local hearings (through the truth commission's Community Reconciliation Process) to reduce their stigma, avoid retribution, and achieve legal finality—even though most had already self-demobilized and returned to their communities.[93] Those hearings provided some measure of shaming and reintegration: "In a number of hearings it was evident the [perpetrators] were 'lowering themselves' before their communities, and that the hearing was at one level a public process of shaming, that concluded with the official re-admittance of the [perpetrators] back into the family."[94] Anecdotal evidence suggests that those hearings have helped some low-level ex-combatants reintegrate into their communities.[95] In one small study, a number of ex-militia "felt that community members were no longer suspicious of them or called them 'militia.'"[96]

Truth commission reports may also aid the political reintegration of ex-combatants. By recognizing the political abuses of previous governments, the Sierra Leone Truth and Reconciliation Commission's final report arguably helped the political reintegration of the RUF rebel group "by signalling that addressing RUF political grievances was deemed integral to the formation of a more equitable Sierra Leonean political landscape."[97] The final report also recommended new institutions and processes to give more political voice to Sierra Leonean youth, whose marginalization had helped fuel the civil war in the first place.[98]

Local justice

"Local justice" is informal, accessible, and participatory dispute resolution, which runs the gamut from cleansing ceremonies in Mozambique and Northern Uganda to state-controlled community courts in Rwanda.[99] In numerous post-conflict settings, purification rituals have been used to help reintegrate former fighters back into their communities.[100] Kees Kingma flagged early on that "[t]hese rituals have an important impact on acceptance by the community, as well as on the state of mind of the ex-combatants themselves."[101] In addition, local justice processes are being increasingly used in conjunction with other transitional justice mechanisms, such as amnesties (as in Uganda) and truth commissions (as in East Timor and Sierra Leone).

Not surprisingly, the IDDRS, with its emphasis on community-based reintegration, has stated that "[r]eintegration programmes for ex-combatants should … support the establishment of local conflict-resolution mechanisms that can work towards finding equitable and sustainable solutions to potential conflict about access to land and other resources."[102] However, that support for local justice has to be read alongside its injunction that "DDR programmes shall not reconstitute traditional power structures that may have contributed to the outbreak of violent conflict in the first place, but instead shall encourage reconciliation and the inclusion of all stakeholders."[103] The new IDDRS transitional justice module makes the point emphatically: "Before establishing a link with locally based processes, DDR programmes must ensure that they are legitimate and that they respect international human rights standards, including that they do not discriminate, particularly against women, and children."[104] This seems to rule out the use of local justice, given that most of these mechanisms violate international human rights standards.[105]

Reparations

Reparations programs, where they exist, are largely disconnected from DDR. Pablo de Greiff argued that "Providing benefits to ex-combatants without attending to the claims of victims not only leaves victims at a comparative disadvantage but gives rise to new grievances, which may exacerbate their resistance against returning ex-combatants."[106] Reparations may also provide a (partial) solution to a problem that bedevils DDR programs: the low numbers of female ex-combatants enrolled. Annan and Patel have suggested that "Reparations programmes can provide benefits to women and children associated with armed groups and forces who experienced high levels of victimization, but are averse to participating in a DDR process that may again put them into close proximity with ex-combatants."[107]

Vetting and screening

Many DDR programs offer some ex-combatants the opportunity to be reintegrated into the (supposedly reformed) security sector. Vetting those ex-combatants for human rights abuses ensures that they are not employed in the public sector. The IDDRS's transitional justice module proposes that DDR programs "consider" screening ex-combatants (essentially, a preliminary vetting) for gross human rights abuses—even though it recognizes that, in some contexts, "it will deter combatants from entering the DDR programme."[108] It further recommends that, "at a minimum," ex-combatants credibly alleged to have engaged in gross human rights abuses should not receive DDR benefits.[109]

In practice, DDR programs have been very reluctant to engage in any human rights screening. The initial World Bank strategy recommended screening ex-combatants in the Democratic Republic of Congo for war crimes, but the UN peacekeeping mission never attempted that.[110] The Rwandan agency in charge of DDR also decided not to screen ex-combatants for genocide or other crimes.[111] In addition, there would be serious due process concerns about screening ex-combatants based on allegations.

Conclusion

The IDDRS created unreasonably high expectations of what DDR can realistically accomplish. It is still unclear whether DDR programs actually have any positive impact on the reintegration of ex-combatants. Following Pugel, then, DDR practitioners should take a minimalist approach, focusing on short-term security and ex-combatants, while leaving longer-term reintegration mostly to transitional justice and development actors who are better equipped to deal with other war-affected groups and communities.

This chapter has described how transitional justice might aid peacebuilding by easing the social reintegration of former combatants. Ex-combatants may reintegrate more successfully if given public spaces, such as those provided by truth commissions and local justice processes, where they can apologize and perhaps undergo purification rituals.[112] Such actions may reduce the fears that ex-combatants and receiving communities often have of one another. Transitional justice mechanisms, particularly reparations, may help blunt the resentment and envy that victims and communities sometimes feel toward returning ex-combatants who receive reinsertion and reintegration assistance. They also may assure victims and receiving communities that perpetrators of international crimes will pay some price for their actions, whether through being punished or publicly shamed or forced to make reparation. Finally, transitional justice mechanisms may help individualize responsibility, so that victims and communities do not perceive all ex-combatants as having committed international crimes.[113] Overall, then, these mechanisms may help reduce reprisal, stigmatization, or discrimination against ex-combatants among victims and receiving communities—something that will benefit their social reintegration.

If transitional justice is supposed to assist the reintegration of ex-combatants, then we need to know more about the dynamics of reintegration and the obstacles it confronts. Several scholars have pointed to the need for better empirical studies to measure reintegration of ex-combatants.[114] We also need more empirical research into how transitional justice affects the reintegration of ex-combatants. A particularly salient issue at the moment is how International Criminal Court (ICC) arrest warrants are impacting DDR programs and reintegration.[115] Once policymakers and practitioners have a solid evidence base, it will be easier to coordinate DDR and transitional justice in the field.

Notes

1 Lars Waldorf would like to thank Ana Cutter Patel and Pablo de Greiff for involving him in the research project on Transitional Justice and DDR that they spearheaded at the International Center for Transitional Justice (ICTJ).

2 The term "post-conflict" will be used as shorthand for the period following a (formal or informal) peace accord. In fact, many post-conflict states exist in a limbo of what the anthropologist Paul Richards terms "no peace, no war." Paul Richards, "New War: An Ethnographic Approach," in Paul Richards (ed.), *No Peace, No War: An Anthropology of Contemporary Armed Conflicts* (Oxford: James Currey, 2005), pp. 13–14. Similarly, Robert Muggah points out that violence often increases after peace agreements. Robert Muggah, "No Magic Bullet: A Critical Perspective on Disarmament, Demobilization and Reintegration (DDR) and Weapons Reduction in Post-Conflict Contexts," *Round Table*, 94 (2005), pp. 240–42.

3 On liberal peacebuilding generally, see Edward Newman, Roland Paris, and Oliver P. Richmond (eds), *New Perspectives on Liberal Peacebuilding* (Tokyo: United Nations University, 2010); and Roland Paris, *At War's End: Building Peace after Civil Conflict* (Cambridge: Cambridge University Press, 2004). For the link between transitional justice and liberal peacebuilding, see Chandra Lekha Sriram, "Justice as Peace? Liberal Peacebuilding and Strategies of Transitional Justice," *Global Society*, vol. 21 (2007), pp. 579–91.

4 ICTJ has sought to persuade policymakers that DDR and transitional justice are complementary peacebuilding processes. See Jeannie Annan and Ana Cutter Patel, "Critical Issues and Lessons in Social Reintegration: Balancing Justice, Psychological Well Being, and Community Reconciliation" (Bogota: CIDDR, 2009); Roger Duthie,

"Transitional Justice and Social Reintegration," in Stockholm Initiative on Disarmament Demobilisation Reintegration, *Background Studies* (Stockholm: Ministry for Foreign Affairs, 2005); Ana Cutter Patel, Pablo de Greiff, and Lars Waldorf, *Disarming the Past: Transitional Justice and Ex-Combatants* (New York: SSRC, 2010); and Ana Cutter Patel, "Transitional Justice and DDR," in Robert Muggah (ed.), *Security and Post-Conflict Reconstruction: Dealing with Fighters in the Aftermath of War* (Abingdon: Routledge, 2009). For a similar perspective from scholars not associated with ICTJ, see Chandra Lekha Sriram and Johanna Herman, "DDR and Transitional Justice: Bridging the Divide?" *Conflict, Security & Development*, 9 (2009), pp. 455–74.

5 United Nations, "The Rule of Law and Transitional Justice in Conflict and Post-Conflict Societies: Report of the Secretary-General," UN Doc S/2004/616 (August 23, 2004), para. 21. For further reframing of the peace versus justice debate, see, e.g., Priscilla Hayner, *Negotiating Justice: Guidance for Mediators* (Geneva: The Centre for Humanitarian Dialogue, 2009).

6 United Nations, "2005 World Summit Outcome," UN Doc A/Res/61 (October 24, 2005). In his 2009 report on peacebuilding, UN Secretary-General Ban Ki Moon reiterated "the interlinked and mutually reinforcing nature" of "development, peace and security and human rights." United Nations, "Report of the Secretary-General on Peacebuilding in the Immediate Aftermath of Conflict," UN Doc A/63/881-S/2009/304 (New York: UN, 2009), para. 18.

7 Department of Peacekeeping Operations (DPKO), *IDDRS: Transitional Justice and DDR*, section 6.20, p. 1.

8 DPKO, *IDDRS*, op. cit., sec. 2.10, p. 4.

9 For brief historical overviews of DDR, see Robert Muggah, "Introduction: The Emperor's clothes?" in Robert Muggah (ed.), *Security and Post-Conflict Reconstruction: Dealing with Fighters in the Aftermath of War* (Abingdon: Routledge, 2009), pp. 4–6; Macartan Humphreys and Jeremy M. Weinstein, "Demobilization and Reintegration," *Journal of Conflict Resolution*, 51 (2007), pp. 531–32.

10 United Nations, "Report of the High-Level Panel on Threats, Challenges and Change," UN Doc A/59/565 (December 2, 2004), paras 227 and 228.

11 Albert Carames, Vicenc Fisas, and Daniel Luz, "Analysis of Disarmament, Demobilization and Reintegration (DDR) Programmes Existing in the World during 2005" (Barcelona: Escola de cultura de pau, 2006), p. 9. Most DDR programs are run by national governments with funding from multi-lateral donors (particularly the United Nations and the World Bank) and bi-lateral donors.

12 There is the risk that DDR programs create incentives for non-combatants to join armed groups in order to become eligible for DDR benefits. As the IDDRS puts it:

> Ideally, DDR should be a one-time intervention, done correctly the first time and never to be repeated again. Otherwise, no matter what safeguards are put in place, the rewards people think they receive from taking part in DDR can become an incentive for them to participate in future conflicts.
>
> DPKO, *IDDRS*, op. cit., sec. 4.30, p. 17

This reflects the negative experiences encountered with weapons buy-back programs.

13 DPKO, *IDDRS*, op. cit., sec. 4.30, p. 20. Anders Nilsson rightly notes that retroactive DDR may be needed for individuals or groups that self-demobilized. Anders Nilsson, "Reintegrating Ex-Combatants in Post-Conflict Societies" (Stockholm: Swedish International Development Cooperation Agency, 2005), p. 17. In Tajikistan, reintegration occurred without much disarmament or demobilization. Stina Torjesen and S. Neil MacFarlane, "Reintegration before Disarmament: The Case of Post-Conflict Reintegration in Tajikistan," in Robert Muggah (ed.), *Security and Post-Conflict Reconstruction: Dealing with Fighters in the Aftermath of War* (Abingdon: Routledge, 2009), pp. 47–66.

14 DPKO, *IDDRS*, op. cit., sec. 4.10, p. 3.

15 DPKO, *IDDRS*, op. cit., sec. 4.20, pp. 1–2.
16 DPKO, *IDDRS*, op. cit., sec. 1.20, p. 6.
17 DPKO, *IDDRS*, op. cit., sec. 1.20, p. 19. It is now generally recognized that "reintegration" is a somewhat misleading term, as many ex-combatants do not return to their home communities. This can be for any number of reasons: (1) some never left in the first place; (2) some search for economic betterment in urban areas; (3) some fear returning to communities they or their armed groups have harmed; or (4) some no longer have communities left to return to.
18 DPKO, *IDDRS Operational Guidelines* (New York: UN, no date), sec. 2.30, p. 45. See DPKO, *IDDRS*, op. cit., sec. 4.10, p. 10.
19 See Nilsson, "Reintegrating Ex-Combatants," pp. 15–17; Beatrice Pouligny, "The Politics and Anti-Politics of Contemporary 'Disarmament, Demobilization and Reintegration' Programs" (Paris: CERI, 2004), p. 7.
20 For overviews, see Luisa Maria Dietrich Ortega, "Transitional Justice and Female Ex-Combatants: Lessons Learned from International Experience" and Roger Duthie and Irma Specht, "DDR, Transitional Justice, and the Reintegration of Former Child Combatants" in Ana Cutter Patel, Pablo de Greiff, and Lars Waldorf, *Disarming the Past: Transitional Justice and Ex-Combatants* (New York: SSRC, 2010). For specific case studies on gender and DDR, see Kathleen M. Jennings, "The Political Economy of DDR in Liberia: A Gendered Critique," *Conflict, Security & Development*, 9 (2009); Kimberly Theidon, "Reconstructing Masculinities: The Disarmament, Demobilization and Reintegration of Former Combatants in Colombia," *Human Rights Quarterly*, vol. 31 (2009).
21 By contrast, the IDDRS explicitly states that weapons possession should not be an entry requirement for DDR programs, particularly for children. DPKO, *IDDRS*, op. cit., sec. 4.10, pp. 9, 11.
22 DPKO, *IDDRS*, op. cit., sec. 4.10, p. 11.
23 Nilsson, "Reintegrating Ex-Combatants," p. 72.
24 Muggah, "Introduction," p. 3; see Leontine Specker, "The R-Phase of DDR Processes" (The Hague: Netherlands Institute of International Relations, 2008), pp. v, 5–9.
25 Mark Knight and Alpaslan Özerdem, "Guns, Camps and Cash: Disarmament, Demobilization and Reinsertion of Former Combatants in Transitions from War to Peace," *Journal of Peace Research*, 41 (2004), pp. 499–516.
26 United Nations, "Disarmament, Demobilization and Reintegration: Report of the Secretary-General," A/60/705 (New York: UN, 2006), p. 3.
27 United Nations, "Disarmament, Demobilization and Reintegration," op. cit., p. 9. These principles are fleshed out in considerable detail in DPKO, IDDRS, op. cit., sec. 2.10, pp. 8–15. Importantly, the *IDDRS* clarifies that "national ownership involves more than just central government leadership: it includes the participation of a broad range of State and non-State actors at national, provincial and local levels," DPKO, *IDDRS*, op. cit., sec. 2.10, p. 12.
28 DPKO, *IDDRS*, op. cit., sec. 1.10, p. 2.
29 Robert Muggah, Mats Berdal, and Stina Trojesen, "Conclusions: Enter an Evidence-Based Security Promotion Agenda," in Robert Muggah (ed.), *Security and Post-Conflict Reconstruction: Dealing with Fighters in the Aftermath of War* (Abingdon: Routledge, 2009), p. 277.
30 Robert Muggah, Desmond Molloy, and Maximo Halty, "(Dis)integrating DDR in Sudan and Haiti? Practitioners' Views To Overcoming Integration Inertia" in Robert Muggah (ed.), *Security and Post-Conflict Reconstruction: Dealing with Fighters in the Aftermath of War* (Abingdon: Routledge, 2009), p. 215.
31 Muggah, "Introduction," op. cit., p. 6.
32 Kathleen Jennings, "Unclear Ends, Unclear Means: Reintegration in Postwar Societies—The Case of Liberia," *Global Governance*, 14 (2008), p. 341. See Nicole Ball and Luc van de Goor, "Disarmament, Demobilization and Reintegration: Mapping Issues,

Dilemmas and Guiding Principles" (The Hague: Netherlands Institute of International Relations, 2006), p. 1.

33 Most DDR programs focused on the more easily deliverable and measurable goals of disarmament and demobilization. See, e.g., Muggah, "No Magic Bullet," op. cit., p. 246; Jennings, "Unclear Ends," op. cit., pp. 333–34.

34 As Paul Collier and Anke Hoeffler contend, the larger the pool of unemployed young men, the greater the risk of conflict. Paul Collier and Anke Hoeffler, "Military Expenditure in Post-Conflict Societies" (Centre for the Study of African Economics, Oxford University, April 8, 2004).

35 Nat J. Colletta, Markus Kostner, and Ingo Wiederhofer, "Disarmament, Demobilization, and Reintegration: Lessons and Liabilities in Reconstruction," in Robert I. Rotberg (ed.), *When States Fail: Causes and Consequences* (Princeton, NJ: Princeton University Press, 2004).

36 See DPKO, *IDDRS*, op. cit., sec. 2.10, 6.

37 Muggah, "Introduction," op. cit., p. 3. In their study of DDR in Afghanistan, Bhatia and Muggah found that "repeated DDR activities failed to sufficiently account for the complex motivations and interests of commanders, rank and file and their layered relationships with communities. Instead, interventions advanced a simple economic bias treating beneficiaries as a homogenous caseload who would respond rationally to monetary incentives." Muggah, "Introduction," op. cit. p. 18; Bhatia and Muggah, "Demobilization in Afghanistan," p. 154. On the motivations of militias and rebel groups more generally, see Chris Alden, Monika Thakur, and Matthew Arnold, *Militias and the Challenges of Post-Conflict Peace: Silencing the Guns* (London: Zed Books, 2011); Jeremy M. Weinstein, *Inside Rebellion: The Politics of Insurgent Violence* (Cambridge: Cambridge University Press, 2007).

38 Macartan Humphreys and Jeremy Weinstein, "Demobilization and Reintegration in Sierra Leone: Assessing Progress," in Robert Muggah (ed.), *Security and Post-Conflict Reconstruction: Dealing with Fighters in the Aftermath of War* (Abingdon: Routledge, 2009), p. 56.

39 DPKO, *IDDRS*, op. cit., sec. 4.30, p. 3.

40 DPKO, *IDDRS*, op. cit., sec. 4.30, p. 3.

41 DPKO, *IDDRS*, op. cit., sec. 2.20, p. 8. The Stockholm Initiative proposed creating a multi-donor trust fund that would support the needs of both ex-combatants and their receiving communities: Stockholm Initiative on Disarmament Demobilization Reintegration, "Final Report" (Stockholm: Swedish Ministry of Foreign Affairs, 2006), pp. 35–36. This assumes that international and national actors will be willing to provide a roughly equal measure of assistance to local communities and other war-affected groups (such as victims) even though they do not present short-term threats to security in the way that ex-combatants do. See Jennings, "Unclear Ends," op. cit., p. 341.

42 Annan and Patel, "Critical Issues and Lessons in Social Reintegration," p. 10 (citing T. Bouta, "Assessment of the Ituri Disarmament and Community Reinsertion Program" (The Hague: Netherlands Institute of International Relations, 2005)). Similarly, the inclusion of communities as beneficiaries in the DDR program in Timor-Leste "resulted in the setting of unclear goals, and less sure-footed implementation." Gordon Peake, "What the Timorese Veterans say: Unpacking DDR in Timor-Leste" in Robert Muggah (ed.), *Security and Post-Conflict Reconstruction: Dealing with Fighters in the Aftermath of War* (Abingdon: Routledge, 2009), p. 166.

43 See Annan and Patel, "Critical Issues and Lessons in Social Reintegration," op. cit., p. 10. However, there is an increased focus on community in what is termed Second Generation DDR programs (where the preconditions for traditional DDR are missing). See United Nations Department of Peacekeeping Operations, *Second Generation Disarmament, Demobilization and Reintegration Practices in Peace Operations* (New York: DPKO, 2010); Nat J. Colletta and Robert Muggah, "Context Matters: Interim Stabilization and Second Generation Approaches to Security Promotion," *Conflict, Security & Development*, 9 (2009), p. 444.

44 James Pugel, "Measuring Reintegration in Liberia: Assessing the Gap between Outputs and Outcomes," in Robert Muggah (ed.), *Security and Post-Conflict Reconstruction: Dealing with Fighters in the Aftermath of War* (Abingdon: Routledge, 2009), p. 90; Ball and van de Goor, "Disarmament, Demobilization and Reintegration," op. cit., p. 3.

45 Pugel, "Measuring Reintegration in Liberia," op. cit., p. 90.

46 World Bank, *Multi-Country Demobilization and Reintegration Program Final Report*, pp. 4, 50.

47 For primarily quantitative studies, see, e.g., Humphreys and Weinstein, "Demobilization and Reintegration," op. cit.; Ana M. Arjona and Stathis Kalyvas, "Preliminary Results of a Survey of Demobilized Combatants in Colombia" (unpublished draft, 2006). For qualitative studies, see Rosalind Shaw, "Linking Justice with Reintegration? Ex-Combatants and the Sierra Leone Experiment" in Rosalind Shaw and Lars Waldorf (eds), *Localizing Transitional Justice: Interventions and Priorities after Mass Violence* (Palo Alto: Stanford University Press, 2010), pp. 111–34; Kimberly Theidon, "Transitional Subjects: The Disarmament, Demobilization and Reintegration of Excombatants in Colombia," *International Journal of Transitional Justice*, vol 1. (2007), pp. 66–99.

48 DPKO, *IDDRS*, op. cit., sec. 4.30, pp. 14–15. Specker makes the same point. Specker, op. cit., pp. vi, 22.

49 Nilsson, "Reintegrating Ex-Combatants," p. 35. Jennings makes a similar critique, while also offering suggestions for how to evaluate reintegration. Jennings, "Unclear Ends," op. cit., pp. 327–38.

50 Muggah, "Introduction," op. cit., p. 15.

51 Humphreys and Weinstein, "Demobilization and Reintegration," op. cit., p. 549.

52 Humphreys and Weinstein, "Demobilization and Reintegration," op. cit., p. 560.

53 Peter Uvin, *Ex-Combatants in Burundi: Why They Joined, Why They Left, How They Fared* (Washington, DC: The World Bank/Multi-Country Demobilization and Reintegration Program, 2007).

54 Jennings, "Unclear Ends," op. cit., p. 338.

55 Torjesen and MacFarlane, "Reintegration before Disarmament," op. cit., p. 47.

56 See Sarah Michael, *Reintegration Assistance for Ex-Combatants: Good Practices and Lessons for the MDRP* (Washington, DC: The World Bank Multi-Country Demobilization and Reintegration Program, 2006), pp. ii, 2–3; but see Anna Borzello, "The Challenge of DDR in Northern Uganda: The Lord's Resistance Army," *Conflict, Security & Development*, 7 (2007), p. 403.

57 Uvin, *Ex-Combatants in Burundi*, op. cit., p. 21.

58 Christopher Blattman and Jeannie Annan, "Child Combatants in Northern Uganda: Reintegration Myths and Realities," in Robert Muggah (ed.), *Security and Post-Conflict Reconstruction: Dealing with Fighters in the Aftermath of War* (Abingdon: Routledge, 2009), p. 112.

59 Peter Barron, "Getting Reintegration Back on Track: Problems in Aceh and Priorities for Moving Forward," Conference on Aceh at Harvard University, October 24–27, 2007, p. 9. He recommended basing payments on needs rather than on ex-combatant status. Ibid.

60 Humphreys and Weinstein, "Demobilization and Reintegration," op. cit., p. 533.

61 Humphreys and Weinstein, "Demobilization and Reintegration in Sierra Leone," op. cit., p. 60.

62 Though it is important to acknowledge that those reintegration difficulties existed even though Sierra Leone had a truth commission and international-national criminal tribunal.

63 United Nations, "The Rule of Law and Transitional Justice," op. cit., para. 8.

64 I use these terms differently from Olsen, Payne, and Reiter, who associate them with different transitional justice mechanisms: maximalist (trials), minimalist (amnesties), moderate (truth commissions), and holistic (a mix of mechanisms). Tricia D. Olsen,

Leigh A. Payne, and Andrew G. Reiter, *Transitional Justice in Balance: Comparing Processes, Weighing Efficacy* (Washington, DC: United States Institute of Peace Press, 2010), p. 16–25.

65 DPKO, *IDDRS*, op. cit., sec. 6.20, pp. 5–7. As the UN High Commissioner for Human Rights stated, "the legal framework governing the disarmament, demobilization and reintegration process of illegal armed groups should guarantee the rights to truth, justice and reparations." UN Commission on Human Rights, "Study on the Right to the Truth, Report of the Office of the United Nations High Commissioner for Human Rights, 8 February 2006," UN Doc E/CN.4/2006/91, para. 16 and n. 28.

66 DPKO, *IDDRS*, op. cit., sec. 6.20, pp. 19–20. On the use of amnesties, see Mark Freeman, "Amnesties and DDR Programs," in Patel, de Greiff, and Waldorf, *Disarming the Past*, op. cit.

67 DPKO, *IDDRS*, op. cit., sec. 6.20, pp. 26–27.

68 Duthie, "Transitional Justice and Social Reintegration," op. cit., p. 230.

69 DPKO, *IDDRS*, op. cit., sec. 6.20, p. 2.

70 DPKO, *IDDRS*, op. cit., sec. 6.20, p. 4. Knight and Özerdem see DDR as creating a new social contract between ex-combatants and both the state and society. Knight and Özerdem, "Guns, Camps and Cash," op. cit., pp. 506, 513.

71 For a recent statement of his argument, see Pablo de Greiff, "Establishing Links between DDR and Reparations" in Patel, de Greiff, and Waldorf, *Disarming the Past*, op. cit.

72 DPKO, *IDDRS*, op. cit., sec. 6.20, p. 2.

73 Muggah, Molloy, and Halty, "(Dis)integrating DDR in Sudan and Haiti?" op. cit., p. 207.

74 Ibid., p. 218.

75 Diplomat, interview by the author, Kigali, May 23, 2006.

76 Theidon, "Reconstructing Masculinities," op. cit., p. 2.

77 De Greiff, "Establishing Links between DDR and Reparations," op. cit., p. 148.

78 DPKO, *IDDRS*, op. cit., sec. 6.20, pp. 18–28.

79 United Nations, "Report of the Secretary-General on Peacebuilding," para. 20.

80 Ibid., This echoes Roland Paris's influential critique of liberal peacebuilding. Paris, *At War's End*, op. cit.

81 Sriram, "Justice as Peace?" op. cit.

82 DPKO, *IDDRS*, op. cit., sec. 6.20, pp. 25–26. Sriram and Herman correctly note that "it is not possible to formulate a template for sequencing DDR and transitional justice" given the wide variation in country contexts. Sriram and Herman, "DDR and Transitional Justice," op. cit., p. 468.

83 DPKO, *IDDRS*, op. cit., sec. 6.20, p. 25. Though realistically, it recognizes that DDR and reparations programs are likely to remain uncoordinated in the near future because "while DDR is funded, reparations are not." Ibid.

84 This is discussed in greater detail in Patel, de Greiff, and Waldorf, *Disarming the Past*, op. cit. The best overview is Patel, "Transitional Justice and DDR," op. cit. Nine individual case studies, commissioned by ICTJ, are available at <*http://ictj.org/our-work/research/disarmament-demobilization-and-reintegration*>.

85 See United Nations, "The Rule of Law and Transitional Justice," op. cit., para. 10.

86 DPKO, *IDDRS*, op. cit., sec. 2.20, p. 9.

87 DPKO, *IDDRS*, op. cit., sec. 6.20, p. 19.

88 See Freeman, "Amnesties and DDR Programs," op. cit.; Louise Mallinder, *Amnesty, Human Rights and Political Transitions: Bridging the Peace and Justice Divide* (Oxford: Hart, 2008), pp. 379–402.

89 Eric Witte, "Beyond 'Peace vs. Justice': Understanding the Relationship Between DDR Programs and the Prosecution of International Crimes," in Patel, de Greiff, and Waldorf, *Disarming the Past*, op. cit., p. 88.

90 On Colombia, see, e.g., Kimberly Theidon, "Transitional Subjects," op. cit., pp. 70–73; Catalina Diaz, "Colombia's Bid for Justice and Peace" (Nuremberg: Working Group on Development and Peace [FriEnt], 2007); Sergio Jaramillo, Yanet Giha, and Paula Torres, *Disarmament, Demobilization and Reinsertion Amidst the Conflict: The Case of Colombia* (New York: International Center for Transitional Justice, 2009).

91 DPKO, *IDDRS*, op. cit., sec. 6.20, p. 8. See Patel, "Transitional Justice and DDR," op. cit. p. 254.

92 For more detail, see Lars Waldorf, "Ex-Combatants and Truth Commissions," in Patel, de Greiff, and Waldorf, *Disarming the Past*, op. cit.

93 Piers Pigou, "The Community Reconciliation Process of the Commission for Reception, Truth and Reconciliation" (Dili: United Nations Development Programme Timor-Leste, 2004), pp. 50, 76–78.

94 Pigou, "The Community Reconciliation Process," op. cit., p. 66. Kelsall and Shaw made similar observations about local TRC hearings in Sierra Leone. Tim Kelsall, "Truth, Lies, Ritual: Preliminary Reflections on the Truth and Reconciliation Commission in Sierra Leone," *Human Rights Quarterly*, 27 (2005), pp. 379–80; Shaw, "Linking Justice with Reintegration?" op. cit.

95 Pigou, "The Community Reconciliation Process," op. cit., p. 81.

96 Judicial System Monitoring Programme (JSMP), "Unfulfilled Expectations: Community Views on CAVR's Community Reconciliation Process" (Dili: JSMP, 2004), p. 17.

97 Keiran Mitton, "Engaging Disengagement: The Political Reintegration of Sierra Leone's Revolutionary United Front," *Conflict, Security & Development*, 8 (2008), p. 205.

98 Mitton, "Engaging Disengagement," op. cit., p. 205. As Mitton makes clear, however, this effort at political reintegration was severely hampered by the failure of economic reintegration.

99 This underscores the need to distinguish carefully between bottom-up local initiatives and top-down state informalism. See Lars Waldorf, "Mass Justice for Mass Atrocity: Rethinking Local Justice as Transitional Justice," *Temple Law Review*, vol. 79 (2006).

100 Annan and Patel, "Critical Issues and Lessons in Social Reintegration," op. cit., p. 11. Kees Kingma, "The Impact of Demobilization in Eritrea," in Kees Kingma (ed.), *Demobilization in Sub-Saharan Africa* (London: Palgrave, 2000), p. 224. He linked these ceremonies to payments by ex-combatants to village elders. Ibid., pp. 223–24.

101 Kees Kingma, "The Impact of Demobilization," op. cit., p. 224.

102 DPKO, *IDDRS*, op. cit., sec. 4.30, p. 33.

103 DPKO, *IDDRS*, op. cit., sec. 2.30, p. 6.

104 DPKO, *IDDRS*, op. cit., sec. 6.20, p. 27. The exact same language is in Annan and Patel, "Critical Issues and Lessons in Social Reintegration," op. cit., p. 12.

105 See Department for International Development (DFID), "Non-state Security and Justice Systems" (London: DFID, 2004).

106 Pablo de Greiff, "Establishing Links Between DDR and Reparations," in Patel, de Greiff, and Waldorf, *Disarming the Past*, op. cit., p. 150.

107 Annan and Patel, "Critical Issues and Lessons in Social Reintegration," op. cit., p. 14.

108 DPKO, *IDDRS*, op. cit., sec. 6.20, p. 25.

109 DPKO, *IDDRS*, op. cit., sec. 6.20, p. 25.

110 World Bank, *Greater Great Lakes Regional Strategy for Demobilization and Reintegration* (Washington, DC: World Bank, 2002), 20.

111 Lars Waldorf, "Transitional Justice and DDR in Post-Genocide Rwanda" (New York: International Center for Transitional Justice, 2009).

112 This is much less the case for female ex-combatants who often quietly self-demobilize to avoid shaming themselves and their families: for example, one talked about her "fear of people's mouths." Chris Coulter, "Reconciliation or Revenge: Narratives of Fear and Shame among Female Ex-Combatants in Sierra Leone" (Uppsala: Department of Cultural Anthropology and Ethnology, 2006).

113 Several studies, however, have raised questions about whether transitional justice mechanisms do, in fact, individuate guilt. See Eric Stover and Harvey M. Weinstein (eds), *My Neighbor, My Enemy: Justice and Community in the Aftermath of Mass Atrocity* (Cambridge: Cambridge University Press, 2004).

114 See Humphreys and Weinstein, "Demobilization and Reintegration in Sierra Leone," op. cit., pp. 64–67; James Pugel, "Measuring Reintegration in Liberia," op. cit., pp. 89–90.

115 See Patel, "Transitional Justice and DDR," op. cit. p. 250.

5 Centralizing legal pluralism? Traditional justice in transitional contexts

Rosemary Nagy

Introduction

While the parameters of transitional justice as a field of practice and normative inquiry are contested, it has nevertheless cohered as a mainstream norm over the last few decades, institutionalized in international law and transnational practice.[1] I refer to this mainstreamed, international legalist paradigm as a centralizing force within transitional justice. That is, the increased judicialization of conflict management brings an array of transitional societies into the fold of international institutions, legal norms, and a global transitional justice industry. The advantages of this include universal standards of accountability and increased know-how through resource- and information-sharing. But international standardization has also produced "legal transplants" and "one-size-fits-all" solutions that lack social and cultural connections at the local level. Transitional justice in such instances not only fails to "deal with the past" sufficiently in terms of truth, justice, or reconciliation at the level of ordinary individuals; it is also ill-suited for building a sustainable, internal culture of peace from the "bottom up."

Transitional justice practitioners and researchers have widely acknowledged this flaw, and the recent turn toward localized, "traditional" forms of justice is represented as an important corrective.[2] As noted by the UN Secretary-General in his 2004 report on transitional justice, "due regard must be given to indigenous and informal traditions for administering justice or settling disputes ... Where these are ignored or overridden, the result can be the exclusion of large sectors of society from accessible justice."[3] Traditional justice, which has been pursued after conflict in places such as Mozambique, Rwanda, Sierra Leone, East Timor, Burundi, and Uganda, represents a pluralization of transitional justice. "Pluralization" as I intend it has two related meanings. First, it represents a diversification and localization that moves away from internationally centralized modes of justice. Second, where traditional mechanisms operate alongside formal institutions, whether national or international, they are in a situation of legal pluralism, which may be defined as "two or more legal orders within the same social field."[4]

This chapter applies insights from the study of legal pluralism to identify and analyze the socio-legal and political forces at work in the turn to traditional justice. Using the Rwandan and Ugandan experiences for illustration, the chapter seeks to theorize trends within transitional justice in order to instigate further research. In particular, I hypothesize that, just as customary law was "made" through its interaction with colonialism, so too is traditional justice now "made" through its interaction with international transitional justice *as mediated by the state.* My concern is less about the "invention" of tradition, for no tradition is static, than about the ways in which traditional justice might help to consolidate state power at the expense of truth, justice, reconciliation, and durable peace.

Three main concerns animate the chapter. First, insofar as a central concern about the legality of traditional mechanisms exists, I argue that we cannot afford to isolate law from politics.[5] Second, efforts to pluralize transitional justice may actually result in it being doubly subject to centralizing forces, that is, both from international actors and from the state. This undermines the ostensible goal of creating a kind of justice that resonates with individuals and communities. Third, because traditional mechanisms should be pursued "in conformity with both international standards and local tradition," in practice this means that traditional practices may be codified and made more like the formal criminal proceedings they were intended to replace.[6] Thus there may be a risk of "one-sizing" traditional justice.

Through these lines of argument, I aim to strengthen the linkages between transitional justice and peacebuilding by expanding the typical transitional justice preoccupation with human rights concerns and legal procedures to include thinking more explicitly about relations of power. It is crucial to locate traditional mechanisms within their broader (global, national, local) socio-political environments and to ask whether the use of traditional justice will, in fact, help move a society toward positive peace, understood here as the absence of social injustice and structural violence.[7] I do not mean that traditional mechanisms themselves should necessarily address some of the more affirmative aspects of social justice associated with positive peace. Rather, my concern lies with the ways in which transitional justice might ignore, reproduce, or aggravate conditions of structural violence.[8] As I will discuss below, there is evidence to suggest that Rwanda's *gacaca* courts exacerbate conditions of structural violence by helping the state to prescribe reconciliation in coercive and unpopular ways. While I do not make as strong a claim with respect to Uganda's proposed use of *mato oput* and other traditional practices, there are nevertheless similar and worrying dynamics in the nexus of centralizing and pluralizing forces there, which I map below. Before turning to the Rwandan and Ugandan examples, I first elaborate upon the chapter's theoretical framework in the next section. The study of legal pluralism remains a relatively untapped resource in transitional justice. While the peacebuilding literature does engage legal pluralism to a greater degree, it tends to focus on constitution-making and security sector reform within a legally plural municipal system, rather than looking at specific transitional justice measures under globalized legal pluralism.

Theoretical framework: insights from the study of legal pluralism

The study of legal pluralism originated in anthropological efforts to understand social ordering outside of "lawyers' law," looking in particular at the role of customary or religious law under colonialism. One of the key arguments forged within this "classic" legal pluralism was that traditional or customary law was not a static or self-contained thing of the past but, rather, shaped through complex interactions with administrative law under colonial indirect rule.[9] Customary law was "made, not found."[10] Following the shift from colonialism to globalization, the "new" legal pluralism has grown to consider the multiplicity of state, infra-state, transnational, and global legal orders. Whether analyzing classic or new constellations, legal pluralists rail against positivist conceptions of law as a closed, autonomous system, seeing it instead as embedded within relations of unequal power where there is both domination and resistance. Law is not simply a set of rules, but constitutive of and constituted by social, economic, and political relations.

Transitional justice represents an archetype of the "new" legal pluralism insofar as it takes place through the interpenetration of a variety of legal and normative orders across different socio-legal fields at the international, transnational, state, and community levels. Moreover, the post-conflict use of traditional mechanisms is reminiscent of studies in "classic" legal pluralism, which focuses on the interactions between indigenous and Western law. These two forms of legal pluralism are intertwined and result in a complex array of complementary and conflicting transitional justice processes, norms, goals, and outcomes. Paradoxically, however, notwithstanding its pluralization, transitional justice is also subject to centralizing forces that render it internally coherent and increasingly standardized.

My use of the word "centralizing" plays upon earlier debates in legal pluralism, in which scholars such as John Griffiths defined it in contradistinction to "legal centralism."[11] Legal centralism (if this ever really existed as a social scientific position) holds that law emanates only from the state and is administered by an exclusive set of institutions.[12] Legal pluralists, in contrast, emphasize the ways in which state law is adapted, ignored, or resisted, and they point to non-state forces of social regulation. One need not deny the importance of the state in making law to be a legal pluralist. Indeed, the use of traditional justice in post-genocide Rwanda (and potentially also in Uganda) involves what is sometimes called "state legal pluralism," where customary law is incorporated into state law, resulting in the coincidence of two or more bodies of (sometimes inconsistent) legal norms.[13] Rather, for my purposes, the point to draw is that law is heterogeneous and subject to "the political mobilization of competing social forces"[14] across interdependent webs of "semi-autonomous social fields."[15]

In transitional justice processes, centralization occurs not at the level of the state but at an international level. Since there is no world state, "centralization" in my sense refers to the standardization of transitional justice through "an international web of individuals and institutions whose internal coherence is held together by common concepts, practical aims, and distinctive claims for legitimacy."[16] Admittedly, this is a rather nebulous approach to centralization, especially since I have already stated that transitional justice is pluralistic in nature (and international coordination is, admittedly, fairly unwieldy). However, I posit that transitional justice is increasingly being driven by an internationally standardized set of normative assumptions and institutional responses. This has developed through policy documents such as the UN Secretary-General's *Report on the Rule of Law and Transitional Justice in Conflict and Post-conflict Societies* and manuals from the Office of the High Commissioner for Human Rights on truth commissions, vetting, rule of law reform, prosecution, and reparation;[17] the involvement of expert consultants and international transitional justice NGOs in different countries; standardized database packages for managing information; the creation of the *ad hoc* tribunals and later the International Criminal Court; and the development of a "right to truth" and a "right to reparation" under customary international law.[18]

The production of transitional justice policies, norms, and institutions from "on high," so to speak, gives rise to the common complaint that transitional justice is "externalized" from the lives of ordinary people.[19] Consequently, transitional justice can neither contribute to the peacebuilding goal of "moving a given population from a condition of extreme vulnerability and dependency to one of self-sufficiency and well-being,"[20] nor assist in rebuilding fractured relationships from the bottom up. In part, this is due to the ways in which the centralization of transitional justice is driven by legalistic approaches that are technocratic and prone to replication.[21] The centrality of law in "dealing with the past" is not unsurprising, of course. Law speaks to qualities such as rationality, certainty, objectivity, universality, and uniformity that are highly prized in times of profound social rupture. However, as McEvoy points out, "because transitions from conflict shine a harsh light on the contingent and political nature of legality … legal formalism becomes the default position for many lawyers working in this field."[22] On this view, law is "there," to be codified and applied; it is a closed system of knowledge and stands apart from politics, social structures, cultural meanings and so forth. This attitude flies in the face of legal pluralists' main contention that law is not a closed system but subject to the complex interaction of various socio-political forces.

The consequent complaint regarding formal legal approaches is that transitional justice and peacebuilding more broadly fail sufficiently to grasp or respond to the lived experiences of atrocity and conflict. Traditional mechanisms, in contrast, offer ordinary persons greater involvement in and access to transitional justice than that provided by remote, formal institutions or technocratic reforms. Anchored in local rituals and indigenous practices, traditional mechanisms promise deeper cultural legitimacy and local ownership. They provide alternate paths to justice, including restorative justice, in broadly participatory forums that aim to reintegrate combatants/perpetrators, victims, and communities. Traditional justice represents a pluralizing move away from "one-size-fits-all" solutions and one that is often explicitly juxtaposed against the legal centralism of "Western" justice.

Yet, traditional justice is not typically designed to deal with mass atrocity. Nor is it consistent with international human rights standards when harsh corporal punishment or the "restitution" of women as brides are involved. Moreover, "tradition" itself may be a victim of conflict through the disruption of community life, the artificial environment of a refugee camp, the dislocation of families, or the erosion of social capital.[23] Thus, not surprisingly, custom will be reinvented or adapted to post-conflict settings. Hence, it may be more fitting to speak of "tradition-inspired" justice. In the following two examples of the experiences of Rwanda and Uganda, I ask how the adaptation and "*conforming*" of tradition to international standards are taken up in the push and pull between the centralization and pluralization of transitional justice.[24] How does the discursive and practical interaction of international, national, and local socio-legal fields shape "tradition" and what consequences might this have for peace and justice?[25]

Post-genocide justice in Rwanda: the *gacaca* courts

In the early aftermath of the genocide, the International Criminal Tribunal for Rwanda (ICTR) was established by the United Nations over the protests of the Rwandan government, which used its seat on the Security Council to vote against it. Although Kigali had originally asked for international assistance, it was unhappy with: the tribunal's jurisdictional mandate; sharing the Prosecutor's office and appeals chamber with the International Criminal Tribunal for the Former Yugoslavia (ICTY); locating the tribunal in Tanzania rather than in Rwanda; and not including the death penalty for leaders of the genocide. In many respects, then, the ICTR is an externalized form of justice, and its remoteness to peasant Rwandans is fairly notorious.[26] Relations between the Rwandan Patriotic Front (RPF) government and the ICTR have been strained at times, with the RPF refusing on occasion to cooperate and managing to block prosecution of war crimes alleged to have been committed by its military wing during the war.

The ICTR was only ever intended to prosecute a handful of cases; the bulk of trials were to be domestic. This plurality of post-genocide legal orders is hierarchical, with the Tribunal exercising primacy over the jurisdiction of national courts.[27] Through prosecutorial discretion the primacy rule may function as a complementary distribution of labor to various national jurisdictions, particularly now that the ICTR has a "completion strategy."[28] But it also acts as a centralizing mechanism. Drumbl argues that the overall effect of primacy "is to induce national courts that seek jurisdiction to conform to a variety of modalities that mimic those found in international criminal law regarding sanction (i.e. no death penalty) and procedure (i.e. a fair trial)."[29] Most explicitly in the case of Rwanda, which until recently had the death penalty, this resulted in its vulnerability to being denied jurisdiction over top-ranking perpetrators.[30]

Moreover, the government of Rwanda argued that international standards of due process were far too time-consuming at national courts, where the bulk of genocide prosecutions were slated to occur. By 1998 it was apparent that it would take over 100 years to process the approximately 120,000 genocide suspects languishing under deplorable prison conditions.[31] And, as with formal processes at the international level, ordinary Rwandans were estranged from the trials in Kigali due to difficulties of access and a lack of literacy or familiarity with formal procedures. Thus, the establishment of the pilot *gacaca* courts in 2002 was in explicit rejection of "classic" or "Western" justice. The Rwandan government sought a speedier process in what it claimed would be a culturally legitimate forum that would enable ordinary Rwandans to deal with the genocide in a face-to-face process.

Inspired by traditional practices translated as "justice on the grass," the reinvented *gacaca* courts were first codified in Organic Law No. 40 of 2001 (*Setting up Gacaca Jurisdictions*) and given a jurisdictional competence like that of formal courts. Unlike formal courts, however, *gacaca* is broadly participatory. There is an abundant literature on the workings and modifications of *gacaca* over the years, and so I will not rehearse that in detail here.[32] Briefly, there are approximately 12,000 *gacaca* courts operated by 250,000 elected lay judges (*Inyangamugayo* or "persons of integrity"). All genocide suspects except for accused leaders and rapists are prosecuted in the *gacaca* courts (as of 2008 rapists also come under *gacaca*'s jurisdiction). All community members over the age of 18 are expected to attend their local *gacaca* sessions both in the investigative phase, where community members helped determine victims and suspects, and in the trial phase, where witnesses corroborate, revise, or reject the evidence presented. Perpetrators are expected to confess and apologize in exchange for a reduced sentence, survivors to forgive, and the *Inyangamugayo* to judge innocence or guilt and to mete out the penalty in accordance with legislated guidelines. The government's claim is that *gacaca* will become "the basis of collaboration and unity, mainly because when the truth will be known, there will be no more suspicion, the author will be punished, justice will be done to the victim and to the innocent prisoner who will be reintegrated in the Rwandan society."[33]

As I have argued elsewhere,[34] the international attention directed toward *gacaca*, particularly during its pilot phase, fixated on the legality of the courts. Early on, Amnesty International and Human Rights Watch expressed concerns about *gacaca*'s lack of defense counsel, potential use of hearsay evidence and false accusations, and the poor training of lay judges.[35] While these NGOs sought in part to use law as a stop on the RPF's growing authoritarianism, they faced attack for an "absolutist" insistence on "rigid" and "universalizing" standards that would simply return *gacaca* to the formal juridical model which had already proven expensive, slow, and removed.[36] *Contra* the centralized modality of response, argued defenders of *gacaca*, there is more than one way of doing things. Yet, these sophisticated arguments for the pluralization of justice ended up speaking to the "prima facie" legality of "*gacaca* as *gacaca*."[37] *Gacaca*, however, is not a self-contained legal process simply aimed at community-level reconciliation; it is also part of a larger effort to consolidate state power. If the description of *gacaca* in the paragraph above pertained to the government's ideal, we see below that *gacaca* in practice has involved state coercion.

"To forgive *is* the law": reconciliation and the politics of the state[38]

The RPF operates as a one-party state under the guise of multi-party democracy. It has silenced, jailed, and disappeared political opponents; it has "Tutsified" state institutions; co-opted or attacked non-governmental organizations; rigged elections; and restricted freedoms of the press, association, and movement.[39] These violations are generally tolerated by the international community, in part due to profound guilt over its inaction in 1994—a guilt that is instrumentalized by the RPF as it claims moral legitimacy for ending the genocide.[40] In some respects, it may be that a legalistic, technocratic approach (which has dominated regime/donor/INGOs' implementation of *gacaca*) provides "a safeguard in interactions with government officials."[41] Yet the consequence is a failure to scratch below the surface of what Ingelaere calls the RPF's cultivated aesthetics of progress.[42] Take, for instance, the policy of national unity and reconciliation. According to the Rwandan constitution, it is illegal to identify as Hutu, Tutsi, or Twa: there are only Rwandans. However, this artifice of reconciliation, as I will discuss further below, papers over the lived experience of ethnicity both during and after the genocide. It also enables charges of "divisionism" against political critics. Thus, to claim narrowly that "we only apply the law" is to ignore the profoundly political uses of *gacaca* in an intolerant and repressive environment.[43]

Although *gacaca* appears as a pluralization of transitional justice from the international perspective, from a more localized perspective we see that *gacaca* operates within a dense network of unequal relations of power. The Rwandan state was reorganized after the genocide but remains highly centralized, with administrative units at the provincial, district, sector, and cell levels. Below this are the *nyumbakumi* officials who are responsible for ten households. The *nyumbakumi* are heavily involved in the administration of *gacaca*, as are officials from the National Service of *Gacaca* Jurisdictions (NSGJ) based in Kigali. Together they work to "sensitize" the local population to *gacaca*, to monitor and instruct the proceedings, and to assist judges in the gathering of information. Such extensive state control in a "grassroots" forum has "often led to manipulation and derailing of the process by various actors, reducing judges' room for maneuver when they are torn between the parties and the administrative authorities."[44] Thus, the community-driven spontaneity of traditional *gacaca* is largely eclipsed in the contemporary state-orchestrated process. We see this not least in the government's resort to military round-ups for attendance, and state fines or imprisonment for absenteeism: *gacaca* is, as Waldorf puts it, an "unpopular popular justice."[45]

Moreover, *gacaca* serves to reinforce a particular vision of the past and future. First of all, *gacaca* appears as a form of "victors' justice" because war crimes committed by RPF soldiers are outside its jurisdiction. In spite of the government's emphasis on ending the culture of impunity, which it sees as a significant factor in the genocide, the exclusion of RPF crimes fails to counteract Hutu extremists' "double genocide" ideology or to grapple with the complexities of Rwanda's cycles of violence.[46] Second, the collectivization of Hutu guilt is reinforced through the potential processing of over 1 million cases in the *gacaca* courts. The government does not sufficiently explain the difference between the number of cases and the number of persons tried.[47] Consequently, the perception created is that over half the adult male Hutu population is responsible for the genocide.[48] Waldorf details how this serves to "exert a degree of social control over the Hutu majority" and could also be used "to disenfranchise a sizable proportion of eligible Hutu voters."[49] Since 2004 a small space has opened up for recognizing the "righteous" Hutus who saved people during the genocide.[50] But, overall, *gacaca* is not a forum that allows Hutus to voice their suffering, at the hands of the RPF or otherwise, during the war and genocide. Only Tutsis are able to call themselves survivors and thus be eligible for state assistance.

Not surprisingly, many Hutu are unwilling to participate in *gacaca* because of its selectivity, its harsh penalties (sometimes motivated by land grabs), and the ways in which *gacaca* is used to settle old disputes. People are unwilling to defend the accused for fear of being accused themselves and the practice of *ceceka* (Kinyarwanda for "be quiet" or "shut up") is a tacit agreement amongst Hutus not to testify against one another.[51] This shifts the evidentiary burden to survivors, most of whom were in hiding and did not witness crimes of genocide. On numerous occasions survivors (and judges) have been intimidated, attacked, or killed.[52] For survivors, *gacaca* may appear as a "disguised amnesty" that produces prison releases and lightened sentences. They receive no compensation, despite legislation to the contrary. There is no direct restitution to victims of physical violence other than a forced apology, though community service (to the state) is also required. Restitution does exist for victims of property crimes; this is the sole area where the aggrieved parties or, in the absence of their agreement, the *inyangamugayo*, determine the amount in a customary manner.

Moreover, survivors *must* forgive; this is understood to be the law. In this, *gacaca* is part of a larger set of controls on Tutsi victimhood: commemorative practices, such as the public display of skulls and bones or required attendance at National Week of Mourning events, operate at the behest of the government and against the wishes of many Tutsi survivors.[53] Rwandans "pretend peace"[54] because to do otherwise is to risk being "un-Rwandan," a label wrought with potential repercussions including fines or imprisonment. But the appearance of reconciliation belies widening socio-economic inequality (despite economic growth),[55] the increasing political dominance of a small clique of Anglophone Tutsi elite, and growing state authoritarianism.

The reasons why people killed, resisted, or stood by during the genocide are complex, having to do with relational dynamics of power, opportunism, insecurity, and fear.[56] Though the relationship between agency and structure is beyond my scope here, I am equally persuaded by Uvin's argument that the genocide was predicated upon structural violence. Profound poverty and inequality, social and political exclusion, and hopelessness help in part to explain why elite messages of extremism and hate "fell on fertile ground" and were actively taken up in complex ways.[57] Today, such conditions of structural violence have not abated, particularly amongst the poorest Rwandans, for whom poverty rather than ethnicity may be an overriding social marker. A negative peace may exist, but positive peace remains out of grasp for ordinary Rwandans whose daily interactions with local and NSGJ officials at the *gacaca* courts reinforce the top-down power of the state. Some authors have warned that the "renewal" of structural violence in post-genocide Rwanda may "eventually again lead to acute violence."[58] Granted, there may be individual instances of closure during *gacaca*, bodies may be located and exhumed, or patterns of perpetration exposed. But because truth can only be revealed in a state-sanctioned manner and under conditions of extreme poverty and distrust, the general perception is that truth is partial and reconciliation is a facade. The struggle to undertake truth, justice, and reconciliation at the community level is inexorably linked to the authoritarian exercise of state power. Because lies, distrust, fear, and insecurity permeate *gacaca* overall, this undermines building an internal culture of peace, as well as individual and community well-being.

Peace through justice? Northern Uganda

As with the ICTR, the International Criminal Court is a centralizing mechanism of transitional justice. Unlike in Rwanda, however, transitional justice is being applied in Uganda in the midst of a conflict punctuated by numerous failed peace talks. The conflict in Northern Uganda between the Lord's Resistance Army (LRA) and the Ugandan government under President Yoweri Museveni once extended over the Acholi, Lango, and Teso regions. Over 25 years old, this conflict was once characterized as "one of the worst humanitarian crises in the world because of the extensive and prolonged displacement" of an estimated 80–90 percent of the Acholi population.[59] The LRA abducted an estimated 30,000 to 45,000 children and adults. They were brutally initiated into conscription, often forced to kill their own family members or to undergo severe beatings, and girls are additionally subjected to forced marriage. The Acholi population was terrorized and mutilated by the LRA; in turn, the Ugandan government was responsible for the forced displacement of people into camps where "protection" can "turn out to be a nightmare."[60] Kampala also chronically neglected the region, which is severely and disproportionately impoverished compared to the rest of the country.

After years of unsuccessful military offensives, the government acceded to pressure from local Acholi leaders to offer amnesty as a means of ending the conflict and allowing abductees to return home. The Amnesty Act of 2000 provides amnesty and material support to any rebel who voluntarily "comes out of the bush" and surrenders arms. At least 12,000 LRA "reporters" have returned, including Sam Kolo, the LRA's alleged second-in-command.[61] The conflict dragged on, however, and in December 2003 President Museveni asked the ICC to investigate the LRA's actions in Northern Uganda.[62] In 2005 the ICC unsealed its warrants of arrest for five LRA commanders, including its notorious leader, Joseph Kony. Local Acholi people feared the indictment would give the President leave to step up the military campaign and exacerbate LRA violence, thereby endangering their children's safety as well spoiling peace talks.[63] Indeed, the peace talks led by Ugandan government minister Betty Bigombe failed in 2005, and she has blamed the Court in part for not waiting long enough before unsealing the indictments.

However, in 2006 the Juba peace process was initiated. Although the Juba peace process failed to reach final agreement, it did result in a signed Agreement on Comprehensive Solutions to the Conflict, including Agenda Item 3, Agreement on Accountability and Reconciliation (AAR). This Agreement and its Annexure set out a broad framework for transitional justice, including promising "to address conscientiously the question of the ICC arrest warrants" (AAR art. 14.6), to establish a War Crimes Division of the High Court (Annexure art. 7), and to establish traditional justice mechanisms such as *mato oput* as a "central part of the framework for accountability and reconciliation" (AAR art. 3.1; Annexure art. 19–22). But Kony repeatedly failed to sign the Final Peace Agreement, insisting that the ICC indictments first be revoked and citing the need for clarification on whether undergoing *mato oput* obviates criminal prosecution for war crimes and crimes against humanity.[64]

While many factors beyond the scope of this chapter are at stake, it is not unreasonable to speculate that the ICC indictments have played a role in impeding peace and destabilizing the region. At the very least, the ICC's intervention forced the simultaneous pursuit of peace *and* justice, thereby eclipsing what many saw as the only viable path: "peace now, justice later."[65] While some Acholi supported the ICC intervention, according to one survey at the height of negotiations in 2007, 84 percent of respondents indicated willingness to accept amnesty if it were the only means to peace.[66] Of course, neither lifting the indictments nor signing a piece of paper are themselves guarantees of peace.[67] While the ICC could be persuaded to drop its prosecution "in the interests of justice," as per Article 53 of the Rome Statute, the Office of the Prosecutor states that "there is a difference between the concepts of the interests of justice and the interests of peace and that the latter falls within the mandate of institutions other than the Office of the Prosecutor."[68] Political and moral considerations about what justice might mean in the midst of poverty and conflict are isolated from technical appraisals of who has the authority to suspend a prosecution.[69] "Justice" is narrowed to individual criminal accountability for the most serious crimes and the presumption is in favor of investigation or prosecution.[70] In this way, the legalism of the ICC indictments (whether prosecuted or not) is prioritizing a mode of justice that does not attend to the complexities of the conflict.

To be clear, however, this mode of justice in all likelihood also suits the Ugandan government. First, consistent with the general critique of legalism, international justice can neither address nor modulate the socio-economic roots of the conflict, most especially Kampala's chronic neglect of the north. Second, the Rome Statute does not allow for the prosecution of crimes committed prior to 2002.[71] Failing to prosecute crimes perpetrated during the first 15 years of conflict in Northern Uganda will necessarily produce a limited narration of violence and accountability. Third, this narration of violence and accountability is one-sided. The ICC's unwillingness to investigate or prosecute the Ugandan Patriotic Defence Forces (UPDF) for their alleged war crimes shows a selectivity that will greatly impede its ability to establish justice or the rule of law within Uganda.[72] Moreover, as Finnström argues, by ignoring UPDF crimes, the ICC has reinforced the Ugandan government's discursive positioning of the LRA as an organization of children and criminals, devoid of political subjectivity, who surrender to an untouchable and superior government for amnesty.[73] This is not to deny the monstrosity of LRA crimes or to morally equate violations on both sides. But formal accountability for violations committed by both sides of the conflict could help forge the terrain for peacebuilding and reconciliation.

Fourth, formal criminal justice alone cannot attend to the complexities of the conflict, especially the abduction of children, and subsequent needs of peacebuilding. At the community level, the desire to return and integrate abductees has been readily apparent in people's calls for traditional justice. Although Northern Uganda's victims of violence by no means speak in a single voice (and not all victims are Acholi), there is vocal antipathy from Acholi Elders, Chiefs, and religious leaders toward international justice. They see it as an externalized form of Western justice and fear it would wreck the peace process. The imposition of victors' justice inscribes an "us-versus-them" mentality which is hierarchical whereas, in comparison, traditional rituals have the potential to operate as a mode of conflict resolution between equals.[74] As Baines convincingly argues, because many perpetrators were abducted as children, "the search for 'pure victims' and 'tainted perpetrators' will ultimately set up the process for exclusion, dehumanisation and future violence."[75] She raises the case of indicted LRA leader Dominic Ongwen, who was abducted at age ten, arguing that individualized prosecution fails to explain why the abduction and abuse of children were normalized in the broader context of forced displacement and structural violence.[76]

As Quinn notes in this volume, now that the height of the conflict has passed, the people of Northern Uganda *do* want justice.[77] Events have fluctuated over the years, but it now seems that the preferred alternatives in Uganda are: the prosecution of those who bear the greatest responsibility for war crimes in the new division of the Ugandan High Court; amnesty for the rank-and-file LRA; a truth commission; and the use of traditional practices aimed at the cleansing and reintegration of some combatants.[78] The ICC supports the use of traditional justice as a "complementary" process at the local level.[79] The Government of Uganda, through its Justice, Law and Order Sector Transitional Justice Working Group, appears to be in the process of determining the inclusion of customary law within the War Crimes Division of the High Court.

It has been suggested that 90 percent of perpetrators will be dealt with through traditional justice,[80] including many mid-to-high-ranked commanders who, like Ongwen, were once abducted children. Traditional mechanisms include numerous elements—cleansing and welcoming, retribution and punishment, truth-telling and dialogue, reparation, and reconciliation and forgiveness.[81] Some of the more well-known ceremonies are *mato oput* ("drinking the bitter herb"), *nyono tong gweno* ("stepping of the egg"), and *gomo tong* ("bending the spear"). However, there is little clarity or consensus about the application of traditional mechanisms for war crimes and crimes against humanity, especially gender-based violence. For example, cultural institutions are the traditional preserve of elder males along certain bloodlines. Given the specific needs of women and girls who have been targeted in sexual and gender-based ways, it is not at all evident, contrary to what Latigo claims, that their involvement in playing "complementary roles … to their adult male counterparts without *undue* discrimination" will be sufficient.[82]

Moreover, there may be a distinct political agenda at work in relying primarily upon Acholi mechanisms. Tim Allen argues:

> Using "traditional justice" risks implying that the government and the rest of the country have nothing to do with the northern conflict, and also that northern Ugandans need their own special justice measures, because they are not yet ready for modern ones … The obsession of so many concerned about the suffering in northern Uganda with "traditional justice" inadvertently reinforces a tendency to demonise the people of the region. For political and historical reasons, the Acholi in particular are caricatured as innately violent and primitive. They are therefore thought to be less concerned about terrible acts than other populations. In Kampala, this is offered as an explanation for their willingness to forgive, and it is common to hear comments about leaving the uncivilised northerners to their own devices. The campaign for regionally and "tribally" specific traditional justice has done nothing to promote national integration.[83]

While I would modulate Allen's tendency to treat international justice as untainted by self-interest or social invention,[84] the relevant caution here is about the appropriation of tradition. This warning resounds particularly in light of developments in Rwanda, where we see traditional justice being pursued for state purposes beyond truth, justice, or reconciliation. It is odd, then, given Allen's immense critique of the state's politicization of tradition in Uganda, that he points to *gacaca* as a potential model for a national initiative of traditional justice in Uganda.[85]

It remains to be seen how traditional mechanisms will be incorporated into a full-blown national process of transitional justice, though the non-governmental Beyond Juba Project calls for a "multi-tiered" approach at the clan, tribe, and national levels. It is possible that the codification of tradition will be seen as necessary, both to meet international standards and to standardize accountability. This might weaken the "many resonances and associations of lived rituals."[86] Moreover, it would bring traditional practices further under the purview of the state. Cultural institutions have only been recently revived in Uganda and over the course of the conflict their legitimacy and status have been weakened.[87] In this, cultural leaders both face an uphill struggle and stand to gain much from the development of traditional justice. Traditional leaders and institutions are financially supported by the government, which to an extent has co-opted traditional leaders by relying on them to help implement government policy.[88] A strong government hand would likely inform justice on the ground, given that there has been little input from cultural institutions and traditional leaders as to how to codify or formalize traditional practices.[89] Thus, although the push for traditional justice may truly have come "from below" within certain sectors of Acholi society (as did not really occur in Rwanda), institutionalization may render it increasingly subject to state power and Museveni's interests in controlling national discourses of peace, justice, and reconciliation.

Conclusion: centralizing legal pluralism?

The turn to tradition within transitional justice is primarily recognized as a corrective to the flaws of "one-size-fits-all" solutions. Yet, just as customary law was "made" through its interaction with colonialism, so too is traditional justice now "made" through its interaction with international transitional justice as mediated by the state. In Rwanda, although *gacaca* emerged in resistance to the centralizing pressures of international legalism, it is less an example of pluralization "from below" than it is a creature of state power. *Gacaca* is codified and administered by the state, and its daily operation is constrained by state-sanctioned narratives of national unity and reconciliation. Are similar mechanics at work in Uganda? While it may yet be too early to tell, there is some foreshadowing of tradition being appropriated for the consolidation of state power through local traditional leaders. If so, rather than laying the foundations for national peace, this approach risks socially isolating the Acholi people from the rest of the country, isolating LRA crimes from broader structural violence, and ignoring UPDF crimes.

In Rwanda, it is becoming very clear that transitional justice is not functioning as an instrument of peacebuilding. Traditional justice has the potential to build peace and stability from the "bottom up" in line with community needs and values. But this is not occurring. Instead, *gacaca* is an instrument of authoritarian state power that exacerbates conditions of structural violence. One obvious response to state authoritarianism is the application of international pressure for such processes to meet basic human rights standards. Yet, when international standards are applied to traditional mechanisms—and this is often done for the sake of protecting the rights of victims and perpetrators—we risk "one-sizing" traditional justice. This is not to discount the normative ideal that perpetrators of crimes against humanity ought to be held to similar standards of accountability across the globe. Rather, this chapter cautions that efforts to pluralize transitional justice in response to centralized flaws may instead result in tradition being doubly subject to centralizing forces. That successor states often use transitional justice to consolidate their new regimes is not surprising or unusual. What is perhaps different in these situations, however, is that traditional justice is recommended as a popular, accessible, community-based form of justice that helps to embed both cultures and structures of peace. But, as the analytical theory in this paper suggests, tradition is located within complex interrelations of power that span from the local to the international. In the dynamics of legal pluralization and centralization, these relations of power potentially converge to give the state, and not conflict-affected populations, control over justice and reconciliation such that cultures and structures of peace are undermined.

Notes

1 I would like to thank Chandra Lekha Sriram for her guidance and my fellow authors for their excellent suggestions and questions at our authors' meeting, especially Lars Waldorf, Par Engstrom, Joanna Quinn, and Stephen Brown. I would also like to thank Franklin Oduro for comments on an early version of this paper. Emily Gillespie has my gratitude for her assistance with the references. All errors or omissions are mine.

2 I will use "traditional justice," "indigenous justice," and "custom" or "customary law" interchangeably. Rather than putting these terms in quotations throughout, I note here the changing, even volatile, nature of tradition, as well as the porous boundaries of indigeneity.

3 United Nations Secretary-General, *Report on the Rule of Law and Transitional Justice in Conflict and Post-conflict Societies*, UN Doc S/2004/616 (3 August 2004), available at <*www.un.org/Docs/sc/sgrep04.html*>, para. 36, accessed 8 June 2008.

4 Sally Engle Merry, "Legal Pluralism," *Law and Society Review*, vol. 22, no. 5 (1988), pp. 869–96, 870.

5 On the prevalence of law and legalism within transitional justice, see Kieran McEvoy, "Letting Go of Legalism: Developing a 'Thicker' Version of Transitional Justice," in Kieran McEvoy and Lorna McGregor (eds), *Transitional Justice From Below: Grassroots Activism and the Struggle for Change* (Oxford and Portland, OR: Hart, 2008), pp. 15–45; Christine Bell, "Transitional Justice, Interdisciplinarity and the State of the 'Field' or 'Non-Field,'" *International Journal of Transitional Justice*, vol. 3, no. 1 (2009), pp. 5–27.

6 United Nations Secretary-General, *Report on the Rule of Law and Transitional Justice in Conflict and Post-conflict Societies* (2004), available at <*www.unrol.org/files/2004%20report.pdf*>, accessed 29 July 2011.

7 Johan Galtung, "Violence, Peace, and Peace Research," *Journal of Peace Research*, vol. 6, no. 3 (1969), pp. 167–91.

8 On these limits of transitional justice, see Wendy Lambourne, "Transitional Justice and Peacebuilding after Mass Violence," *International Journal of Transitional Justice*, vol. 3, no. 1 (2009), pp. 28–48; Zinaida Miller, "Effects of Invisibility: In Search of the 'Economic' in Transitional Justice," *International Journal of Transitional Justice*, vol. 2 (2008), pp. 266–91; Rosemary Nagy, "Transitional Justice as Global Project: Critical Reflections," *Third World Quarterly*, vol. 29, no. 2 (2008), pp. 275–89.

9 I borrow Merry's distinction between "classic" and "new" legal pluralism. Merry, "Legal Pluralism," op. cit., p. 872.

10 Martin Chanock, *Law, Custom and Social Order: The Colonial Experience in Malawi and Zambia* (New York: Cambridge University Press, 1985) cited in Sally Engle Merry, "From Law and Colonialism to Law and Globalization," *Law and Social Inquiry*, vol. 28, no. 2 (2003), pp. 569–90.

11 John Griffiths, "What is Legal Pluralism?" *Journal of Legal Pluralism and Unofficial Law*, vol. 24 (1986), pp. 1–55.

12 See Brian Z. Tamanaha, "The Folly of the 'Social Scientific' Concept of Legal Pluralism," *Journal of Law and Society*, vol. 20, no. 2 (1993), pp. 192–217, 298.

13 Gordon R. Woodman, "Legal Pluralism and the Search for Justice," *Journal of African Law*, vol. 40, no. 2 (1996), pp. 152–67, 158. State legal pluralism is mapped alongside international legal/normative orders in this research.

14 Boaventura de Sousa Santos, *Toward a New Legal Common Sense*, 2nd ed. (London: Butterworths, 2002; reprint, 2nd ed.), p. 85.
15 Sally Falk Moore, "Law and Social Change: The Semi-Autonomous Social Field as an Appropriate Subject of Study," *Law and Society Review*, vol. 7, no. 4 (1973), pp. 719–46.
16 Paige Arthur, "How 'Transitions' Reshaped Human Rights: A Conceptual History of Transitional Justice," *Human Rights Quarterly*, vol. 31, no. 2 (2009), pp. 321–67, p. 324.
17 The Office of the High Commissioner for Human Rights series, "Rule of Law Tools for Post-Conflict States," are available at <*www.ohchr.org/EN/PUBLICATIONS RESOURCES/Pages/SpecialIssues.aspx*>, accessed 10 June 2011.
18 *Velásquez-Rodríguez v. Honduras*, Judgment of July 21, 1989, Inter-Am. Ct. H.R. (Ser. C) No. 7 (1989); *Study on the Right to Truth* (Report of the United Nations High Commissioner for Human Rights) UN Doc E/CN.4/2006/91 (8 February 2006); UN General Assembly Resolution 60/147, *Basic Principles and Guidelines on the Right to Remedy and Reparation for Victims of Gross Violations of International Human Rights Law and Serious Violations of International Humanitarian Law*, U.N. Doc E/CN.4/2005/59 (16 December 2005).
19 Chandra Lekha Sriram and Brad Roth, "Externalization of Justice: What Does it Mean and What is at Stake?" *Finnish Yearbook of International Law*, vol. 12 (2001), pp. 2–6; Mark A. Drumbl, *Atrocity, Punishment and International Law* (Cambridge: Cambridge University Press, 2007), p. 127ff.
20 Lederach, cited in Rama Mani, *Beyond Retribution: Seeking Justice in the Shadows of War* (Malden, MA: Polity, 2002), p. 14.
21 For examples, see Chandra Lekha Sriram, Johanna Herman, and Olga Martin-Ortega (eds), *Peacebuilding and the Rule of Law in Africa: Just Peace?* (New York: Routledge, 2010); Augustine S. J. Park, "Consolidating Peace: Rule of Law Institutions and Local Justice Practices in Sierra Leone," *South African Journal on Human Rights*, vol. 24, no. 3 (2008), pp. 536–64; Kirsti Samuels, "Rule of Law Reform in Post-Conflict Countries: Operational Initiatives and Lessons Learnt," *Social Development Papers: Conflict Prevention and Reconstruction*, no. 37 (2006), available at <*http://siteresources.worldbank.org/INTCPR/Resources/WP37_web.pdf*>, accessed on 12 June 2011.
22 McEvoy, "Letting Go of Legalism," op. cit., p. 19.
23 Luc Huyse, "Conclusions and Recommendations," in Luc Huyse and Marc Salter (eds), *Traditional Justice and Reconciliation after Violent Conflict: Learning from African Experiences* (Stockholm: International IDEA, 2008), pp. 185–86, 181–98.
24 See UNSG, *Report on the Rule of Law*, op. cit.
25 By "socio-legal fields" I mean structured social spaces.
26 See Peter Uvin and Charles Mironko, "Western and Local Approaches to Justice in Rwanda," *Global Governance*, vol. 9, no. 2 (2003), pp. 219–31.
27 This is often referred to as "stratified concurrent jurisdiction," whereby the ICTR is entitled but not obliged to exercise jurisdiction to the exclusion of the national court system. The division of labor is such that the Tribunal prosecutes leaders and organizers, whereas more "ordinary" perpetrators are prosecuted at home. See Chandra Lekha Sriram, "Revolutions in Accountability: New Approaches to Past Abuses," *American University International Law Review*, vol. 19 (2003), pp. 301–428. On the weak rationale for stratified concurrent jurisdiction, see Madeleine H. Morris, "The Trials of Concurrent Jurisdiction: The Case of Rwanda," *Duke Journal of Comparative and International Law*, vol. 7 (1997), pp. 349–74.
28 Mohamed M. El Zeidy, "From Primacy to Complementarity and Backwards: (Re)-Visiting Rule 11 Bis of the Ad Hoc Tribunals," *International & Comparative Law Quarterly*, vol. 57, no. 02 (2008), pp. 403–15.
29 Drumbl, *Atrocity, Punishment and International Law*, op. cit., p. 139.
30 Ibid., pp. 139–40.
31 National Service of Gacaca Jurisdictions, "Context or historical background of Gacaca Courts," (n.d.), available at <*www.inkiko-gacaca.gov.rw/En/Generaties.htm*>, accessed 13 June 2011.

32 See Susan Thomson and Rosemary Nagy, "Law, Power and Justice: What Legalism Fails to Address in the Functioning of Rwanda's *Gacaca* Courts," *International Journal of Transitional Justice*, vol. 5, no. 1 (2011), pp. 11–30; Lars Waldorf, "Mass Justice for Mass Atrocity: Rethinking Local Justice as Transitional Justice," *Temple Law Review*, vol. 79, no. 1 (2006), pp. 1–87; Susanne Buckley-Zistel, "'We are Pretending Peace'—Local Memory and the Absence of Social Transformation and Reconciliation in Rwanda," in Phil Clark and Zachary D. Kaufman (eds), *After Genocide: Transitional Justice, Post-conflict Reconstruction and Reconciliation in Rwanda and Beyond* (New York: Columbia University Press, 2009), pp. 125–44; Phil Clark, "Hybridity, Holism, and 'Traditional' Justice: The Case of the Gacaca Courts in Post-Genocide Rwanda," *George Washington International Law Review*, vol. 39 (2007), pp. 765; Max Rettig, "Gacaca: Truth, Justice and Reconciliation in Post-Conflict Rwanda," *African Studies Review*, vol. 51, no. 3 (2008), pp. 22–50; Bert Ingelaere, "The Gacaca Courts in Rwanda," in Luc Huyse and Marc Salter (eds), *Traditional Justice and Reconciliation after Violent Conflict: Learning from African Experiences* (International Institute for Democracy and Electoral Assistance, 2008), pp. 24–59; African Rights, *Gacaca Justice: A Shared Responsibility* (2003). See also the series of reports by Penal Reform International at <*www.penalreform.org*> as well as the Rwandan government's *gacaca* website at <*www.inkiko-gacaca.gov.rw*>.

33 Inkiko-Gacaca website, "Objectives," at <*www.inkiko-gacaca.gov.rw/En/EnObjectives.htm*> accessed 22 July 2010. On the coercive aspects of these expectations, see Thomson and Nagy, "Law, Power and Justice," op. cit.; Ingelaere, "The Gacaca Courts in Rwanda," op. cit.

34 Rosemary Nagy, "Whose Justice? Gacaca, National Trials and the International Criminal Tribunal for Rwanda," in Joanna R. Quinn (ed.), *Reconciliation(s): Transitional Justice in Post-conflict Societies* (Kingston, ON: McGill-Queen's University Press, 2009).

35 Amnesty International, "Gacaca: A Question of Justice" (2002), available at <*www.amnesty.org/en/library/info/AFR47/007/2002*>, accessed 17 August 2011; Kenneth Roth and Alison Des Forges, "Justice or Therapy?" *Boston Review*, vol. 27, no. 3–4 (2002), available at <*http://bostonreview.net/BR27.3/rothdesForges.html*>, accessed 17 August 2011.

36 Ariel Meyerstein, "Between Law and Culture: Rwanda's *Gacaca* and Postcolonial Legality," *Law & Social Inquiry*, vol. 32, no. 2 (2007), pp. 467–508. See also Anuradha Chakravarty, "Gacaca Courts in Rwanda: Explaining Divisions within the Human Rights Community," *Yale Journal of International Affairs*, vol. 1, no. 2 (2006), pp. 132–45.

37 E.g. Timothy Longman, "Justice at the Grassroots? Gacaca Trials in Rwanda," in Naomi Roht-Arriaza and Javier Mariezcurrena (eds), *Transitional Justice in the Twenty-First Century* (New York: Cambridge University Press, 2006), pp. 206–28; Meyerstein, "Between Law and Culture," pp. 467–508; Clark, "Hybridity, Holism, and 'Traditional' Justice," p. 765. Certainly, these authors are aware of *gacaca*'s potential for social control; however, they chose to respond largely within the terms of the legalist critique. Longman now seems less optimistic: see Timothy Longman, "An Assessment of Rwanda's *Gacaca* Courts," *Peace Review*, vol. 21, no. 3 (2009), pp. 303–12.

38 Local government official quoted in *Penal Reform International* (*PRI*), PRI Research Team on Gacaca Report III (2002), p. 23.

39 See Amnesty International, "Rwanda Country Report" (2011), available at <*www.amnesty.org/en/region/rwanda/report-2011*>, accessed 13 June 2011; Nyamwasa, General Kayumba *et al.*, "Rwanda Briefing" (August 2010), available at <*http://rwandinfo.com/documents/Rwanda_Briefing_August2010_nyamwasa-et-al.pdf*>, accessed 11 June 2011; Susan M. Thomson, "Collateral Damage," *Mail and Guardian*, 20 July 2010, available at <*http://za.mg.co.za/article/2010-07-20-collateral-damage*>, accessed 20 July 2010; Kenneth Roth, "The Power of Horror in Rwanda," *Los Angeles Times* (11 April 2009), available at <*www.hrw.org/en/news/2009/04/11/power-horror-rwanda*>, accessed 1 July 2010; Filip Reyntjens, "Post-1994 Politics in Rwanda: Problematising 'Liberation' and 'Democratisation'," *Third World Quarterly*, vol. 27, no. 6 (2006), pp. 1103–17.

40 See Paul Gready, "Civil Society and Policy-making in Rwanda: A Case Study of Land Reform and the Gacaca Courts," London School of Economics, available at <*www.lse.ac.uk/collections/NGPA/publications/WP32_Rwanda_Gready_Web.pdf*>, accessed 17 August 2011; Eugenia Zorbas, "'Keep Out of our Affairs': How the Post-genocide Government in Rwanda Manages Relations with Donors" paper presented at International Studies Association, Chicago, 2007.

41 Ingelaere, "The Gacaca Courts in Rwanda," op. cit., p. 53.

42 Bert Ingelaere, "Do We Understand Life after Genocide? Center and Periphery in the Construction of Knowledge in Postgenocide Rwanda," *African Studies Review*, vol. 53, no. 1 (2010), pp. 41–59.

43 Thomson and Nagy, "Law, Power and Justice," op. cit., p. 12; Ingelaere, "The Gacaca Courts in Rwanda," op. cit.

44 See Prison Reform International, *The Contribution of the Gacaca Jurisdictions To Resolving Cases Arising from the Genocide* (22 July 2010), available at <*www.penalreform.org/publications/final-monitoring-and-research-report-gacaca-process*>, p. 45, accessed 22 July 2010.

45 Ingelaere, "The Gacaca Courts in Rwanda," op. cit., p. 55.

46 Nigel Eltringham, *Accounting for Horror: Post-Genocide Debates in Rwanda* (London, England: Pluto Press, 2004), p. 145; see also Ingelaere, "The Gacaca Courts in Rwanda," op. cit., p. 56.

47 See the online discussion on the challenges of calculating the number of persons tried on the Transitional Justice Listserve of April 20–21, 2010 (on file with author).

48 See Klaas de Jonge, "PRI's Research on Rwanda," May 2010, available at <*www.penalreform.org/publications/pri%E2%80%99s-research-gacaca-klass-de-jonges-commentary*>, p. 6, accessed 20 July 2010.

49 Waldorf, "Mass Justice for Mass Atrocity," op. cit., p. 82.

50 PRI, *The Contribution of the Gacaca Jurisdictions To Resolving Cases Arising from the Genocide*, p. 49.

51 Rettig, "Gacaca," op. cit., pp. 22–50, 40; Susan M. Thomson, "Resisting Reconciliation: State Power and Everyday Life in Post-Genocide Rwanda" (Doctoral dissertation, Dalhousie University, 2009), ch. 6.

52 Human Rights Watch, *There Will be No Trial* (2007), available at <*www.hrw.org/en/node/10839/section/1*>, accessed 17 August 2011.

53 Waldorf, "Mass Justice for Mass Atrocity," op. cit., p. 37; Thomson, "Resisting Reconciliation," op. cit., 170ff.

54 Buckley-Zistel, "We are Pretending Peace," op. cit. See also Ingelaere, "Do We Understand Life after Genocide?" op. cit.

55 UNDP, "Turning Vision 2020 into Reality: From Recovery to Sustainable Human Development" (National Report, Rwanda, 2007), available at <*http://hdr.undp.org/en/reports/nationalreports/africa/rwanda/name,3322,en.html*>, accessed 10 December 2010.

56 See Scott Strauss, *The Order of Genocide* (Ithaca, NY and London: Cornell University Press, 2006); Lee Ann Fujii, *Killing Neighbors: Webs of Violence in Rwanda* (Ithaca, NY and London: Cornell University Press, 2009).

57 Peter Uvin, *Aiding Violence: The Development Enterprise in Rwanda* (West Hartford, CT: Kumarian Press, 1998), p. 68. For the relationship between acute and structural violence in other contexts, see Paul Farmer, *Pathologies of Power: Health, Human Rights and the New War on the Poor* (Berkeley and Los Angeles: University of California Press, 2003); Galtung, "Violence, Peace, and Peace Research," op. cit.

58 Filip Reyntjens, "Rwanda, Ten Years On: From Genocide to Dictatorship," *African Affairs*, vol. 103 (2004), pp. 177–210, 210. See also Nyamwasa *et al.*, "Rwanda Briefing," op. cit.

59 Human Rights Watch, *Uprooted and Forgotten: Impunity and Human Rights Abuses in Northern Uganda* (19 September 2005), available at <*www.hrw.org/reports/2005/09/19/uprooted-and-forgotten*>, p. 14, accessed 17 August 2011.

60 Ibid., p. 33.

61 The Amnesty Act applies to all rebel groups. The Ministry of Internal Affairs lists 21,783 reporters from 27 rebel groups for 2000–06; 12,119 of these were from the LRA, available at <*www.mia.go.ug/page.php?1=reporters&&2=Reporters%20Granted%20Amnesty*>, accessed 31 January 2010.

62 It has now emerged that Chief Prosecutor Luis Moreno-Ocampo invited President Museveni to seek ICC intervention. Although Moreno-Ocampo has stated that he has the authority to investigate any crimes, not just LRA crimes, no action has been taken in this regard. The main justification has been that UPDF crimes simply do not compare to those of the LRA in terms of gravity. Nicholas Waddell and Phil Clark (eds), *Courting Conflict? Justice, Peace and the ICC in Africa* (London: Royal African Society, March 2008), p. 43.

63 For a qualitative discussion, see Tim Allen, *Trial Justice: The International Criminal Court and the Lord's Resistance Army* (London; New York: Zed Books, 2006), ch. 5. While Pham *et al.* found that 84% of their respondents supported international involvement in accountability, there was a vast difference of opinion in Acholi and non-Acholi districts. Acholi respondents favored "peace with amnesty," while non-Acholi respondents preferred "peace with trials and punishment." Phuong Pham *et al.*, *Forgotten Voices: A Population-Based Survey of Attitudes About Peace and Justice in Northern Uganda* (July 2005), available at <*http://reliefweb.int/sites/reliefweb.int/files/resources/A1AABC919BF22E384925704A0022B98D-hrc-uga-25jul.pdf*>, pp. 33–34, accessed 17 August 2011.

64 Isaac Vuni, "Ugandan LRA Fails To Sign Final Peace Deal at Riikwnbwa," *Sudan Tribune* (13 April 2008), available at <*www.sudantribune.com/spip.php?article26734*>, accessed 7 May 2009; IRIN, "LRA Sticks to its Guns, Yet Ready To Sign Peace Deal," (27 March 2008), available at <*www.irinnews.org/Report.aspx?ReportId=77481*>, accessed on 7 May 2009.

65 For example, Lucy Hovil and Joanna Quinn. *Peace First, Justice Later: Traditional Justice in Northern Uganda*, Refugee Law Project Working Paper No. 17. Kampala, Uganda: Refugee Law Project, 2005.

66 Pham *et al.*, *Forgotten Voices*, op. cit., p. 4.

67 J. N. Clark, "The ICC, Uganda and the LRA: Re-Framing the Debate," *African Studies*, vol. 69, no. 1 (2010), pp. 141–60.

68 Office of the Prosecutor of the International Criminal Court, *Policy Paper on the Interests of Justice* (September 2007), available at <*www.icc-cpi.int/NR/rdonlyres/772C95C9-F54D-4321-BF09-73422BB23528/143640/ICCOTPInterestsOfJustice.pdf*>, p. 1, accessed 17 August 2011.

69 Issaka K. Souaré, "The International Criminal Court and African Conflicts: The Case of Uganda," *Review of African Political Economy*, vol. 36, no. 121 (2009), pp. 369–88, 376.

70 Office of the Prosecutor of the ICC, *Policy Paper on the Interests of Justice*, op. cit., p. 3.

71 In contrast, the War Crimes Division will be eligible to try any crimes committed since 1987. However, as Quinn notes in this volume, the GOU's commitment to accountability is on paper only.

72 See Adam Branch, "Uganda's Civil War and the Politics of ICC Intervention," *Ethics & International Affairs*, vol. 21, no. 2 (2007), pp. 179–98, 188–89.

73 Sverker Finnström, "Reconciliation Grown Bitter? War, Retribution, and Ritual Action in Northern Uganda," in Rosalind Shaw and Lars Waldorf (eds), *Localizing Transitional Justice: Interventions and Priorities after Mass Violence* (Stanford: Stanford University Press, 2010), pp. 135–56, 151.

74 Ibid., pp. 151–53. Notably, though, Finnström does not address gendered or social inequalities that might exist at the local level.

75 Erin Baines, "Complex Political Perpetrators: Reflections on Dominic Ongwen," *Journal of Modern African Studies*, vol. 47, no. 2 (2009), pp. 163–91, 181.

76 Ibid., p. 183.

77 See the chapter by Quinn, "The Supposed Accountability/Peacebuilding Dilemma in Uganda," in this volume.

78 The National Reconciliation Bill provides for the institution of a "National Reconciliation Forum," which functions basically as a truth commission. It would operate in conjunction with the Amnesty Commission, Human Rights Commission, Equal Opportunities Commission, and traditional justice institutions and religious representatives. The 2009 draft bill is available at <*www.iccnow.org/documents/TRC_Bill_-for_Uganda_2009.pdf*> (accessed 19 November 2010).

79 Office of the Prosecutor of the ICC, *Policy Paper on the Interests of Justice*, op. cit., p. 8.

80 "Report on the Proceedings of the JLOS Transitional Justice Working Group Roundtable Discussions," Cape Town, South Africa, jointly hosted by CSVR, IJR and the Beyond Juba Project (2–5 February 2009), available at <*www.beyondjuba.org/conferences_seminars.php*>, accessed 7 February 2010.

81 Beyond Juba Project, "Tradition in Transition," Working Paper No. 1 (July 2009), available at <*www.beyondjuba.org/working_papers/BJP.WP1.pdf*>, accessed 17 August 2011.

82 James Ojera Latigo, "Northern Uganda: Tradition-based Practices in the Acholi Region," in Luc Huyse and Marc Salter (eds), *Traditional Justice and Reconciliation after Violent Conflict: Learning from African Experiences* (Stockholm: International Institute for Democracy and Electoral Assistance, 2008), pp. 85–120, 112. *Emphasis added.* Latigo dismisses gender inequality in this single sentence.

83 Tim Allen, "Ritual (Ab)use? Problems with Traditional Justice in Northern Uganda," in Nicholas Waddell and Phil Clark (eds), *Courting Conflict? Justice, Peace and the ICC in Africa* (Royal African Society, 2008), pp. 47–54, 52–53.

84 See Kamari Maxine Clarke, *Fictions of Justice: The International Criminal Court and the Challenge of Legal Pluralism in Sub-Saharan Africa* (New York: Cambridge University Press, 2009), p. 21; Finnström, "Reconciliation Grown Bitter?" op. cit., p. 147.

85 Allen, "Ritual (Ab)use?" op. cit., p. 51.

86 Ibid., p. 50.

87 Erin K. Baines, "The Haunting of Alice: Local Approaches to Justice and Reconciliation in Northern Uganda," *International Journal of Transitional Justice*, vol. 1, no. 1 (2007), pp. 91–114, 106; Joanna R. Quinn, "Accountability and Reconciliation: Traditional Mechanisms of Acknowledgement and the Implications of the Juba Peace Process," paper presented at Reconstructing Northern Uganda, University of Western Ontario, London 9 April 2008, p. 15.

88 Joanna R. Quinn, "Tradition?! Traditional Cultural Institutions on Customary Practices in Uganda," paper presented at International Studies Association, New York, 16 February 2009, p. 19.

89 Ibid., p. 22.

Part II

Country case studies

6 Peacebuilding and transitional justice in Cambodia: Attempts at DDR and the rise of victim-centered justice

Johanna Herman

Introduction

After a 30-year wait, the top leaders of the Khmer Rouge are finally facing justice at the Extraordinary Chambers in the Courts of Cambodia (ECCC). As the negotiations, preparations, and creation of this formal transitional justice mechanism took place, there was a great deal of international support for peacebuilding activities in the country. This peacebuilding assistance followed three decades of conflict in Cambodia during 1967–99.[1] The Khmer Rouge, led by Pol Pot, gained control of the country in 1975–78 and carried out mass human rights abuses, including the forced evacuation of the cities, overwork, starvation, and killing of "enemies of the revolution" through purges.[2] It is estimated that up to 2 million Cambodians were killed during this period.[3] This was followed by the invasion of the country by Vietnam in 1978 and a decade of civil war and attempts at political settlement. The Agreements on the Comprehensive Political Settlement of the Cambodia Conflict (Paris Peace Agreements) were signed in Paris in 1991, and elections were successfully carried out in 1993, although the Khmer Rouge did not participate and carried on fighting. The fragility of the peace process was demonstrated by the 1997 coup by co-Prime Minister Hun Sen, which also led to factional fighting. The remaining Khmer Rouge leaders were finally captured in December 1998 and March 1999.[4]

Over the past 15 years, the country has entered a period of stability with strong economic growth. However, there are still a number of concerns. Despite the huge amounts of foreign assistance provided to the country, there is still widespread corruption, impunity for human rights abuses, restriction of freedom of expression, and growing power of the Prime Minister and Cambodian People's Party (CPP). Freedom House, for instance, has stated that "authoritarianism has become normalized in Cambodia."[5] There was little attempt at accountability for crimes committed under the Khmer Rouge until the establishment of the ECCC, which delivered its first verdict in July 2010.

This chapter examines the relationship between peacebuilding and transitional justice activities in Cambodia and the inclusion of victims' rights at the ECCC.[6] It first looks at how there have been a number of unsuccessful attempts at disarmament, demobilization, and reintegration (DDR) and the amnesties of the

1990s. It then explores the establishment of the ECCC and the participation of victims as an important innovation within an internationalized tribunal, examining also the evolution of victim reparations at the court. This particular aspect might be the lasting legacy of the ECCC.

Peacebuilding in Cambodia

The United Nations Advance Mission in Cambodia (UNAMIC) was the first UN mission, established in October 1991, to assist the Cambodian parties in maintaining the ceasefire of 1 May 1991. It was succeeded in February 1992 by the United Nations Transitional Authority in Cambodia (UNTAC), as agreed in the Paris Peace Agreements, and established by Security Council Resolution 745. Its mandate was as follows: supervise the ceasefire and the withdrawal of foreign military assistance and of foreign forces; regroup, canton, and disarm all armed forces of the Cambodian parties; ensure 70 percent demobilization; control and supervise the activities of the administrative structures, including the police; ensure respect of human rights; and organize and conduct free and fair elections. In total US $1.6 billion was spent on both UN missions.[7] UNTAC supported the elections in May 1993, which were won by the royalist political party Front Uni National pour un Cambodge Indépendant, Neutre, Pacifique, et Coopératif (FUNCINPEC). UNTAC's support is often seen as an example of a successful UN mission assisting the transition to civil rule.[8]

After the withdrawal of UNTAC in September 1993 following the promulgation of the new Constitution and inauguration of the new government, UN agencies remained in the country to support reconstruction and development. In 1993, as required in the Paris Peace Agreement, a Special Representative for Human Rights was appointed by the Secretary-General, who also appointed a representative for Cambodia to serve as liaison with the domestic government, to monitor the political situation, and to report on developments relating to peace and security.[9] UNTAC left behind a fragile peace, with the leaders of FUNCINPEC and the CPP, Prince Ranariddh and Hun Sen, as co-Prime Ministers. FUNCINPEC had won the election, but the CPP controlled the army, lower-level bureaucracy, and the police.[10] This instability led to five coups in 1993–97, while the fighting with the Khmer Rouge continued. Although UNTAC achieved a great deal, there were missed opportunities to assist the state and economy. The weakness of the state, poverty, inequality, and bureaucratic stalemate led Michael Doyle to state in 2001 that "the peacebuilding deficit continues to shape and misshape the process of Cambodian development."[11] Institution building—particularly of the justice system, rule of law, and democratic governance—has been heavily criticized. Other peacebuilding-related activities such as rebuilding of infrastructure and support to social and economic development have been more successful.

Despite the internal turbulence, international support to Cambodia across a wide range of activities continued with more than US $5 billion in aid disbursed between 1998 and 2008.[12] However, the structural problems within the country mean that recovery in the post-conflict period is slow. Cambodia ranks 124th out of 169 countries in the 2010 Human Development Index and remains one of the poorest countries in Asia. Nonetheless, it has more than doubled its income per capita from $285 in 1997 to $593 in 2007.[13] This growth has profoundly changed the economy,[14] but the establishment of democratic institutions and promotion of rule of law has not resulted in a similar transformation in the civil sphere. This is a key area of attention for the UN country team, with a focus on corruption and rule of law, and good governance and the protection of human rights more broadly.[15]

DDR

There have been a number of attempts at DDR in Cambodia: UNTAC initially had responsibility for a DDR process in 1992, and then there were two attempts by the World Bank under the Cambodian Veterans' Assistance Program (CVAP) in 1994–96 and in 2000–02. The Paris Peace Agreements stated that all parties, the Khmer People's National Liberation Front (KPNLF), FUNCINPEC, CPP, and the Khmer Rouge, would demobilize 70 percent of their forces, which was aimed to be completed prior to the end of the process of registration for elections. The parties also undertook to demobilize the remaining forces after the elections.[16] UNTAC aimed to regroup and canton 200,000 regular troops, disarm 420,000 combatants, and guard 300,000 weapons and 80 million rounds of ammunition. However, although the cantonment and regrouping did begin, the Khmer Rouge refused to cooperate and began fighting again. As a result, only 36,000 troops were demobilized by the end of the program in May 1992 and the Secretary-General reported to the Security Council that the cantonment, disarmament, and demobilization process had been suspended.[17] This first DDR process ceased when the Khmer Rouge withdrew from the peace process in 1992.[18]

FUNCINPEC, KPNLF, and the CPP formed a single army, the Royal Cambodian Armed Forces (RCAF) in 1993. Immediately after the elections, 20,000 FUNCINPEC and KPNLF soldiers were integrated into RCAF, as well as defecting Khmer Rouge soldiers.[19] The integration process was highly unsuccessful, with the different units suspicious of each other and a general lack of discipline in the military.[20] This meant that a second phase of DDR was needed to lower the number of RCAF forces, which were then estimated at 155,000. This took the form of CVAP, which began to be prepared by the World Bank and the government from 1995. It focused on 40,000 RCAF and 3,000 Khmer Rouge soldiers and aimed at providing assistance to the disabled, the sick, and the spouses of deceased soldiers.[21] However, this first version of CVAP was never implemented due to political uncertainty as tension mounted in 1995–96 between CPP and FUNCINPEC. This culminated in the successful 1997 coup, with one Cambodian general quoted as stating that "recruitment was more important for stability than demobilization."[22]

A second attempt at CVAP, and the third round of DDR, started in 1999 with the objective of demobilizing 30,000 soldiers and also contributing to the reallocation of budget to the social sectors.[23] At that point military spending was 40 percent of the country's total budget. The project was designed with two phases of discharge and demobilization, with 15,000 soldiers in each phase. Some 80 percent of combatants in the first phase were to be made up of soldiers above retirement age, ill, or disabled. In the second phase, a higher proportion of healthy and below-retirement-age soldiers were to be included. The World Bank stated that "an unintentional consequence of the Paris Peace Agreement … was to encourage all factions to integrate as many of their respective combatants as possible within the RCAF to preserve their respective military power and to leverage their respective political power."[24] This obviously ran counter to the demobilization attempts of UNTAC and explained why RCAF numbers were so high. By the end of the project, only 15,000 soldiers had been successfully demobilized and received reinsertion and reintegration packages.[25] CVAP ended abruptly, with the second phase not yet initiated after the World Bank found procurement irregularities, and the project closed on 31 December 2004.[26] It was an acrimonious end to the project with the government refusing to work with the World Bank on future demobilization.[27] The three rounds of attempted DDR left RCAF numbers still high, at around 110,000.[28]

International donors and actors also regarded security sector reform (SSR) as vital to peacebuilding in Cambodia and as such it is inextricably linked with DDR. Links between the military and the CPP were regarded as one of the biggest problems with democratization in Cambodia, and in addition the RCAF consumed over 50 percent of the national budget.[29] The demobilization program in Cambodia was one part of downsizing the military spending and redirecting it towards social spending.[30] Further to this, an important focus for SSR was governance within the military. This reflects the broader challenges facing good governance in Cambodia as a whole. Patronage networks, relying on informal relationships and material inducements, are the basis of Cambodian politics and public life and have a broad impact in terms of corruption and limiting genuine political participation.[31] The Royal Government of Cambodia (RGC) tries to demonstrate that democratic principles and civil liberties are upheld in order to ensure continuing international support, but political violence and politics based on personal networks and corruption persist.[32]

This political and social context makes it particularly hard to institutionalize formal rules within the military. There was no associated program along with the DDR program to improve military accountability, leading to the criticism that "emphasis has been placed on reducing its size and political influence without the groundwork being laid for cost effectiveness and greater accountability."[33] The lack of progress in institutionalizing integrity and professionalism facilitated illegal activity and a situation where the primary mission of the army and police was to protect their political patrons and ensure economic survival.[34] This lack of accountability accorded to the security forces is demonstrated by the fact that the RCAF, military police, and police are heavily implicated in illegal logging in the country.[35] Global Witness alleges that RCAF units carry out illegal logging operations in order to enrich their commanders, including in protected areas.[36]

RCAF and the police are able to engage in other illegal activities, including trafficking in drugs, arms, illegal immigrants, and the sex trade.[37] The fact that the army and police are able to engage in illegal activities due to "impunity and protection granted to them by top political and military leaders" demonstrates the fundamental structural problems in carrying out any SSR in Cambodia.[38] The absence of accountability and democratic governance in the security sector mirrors many of the problems of carrying out DDR where there is little political will and reliance on patronage, rather than strong democratic institutions.

DDR, amnesties, and transitional justice

There had been few attempts at justice for Khmer Rouge perpetrators before the establishment of the ECCC. The Vietnamese-backed government punished a number of Khmer Rouge foot-soldiers, although the total number is not known.[39] The attitude of the new government elected after the peace process was that those who defected were welcomed and those captured would have to undergo re-education.[40] The priority was reconciliation and stability and so there was little concern with accountability. In the 1990s, neither FUNCINPEC nor the CPP wished to push for trials since there was competition between them to attract defectors to their parties.[41] Instead, there was a focus on amnesty in order to encourage defections. The Cambodian amnesties were primarily put into place to weaken the Khmer Rouge and provided no accountability. Neither did they provide benefits to victims or provide information regarding the crimes of the defectors.[42] In the words of Sok An, Deputy Prime Minister:

> The "win-win" policy initiated … five facets: "divide, isolate, finish, integrate and develop," in which the Khmer Rouge political and military structure was ended. Those Khmer Rouge who defected were assured of their physical safety and survival, the right to work and to carry out their professions, and the security of their property.[43]

The first amnesty was put into place after the Paris Peace Agreement and renewal of conflict by the Khmer Rouge. As part of the approach of "political reconciliation," the RGC passed a law in 1994 to outlaw the Khmer Rouge with a six-month amnesty period.[44] Under Article 5 of the law, a six-month amnesty was provided for those Khmer Rouge who defected during this period, allowing them "to return to live under the authority in the Royal Government of Cambodia, without facing punishment for crimes which they have committed."[45] Under Article 6, it excluded "leaders" of the Khmer Rouge.[46] The King was also allowed to give royal pardon or amnesty under Article 7.[47] During the six-month amnesty period there were 7,000 defections (there had previously been 3,000 in total in 1992–94).[48] The government extended the amnesty period indefinitely and committed to the protection of everyone who defected. This can be classed as a "non-self amnesty," given by a state to benefit its opponents as an incentive to finish fighting.[49]

However, 2,970 Khmer Rouge defectors were given positions within the RCAF and returned to the conflict.[50] Even high-profile commanders were given positions in RCAF with punishment set aside to encourage defections.[51] Therefore amnesties under the 1994 law ensured that there were thousands of Khmer Rouge integrated into the RCAF, but there was little vetting done, affecting the potential for successful SSR. The lack of understanding regarding vetting is shown by one RCAF general, who claimed that the Khmer Rouge could *only* be deputies and could not be in command of armed units.[52] Unfortunately this culture of impunity in the security forces continues to the present day with claims that members and units of RCAF have been implicated in gross human rights violations dating from the coup in 1997 and ongoing abuses since then.[53] With ongoing widespread impunity, a vetting process for previous crimes would have been extremely challenging to implement.

Although the 1994 amnesty excluded "leaders," a later royal decree granted both an amnesty and pardon to Ieng Sary, Vice-Prime Minister of the Khmer Rouge. In 1979, Sary and Pol Pot, leader of the Khmer Rouge, had been found guilty of genocide *in absentia* in what has widely been considered a show trial that failed to follow due process.[54] Sary was given a pardon in September 1996 both for the death sentence that he received at this trial and for any penalties stipulated under the 1994 law outlawing the Khmer Rouge.[55] This was crucial in the final collapse of the Khmer Rouge. The CPP expected all Khmer Rouge to join the party and consolidate their power over FUNCINPEC. Prime Minister Hun Sen, for his part, wanted the credit for defeating the Khmer Rouge. This pardon was considered necessary for the peace process despite outrage from the international community and human rights groups. The King sent a letter to Amnesty International stating that the government would support the judgment of any future tribunal that would try Ieng Sary or other Khmer Rouge leaders.[56] The amnesty did not appear to provide any protection to Sary for criminal acts that he may have committed after the trial and before 1996.[57] This led to a further 3,000 defections and in 1996 Ieng Sary passed official control of 4,400 combatants to the government.[58]

The use of amnesties in Cambodia has not prevented the work of the ECCC. Since the 1994 amnesty was confined to subordinates, this meant that there was no bar to the ECCC carrying out its mandate regarding prosecution of the leaders and most senior Khmer Rouge. In addition, this focus meant that important eyewitnesses were willing and able to provide evidence to the tribunal.[59] During the first trial of Kaing Guek Eav, head of the S-21 prison, a number of guards testified. Ieng Sary was the focus of the 1996 amnesty, leaving other high-level officials still open to prosecution.[60] Ieng Sary appealed against investigation and provisional detention based on the royal pardon and amnesty, but the Office of the Co-Investigating Judges held that these did not apply. Sary appealed against the subsequent Closing Order (indictment) issued by the Co-Investigating Judges, claiming that the pardon was valid in Cambodia and applicable to the ECCC and that the scope of amnesty protected him from prosecution.[61] However, the Pre-Trial Chamber found that the pardon from the 1979 tribunal had no effect on the possibility to institute future prosecutions "as the amnesty was not related to acts allegedly committed." Regarding the 1994 Law, the Pre-Trial Chamber found that it did not prevent Sary's prosecution for the crimes of genocide, crimes against humanity, grave breaches of the Geneva Conventions, and homicide, torture, and religious persecution before the ECCC, and that a blanket amnesty would be inconsistent with the international obligations of Cambodia.[62] Sary's lawyers then filed the same objections regarding the royal pardon and amnesty and an objection regarding double jeopardy with the Trial Chamber. In November 2011, the Trial Chamber found that these objections did not bar the prosecution of Sary at the ECCC and Sary's team subsequently appealed to the Supreme Court Chamber.[63] In the opening statements to his trial in June 2011, these questions of the pardon and of double jeopardy had been raised by Ieng Sary's lawyers as forming the basis of his defense.[64] This was reiterated in his statement in November 2011, in which Sary declared that, although he respected the Trial Chamber's decision that the Royal Pardon and Amnesty did not apply in the ECCC, he was troubled by the Trial Chamber's refusal to delay proceedings until the Supreme Court Chamber ruled on his appeal of the matter.[65]

There was no parallel transitional justice process to accompany the amnesties, which would have helped to ensure what Mark Freeman calls "maximum external coherence," ensuring a balance between enhancements of perpetrators' and victims' rights.[66] Discussions regarding the possibility of international assistance for Khmer Rouge crimes only really started from April 1997, a number of years after the first amnesty.[67] During the later version of CVAP, when the negotiations of the tribunal were ongoing, there was no linkage made between DDR and accountability processes. This lack of engagement is unsurprising, when the Cambodian experience demonstrates the difficulties and challenges involved in implementing a comprehensive DDR process. There are many factors that affect whether DDR is successful, without even trying to consider its impact on transitional justice processes in a country. Therefore, consideration of the relationship between DDR and transitional justice must go beyond an assumption that activities will achieve their goals, and must engage with examples of failed processes or at least the numerous challenges to such a relationship. The political context had a significant impact, as demonstrated by the aborted attempt at CVAP in 1994/95 and the premature closing of the second attempt at CVAP. The World Bank had admitted that it underestimated the extent to which this politically charged atmosphere would affect the DDR program. Despite the specific procedures and guidelines of the DDR program, the World Bank found that these were not enough where "governance and rule-of-law are weak and there is seldom any follow up of problems to reduce incentives not to abuse this."[68] With such fundamental and structural problems in carrying out DDR in the country, not much thought was given to additional challenges—such as supporting or linking with transitional justice. Furthermore, the focus of the DDR programs was on demobilization as opposed to reintegration, meaning that there was less potential for a relationship between DDR and transitional justice (see Waldorf's chapter in this volume). In addition, as will be explored below, the tortuous negotiation process for the ECCC left no space to raise the subject of linking initiatives.

The impact on victims of the lack of coherence between DDR, amnesties, and transitional justice in Cambodia can be seen in the results of a nationwide population survey carried out in 2008 by the Human Rights Center, University of California, Berkeley.[69] One-third to half of respondents claimed they were uncomfortable interacting with former members of the Khmer Rouge in various situations. For example, over 40 percent were uncomfortable living in the same community, having their children marry former Khmer Rouge members, living as a close neighbor, and working together.[70] A total of 83 percent harbored feelings of animosity towards Khmer Rouge members responsible for violent acts.[71] There were 90 percent who believed that it was important to hold those who were responsible to account, and 50 percent believed these should be leaders or officials, while 20 percent thought accountability was needed for the Khmer Rouge regime in general. In terms of what was understood by accountability, nearly 50 percent wanted them put on trial, while around 20 percent spoke generally of punishment. Although there is a diversity of opinion, with one-third of respondents saying they had forgiven the Khmer Rouge, this survey does demonstrate negative attitudes towards former Khmer Rouge members and the desire for justice.

Victim-centered justice in Cambodia

Establishment of the Extraordinary Chambers in the Courts of Cambodia

As mentioned above, apart from the show trials of Ieng Sary and Pol Pot, the question of accountability for human rights abuses during the period of Khmer Rouge rule was not a priority for the RGC. In 1997, the Cambodian co-Prime Ministers requested assistance from the UN concerning this question, and the UN appointed a Group of Experts to provide a report on the options available for bringing to justice those most responsible for the atrocities.[72] Their report found that due to the problems in the Cambodian domestic judicial system, such as government interference, corruption, and lack of capacity, an international criminal tribunal would be the best option, located outside of the country.[73]

However, by the time the report was presented to the General Assembly in 1999 the political situation in Cambodia had changed. As explained by Thomas Hammarberg, former Special Representative of the UN Secretary-General for Human Rights in Cambodia, during this period there were important defections by key Khmer Rouge leaders, which led the RGC to respond to the report with the statement that "the trials of Khmer Rouge leaders would panic other former Khmer Rouge officers and rank and file … renewing the guerrilla war in Cambodia."[74] With the collapse of the Khmer Rouge militarily and politically, it became apparent that the tribunal had only been considered useful to defeat the Khmer Rouge and that an international tribunal was no longer considered important by the RGC.[75] The RGC was only willing to consider a national trial for Ta Mok (who unlike the other leaders had not surrendered, but was arrested) leading to an impasse between the UN and RGC. Finally, the suggestion of a hybrid model seemed to find a middle ground between the two parties. The hybrid model would have a mix of international judges and Cambodian judges, use a mixture of domestic and international law, and be located in Phnom Penh. Nonetheless, this model still caused problems in negotiations. The RGC wanted a majority of Cambodian judges and the UN wanted a majority of international judges in order to try to prevent the problems of government interference or influence. Finally, the concept of "supermajority" decision-making was introduced. Following this rule, even though Cambodian judges would be in the majority, at least one foreign judge would have to agree with the Cambodian judges. This was an attempt to circumvent the problems of the domestic system by ensuring that the Cambodian judges could not just outvote the international judges, thus supporting independent decision-making by the ECCC. The agreement between the UN and RGC was signed in June 2003 and approved by the National Assembly and Senate in October 2004.

The ECCC is mandated:

> to bring to trial senior leaders of Democratic Kampuchea and those most responsible for the crimes and serious violations of Cambodian penal law, international humanitarian law and custom and international conventions recognized by Cambodia that were committed during the period from 17 April 1975 to 6 January 1979.[76]

The ECCC has a Pre-Trial Chamber and Trial Chamber with five judges (three Cambodian and two international) and the Supreme Court Chamber has seven judges (four Cambodian and three international). In accordance with the supermajority rule, the Pre-Trial Chamber and Trial Chamber need four votes for a decision and the Supreme Court Chamber needs five.

The ECCC is unique compared with other hybrid tribunals and the *ad hoc* international tribunals, since it operates within a civil law system (inquisitorial) rather than common law (adversarial). There are two co-prosecutors, (one Cambodian and one international) and also two co-investigating judges (one Cambodian and one international). This model with prosecutor and investigating judges reflects the Cambodian domestic justice system. The co-prosecutors carry out a preliminary investigation and file an Introductory Submission in order for the suspect(s) to be arrested. The co-investigating judges then examine the evidence and decide whether to charge the suspect. They carry out their own investigation and decide whether to issue a Closing Order, which sends the charged person to trial. Other organs of the ECCC, the Defense Support Section (DSS), Office of Administration, and Victims Support Section also have half Cambodian and half international staff.

The ECCC began its operations in February 2006. The internal rules were finally agreed upon in 2007 and by November 2007 five suspects were arrested and taken into custody. The trial of Kaing Guek Eav (known as Duch), the former head of the S-21 prison, began in March 2009 and the verdict was delivered on 26 July 2010. Duch was found guilty of crimes against humanity and grave breaches of the Geneva Conventions. The co-prosecutors, Duch, and civil parties appealed the Trial Chamber's judgment and, in February 2012, the Supreme Court Chamber increased Duch's sentence from 30 years to life imprisonment. The second trial of four Khmer Rouge leaders has recently begun: Ieng Sary, former Deputy Prime Minister and former foreign minister; his wife, Ieng Thirith; Khieu Samphan, President during the Khmer Rouge; and Nuon Chea, the second-in-command to Pol Pot. They have been charged with crimes against humanity, war crimes, and genocide. Although the Trial Chamber found Ieng Thirith unfit to stand trial and ordered her release, the co-prosecutors appealed this decision. The Supreme Court Chamber granted the appeal and she is currently detained pending further medical opinion.[77] The judicial investigation of five more suspects (the names are confidential and they are known as Cases 003 and 004) is ongoing and proving highly controversial, with allegations of political interference in the work of the ECCC. Prime Minister Hun Sen and other senior members of the RGC have openly spoken out against any further prosecutions. The progress of Cases 003 and 004 has resulted in complaints against the co-investigating judges, leading to the resignation of the international co-investigating judge in October 2011, citing the attempted interference by Cambodian government officials.[78] The Cambodian Supreme Council of the Magistracy did not appoint the UN choice for international co-investigating judge (the current reserve international co-investigating judge) although it was required to do so.[79] Nevertheless, the reserve international judge carried out his duties until he tendered his resignation, citing obstruction by his Cambodian counterpart. This led the Secretary-General to initiate a new process for the selection of both a new international co-investigating judge and a new reserve international co-investigating judge and to state that the RGC "should afford the new international co-investigating judge every assistance and full cooperation to carry out his or her functions."[80]

Participation of victims at the Extraordinary Chambers in the Courts of Cambodia

At the ECCC, victims of crimes alleged to have been committed by the accused can act as complainants or civil parties to the trial. Victims can act as a civil party, not only in support of the prosecution, but also to seek collective and moral reparations in their own right.[81] Anyone who has suffered physical, psychological, or material harm as a direct consequence of the Khmer Rouge regime can apply to become a civil party. Once admitted as a civil party, they have the same rights as every other party to the proceedings and are eligible for reparations. Although the ECCC is the first internationalized tribunal where victims can participate in this way, this aspect developed quite late. Over the past decade, there has been a growing focus on the rights of victims at international and internationalized tribunals. Although victims could participate as witnesses at the International Criminal Tribunal for Rwanda (ICTR) and International Criminal Tribunal for the Former Yugoslavia (ICTY), their participation was restricted by the requirements of the prosecution. The *UN Basic Principles on the Rights to a Remedy and Reparation for Victims of Gross Violations of International Human Rights Law and Serious Violations of International Humanitarian Law* adopted by the General Assembly in December 2005 marked an evolution in the role of victims and they can now participate in various capacities at the International Criminal Court and the Special Tribunal for Lebanon, as well as the ECCC.

During the negotiations for the ECCC in the late 1990s, victim participation was not seen as important or central to the suggested mandate of the tribunal. In the first reports of the Secretary-General updating the General Assembly about the development of the ECCC (2003–05), there is no information regarding the participation of victims.[82] It was only when the Internal Rules were drafted in 2007 that a Victims Unit was established and a Practice Direction on Victim Participation was issued elaborating on their role. The Victims Unit was a late addition, and resulted in a request for increased budget. This inclusion of victim participation in the Internal Rules was unique and due to the hybrid nature of the court. The Criminal Procedure Code of Cambodia states that civil parties have the same right to be heard as other parties to criminal proceedings and allows their involvement through all the stages of the trial. Once the rule was established, Cambodian NGOs recognized the importance of the mechanisms and played an instrumental role in supporting the ECCC's work in this area, resulting in a high number of applications.[83] However, it has not been easy to adapt this mechanism to cases concerning mass atrocity crimes. A number of challenges arose during the first trial, resulting in significant alterations to the victim participation process. The ECCC had to make a number of decisions in order to streamline the process while balancing the rights of victims.

During the trial of Duch, 90 civil parties participated, divided into four groups.[84] As mentioned, civil parties have the same rights as other parties and so are allowed to ask questions of witnesses, experts, and the accused through their lawyers. Each group had one international and one Cambodian lawyer, which meant that, after the prosecution and defense, there could be questions from a further eight lawyers. There was often repetitive questioning and this slowed down the trial. Subsequently, in June 2009, the Trial Chamber introduced time limits to questioning. It was clear, however, that there would still need to be further changes. With four defendants and 3,850 civil parties, it soon became clear that this model would be untenable for the second trial. Therefore, instead of having one international and one Cambodian lawyer representing each civil party group, there is one international lead co-lawyer and one Cambodian lead co-lawyer representing all civil parties as a consolidated group.[85] This model will hopefully facilitate coordination, but it remains to be seen how it will work during the second trial, and to what extent all civil parties will feel included.

Reparations and the Victims Support Section

The Group of Experts' report in 1999 recommended that monetary reparations be awarded to victims from the wealth of Khmer Rouge leaders convicted by the tribunal.[86] During the process of negotiation, there was a great deal of advocacy from both Cambodian and international NGOs regarding the fact that there were no provisions for reparations.[87] Eventually, the Internal Rules allowed for "moral and collective reparations" to be awarded to the victims. It was unclear what this meant, and the four groups of civil parties in the Duch trial put forward a number of requests, such as access to medical care and education, a national commemoration day, and construction of pagodas. In the Berkeley Human Rights Center survey, the types of reparations most requested by victims were social services, infrastructure, economic development programs, and memorials.[88] Disappointingly, the verdict of the Duch trial provided extremely limited reparations. First, the names of the 66 civil parties and their relatives who died were included in the judgment. Second, the ECCC compiled all statements of apology made by Duch during the trial into a 27-page document and published 10,000 copies for distribution.[89] Other requests were considered outside the competence of the ECCC or lacking specificity. This led to great disappointment on behalf of the civil parties and criticism over the lack of initiative from the ECCC.[90] The Supreme Court Chamber took the same restrictive view of reparations at the Duch appeal, stating that it had no jurisdiction to grant requests that would need the involvement of Cambodian authorities to be realized.[91]

However, a number of changes to the rules regarding reparations should provide more opportunities to think creatively in the second trial. The mandate of the former Victims Unit, now called the Victims Support Section, has been expanded to support these changes. There will now be a single claim for collective and moral reparation from all the civil parties, which can seek a limited number of awards.[92] As stated in Rule 23, the Chamber may a) order that the costs of the award shall be borne by the convicted person or b) recognize that a specific project may be implemented, which should have been designed or identified in cooperation with the Victims Support Section and have secured external funding.[93] However, there is still concern regarding the funding of such awards.[94]

The new mandate of the Victims Support Section includes the development and implementation of non-judicial programs and measures addressing the broader interests of victims.[95] These can be developed with external governmental and non-governmental organizations. These non-judicial measures are particularly important and relevant when 90 percent of respondents to the Berkeley Human Rights Center survey believed it was important to provide symbolic reparations, the majority believing that reparations should go to the community and only 11 percent believing that they should go to individuals only.[96]

Non-judicial initiatives

In the absence of an official truth commission process in Cambodia, the need for memorialization and reconciliation initiatives has been filled by NGOs and civil society. The Victims Support Section has the opportunity to work with civil society, drawing on the expertise of Cambodian NGOs to develop the non-judicial measures and externally funded projects that can be awarded as moral and collective reparations.

The Documentation Center of Cambodia (DC-Cam) has carried out a wide range of activities to support its aim of documenting the crimes and atrocities of the Khmer Rouge era. It has the largest collection of primary documents on the Khmer Rouge and has catalogued approximately 155,000 pages of primary Khmer Rouge documents and more than 6,000 photographs.[97] One of its projects, the Genocide Education Program, developed a textbook on the Khmer Rouge period, and assisted the Ministry of Education in training nearly 4,000 teachers on how to use the text.[98] A wide variety of materials have been produced, including posters, guidance for teachers, and workbooks for students. This is a particularly important project since very little on the subject has been taught in Cambodian schools in the past. Furthermore, DC-Cam has begun advocacy regarding a truth and reconciliation process that fits the social and cultural context of Cambodia. One of its proposals is to build on the experience of this Genocide Education Program to start a project on memory and reconciliation. The project proposal is for trained teachers to use the knowledge gained through training to expand their activities from teaching to broader community outreach. The main project activity will be to collect testimony from Cambodians about their experiences under the Khmer Rouge. The goals are to "establish a big picture narrative of this important period of Cambodian history … an environment that fosters social healing … engaging communities in narrative."[99]

The Transcultural Psychosocial Organization (TPO Cambodia) provides a great deal of psychological support and counseling to civil parties and witnesses at the ECCC, and has also developed a treatment approach that is appropriate to the specific cultural and human rights dimensions of mental health in Cambodia. Victims of the Khmer Rouge talk about their experience and write a testimony of what they have experienced. This is then read aloud during a Buddhist ceremony in the presence of other victims or members of their community. This ceremony allows them to express their traumatic experiences and honor the spirits of the dead, as well as documenting the human rights violations that they have suffered.[100] This mixture of testimony, therapy, and spirituality has achieved very positive results.[101]

The International Center for Conciliation (ICfC) has a "Justice and History Outreach Project," which focuses on empowering communities. ICfC worked with Youth for Peace (YFP), a local NGO, to work with six villages to develop goals to engage with and heal from the past.[102] YFP had found in its previous work that many young people do not believe that atrocities took place[103] and so the project also facilitated communication with the younger generation and in addition provided information concerning the ECCC. The project was very intensive, with a number of stages, including ICfC staff spending ten days living in the village. ICfC staff helped villagers and YFP to design and organize activities to meet their own needs, including village dialogues, visits to Phnom Penh to sites such as S-21, the ECCC, and Cheung Ek (the Killing Fields), and the construction of memorials.[104] The project was seen as an effective way of bringing young people together with Khmer Rouge survivors and provided a space for sharing and learning about their experiences.[105] Participants also reported a greater sense of community, greater self-disclosure of their experiences under the Khmer Rouge, and fewer social constraints in talking with others.[106] Although this is a small project, involving five or six villages a year, it has had a lasting impact on the communities involved. These are just a few examples of initiatives that have been undertaken; there are many more for the Victims Support Section to draw on for the broader benefit of victims.

Conclusion

It is clear that peacebuilding and transitional justice activities in Cambodia faced an extremely challenging context. The desire for amnesty and will to move forward with accountability very much relied on the RGC's position. The experience in Cambodia makes clear that any consideration of sequencing of peacebuilding and transitional justice activities predominantly relies on the context. There was no possibility to plan sequencing or engagement between DDR and transitional justice, and a much more pragmatic approach was needed and taken. The final structure of the ECCC was the product of lengthy negotiations between two parties with very different goals, resulting in a compromised tribunal. The attempts at DDR should be evaluated against the backdrop of ongoing problems with corruption and lack of rule of law in the country.[107] Even the ECCC has not been immune to these accusations, with ongoing controversy regarding additional prosecutions and claims of political interference. If these problems tarnish the reputation of the ECCC, victim participation has the potential to be its lasting legacy, with a number of lessons for other countries regarding management of the process. This provides another example of the necessity of taking a pragmatic approach and taking advantage of opportunities as and when they arise. Although the participation of victims was not planned for during the negotiations and the early years of the ECCC, from 2007 and with support from civil society, this aspect has become vital to the Court's work. Despite the difficulties with the numbers of civil parties during the trial of Duch, their testimonies and presence were extremely important. With the thousands of civil parties in the second trial, there is still a lot of work to be done to ensure that their participation is meaningful and that the non-judicial measures to be developed by the Victims Support Section are designed in a collaborative manner with those they are meant to benefit. This will provide a basis for victim-centered justice for the ECCC and an example for other courts and tribunals.

Notes

1 See Ben Kiernan, "Conflict in Cambodia 1945–2002," *Critical Asian Studies*, vol. 34, no. 4 (2002), pp. 483–95. I define the conflict period from the outbreak of civil war in Cambodia to the final surrender and capture of the Khmer Rouge leaders.

2 David Chandler, *A History of Cambodia* (Boulder, CO: Westview, 2008), p. 259.
3 Ibid., pp. 256–57.
4 Kiernan, "Conflict in Cambodia 1945–2002," op. cit., p. 492.
5 Freedom House, *Countries at the Crossroads. Country Report – Cambodia.* 2010, available at <*www.freedomhouse.org/template.cfm?page=140&edition=9&ccrpage=43&ccrcountry=179*>.
6 For a detailed exploration about the relationship between peacebuilding and transitional justice, see Chandra Lekha Sriram and Johanna Herman, "DDR and Transitional Justice: Bridging the Divide?" *Journal of Conflict, Security & Development*, vol. 9, no. 4 (December 2009) and Chandra Lekha Sriram, Olga Martin-Ortega, and Johanna Herman, "Beyond Justice Versus Peace: Transitional Justice and Peacebuilding Strategies," in Karin Aggestam (ed.), *The Study of Just and Durable Peace* (London: Routledge, 2012).
7 UN, "Cambodia UNTAC: Facts and Figures," available at <*www.un.org/en/peace keeping/missions/past/untacfacts.html*> (last accessed July 1st 2011).
8 Michael W. Doyle and Nicholas Sambanis, *Making War and Building Peace* (Princeton, NJ: Princeton University Press, 2006).
9 Agreement on a Comprehensive Political Settlement of the Cambodia Conflict, Article 17. United Nations, Department of Public Information, Agreements on a Comprehensive Political Settlement of the Cambodia Conflict: Paris, 23 October 1991, January 1992, 7–40.
10 Michael W. Doyle, "Peacebuilding in Cambodia: Legitimacy and Power," in Elizabeth M. Cousens and Chetan Kumar (eds), *Peacebuilding as Politics* (Boulder, CO: Lynne Rienner, 2001), p. 92.
11 Ibid., p. 103.
12 Ek Chanboreth and Sok Hach, "Aid Effectiveness in Cambodia," Wolfensohn Center for Development Working Papers, No. 7, December 2008. Available at <*www.brookings.edu/papers/2008/12_cambodia_aid_chanboreth.aspx*>.
13 It is highly unlikely that the country will continue this scale of growth. See World Bank, *Sustaining Rapid Growth in a Challenging Environment: Cambodia Country Economic Memorandum*, February 2009, p. ix.
14 Ibid., p. xi.
15 United Nations and Kingdom of Cambodia, United Nations Development Assistance Framework 2006–10, pp. 14–15.
16 Agreement on a Comprehensive Political Settlement of the Cambodia Conflict, op. cit., Annex 2, Article V, para 1–2.
17 Centre for International Cooperation and Security, "Disarmament, Demobilisation and Reintegration (DDR) and Human Security in Cambodia" (University of Bradford: July 2008), p. 10.
18 Peter Bartu and Neil Wilford, *Transitional Justice and DDR: The Case of Cambodia* (New York: ICTJ, 2009), p. 6.
19 Dylan Hendrickson, "Cambodia's Security-sector Reforms: Limits of a Downsizing Strategy," *Conflict, Security & Development*, vol. 1, no. 1 (2001), p. 74.
20 Bartu and Wilford, *Transitional Justice and DDR*, op. cit., p. 13.
21 Ibid., p. 14.
22 Ibid.
23 World Bank, *Implementation Completion Report*, Report No: 36269, May 22, 2006, p. 4.
24 Ibid.
25 Ibid., p. 6.
26 World Bank press release, "Cambodia: World Bank Sanctions Thales Engineering and Consulting S.S. and Others in Demobilization Project," 22 November 2004.
27 World Bank, *Implementation Completion Report*, op. cit., p. 15.
28 Bartu and Wilford, *Transitional Justice and DDR*, op. cit., p. 22.
29 Hendrickson, "Cambodia's Security-sector Reforms," op. cit., p. 70.
30 World Bank, *Implementation Completion Report*, op. cit., p. 2.

31 Kheang Un, "Patronage Politics and Hybrid Democracy: Political Change in Cambodia, 1993–2003," *Asian Perspective*, vol. 29, no. 2 (2005), pp. 203–30.
32 Joakim Öjendal and Mona Lilja, "Beyond Democracy in Cambodia: Political Reconstruction in a Post-conflict Society?" in Joakim Öjendal and Mona Lilja (eds), *Beyond Democracy in Cambodia: Political Reconstruction in a Post-conflict Society?* (Copenhagen: Nias, 2009), p. 7.
33 Hendrickson, "Cambodia's Security-sector Reforms," op. cit., p. 79.
34 Ibid., p. 72.
35 Global Witness, "Cambodia's Family Trees: Illegal Logging and the Stripping of Public Assets by Cambodia's Elite," June 2007, p. 6.
36 Ibid, p. 14.
37 Ibid., p. 73. Hendrickson, op. cit., and Global Witness, op. cit., p. 12.
38 Hendrickson, op. cit., p. 72.
39 Suzannah Linton, "Putting Cambodia's Extraordinary Chambers into Context," *Singapore Year Book of International Law*, vol. 11 (2007), p. 212.
40 Ibid.
41 Thomas Hammarberg, "Efforts To Establish a Tribunal Against the Khmer Rouge Leaders: Discussions between the Cambodian Government and the UN," paper presented at a seminar organized by SIDA, Stockholm, 29 May 2001, p. 1–2.
42 Ronald C. Slye, "The Cambodian Amnesties: Beneficiaries and the Temporal Reach of Amnesties for Gross Violation of Human Rights" (21 August 2003), *bepress Legal Series*, Working Paper 33, p. 26.
43 Sok An, "Closing Remarks for the International Conference, Dealing with a Past Holocaust and National Reconciliation: Learning from Experiences," available at <*www.eccc.gov.kh/sites/default/files/media/dealing_with_a_past_holocaust.pdf*> (last accessed 1 July 2011).
44 Linton, "Putting Cambodia's Extraordinary Chambers into Context," op. cit., p. 213. Also see Law on the Outlawing of the "Democratic Kampuchea" Group (English translation based on the text published by the Phnom Penh Post, vol. 3, no. 14, 15–28 July 1994), available at <*www.cambodia.gov.kh/krt/pdfs/Law%20to%20Outlaw%20DK%20Group%201994.pdf*> (last accessed 1 July 2011).
45 Law on the Outlawing of the "Democratic Kampuchea" Group, op. cit.
46 Ibid.
47 Ibid.
48 Bartu and Wilford, "Transitional Justice and DDR," op. cit., pp. 11, 15.
49 Mark Freeman, *Necessary Evils: Amnesties and the Search for Justice* (Cambridge: Cambridge University Press, 2009), pp. 152–53.
50 Bartu and Wilford, "Transitional Justice and DDR," op. cit., p. 15.
51 Ibid.
52 Ibid., p. 22.
53 Human Rights Watch testimony to the Tom Lantos Commission, 10 September 2009.
54 Linton, "Putting Cambodia's Extraordinary Chambers into Context," op. cit., p. 211.
55 Royal Decree, NS/RKT/0996/72, unofficial translation provided by ECCC, available at <*www.eccc.gov.kh/sites/default/files/legal-documents/pardon_foriengsary.pdf*> (last accessed 2 September 2011).
56 Seth Mydans, "An Amnesty in Cambodia," *The New York Times*, 18 September 1996.
57 Slye, "The Cambodian Amnesties," op. cit., p. 5.
58 Bartu and Wilford, "Transitional Justice and DDR," op. cit., p. 16.
59 Slye, "The Cambodian Amnesties," op. cit., pp. 15–16.
60 Ibid., p. 16.
61 Case of Ieng Sary 002/19-09-2007-ECCC/OCIJ (PTC75), Ieng Sary's Appeal against the Closing Order, 25 October 2010, para. 50.

62 Case of Ieng Sary, 002/19-09–2007-ECCC/OCIJ (PTC75), Decision on Ieng Sary's Appeal against the Closing Order, 11 April 2011, paras 197–201.
63 Case of Ieng Sary, 002/19-09–2007-ECCC/TC, Ieng Sary's request to stay the commencement of the trial proceedings until the final determination of Ieng Sary's preliminary objections regarding the royal pardon and amnesty and *ne bis in idem*, paras 1–17.
64 Reuters, "Khmer Rouge Commanders Go On Trial in Cambodia," Monday 27 June 2011.
65 Christine Evans, "Preview of the Defense: Khieu Shamphan and Ieng Sary Respond," *Cambodia Tribunal Monitor*, 23 November 2011.
66 Freeman, *Necessary Evils*, op. cit., p. 132.
67 Hammarberg, "Efforts To Establish a Tribunal Against the Khmer Rouge Leaders, op. cit., p. 2.
68 World Bank, *Implementation Completion Report*, op. cit., p. 21.
69 Phuong Pham *et al.*, "So We Will Never Forget: A Population-based Survey on Attitudes about Social Reconstruction and the Extraordinary Chambers in the Courts of Cambodia" (Berkeley, CA: Human Rights Center, January 2009).
70 Ibid., p. 28.
71 Ibid., p. 29.
72 General Assembly resolution 52/135 "Situation of Human Rights in Cambodia" 12 December 1999, UN doc A/RES/52/135.
73 UN, *Report of the Group of Experts for Cambodia Established Pursuant to General Assembly Resolution 52/135*, paras 171, 178–79.
74 Hammarberg, "Efforts to Establish a Tribunal Against the Khmer Rouge Leaders," op. cit., p. 10.
75 Ibid., p. 11.
76 Law on the Establishment of the Extraordinary Chambers, with inclusion of amendments as promulgated on 27 October 2004, Chapter I, Article 1.
77 Open Society Justice Initiative, "Recent Developments at the Extraordinary Chambers in the Courts of Cambodia" (Open Society Foundation: February 2012), pp. 17–18.
78 Ibid., pp. 20–21; Open Society Justice Initiative, "Recent Developments at the Extraordinary Chambers in the Courts of Cambodia" (Open Society Foundation: June 2011), pp. 7–22 and Open Society Justice Initiative, "Recent Developments at the Extraordinary Chambers in the Courts of Cambodia" (Open Society Foundation: November 2011).
79 United Nations, "Statement Attributable to the Spokesperson for the Secretary-General on the Extraordinary Chambers in the Courts of Cambodia," New York, 30 March 2012.
80 Ibid.
81 ECCC, Internal Rules, Rule 23, 12 June 2007.
82 UN, *Reports of the Secretary-General on Khmer Rouge Trial*, UN doc. A/57/769, 21 March 2003; UN doc. A/58/617, 3 December 2003; UN doc. A/59/432, 12 October 2004; UN doc. A/60/565, 25 November 2005.
83 See Johanna Herman, "Reaching for Justice: The Participation of Victims at the Extraordinary Chambers in the Courts of Cambodia," CHRC Policy Paper no. 5, September 2010, available at <*www.uel.ac.uk/chrc*>.
84 Although ultimately only 66 were given the status of civil parties in the final judgment. This has now been changed so that the status of civil parties was decided before the second trial.
85 ECCC, Internal Rules (Rev. 5), as revised on 9 February 2010.
86 UN, *Report of the Group of Experts for Cambodia*, op. cit., paras 212, 219.
87 Suzannah Linton, "Comments on the Draft Agreement between the UN and Cambodia," *Searching for the Truth*, issue 40 (2003), Magazine of Documentation Center of Cambodia, available online at <*www.dccam.org/Tribunal/Analysis/Comments_Regarding_ Draft_Agreement.htm*> (last accessed 1 July 2011).

88 Phuong Pham *et al.*, "So We Will Never Forget," op. cit., p. 44.
89 Kong Sothanarith, "Court Begins Reparations Campaign," Voice of America, 20 February 2012.
90 John D. Ciorciari, "The Duch Verdict," *The Cambodia Tribunal Monitor*, 28 July 2010, available at <*http://cambodiatribunal.org/images/CTM/the%20duch%20verdict.pdf*> (last accessed 19 April 2011); James O'Toole, "Reparations Remain a Key Issue," *The Phnom Penh Post*, 27 July 2010; Sam Rith, "KRT Civil Parties Plan Appeal," *The Phnom Penh Post*, 24 August 2010.
91 Open Society Justice Initiative, "Recent Developments at the Extraordinary Chambers in the Courts of Cambodia" (Open Society Foundation: February 2012), p. 13.
92 ECCC, Internal Rules (Rev. 5), as revised on 9 February 2010.
93 ECCC, Internal Rules (Rev. 6), as revised on 17 September 2010.
94 FIDH and CHRAC, 'The New ECCC Internal Rules: Effective Victim Participation and Reparation Advanced, but Implementation Not Yet Guaranteed,' 14 October 2010, <*www.fidh.org/The-New-ECCC-International-Rules-Effective-Victim*> (accessed 31 March 2011).
95 ECCC, Internal Rules (Rev. 6), Rule 12.
96 Phuong Pham *et al.*, "So We Will Never Forget," op. cit., p. 44.
97 DC-Cam website, History and Description of DC-Cam (no date), available at <*www.dccam.org/Abouts/History/Histories.htm*> (last accessed April 2011).
98 Author interview, Phnom Penh, September 2009. For further information on the project, please see <*www.dccam.org/Projects/Genocide/Genocide_Education.htm*> (last accessed April 2011).
99 DC-Cam, "Complementary Justice: Designing a Mechanism for Memory and Reconciliation in Cambodia," *Searching for the Truth*, English Edition, 1st Quarter (2011), pp. 1–9, available at <*www.dccam.org/Projects/Magazines/Image_Eng/pdf/1st_Quarter_2011.pdf*>.
100 TPO, "Justice and Healing in Times of the Khmer Rouge Tribunal," available at <*www.tpocambodia.org/index.php?option=com_content&view=article&id=48&Itemid=60*>.
101 Author interview, Phnom Penh, May 2010.
102 Nigel Field *et al.*, "Dealing with the Past: An Evaluation of the ICFC's Justice and History Outreach Project," August 2009, p. 6. Copy with author.
103 Interview, Phnom Penh, September 2009, and see Mark Channsitha, "Evaluation Report for Youth for Peace 2008," Centre for Peace and Conflict Studies, Phnom Penh, April 2008, p. 25. Copy with author.
104 Field *et al.*, "Dealing with the Past," op. cit., p. 7.
105 Channsitha "Evaluation Report," op. cit., pp. 26–27.
106 Field *et al.*, "Dealing with the Past," op. cit., p. 33.
107 Kheang Un, "The Judicial System and Democratization in Post-Conflict Cambodia," in Joakim Öjendal and Mona Lilja (eds), *Beyond Democracy in Cambodia: Political Reconstruction in a Post-Conflict Society* (Copenhagen: NIAS Press, 2009) pp. 70–100.

7 Unfinished business: Peacebuilding, accountability, and rule of law in Lebanon

Chandra Lekha Sriram

Introduction

Much of the time, transitional justice measures are developed alongside the implementation of peace agreements and peacebuilding efforts, and are expected by their framers and advocates to contribute to peace. The claim is that accountability measures can help to deter future violence and prevent revenge attacks, demonstrate and help to reinstall the rule of law and democracy, and contribute in so doing to longer-term stability. And indeed, transitional justice measures are expected to work alongside specific measures of peacebuilding, such as rule of law promotion, security sector reform, and disarmament, demobilization, and reintegration of ex-combatants. Increasingly those developing such measures of peacebuilding are expected to take transitional justice measures into account.[1] What happens, however, when a transitional justice measure is developed decades after the end of the conflict, where such standard measures of peacebuilding were not pursued, or are incomplete? Can a transitional justice mechanism have the desired effects? And what if that mechanism is not designed to address the wide range of past violations of international human rights or international humanitarian law, but a more recent, and far narrower, set of political crimes?

This chapter considers the prospects for the Special Tribunal for Lebanon (STL) to have any serious impact on the country itself, against the backdrop of long-term reconstruction but limited efforts that might be construed as peacebuilding. It argues that, while Lebanon has undergone extensive reconstruction since the end of its brutal civil war, no serious peacebuilding efforts were undertaken. Indeed, many of the changes that a post-conflict society is expected to undergo, arising from demobilization of large numbers of fighters, and reform of the justice and security sector, did not take place. In this context, accountability for the abuses committed during the war and in the subsequent 15 years under Syrian occupation has yet to take place and seems unlikely. The STL is nonetheless often expected to operate as a mechanism analogous to ordinary transitional justice mechanisms, yet it does not have the remit to address the legacy of conflict and occupation. Instead, its mandate is limited to the assassination of former Prime Minister Rafik Hariri and related assassinations. It seems unlikely that it can have the effect expected of transitional justice mechanisms generally, and ascribed by the advocates of the STL specifically, of promoting human rights and accountability, or even peacebuilding. Rather, after two decades of reconstruction, the tribunal is unlikely to contribute to peace and may run the risk of promoting conflict should it try defendants, whether in person or *in absentia*.

A note on the place of a case study in Lebanon in a volume on transitional justice and peacebuilding; this might, and perhaps should, strike some readers as odd, given that Lebanon presents us with what one of our authors has termed a "no-no" case: no transitional justice, and no peacebuilding.[2] First, the study of Lebanon's experience provides a useful counterpoint to the study of countries in which one or more mechanism of each has been deployed over time, helping us to understand at least one possible result of failure to take either seriously. While every situation is different, given that we frequently scrutinize and criticize mechanisms that exist as though their absence *might* be a preferable option, there is much to be learned from study of their absence in Lebanon. Second, and perhaps more importantly, given the tendency towards proliferation of mechanisms of transitional justice, it is important to closely scrutinize them and ask whether they are genuinely dedicated to certain core goals of human rights and accountability, or whether they serve other, political purposes. Here, the STL looks like a transitional justice instrument, but it is worth asking, as with the use of certain transitional justice mechanisms in Colombia, whether that means that transitional justice is actually underway.[3]

Background: the conflict and its termination

Lebanon experienced a brutal civil war during 1975–90 and a brief resurgence of violence following the assassination of former Prime Minister Rafik Hariri in 2005. The conflict was based on sectarian violence amongst militias and between the militias and the government, with significant regional dimensions. In 1976 Syria invaded Lebanon, with what it would later recast as an Arab Deterrent Force, or a peacekeeping force, and remained an occupying power. Israel also invaded southern Lebanon, in 1978, and put in place a "buffer zone" which remains today. The UN Interim Force in Lebanon peacekeeping force was put in place in southern Lebanon in 1978 to monitor Israeli withdrawal, and remains in place today.

Official estimates of casualties during the civil war are of about 145,000 deaths of which some 90 percent were civilians, 185,000 wounded, 2,000 women killed for having been raped, and 800,000 displaced.[4] In addition to Lebanese citizens killed and displaced during the conflict, many disappeared and their numbers and fate have still not been determined, although official estimates stand at about 17,000.[5] Others disappeared or have been held in Syrian prisons, many as political prisoners, although this is a charge that Syria denies.[6]

In 1989, the Ta'if agreement was negotiated by surviving members of the prewar Parliament, with brokerage by regional states, which proposed to heal national rifts and promote reconciliation (it was also titled the Charter of National

Reconciliation), develop administrative and political reforms, disarm militias, reaffirm sovereignty, and engage in "Lebanonization."[7] While it reinforced the need for Israeli withdrawal, it emphasized the importance of Syrian-Lebanese relations. Lebanon remained, following the end of the conflict, under heavy Syrian influence. While under the Ta'if agreement Syrian troops, then at a strength of 40,000, were to be redeployed to the Bekaa valley and removed, they remained in the country and were only fully removed in 2005 under heavy international pressure (UNSC resolution 1559).

The Hezbollah militia continues to maintain significant control in southern Lebanon and poor suburbs of Beirut and has not demobilized. In 2006, a short war between Israel and Hezbollah militants operating in southern Lebanon further devastated the country.

Meanwhile, the politics are shaped not only by confessionalism, discussed further below, but by rivalries between the 8 March and 14 March coalitions. These coalitions are particularly split over the creation and operation of the Special Tribunal. The 8 March coalition, comprised of the Shiite parties Amal and Hezbollah, allied with the Free Patriotic movement, refers to the date of a rally organized in 2005 to thank Syria for its involvement in the country. They view the creation of the tribunal as external interference in Lebanon. The 14 March coalition refers to the date in 2005 in which 1 million Lebanese protested in the streets, calling for Syrian withdrawal and an international investigation of the Hariri assassination. The coalition comprises the largely Sunni Future Movement founded by Hariri, several Christian parties, the Lebanese Forces (LF, formerly a militia within the Christian-dominated Lebanese Front, now a political party), and the Progressive Socialist Party, and supports the tribunal and rejects Syrian involvement in Lebanon.[8]

Challenges for peacebuilding

The situation in Lebanon was somewhat unique in that much of the primary post-conflict economic reconstruction activities were not only internationally, but also internally, generated and regionally supported, particularly with the support of wealthy Prime Minister Rafik Hariri, who was able to obtain a mix of grants and loans from oil-rich Gulf states alongside Western donors. The emphasis, however, has been less on peacebuilding and more on physical reconstruction, with Gulf donors and Hariri emphasizing infrastructure projects and Western donors emphasizing technical support to governance reform.[9] If it is difficult, approximately 20 years after the Ta'if agreement, to characterize most activities seeking to rebuild Lebanon as peacebuilding rather than reconstruction, this may be in significant part due to the environment in which any peacebuilding might be attempted.

Governance, sectarianism, and clientelism

There are significant structural challenges to long-term peacebuilding in Lebanon.[10] The country is technically a parliamentary democracy, with power-sharing in governance.[11] However, because of the dominance of political parties by particular sectarian groups traditionally and the consolidation of power in the hands of a few powerful politicians, political parties lack much significance. The prevalence of clientelism increases this phenomenon. While the Ta'if agreement sought to break clientelism by stipulating that voting be in governates, or large administrative units, elections have regularly violated its terms with district-based and uni-confessional voting. The Lebanese Constitution of 1926, as amended in 1990, stipulates the abolition of confessionalism in article 95, but has yet to be implemented.[12] Power-sharing arrangements have been used repeatedly to address immediate crises of governance, often leaving underlying grievances unaddressed.

It is unclear whether peacebuilding in any traditional sense, including the (re)building of a strong and unitary state, is feasible in the country. Sectarian parties have an interest in a weak state so that they are able to pursue their own interests, according to some experts, and individuals define themselves as much or more through sectarian identities than as Lebanese.[13] One observer, pointing out that state weakness left vacuums that were filled by Hezbollah, Saad Hariri, Walid Jumblatt, and Christian factions, suggested that there were really many small strong states within a weak larger state.[14] Further, each sectarian group has its own regional patrons, variously Saudi Arabia, Egypt, Jordan, Syria, and Iran. These factors make state consolidation difficult.

The regional environment

Any efforts at building peace and promoting justice in Lebanon do not operate in a vacuum. Obviously, Lebanon is in an unstable region and subject to influences from regional powers noted above, even after the Syrian withdrawal from its territory. Israel only withdrew from a security zone that it occupied in the south of the country in 2000 and in 2006 fought a war with Hezbollah. The presence of a large number of Palestinian refugees living in poor conditions in refugee camps is a source of both political dispute and security concerns. Many observers suggest that genuine peace in Lebanon will not be feasible in the absence of a broader regional settlement, which would include a fair solution for Palestinians.[15]

Unfinished demobilization of combatants

The Ta'if agreement sparked new fighting between the Lebanese Forces (the largest militia) and the interim prime minister, General Michel Aoun, in 1990. There was provision for disarmament, demobilization, and reintegration of ex-combatants (DDR), but its implementation was not internationally supported, and it did not extend to all fighting forces. A general amnesty, offering militia leaders posts in government, helped end the fighting, and some 50,000 fighters from 24 militias disarmed by April 1991. Some militias also had members integrated into the new Lebanon army, although all sought to integrate more members than was feasible. However, while there was widespread disarmament, there was also variation in willingness to hand over or canton weapons. The Druze and Amal militias tended to comply with the process and also handed over heavy weaponry to the Syrians. Former Amal militia were heavily integrated into the state forces because of the group's ties to the state and the rise of its leader, Nabih Berri, to be speaker of the Parliament.

Two critical exceptions are to be noted. Hezbollah, viewed by many as a liberator from Israeli occupation, was allowed to keep its arms. In addition, members of the LF were unable to take full advantage of DDR programs and very few were allowed to be integrated into the new army or civilian posts; instead, they tended to rely upon militia and family networks for reintegration. Many militia members did not seek inclusion in state forces because they had other opportunities, were established in legal businesses, or were engaged in smuggling, which in some cases increased organized criminal activity significantly.[16] The lack of demobilization of Hezbollah enabled it to become a critical power-broker in post-Ta'if Lebanon, and it continues to hold significant power to influence and destabilize politics today.[17]

The lasting impact of the failure to engage in complete DDR in Lebanon, according to one observer, has been not only continued sectarianism, but continued "territorialization of security," with factions controlling different sectors of the country and providing or undermining security. Such groups, including but not limited to Hezbollah, compete with one another and with the legitimate state security providers. The continued possibility of factional violence was demonstrated in the street fighting between Hezbollah and Amal militia members in May 2008.[18]

Sectarianism and the security forces

The possibility of security sector reform is limited, largely for the reasons that have been noted already. The state security forces, the ISF, do not control all the territory, and are widely viewed as being, like the judiciary, politics, and other aspects of public life, shaped by sectarianism and patronage.[19] Militia members were to be incorporated into the ISF following rehabilitation, but in general they were simply incorporated without any rehabilitation process.[20] The army is considered to be a more professional and truly national institution, but it too is affected by sectarianism.[21] And, as one observer noted, without true disarmament of the more general population and militias, which would leave the security forces with the monopoly on weapons and use of force, reform will prove difficult.[22] The army continues to respond to internal security issues rather than confining itself to external security because the ISF has lacked the capacity to control militias or larger demonstrations.[23]

Human rights and rule of law

While the judiciary is formally independent, sectarian divisions are said to interfere in its management by the Supreme Judicial Council.[24] The judiciary is considered widely to be corrupt and subject to political manipulation.[25] More generally, it is very slow and inefficient.[26] However, there are exceptional judges who have displayed independence and professionalism and have applied international human rights and refugee law in their decisions.[27] Thus, while most judges have the proper training, unlike in many countries where capacity-building is a necessary first step, the real challenge is the reform of the politicized environment in which they operate.[28]

There are some positive signs of the prospects for human rights and the rule of law, albeit limited ones. President Michel Suleiman has publicly stated an interest in promoting judicial reform and appointed as minister of the interior a former civil society activist, Ziad Baroud, who has promoted electoral reform. However, Suleiman and Baroud are considered by some observers as weak and/or exceptions to the rule, and reform will prove challenging given the sectarian nature of the polity, as well as the reliance of some judges on political patrons for their positions.[29] The minister of justice, also a reformist, proposed the abolition of the death penalty in the summer of 2009, but it was politically controversial and was not presented to Parliament amid a broader cabinet crisis.[30] The country also ratified the Optional Protocol to the Torture Convention in 2008, which obligates it to create a national office of prevention of torture within a year, which as of this writing has not been created.[31]

Accountability and impunity

The absence of transitional justice mechanisms

In many countries emerging from violent conflict or repression, domestic trials are debated, if not held, and other measures such as commissions of inquiry, reparations, and commemorations may be utilized. However, the Amnesty Law of 1991 (law 94/91) provides for amnesty for all crimes except political assassination, thus making it impossible to try war crimes, crimes against humanity, and forced disappearances domestically. In general, there have been very few prosecutions for clear abuses of human rights or violations of humanitarian law, although there has been selective prosecution.[32] Thus Elias Hobeika, former leader of the LF security agency and implicated in the 1982 Sabra and Shatila massacres, escaped prosecution and was elected to Parliament twice, only to be disgraced (and assassinated) following revelations of his involvement in the massacres in the context of attempts to prosecute Ariel Sharon. However, Samir Geagea, the leader of the Lebanese Forces, was imprisoned for life, accused of responsibility for a church bombing near Beirut in 1994. The LF was outlawed. He was given amnesty by the legislature in 2005.

There has been no plan for broader war crimes or human rights trials, and there are no policies in place for transitional justice mechanisms or a national reconciliation process. Proposals for a national commemorative day for the civil war have been rejected.[33] However, commemorative events in 2005, not long after the assassination of former Prime Minister Hariri, may have marked the beginning of a change in the so-called culture of amnesia. In the absence of official government efforts, civil society organizations in particular have developed memorials and recollection of the events of the civil war through films and documentaries.[34] One former Christian militia leader, M. Assad Shaftari, has also offered an apology.[35]

Nonetheless, there is relatively little public discussion of the past and certainly no shared narrative regarding the conflict, although the latter is often difficult if not impossible. Following the Ta'if accord, a committee was created to develop a history textbook which would be acceptable to all confessional groups. The committee worked for a decade to develop such a textbook, but the end result was not endorsed, which means that different groups continue to learn from different textbooks. Furthermore, different groups receive news from different sources which each have their own particular biases.[36]

There has, similarly, been little done to address the fate of the disappeared or the needs of their relatives.[37] While the government has issued official statistics on those disappeared alongside estimates of the dead and wounded, those are alleged to be inflated. And while there have been two commissions of inquiry into the disappeared, one in 2000 and one in 2001, the first published only a two-page report, and the other none at all, in relation to thousands of potential victims. Two NGOs have brought suit, seeking release of a detailed report; proceedings were pending in 2011.[38] Pursuit of detailed information about, or justice for, the disappeared was impossible during Syrian occupation and remains difficult in light of the 1991 amnesty, political divides, and security concerns. Further, there has historically been a political divide between the two main organizations of families of the disappeared and detained, although that has been bridged to some degree,[39] and more vocal advocacy for information about the disappeared and opening of mass graves has been possible in recent years.

The Hariri tribunal

There was widespread speculation in Lebanon and abroad about who might be responsible, with allegations that Hezbollah members, with Iran's backing, might be responsible, or that Syria might have arranged for Hariri to be killed in order to maintain its influence in the country, or that both were responsible.[40] Many in the international community felt that accountability was important and that Lebanese courts were unlikely to be able to hear cases related to the assassination.[41] Thus the only significant, and the only externally supported, attempt at accountability is the Lebanon Special Tribunal, which was created to prosecute just a few crimes—the 14 February 2005 assassination of former Prime Minister Hariri and several related assassinations.[42] It may be a mistake to treat the tribunal as a mechanism of transitional justice in anything other than form, given that it was created long after the Ta'if agreement, although of course there is no time limitation on accountability mechanisms.[43] Furthermore, the withdrawal of Syria certainly constituted an important transition for the country. The question remains whether it could nonetheless catalyze efforts at broader accountability in the country.

The tribunal's creation

Following the assassination, the United Nations Security Council established the mandate of a commission of inquiry in April 2005.[44] That commission concluded that the assassination was carried out by a group with "extensive organization," and indicated that some evidence pointed to Lebanese and Syrian involvement. It transmitted evidence collected in its investigations to Lebanese judicial authorities and expressed the view that further investigations should be undertaken by domestic judicial and security forces.[45] Whether members of Hezbollah or of the Syrian government are responsible, obtaining custody of them could be difficult.[46]

Following a resolution by the UN Security Council calling for a criminal tribunal in 2006, the UN and the government of Lebanon entered into agreement for the creation of the Special Tribunal for Lebanon to prosecute individuals responsible for the organization of the Hariri assassination and related killings. The creation of the tribunal was endorsed by the Council in 2007.[47] There are 11 judges, of which four are Lebanese. Some scholars have questioned even the presence of four Lebanese judges, arguing that the judiciary is simply too corrupt and politicized to guarantee that their decisions at the tribunal would be impartial.[48]

Controversy over the tribunal: selectivity and politics

The tribunal is controversial because it is only designed to address such a limited set of crimes, given the extensive history of assassinations both during and since the end of the civil war, as well as disappearances and violations of international human rights and international humanitarian law during the armed conflict.[49] Many see the tribunal as politicized and unable to deliver accountability, and a range of civil society organizations that do promote the idea of some form of transitional justice or reckoning with the past do not support the tribunal itself.[50] Families of the thousands of persons who disappeared during the war question the creation of a tribunal to investigate the killings of a few elite with no serious investigations into the fate of their relatives.[51] Indeed, even the international nature of the tribunal, which in form appears similar to hybrid tribunals such as the Special Court for Sierra Leone, but which does not have jurisdiction over any international crimes, might be called into question. As the Regional Representative of the Office of the High Commissioner for Human Rights in Lebanon observed, the internationalization of this particular judicial process is justifiable only either with reference to the inability of Lebanese courts to hear such politically sensitive cases, or because one or more of the perpetrators may be outside of Lebanese territory.[52]

Furthermore, many view the tribunal's creation as having been motivated more by politics than a desire to pursue justice or confront a broader culture of impunity.[53] In particular, France and the USA are said to have used the creation of the tribunal to isolate and in some sense "criminalize" Syria, which is seen by many as at least partially responsible for the assassination. However, the changes in administration in both countries have meant, according to one observer, that their interest in promoting the tribunal has waned, and their fears of destabilizing Syria have increased;[54] given the uprisings in the country and the region, these fears possibly became more acute during 2011. Nonetheless, the faction most supportive of the tribunal is that led by Saad Hariri, the prime minister and former prime minister's son, while the primary opposition faction alleges that the tribunal is politicized.[55]

Tribunal legacy?

There are numerous models of hybrid tribunals, and there is some controversy over whether the Special Tribunal for Lebanon is indeed such a tribunal, although it shares some characteristics with existing hybrid models. Generally, hybrid tribunals share a number of features: they are sited in the country affected by the violence or conflict to be addressed, they utilize international and domestic judges, lawyers, and other court staff, and they prosecute international crimes and may also have some domestic crimes within their remit.[56] The STL shares few of these characteristics: it applies domestic law pertaining to domestic crimes of terrorism and murder, rather than international law crimes such as crimes against humanity or war crimes.[57] It is sited just outside The Hague, nearer to other international criminal tribunals such as the International Criminal Court and the *ad hoc* tribunals for the former Yugoslavia and Rwanda, rather than in Lebanon itself, for reasons of security. It does, however, include domestic and international staff, with Lebanese and international judges, and an international chief prosecutor, head of defense, and registrar.[58] There is thus an argument for treating it as a hybrid.[59]

More importantly for our purposes, the primary arguments for the tribunal are quite similar to those made for hybrid tribunals. Advocates of hybrid tribunals often argue that they should be created to pursue accountability where the domestic judiciary is unable to address serious crimes of the past due to damage, incapacity, or bias. They also argue that they help to address the needs of affected victims and society, sited as they are ordinarily in the country affected. And they are often expected to have a capacity-building and demonstration effect for weak or corrupt national judiciaries, through the inclusion of national staff, presence on the territory affected, and legacy-building through engagement with the domestic judiciary. Similar arguments have been put forth in support of the STL, despite its presence in the Netherlands. Its mixed character is defended as necessary due to the bias and corruption of the judiciary, and advocates emphasize their hopes for a wider legacy for domestic rule of law. The fact that the tribunal will apply purely domestic law but apply international standards regarding the rights of the defendant and due process, among others, has the potential to enhance domestic rule of law in Lebanon by having a more directly analogous relevance, at least for specific crimes.[60] Finally, advocates hope that the tribunal will contribute to, rather than undermine, peace.[61]

It might be hoped that the tribunal, notwithstanding its mandate to try a limited number and type of cases, could reopen broader domestic debates regarding accountability and impunity that might eventually lead to a real impetus for reform of rule of law and/or transitional justice processes, open political space for discussions about the civil war, or even enable reconciliation processes.[62] There is some evidence that the procedures of the tribunal have influenced some domestic legal discussions. Following the release of four generals detained for the tribunal (see below), the minister of justice presented a proposal that would reform the Code of Criminal Procedure setting a limit to the period of detention without charge to a year, albeit much longer than the tribunal's 90-day rule.[63] Advocates argue that the Lebanese judges serving on the tribunal will return to the country with expertise that will be shared with colleagues.[64]

Some argue that the tribunal could serve as an example of impartial justice in operation and could result in justice for a political crime, both rarities in Lebanon.[65] They suggest as well that the tribunal's creation, justified in part with reference to the inability of the Lebanese judiciary to manage a case of this nature, or to act impartially, will draw attention to the need for judicial reform in the country.[66] They note, too, that families of the disappeared have sought to use the creation of the tribunal as an opportunity to draw attention to their concerns.[67] Any such impact, of course, will depend upon effective outreach and, as the outreach office was launched in December 2009, it is as yet too early to assess its effects.[68]

However, the prospect for criminal accountability for other crimes remains unlikely so long as the 1991 amnesty remains in force, and leaders and fighters from various fighting forces who may be responsible for abuses are in office.[69] It is not clear that the tribunal will have any further impact on rule of law promotion in the country.[70] While some discussions regarding the possibility of a truth commission were initiated with the support of the International Centre for Transitional Justice and the International Federation of Human Rights (FIDH), one observer suggests that the 2006 Israeli war with Hezbollah interrupted these discussions, which have not been seriously resumed.[71]

At the same time, the selectivity of the tribunal's mandate may undermine its legitimacy and thus its ability to promote the concept of rule of law more generally, in the absence of any processes to address the legacy of the civil war, the assassinations and disappearances (in Syria as well as Lebanon) since the end of the war, the 2006 war, or the May 2008 violence. Some characterize the tribunal as simply demonstrating that there is a double standard—justice for wealthy elites and no justice for the rest of the populace.[72] The rumors first that Syria, and later Hezbollah, were the primary subjects of investigation have generated concerns, too, about the legitimacy or expedience of any indictments. In January 2011, the prosecutor submitted a sealed indictment request to the pre-trial judge; on 30 June the indictments were confirmed, and eventually the names of four suspects, all with connections to Hezbollah, were released.[73]

Others have suggested that the funds spent on the tribunal would be better spent on domestic judicial reform.[74] The legitimacy of the tribunal is also affected by the perceived lack of transparency—there was no public discussion of the selection process for judges.[75] All of this adds up to an institution that looks like a hybrid tribunal, and might be taken to be part of a transitional justice process, but which may be simply a mechanism without a wider process.

Unique features

The tribunal has a number of unique features, beyond the deviations from the common characteristics of hybrid tribunals noted above. It is noteworthy that it will be an internationalized court trying the crime of terrorism, given that there is no comprehensive agreed definition of the crime of terrorism in international law.[76] It is also unique in that trials *in absentia* are permitted, which critics have argued is inconsistent with international human rights law.[77] The final feature, if utilized effectively, might have the potential for wider impact of the tribunal: the provision for victim participation.[78] Article 17 of the statute, copying the language of article 168 of the statute of the International Criminal Court, permits victims to present their views during the proceedings. The purpose of inclusion of victims in such proceedings, according to one jurist, is not merely judicial, but also serves reparative and symbolic functions for the victims themselves.[79] In theory, such participation might serve symbolic functions for the wider society as well. However, given the relatively limited scope of persons likely to be considered victims for the purposes of the STL, the impact is likely to be limited.[80] In particular, the large number of victims and families of victims, including the disappeared, would not be able to make statements at the STL as the crimes to which they could refer do not fall within the remit of the court. At this stage, in the absence of any criminal proceedings, it is too early to assess the impact of victim participation at the STL.

Legitimacy, politics, and stability: controversy over the four generals

Given the political context and the politicized nature of its creation, the Special Tribunal is viewed by many as politicized and potentially biased itself. This perception may undermine the impact of its operation on Lebanese politics and society, and discussions about accountability, even if it operates in an impartial and independent fashion. Thus, for example, even the tribunal's decision in April 2009 to free four accused pro-Syrian generals who had been detained by the Lebanese government for future prosecution did not prove its independence to some. The four men, former head of the presidential guard Mustafa Hamdan, security services director Jamil al-Sayed, domestic security chief Ali Hajj, and military intelligence chief Raymond Azar, were released after the prosecutor of the tribunal, Daniel Bellemare, requested that they be, on the grounds that there was not sufficiently credible evidence to make it possible for him to bring indictments in the legally mandated time frame of 90 days.[81] A key witness, Mohammed Zuhair Siddiq, a Syrian army deserter, had recanted his original statements incriminating the four, and arrest warrants were issued for him in both Syria and

Lebanon.[82] Following his release, al-Sayed repeatedly made statements calling into question the impartiality of the Lebanese judicial system and high-level politicians. Members of the 8 March faction say that the Lebanese judges at the tribunal itself are corrupt and can be bought off, although they provide no specific evidence for such allegations, and indeed the order by the STL would seem to indicate that this is not the case.[83] One of the detained, al-Sayed, subsequently submitted a claim before the tribunal that he was the victim of arbitrary detention on the basis of libel. The matter has been assigned to a pre-trial judge and al-Sayed has been provided with defense counsel.[84]

The tribunal could, according to some, have a destabilizing effect on Lebanese politics, depending upon whom it chooses to indict.[85] Thus Walid Jumblatt, the leader of the Progressive Socialist Party, originally a supporter of the tribunal, later predicted that there would be chaos when indictments were issued.[86] Some observers are more circumspect, suggesting that the tribunal may have exacerbated existing political divisions, but that it did not create them.[87] Further, while the tribunal was extremely politicized at its creation, given perceptions that it was a tool for the USA, France, and others to demonize Syria, Syria has begun to rebuild relations with regional and international powers. Thus the "shadow of the tribunal" may be lessened.[88] Conversely, indictments could help calm the political situation, ending rumor and speculation, according to one observer.[89] The expectation, and subsequent decision, on indictments of persons connected to Hezbollah generated new speculation about possible political compromise by Saad Hariri and his successor Najib Azmi Mikati, including the possibility of requesting the closure of the tribunal.[90] While this might alleviate immediate domestic political debates and the legitimacy issues that hamper the tribunal, it would also contribute to the already significant trend towards impunity in the country and indeed make future efforts at accountability significantly more difficult.[91] In late 2010, Saudi Arabia and Syria sought to broker a deal that would allow Hariri to distance the government from the tribunal without closing it; this initiative failed. In January 2011, Hezbollah withdrew from the coalition government, prompting its collapse and a continuing parliamentary crisis.[92]

Conclusion

As one analyst asked me, "How can we establish peace with half a justice done?"[93] Despite the passage of 20 years since the Ta'if agreement, it is difficult to say that peace is truly consolidated in Lebanon. This has hampered efforts to pursue accountability, or even establish a shared narrative of the events of the civil war or under occupation, even five years after Syrian withdrawal. The Special Tribunal for Lebanon is ill-suited to engage the larger legacy of the past, given its limited mandate and its curious status as a transitional justice-type mechanism in the absence of an obvious transitional process. And it is unlikely, on the evidence to date, to have the hoped-for effect of promoting efforts at accountability or even truth-telling domestically, engendering frustration and disappointment among victims and families of victims and the missing. Whether the tribunal will undermine stability, should it have any defendants before it, remains to be seen.

Notes

1 *Guidance Note of the Secretary-General. United Nations Approach to Transitional Justice* (March 2010), at <www.unrol.org/files/TJ_Guidance_Note_March_2010FINAL.pdf>.

2 I thank Lars Waldorf for raising provocative questions on this point during the authors' meeting for this project in May 2011, and Jemima García-Godos for providing a helpful set of concepts to which to respond.

3 See, e.g., Maria Paula Saffon and Rodrigo Uprimny, "Uses and abuses of transitional justice in Colombia," in Morten Bergsmo and Pablo Kalmanovitz, eds, *Law in Peace Negotiations* (Oslo: Torkel Opsahl Academic Publisher, 2010), pp. 354–94.

4 These killings are a subset of so-called honor killings, in which the victim is punished for having supposedly brought dishonor to the family; in Lebanon many women who have been raped are subsequently killed by their brothers. United Nations Trust Fund to End Violence Against Women, "Facts and figures on violence against women" (16 February 2007), at <www.unifem.org/campaigns/trust_fund_10th_anniversary/facts_figures.php?page=4>.

5 Marieke Wierda, Habib Nassar, and Lynn Maalouf, "Early reflections on local perceptions, legitimacy and legacy of the Special Tribunal for Lebanon," *Journal of International Criminal Justice*, vol. 5 (2007), pp. 1065–81, at 1068; Iolanda Jaquemet, "Fighting amnesia: Ways to uncover the truth about Lebanon's missing," *International Journal of Transitional Justice*, vol. 3, issue 1 (2008), pp. 1–18, at 1.

6 Author's interview with observer who requested anonymity (Beirut, September 2009).

7 Lebanonization was meant to imply a positive return to control of Lebanese over their own country and the incorporation of various factions in a pluralist political system, but is also often used internationally in a derogatory fashion, to refer to disintegration of a state or foreign control over it.

8 Wierda, Nassar, and Maalouf, "Early reflections," op. cit.

9 Are Knudsen, "Precarious peacebuilding: Post-war Lebanon, 1990–2005," CMI Working Paper (Bergen: Chr. Michelsen Institute, 2005); Christine Sylva Hamieh and Roger MacGinty, "A very political reconstruction: Governance and reconstruction in Lebanon after the 2006 war," *Disasters*, vol. 34 (2010), pp. S103–S123.

10 Martin Kraft, Muzna Al-Mazri, Heiko Wimmen, and Natascha Zupan, "Walking the line: Strategic approaches to peacebuilding in Lebanon" (Bonn: Working Group on Development and Peace, German Development Service, and Heinrich Böll-Stiftung, December 2008), pp. 15–24.

11 See Arab Reform Initiative and Palestinian Center for Policy and Survey Research, "The state of reform in the Arab world 2009–10" (Arab Reform Initiative, March 2010), <www.arab-reform.net>.

12 The Constitution of Lebanon (1926, as amended 1990), at <www.servat.unibe.ch/icl/le00000_.html#A095> (accessed 12 December 2009). See generally Robert Fisk, *Pity the Nation: Lebanon at War* (Oxford: Oxford Paperbacks, 2001); Fawwaz Traboulsi, *A History of Modern Lebanon* (London: Pluto Press, 2007). Sandra Mackey, *Lebanon: A House Divided* (New York: W.W. Norton, 2006). Author's interview with Gaëlle Kibranian, Lebanese Transparency Association (Beirut, September 2009).

13 Kraft, Al-Mazri, Wimmen, and Zupan, "Walking the line," op. cit., pp. 5–6, 20–21; author's interview with Bassel Salloukh, Lebanese American University (Beirut, September 2009); author's interview with Father Fady Fadel, Antonine University (Beirut, September 2009).

14 Author's interview with Sylva Hamieh (speaking in personal capacity) (Beirut, September 2009).
15 Author's interview with Julien Courson, Alef (Beirut, September 2009); author's interview with Kamel Mohanna, Director, Amel Association (Beirut, September 2009).
16 Knudsen, "Precarious peacebuilding," op. cit., pp. 12–13; author's interview with Paul Salem, Director, Carnegie Middle East Center (Beirut, September 2009).
17 Robert Rabil, "Hezbollah: Lebanon's power broker," *The Journal of International Security Affairs*, no. 15 (Fall 2008), at <www.securityaffairs.org/issues/2008/15/rabil.php>.
18 Author's interview with Siad Darwish, Peace Permanent Movement (Beirut, September 2009); Ghaith Abdul Ahad, "Ghaith Abdul Ahad reports on the street battle in Lebanon," *The Guardian* (10 May 2008), at <www.guardian.co.uk/world/2008/may/10/lebanon.syria>.
19 Kraft, Al-Mazri, Wimmen, and Zupan, "Walking the line," op. cit., pp. 10, 33–35; Yezid Sayigh, "'Fixing broken windows': Security sector reform in Palestine, Lebanon, and Yemen," *Carnegie Papers* no. 17 (Beirut: Carnegie Middle East Center, October 2009); author's interview with Salloukh.
20 Author's interview with Salloukh.
21 Aram Nerguizian and Anthony Cordesman, "The Lebanese armed forces: Challenges and opportunities in Post-Syria Lebanon" (Washington, DC: Center for Strategic and International Studies, 10 February 2009); author's interview with Salloukh; author's interview with Hamieh; author's interview with Salem.
22 Author's interview with Darwish.
23 Author's interview with Jeremy Cornforth, Political and Economic Counsellor, Embassy of the United States of America (Beirut, September 2009).
24 Kraft, Al-Mazri, Wimmen, and Zupan, "Walking the line," op. cit., pp. 31–33.
25 Author's interview with Julien Courson, Alef (Beirut, September 2009); expert speaking on condition of anonymity (Beirut, September 2009).
26 Author's interview with Salem.
27 Author's interview with Fateh Azzam, Regional Representative, Office of the High Commissioner for Human Rights (Beirut, September 2009).
28 Author's phone interview with Nadim Houry, Human Rights Watch (Beirut, September 2009).
29 Author's interview with Salloukh author's interview with Darwish; author's interview with Hamieh; author's interview with Salem.
30 "Lebanon: Justice ministry campaigns to abolish death penalty" (29 August 2009), at <www.handsoffcain.info/archivio_news/200908.php?iddocumento=12311666&mover=0> (accessed 12 December 2009); author's interview with Azzam.
31 Expert speaking on condition of anonymity (Beirut, September 2009).
32 Wierda, Nassar, and Maalouf, "Early reflections," op. cit., pp. 1066–69.
33 Knudsen, "Precarious peacebuilding," op. cit., p. 15.
34 Laurie King-Irani, "Commemorating Lebanon's war amid continued crisis," *Middle East Report Online* (14 April 2005), at <http://merip.org/mero/mero041405.html>; author's interview with Siad Darwish, who suggested there was increased openness to transitional justice at the public and political level, referring to television programs with politicians discussing the war, and commemorative events. One observer suggests that the Hariri assassination itself created new political space, by generating international condemnation, some directed at Syria and Iran, lessening Syria's influence in Lebanon; author's interview with Fadel; author's interview with Zeina el-Hélou, Lebanese Centre for Policy Studies (Beirut, September 2009).
35 M. Assad Shaftari, "Letter from a militia leader in Lebanon's civil war," at <www.caritas.org/activities/peace_reconciliation/Peacebuilding_Slideshow.html?cnt=337> (accessed 10 December 2009).

36 United Nations Development Programme Lebanon, *Peace Building Project Newsletter* (1st Quarter 2009) on file with author; Stephen Dockery, "Journalists of all political colors attend media workshop," *The Daily Star* (Beirut, 8 July 2009).
37 Wierda, Nassar, and Maalouf, "Early reflections," op. cit., pp. 1067–68.
38 Jaquemet, "Fighting amnesia," op. cit., pp. 5–6; Amnesty International, "Never forgotten: Lebanon's missing people" (April 2011), at <www.amnesty.org/en/library/asset/MDE18/001/2011/en/4c0716c2-8825-41d6-b816-c678ef4eeb44/mde180012011en.pdf>.
39 Jaquemet, "Fighting Amnesia," op. cit., pp. 6–8. These are the Committee of the Families of the Kidnapped and Disappeared and SOLIDE (Support of Lebanese in Detention and Exile).
40 An article in a German magazine spurred particular controversy in 2009 for alleging that the Special Tribunal had evidence regarding Hezbollah's role in the assassination and was keeping it secret. Erich Follath, "New evidence points to Hezbollah in Hariri murder," *Der Spiegel* (23 May 2009), at <www.spiegel.de/international/world/0,1518,626412-2,00.html>.
41 This view was confirmed by the international inquiry initiated by the UN: *Report of the International Independent Investigation Commission Established Pursuant to Security Council Resolution 1595*, UN Doc. S/2005/662 (20 October 2005).
42 One author, a Lebanese judge involved in the negotiations for the tribunal, says that the extension of the tribunal's jurisdiction to attacks related to, but other than, that of Hariri was to deter the "serial political assassinations" that followed Hariri's. Choucri Sader, "A Lebanese perspective on the Special Tribunal for Lebanon," *Journal of International Criminal Justice*, vol. 5 (2007), pp. 1083–89.
43 Chandra Lekha Sriram, Olga Martin-Ortega, and Johanna Herman, "Justice delayed? Internationalized criminal tribunals and peacebuilding in Lebanon, Bosnia, and Cambodia," *Conflict, Security, and Development*, vol. 11, no. 3 (July 2011).
44 United Nations Security Council Resolution 1595, UN Doc. S/RES/1595 (7 April 2005).
45 *Report of the International Independent Investigation Commission Established Pursuant to Security Council Resolution 1595*, UN Doc. S/2005/662 (20 October 2005).
46 Follath, "New evidence," op. cit.
47 United Nations Security Council Resolution 1664, UN Doc. S/RES/1664 (29 March 2006); United Nations Security Council Resolution 1757, UN Doc. S/RES/1757 (30 May 2007), which includes the statute; for an overview, see International Center for Transitional Justice, *Handbook on the Special Tribunal for Lebanon* (10 April 2008), at <www.ictj.org>.
48 Author's interviews with anonymous sources in Beirut, August–September 2009.
49 Wierda, Nassar, and Maalouf, "Early reflections," op. cit., pp. 1071–72; author's interview with Courson; author's interview with el-Hélou.
50 Author's interview with Darwish.
51 Pamela Badine, Université Saint-Joseph de Beyrouth (Beirut, September 2009), describes their view as it being a matter of "leaders vs people."
52 Author's phone interview with human rights official on condition of anonymity.
53 Wierda, Nassar, and Maalouf, "Early reflections," op. cit., pp. 1072–73.
54 Author's phone interview with human rights official in Lebanon on condition of anonymity. See also Jan Erik Wetzel and Yvonne Mitri, "The Special Tribunal for Lebanon: A court 'off the shelf' for a divided country," *The Law and Practice of International Courts and Tribunals* (2008), pp. 81–114, 111; author's interview with Fadel.
55 Author's interview with Hamieh.
56 Beth Dougherty, "Right-sizing international criminal justice: The hybrid experiment at the Special Court for Sierra Leone," *International Affairs*, vol. 80, no. 1 (March 2004), pp. 311–28; compare Chandra Lekha Sriram, "Wrong-sizing international justice? The hybrid tribunal in Sierra Leone," *Fordham International Law Journal*, vol. 29, no. 3 (February 2006), pp. 472–506; Cesare P. R. Romano, André Nollkaemper, and Jann

K. Kleffner, eds, *Internationalized Criminal Courts: Sierra Leone, East Timor, Kosovo, and Cambodia* (Oxford: Oxford University Press, 2004).

57 Janice Yun, "Special Tribunal for Lebanon: A tribunal of international character devoid of international law," *Santa Clara Journal of International Law*, vol. 7 (2009–10), pp. 181–96; Marko Milanovich, "An odd couple: Domestic crimes and international responsibility in the Special Tribunal for Lebanon," *Journal of International Criminal Justice*, vol. 5 (2007), pp. 1139–52; James Cockayne, "The Special Tribunal for Lebanon: A cripple from birth?" *Journal of International Criminal Justice*, vol. 5 (2007), pp. 1061–64.

58 There is one international Pre-Trial Judge; a Trial Chamber with one Lebanese judge and two international judges, plus two alternate judges, one Lebanese and one international; and an Appeals Chamber with two Lebanese judges and three international judges.

59 On possible criteria for treating a tribunal as a hybrid, see Neha Jain, "Conceptualizing internationalisation in hybrid criminal courts," *Singapore Year Book of International Law*, vol. 12 (2008), pp. 81–95.

60 Wierda, Nassar, and Maalouf, "Early evidence," op. cit., p. 1078.

61 Wetzel and Mitri, "The Special Tribunal for Lebanon," p. 111.

62 Wierda, Nassar, and Maalouf, "Early reflections," op. cit., p. 1077; author's interview with Fadel, who emphasized the possibility of the tribunal's work encouraging reconciliation; author's interview with Cornforth. Courson pointed out that the existence of the tribunal has prompted some Lebanese to speak more openly about the absence of trials for killings of ordinary civilians during the war; author's interview with Iolanda Jaquemet, journalist (Beirut, September 2009).

63 Author's interview with Fadel, who thinks nonetheless that the tribunal is unlikely to influence wider legal reform; author's interview with Nadim Houry, Human Rights Watch (Beirut, September 2009), who noted that, while this would be an advance if passed, it would not affect procedures of the Judicial Council, so its impact would be limited.

64 Author's interview with Cornforth.

65 Author's interview with Azzam.

66 Author's interview with Salloukh.

67 Author's interview with Lynn Maalouf (Beirut, September 2009).

68 Email from Wajed Ramadan, Outreach Officer (23 August 2010), outlining press and other events, including visits by several judges to Lebanon; Tolbert, "Introductory note to the Special Tribunal for Lebanon: Orders regarding the detention of persons and memorandum of understanding," *International Legal Materials*, vol. 48 (April–June 2009), p. 1151; Outreach page of STL website, at <www.stl-tsl.org/sid/146> (accessed 23 August 2010).

69 Author's interview with Fadel.

70 Author's interview with Azzam; author's interview with Hassan Krayem, UNDP policy specialist and scholar at the American University in Beirut (Beirut, September 2009).

71 Author's phone interview with human rights official on condition of anonymity.

72 Author's interview with Houry.

73 Special Tribunal for Lebanon, "STL Prosecutor submits an indictment to the Pre-Trial Judge" (17 January 2011), at <www.stl-tsl.org/sid/239>; UN News Centre, "Lebanon: UN-backed tribunal submits indictment over Hariri's murder" (30 June 2011), at <www.un.org/apps/news/story.asp?NewsID=38902&Cr=hariri&Cr1>; Patrick Galey, "STL: Lebanon must still cooperate with Tribunal," *The Daily Star* (Beirut) (11 August 2011), at <www.dailystar.com.lb/News/Politics/2011/Aug-11/STL-Lebanon-still-must-cooperate-with-tribunal.ashx#axzz1Ui8tGjT3>.

74 Author's interview with Houry, who suggested that many human rights organizations are of this view.

75 Author's interview with Houry.

76 Jan Erik Wetzel and Yvonne Mitri, "The Special Tribunal for Lebanon: A court 'off the shelf' for a divided country," *The Law and Practice of International Courts and Tribunals* (2008), pp. 81–114; Cockayne, "The Special Tribunal for Lebanon," op. cit., p. 1062. Specific terrorist crimes are defined in a range of international and regional agreements, of course.

77 Paola Gaeta, "To be (present) or not to be (present): Trials *in absentia* before the Special Tribunal for Lebanon," *Journal of International Criminal Justice*, vol. 5 (2007), pp. 1165–74; Wayne Jordash and Tim Parker, "Trials *in absentia* at the Special Tribunal for Lebanon: Incompatibility with international human rights law," *Journal of International Criminal Justice*, vol. 8 (2010), pp. 487–509.

78 Cécile Aptel, "Some innovations in the statute of the Special Tribunal for Lebanon," *Journal of International Criminal Justice*, vol. 5 (2007), pp. 1107–24; Jerome de Hemptinne, "Challenges raised by victims' participation in the proceedings at the Special Tribunal for Lebanon," *Journal of International Criminal Justice*, vol. 8 (2010), pp. 165–79.

79 de Hemptinne, "Challenges raised by victims' participation," op. cit., pp. 167–68.

80 The impact of such provisions can be expected to be greater in trials involving large numbers of victims, such as in Cambodia, where the Extraordinary Chambers apply similar provisions.

81 David Tolbert, "Introductory note to the Special Tribunal for Lebanon," op. cit., pp. 1149–51; "Order regarding the detention of persons detained in Lebanon in connection with the case of the attack against Prime Minister Rafiq Hariri and Others," Case No. CH/PTJ/2009/06 (29 April 2009), reproduced in *International Legal Materials*, vol. 48 (April–June 2009), pp. 1152–60; Antonios Tzanakopoulos, "Special Tribunal for Lebanon: The first orders by the Pre-Trial Judge," *ASIL Insights*, vol. 13, issue 11 (7 August 2009), at <*www.asil.org*>. According to the rules of procedure of the tribunal, persons cannot be detained without charges being laid for more than 90 days.

82 "Lebanon frees four generals held in Hariri case," *Al-Arabiya.net* (29 April 2009), at <www.alarabiya.net/articles/2009/04/29/71647.html#001>; "Jamil Sayyad to Saad Hariri: You are your father's killer until you punish forgers," *Al-Manar TV* (30 August 2009), at <www.almanar.com.lb/NewsSite/NewsDetails.aspx?id=101267&language=en>.

83 Author's interview with Hamieh.

84 "Order assigning matter to Pre-Trial Judge," Case No. CH/PRES/2010/01 (15 April 2010); "Appointment of defence counsel. Rule 58 of the *Rules of Procedure and Evidence*," Case No. CH/PTJ/2010/01 (26 April 2010).

85 Comments from observer speaking on condition of anonymity (Beirut, September 2009).

86 "Walid Jumblatt: 'I wish we did not have the tribunal,'" *YaLibnan* (26 September 2010), at <www.yalibnan.com/2010/09/26/jumblatti-wish-we-did-not-have-the-tribunal>.

87 Author's interview with Lynn Maalouf.

88 Paul Salem, "Lebanon's multiple crises risk escalation" (Carnegie Endowment for International Peace, Carnegie Middle East Center, 12 July 2010), at <http://carnegie-mec.org>.

89 Author's interview with official of the European Commission.

90 International Crisis Group, "Trial by fire: The politics of the Special Tribunal for Lebanon," *Middle East Report No. 100* (2 December 2010), p. 37, at <www.crisisgroup.org/~/media/Files/Middle%20East%20North%20Africa/Iraq%20Syria%20Lebanon/Lebanon/100%20Trial%20by%20Fire%20%20The%20Politics%20of%20the%20Special%20Tribunal%20for%20Lebanon.ashx>. One observer discounts the likelihood of serious security risks as a result of any such indictments, but sees the

potential for political weakening of Hariri's position, if not compromise over the tribunal. Author's interview with British Ambassador Frances Guy (Beirut, 9 December 2010). Mikati heads a caretaker government following several unsuccessful attempts to form a government.

91 Author's interview with Ambassador Guy.

92 Tony Karin, "Lebanon government collapse: Hizballah exits cabinet," *Time* (12 January 2011), at <www.time.com/time/world/article/0,8599,2042003,00.html>.

93 Author's interview with el-Hélou.

8 Building peace and delivering justice in Bosnia and Herzegovina: The limits of externally driven processes

Olga Martin-Ortega[1]

Introduction

During the conflict in Bosnia and Herzegovina (1992–95) the civilian population was specifically targeted and suffered forced displacement, massacres, widespread rape, imprisonment in concentration camps, ethnic cleansing, and genocide. During the war 100,000 people were killed and 2.2 million were made refugees; 1.3 million people were internally displaced and up to 15,000 are still missing.[2] All sides of the conflict suffered horrific crimes, but the number of violations committed against the Bosniak[3] population was significantly higher. Ethnic cleansing was not just a consequence of the conflict, but a goal of the nationalist parties, particularly in Serb- and Croat-controlled areas, which implemented policies of forced expulsion of minorities to effectively create ethnically homogeneous areas, many of which remain in place today.[4]

The conflict came to an end through the Dayton General Framework Agreement for Peace (Dayton Peace Accords, DPA). The Agreement aimed to establish the framework of a long-term sustainable peace by including provisions on political structure, security, physical and economic reconstruction of the country, and the new Constitution. Since 1995 an army of international and non-governmental organizations have worked to build a stable, multi-ethnic, and viable democratic country, whilst at the same time establishing institutions to provide justice for the atrocities committed during the conflict. In Bosnia and Herzegovina peacebuilding and justice for the human rights violations committed during the conflict have run parallel from the beginning. In fact, the establishment of justice institutions, mainly the International Criminal Tribunal for the Former Yugoslavia (ICTY), was directly linked to the goal of achieving peace in the region and in the country. The creation of the Tribunal meant the resurgence of justice for war crimes as an interest of the international community, as well as an acknowledgement that justice needed to play an important role in the building of peace. The international intervention in Bosnia therefore marked not only a new era in peacebuilding and international justice but also a transformation of transitional justice. This can be seen as a transformation from nationally driven processes and mechanisms dealing with past atrocities in the context of political transitions to democracy towards internationally led post-conflict (or even during conflict) justice.[5] Bosnia has functioned as an experimental field for peacebuilding as well as for post-conflict justice. This chapter analyzes these processes and mechanisms and discusses how peacebuilding and transitional justice have evolved in the context of the reconstruction of Bosnia and to what extent they have impacted on each other.

Peacebuilding and governance challenges in post-conflict Bosnia

The peace negotiation process, hosted by the USA, brought together the leaders responsible for the extreme nationalistic rhetoric that drove the conflict. The DPA effectively consolidated the ethnically divided territories created by the war through a political structure which included two main entities of roughly the same size (along the wartime front lines): the Federation of BiH, mainly composed of Bosniaks and Bosnian Croats, and Republika Srpska, mainly composed of Bosnian Serbs. A third separate political entity, Brko District, has autonomous status. At state level every institution has to have the necessary representation of the so-called three constituent people, including a shared presidency. The institutional structure is particularly complex as the institutions at state level share competences with the entity institutions. Each entity has its own President, Prime Minister, government, Assembly, and court system, which includes a Supreme Court each and lower-level courts. The Federation is further divided into ten cantons. The institutional fragmentation has undermined the possibilities of building a strong central state.

The need—and urge—to guarantee the end of hostilities and stability led to a power-sharing agreement based on the fragmentation of state power and granting warring factions their quota of power. This effectively provided each ethnic group a share of political power, maintained the external influence of Serbia and Croatia, and allowed for leaders, some of them with war crimes records, to consolidate themselves in powerful positions. Soon after the signature of the DPA the international community rushed to hold elections which cemented the power bases of the ethnically segregated nationalist parties and legitimized their leaders.[6] In subsequent elections moderate cross-cutting parties have failed to gain enough political representation, whilst nationalist parties still enjoy great popular support.[7] All these factors have impeded the ethnic reintegration of previously plural territories, perpetuated the lack of social and political cohesion brought by the war, and encouraged an inefficient, extremely expensive, and dysfunctional governance system which often comes to paralysis at the state level.

The DPA created lead roles for multiple intergovernmental organizations but did not draw a comprehensive strategy for peacebuilding, and at the beginning of the peacebuilding process the agencies were deployed in an uncoordinated manner.[8] The DPA also created the post of an internationally appointed high representative to monitor the implementation of the accord and coordinate the activities for the other agencies. The High Representative (HR) was granted extraordinary powers, including the authority to remove elected officials, enact legislation, and establish new institutions and has used them robustly to erode the power of nationalist and corrupt spoilers. These powers have been particularly instrumental to guarantee refugee return and property restitution and to accelerate the pace of judicial and police reform.

Since 2002, the HR is also the EU Special Representative (EUSR). Once the Office of the HR closes, the EUSR will remain, with the ultimate goal to lead Bosnia to EU membership.[9] The possibility of integration in the EU has made this peacebuilding process relatively different to others analyzed in this volume given the leverage that the international community has been able to assert over the different parties involved. The steps forward and backward on the road to membership to the EU have very often been linked to political negotiations to advance in areas of internal reform, such as police reform, and very significantly to cooperation with the ICTY.

Coming back home: ex-combatants, armed forces, and refugees

One of the main priorities of the DPA was to reverse the impact of the wartime ethnic cleansing policies through the return of refugees and internally displaced persons to their pre-war homes and municipalities. Whilst the agreement contained detailed provisions and mechanisms for such return, provisions on the demobilization of ex-combatants and the reform of the security sectors were scaroe. The way these activities were conducted has had a significant impact on other aspects of peacebuilding as well as on transitional justice initiatives.

DDR and SSR

The DPA generally called for all the parties to disarm and disband all civilian armed groups. NATO's Implementation Force (IFOR), which later became the Stabilisation Force (SFOR), was tasked with the supervision of this process.[10] Right after the war, combatants demobilized in a chaotic way as the armed forces were disintegrating and a large number of irregular combatants were returning home, with no international organization assuming a leadership role for DDR.[11] An estimated 300,000 combatants voluntarily disarmed in 1996 without any assistance, and had to be absorbed by local towns and communities in a form of emergency demobilization.[12] The former combatants re-entered Bosnian society largely unprepared for such a transition, often lacking education and skills and suffering from post-traumatic stress disorder.[13] They returned to their communities in a post-war environment that offered a virtually non-existent economy and no employment opportunities.[14] During this first wave of demobilization, there was no assistance from either the state institutions, which lacked capacity at the time, nor the entity authorities. The help of the international community was limited to the support provided by the World Bank through the Emergency Demobilization and Disarmament Project.[15] Meanwhile, the three ethnic armies remained active, with entity authorities making no formal efforts to downsize them.[16] From 1998, following pressure from the international community, military expenditure was cut by 40 percent and national authorities started to focus on planned demobilization.[17] It was only from 2002 that reintegration became an important focus of the process. The International Organisation for Migration (IOM) provided severance packages, provision of livestock, basic kits to establish business or start agricultural production, vocational training, etc., as well as basic civic education courses which included human rights and democracy among its curricula.[18] But it was not until 2005, after much negotiation between the international community and national authorities, that the three armies were replaced by a single, multinational, and professional force, under the authority of the President of the country.[19] In 2007 the final phase of demobilization was considered completed.

Police reform was overseen by the UN Mission (UNMIBH) and its International Police Task Force, and later assumed by the EU Police Mission (EUPM) in 2003. It proved very difficult to reform the three mono-ethnic police forces, each having its own territorial jurisdiction.[20] Bosnian and Croatian forces merged without the intervention of the international community, but it was the pressure from the EU that triggered the participation of Republika Srpska. The EU Stabilisation and Association Agreement in 2008 was made dependent on advances in police reform, mainly to guarantee its direction at state level and to free it from political interference.[21]

The demobilization and security sector reform processes were not linked to any transitional justice initiative, and they were held independently of the larger efforts to seek justice.[22] This had an important effect, especially with regard to the police, who had been key instruments of ethnic cleansing during the war. During peacetime, they continued to play an important role in supporting nationalist and separatist agendas. Entity police forces refused to cooperate with each other and tended to favor their own ethnic groups in the enforcement of the law, especially in Republika Srpska and the Croatian areas of the Federation.[23] As a consequence of lack of coordination between UNMIBH and EUPM, a large number of police officers remained unvetted.[24] This meant that war criminals remained in the forces, contributing to a climate of impunity and insecurity and obstructing refugee return.[25] Both domestic war trials and cooperation with the ICTY were severely affected by this situation. In addition, only limited attention and funds were dedicated to reintegration of those demobilized, leading some veterans' associations to assume the role of social security networks. This has given them unprecedented power and political influence.[26] They have also managed to secure important funds from private sources, nationalistic political parties, and the governments of the entities.[27] These associations have played an important role in supporting ethnically based authorities and discourses and have negatively influenced the progress towards strengthening the role of the state, vocally protesting against prosecutions, undermining some other transitional justice initiatives, and competing with civilian victims in reparation schemes.[28]

Refugee and IDP return

Refugee and internally displaced person (IDP) return was conceived of as instrumental to reversing ethnic cleansing and reconstituting wherever possible the multi-ethnic composition of the country. The mechanisms and institutional provisions for refugee return were established in Annex 7 of the DPA, which states the rights of refugees and displaced persons as well as the obligation for national authorities in each territory to create the political economic and social conditions conducive to the voluntary return and harmonious reintegration of refugees and displaced persons, without any preference for a particular group (art. 2.1). It also establishes the responsibility to prevent activities within their territories which would hinder or impede the safe return of refugees and displaced persons. To achieve this, it obliges local public officials to repeal domestic legislation and administrative practices with discriminatory intent or effect (art. 1.3.a) and to prosecute, dismiss, or transfer those responsible for serious violations of the basic rights of persons belonging to ethnic or minority groups (art. 1.3.e).

Early on, refugee and IDP return was identified on a technical level with property restitution. In this regard Bosnia is often cited as a success, in which the international community managed to overcome strong domestic political resistance and facilitate the return of over 200,000 claimed properties to their pre-war residents.[29] The process, which was considered concluded in 2004, was full of challenges. The properties left vacant by those who had perished, fled, and in most cases been forcibly displaced had been allocated to the use of IDPs of the new majority ethnicity. However, they were also given to those not necessarily displaced but simply politically well connected: young families, war veterans, and the families of fallen soldiers.[30] In this way, a new ethnic distribution was being consolidated. Local nationalist leaders and local police forces played an important role in obstructing the process of return. Local authorities encouraged members of their own ethnic group not to leave the areas where they had settled after the war and created barriers to the return of the original inhabitants of the territory under their control, whom they referred to as “aliens.”[31] Police refused to evict new residents in certain municipalities.[32] The HR had to make use of his powers to repeal discriminatory laws and even remove obstructive public officials from office in order for the process to be completed. Equally, UNMIBH suspended police officers who failed to assist local authorities.[33]

The success on property return did not automatically mean success in refugee and IDP return, nor did it have an immediate impact on reversing the ethnic cleansing effect. Access to property was not the only obstacle to return. In many cases, security and discrimination concerns prevented families from returning to municipalities where they were no longer the majority ethnic group or where public officials and police were openly hostile to them and where little of the pre-war ties remained. Equally, employment prospects and lack of education opportunities played an important part in the lack of return, with many refugees settling in the host countries, especially in Serbia and Croatia, and IDPs staying in their new municipalities.[34] But, as Nettelfield points out, for many the selectivity of prosecutions meant that those who had perpetrated crimes against them or their families had not been removed from their municipality, and "they found themselves living literally next door to the same people who raped, murdered and forcibly expelled" them.[35] Many chose to reclaim their property to sell it, while others kept their former homes but were reluctant to come back to live in them and establish permanent residence.[36] Even if an estimated half of the displaced population has returned to their pre-war homes,[37] the country has not gone back to the pre-war original ethnic distribution.

Accountability for war crimes: justice as prosecution

Most of the population in BiH was affected by the conflict, which left both a trail of human rights violations and a high level of social destruction and distortion of community life. Segregated communities continue to be affected by nationalist rhetoric today. In addition, there is a very low level of social trust and trust in public institutions.[38]

From the very beginning of the international response to the conflict, justice for the atrocities committed played a central role. Victims of all sides wanted justice for what happened to them and their relatives and there was a high domestic and international demand for fighting impunity.[39] Both victims and the international community identified justice with criminal prosecutions, as will be discussed in more detail below.

Justice in The Hague

The ICTY was created in 1993 whilst the conflict was still ongoing. It was established to put an end to the serious international humanitarian law violations in the territory of the former Yugoslavia and bring to justice those responsible.[40] Since its establishment the ICTY has indicted 161 persons and concluded proceedings for 126 accused; there are ongoing proceedings for 35 accused.

The international community placed high expectations on the international prosecution of war crimes, which was envisioned as contributing more widely to the restoration and maintenance of peace.[41] Supporters expected the ICTY to contribute to the stable development of the rule of law by serving as deterrence and sending a powerful message that impunity would not be tolerated.[42] Even if not explicit in its mandate, it was expected also to contribute to social reconstruction or reconciliation.[43] The assumption of the advocates of the ICTY, including its first President, was that judicial processes facilitate peace and stability in the region by individualizing guilt, addressing the needs of victims and establishing the facts concerning the conflict.[44] It was hoped that criminal prosecutions would promote the restoration of social relations in peacebuilding processes by releasing communities from general guilt. Equally, the recognition of truth through testimony would address the needs of the victims and act as a catharsis, and allow victims to be recognized as such, independently of their ethnic origin.[45]

It is true that prosecutions in The Hague have helped remove the most notorious political leaders from positions of institutional power and marginalize some of the more radical nationalistic groups.[46] This had an important effect on the consolidation of peace and stability in the region. An example is the positive effect on refugee return (despite the problems explored above), with people feeling safer to return to their pre-war municipalities as the court developed its work.[47] A further example is the fact that, as the Court winds down its activities, protests have been less visible and had much less impact on national and local politics. The recent detentions and transfers to The Hague of the last two remaining fugitives, Ratko Mladić and Goran Hadžić, brought several thousand radical followers out onto the streets but did not have a particularly destabilizing effect in Bosnia.

With regards to reconciliation, the impact of the ICTY is far more difficult to assess. If anything, the experience of the ICTY (and the ICTR) has contributed to understanding of the limitations of criminal trials to facilitate social reconstruction and reconciliation, leading to policymakers tempering some of their grand statements over the capabilities of international criminal justice in societies after conflict. The assumptions regarding the expected impact of the ICTY have now been challenged, and more nuanced research work demonstrates the limitations.[48] Several studies have attempted to measure the impact of the ICTY on public opinion and in particular on reconciliation or social repair, including through population surveys.[49] The conclusions, as is often the case with this kind of research, are varied, and on occasion contradictory; therefore they have to be taken with caution. A key lesson from the ICTY for other courts has been the importance of the relationship with people affected by the prosecutions.[50] The legitimacy of the ICTY was greatly affected in the early years by the fact that it was physically and linguistically removed from the region,[51] as well as by the constant political attacks suffered from nationalistic political leaders.[52] The ICTY has since worked to restore such damage through its Outreach Programme, created in 1998. In the years of engagement with local civil society, the population's attitudes towards the international court have changed for the better.[53] Most of the population, even in Republika Srpska, now accept that the establishment of the international tribunal was important, even if they question the quality of its work.[54]

An overall conclusion regarding the impact of 20 years of the ICTY on peacebuilding and transitional justice in Bosnia can only be positive. As Nettelfield's work demonstrates, the international court has played an important role in the cementing of the country's nascent democracy. She finds that the work of the international court has contributed to the process of democratization by "facilitating social mobilization, political participation and the internationalization of human rights norms" as well as having challenged "extreme versions of dominant nationalistic narratives and assisted with the development of democratic institutions to bolster the rule of law."[55] The ICTY enabled Bosnia to address some of the "ghosts of its war time era" by pushing the painful question of "what to do with the past."[56] In this regard, the ICTY has contributed to the development of national accountability processes. It has been instrumental in overseeing national prosecutions, building the capacity of national judicial staff, and the creation of the War Crimes Chambers in Sarajevo, which is now continuing its prosecutorial work. ICTY rulings have made it more difficult for nationalist politicians to manipulate the facts of the conflict and deny the abuses.[57] The progressive advancement in accountability has opened the door for further transitional justice processes, which only years ago seemed nearly impossible in such a divided society, as analyzed below. The deficiencies evidenced by the work of the court have made it clearer that complementary transitional justice mechanisms are needed and have even contributed to an internal demand for such mechanisms.[58]

Impunity at home and the creation of the War Crimes Chamber

The DPA established specific obligations to cooperate with the ICTY (article IX), but was silent on domestic prosecutions. However, once the war was over, the international community discouraged domestic prosecutions. This was mainly because, during and immediately after the war, all sides used civilian and military courts to try the war crimes committed by "the other side." Destruction caused by the war and the lack of qualified personnel contributed to the inability of courts to administer justice efficiently but, most worryingly, the appointment of new judges on ethnic and political grounds in each entity resulted in ethically motivated trials and lack of impartiality.[59] Police forces also played a role in such dubious prosecutions. The ongoing failure to address impunity undermined the rule of law and negatively impacted public confidence in the police and legal system. The complex legal framework brought about by the DPA's territorial and administrative divisions made it more difficult to coordinate procedures between entities and at federal level.

It was only after the international community seriously committed to rule of law reform that prosecutions compliant with international standards at national level were possible. A UN Judicial System Assessment Programme was created in 1998 and in 2002 the HR presented his strategy for the reform of the justice sector.[60] The most important reforms included vetting and reappointment of judicial staff, the reduction of the number of judges and prosecutors, ensuring ethnic representation, the establishment of an independent body for the appointment and review of judges and prosecutors, the passing of new Criminal and Criminal Procedure Codes at state level, the passing of a law on witness protection, and the establishment of the State Court, with jurisdiction for the whole of BiH. Many of the new institutions were created as mixed or hybrid, that is, involving national and international staff and were in great part paid for by the international community.[61] These reforms had a beneficial impact on the functioning of the judicial system and the general trust over the system, which, even if improved, remains low.[62]

Section I of the State Court is the War Crimes Chamber (WCC), with jurisdiction over war crimes, crimes against humanity, and genocide. It is accompanied by a Special Department for War Crimes at the Office of the Prosecutor

(SDWC). Both bodies were established as the result of an agreement reached in January 2003 between the Office of the High Representative (OHR) and the ICTY[63] to provide the justice system with the tools and capacity to prosecute and carry out war crimes trials according to international standards.[64] They were created as national institutions assisted by international judges, prosecutors, and other staff. But, unlike other hybrid tribunals for the prosecution of international crimes, these institutions were envisaged to become fully national after five years. The WCC was officially inaugurated on 9 May 2005 and opened its first trial in September that year. The mandate of international judges and prosecutors, originally due to finish in 2010, was later extended until December 2012.[65] The SDWC and the WCC have been especially successful in prosecuting war crimes, with over 40 verdicts pronounced in appeal and a similar number of cases in first instance.[66]

Underlying the creation of the WCC was the fact that prosecutions at national level, with an increased sense of ownership by the local population, would contribute to the achievement of some of the goals that the ICTY left incomplete: particularly the prosecution of war criminals and aiding national reconciliation.[67] The WCC faced two substantial obstacles for this: an initial suspicion from the general population due to the general lack of satisfaction towards the judicial system[68] and the manipulative discourse of the nationalistic camps, which portrayed it, as they did with the ICTY, as a biased and corrupt institution. Bosnian Serb political leaders have been very vocal in their rejection of the WCC, arguing that it has focused more strongly on the prosecution of Serbs.[69] Serb victim associations, mostly those of veterans of war and former camp inmates, have protested over the lack of prosecutions of Bosnian Muslims and held demonstrations against the State Court.[70]

Lessons learnt from the initial failure of the ICTY to engage with the public led to the establishment of a Public Information and Outreach Section of the State Court (PIOS) from the outset, as well as to initiatives to engage with civil society and local communities, through a Court Support Network. However, funding problems and lack of staff have meant that outreach of the WCC has not been as effective as it should have been.[71] The shift from the initial efforts to partner with civil society and reach key groups has had, according to Barbour, a measurable effect in terms of failing to increase trust in domestic war crimes prosecutions and undermining civil society support.[72] Also, in its six years' practice the WCC shows a poor balance in the protection of witnesses and a failure to explain the prosecutorial processes. It has been particularly problematic for victims and the wider population to understand (in a similar way to the experience of the ICTY)[73] the use of plea agreements, which raise claims of impunity and leniency.[74]

The WCC does not have exclusive jurisdiction; other local courts can also prosecute war crimes, and have been doing so. Trials have been held in both Republika Srpska and the Federation, at district court and cantonal level, respectively. These trials at local level are crucial: the WCC will only deal with higher-level perpetrators, but victims need to see justice served in respect of the lower-level perpetrators, those who actually perpetrated the offence against them, the ones walking free in their community and living next door to their victims.[75] These prosecutions are progressing slowly. Some of the obstacles are technical, such as limited prosecutorial resources and lack of specialization among prosecutors and defense counsels, and deficient witness protection or support systems.[76] But important political obstacles still persist in certain areas where police and authorities are unwilling to investigate certain crimes and where prosecutors, court staff, and witnesses are at risk.[77]

Overall, any assessment of national prosecutions has to be positive, since the WCC is doing very important work and local courts are slowly progressing, despite the problems highlighted. However, there are thousands of violations to investigate, thousands of victims without redress, and potentially thousands of perpetrators who may not be able to be brought to trial.[78] Only through the development of complementary transitional justice mechanisms would it be possible to reach some of these victims and wider civil society.[79] These will be examined in the next section.

Lack of attention to non-prosecutorial measures

The emphasis on criminal trials has made it difficult for the development of other transitional justice mechanisms to accompany the peacebuilding process. The focus on criminal prosecutions resulted from the neglect of other mechanisms by both the international community and national authorities, and, until recently, the general public. In this section we explore the initiatives to conduct truth-seeking investigations and reparations. Unfortunately the scope of this chapter does not allow us to devote analysis to smaller-scale community projects, which are, house by house, school by school, village by village, trying to advance reconciliation and better social relations for a peaceful future.[80]

Truth seeking

Truth-seeking initiatives have so far failed in Bosnia, including two formal attempts to establish a Truth and Reconciliation Commission in 2000 and 2005.[81] The lack of commitment from national authorities played an important role in such failure, as did the lack of support of the international community. In particular, the ICTY was concerned over the potential for a truth commission to act as a parallel rival institution, which would compete with the ICTY's work and financing.[82] But the main concern regarding the establishment of such a body was the potential use of amnesties. The ICTY made it clear that it considered amnesties as infringing on the very mission of the Tribunal.[83] Equally, victims were highly suspicious of this possibility.[84] At the time of drafting these failed institutions, victims did not believe that truth commissions could help in the process of vindication of their rights.[85]

The only truth-seeking process that has succeeded has been a much more limited one: the Commission for Investigation of the Events in and around

Srebrenica between 10 and 19 July 1995 (Srebrenica Commission). It was established in 2003 by the Republika Srpska authorities in response to the resolution of the, now extinct, Human Rights Chamber,[86] but only after the OHR exercised considerable pressure. The main tasks of the Srebrenica Commission, which did not include victim participation, were to locate mass graves and determine the identity of all victims of the genocide. Its work was quite significant in that it reconstructed the involvement of military and police units of Republika Srpska and drafted lists of potential perpetrators. It also discovered 32 unknown graves and established that a total of 7,779 persons went missing in the period covered by the investigation.[87] A similar public investigative body was supposed to establish the events during the siege of Sarajevo, but political obstacles made it impossible.[88]

The lack of official involvement in truth seeking led several civil society organizations to conduct their own investigations and documentation processes. A remarkable example of this is the work of the Research and Documentation Centre in Sarajevo, which has established the most comprehensive database of events that occurred during the war.[89] Since 2005 civil society organizations have been developing a new truth-seeking initiative at regional level: RECOM. The Coalition for RECOM is a coalition of non-governmental organizations from the countries of the former Yugoslavia for the creation of a regional commission for establishing the facts of the conflict. The process of consultation has been impressively wide and detailed.[90] Numerous encounters have been organized between victims' organizations, war veterans' groups, and civil society in general, as well as media personnel, justice system personnel, government officials, and politicians.[91] During the consultations victims have expressed all range of opinions regarding the need for this kind of commission; however, most of those involved seem to agree that a process of this sort is important.[92] From the consultation it has become evident that the only possibility for an investigative commission to be considered successful is if it solely focuses on establishing the facts and drops the goal of reconciliation. The investigative body will be constituted as an international regional organization created by agreement of all the countries in the region, and with its main office in Sarajevo.[93] The initiative faces multiple challenges, from retaining participation of some of the most resistant victims' organizations to gaining the necessary legitimacy and regional credibility from the wider public. But importantly, its success depends on the political will in all countries to sign the international agreement, which is politically very difficult. The organizations involved are hopeful that it will succeed, even while recognizing the difficulties. Some of them, such as the leading Humanitarian Law Centre in Serbia and Documenta in Croatia, believe that a process of social reconstruction has already started: at an informal level the process of RECOM has helped to bring individuals together, promoted dialogue in different communities, and facilitated, although in a limited way, processes of sharing experiences of suffering and mutual recognition of victims from different ethnic groups.[94] Although several political leaders have supported the initiative, the public reactions to the initiatives are mixed. The results of a recent regional signature-gathering campaign (April–June 2011) to pressure governments to sign the RECOM agreement are disappointing in Bosnia, with the leadership of some victims' organizations explicitly boycotting the initiative.[95] There are still doubts as to whether the investigative commission will actually come into being, but what the process shows is a determination on the part of certain civil society organizations to face the past and find a common narrative that would overcome the prospects of a divided future that nationalistic rhetoric continues to aspire for.

Reparations

Together with the deficiencies described in regard to truth-seeking initiatives, the lack of a coherent policy on reparations has impacted negatively on the transitional justice process. Even if the property restitution process can be considered positive from a reparations perspective, the process was conceived as a way to reverse ethnic cleansing rather than specifically as a victim-centered reparations program. Beyond property restitution, reparations have been limited and not systematized. At the international level the ICTY does not provide for reparations; however, it did foresee in its own Rules of Procedure and Evidence that victims could rely on its judgments to seek compensation in a different forum (Rule 106). National court proceedings for compensation for human rights abuses have been rare. The WCC has done little to make up deficiencies in other reparations programs by routinely instructing the victim to take civil action after the criminal trial has been completed, although the Criminal Procedure Code provides for direct compensation for victims. The legal complexities and lack of financial resources prevent most victims from initiating civil procedures. The only judicial resolutions at state level regarding financial reparations have been made by the now extinct Human Rights Chambers.

But a more problematic issue has been that of the divide in the consideration of who is entitled to the reparation. This is closely connected to the question posed by García-Godos regarding "Who is the victim?" in terms of reparations for human rights violations.[96] As García-Godos explores, identification of the victim is vital, that is, determining who is entitled to whatever form of remedy or benefit is to be provided.[97] In Bosnia the legislation enacted and implemented by both territorial entities has emphasized military victims—war veterans and their families—over civilian ones.[98] This has left large groups of civilian victims without financial support and psychosocial attention, which is being carried out by civil society organizations. Equally, the territorial entities have considered victims differently and tended to favor the victims of their own ethnic group.[99] There is increasing popular support for the equal treatment of all victims, regardless of whether they are military or civilian and regardless of the entity or region in which they live. However, in a recent United Nations Development Programme (UNDP) survey on the matter a third of those interviewed still disagreed that all victims should be treated equally.[100] The lack of a comprehensive and victim-centered program of reparations has also brought an even more worrying inequality: that between victims and their perpetrators. As the latest UNDP survey demonstrates, victims of war crimes and their families have in most cases been left to their own resources, "abandoned" as the survey puts it, with no assistance, whilst the accused have benefited from some kind of practical support and assistance from both the international and national criminal system.[101]

All surveys show that Bosnian people also find symbolic reparations important: from monuments and commemorations to public apologies.[102] Symbolic reparations have included the establishment of the Srebrenica-Potocari memorial and the reconstruction of sites destroyed during the war, such as the Banja Luka Mosques.[103] However, the installation of monuments and memorials has been politically charged. The memorial for the genocide in Srebrenica was only established after considerable pressure from the international community.[104] Memorials have been the source of grievance aggravation among communities. They have tended to be built along ethnic lines and with underlying political causes. In each village or site of horrific violations people remember the victims of their own group, leaving little option for the commemoration of all victims. Over the last few years there has been a proliferation of public apologies. In 2004 the President of Serbia, Boris Tadić, apologized for the crimes committed to the citizens of Bosnia in the name of the Serbian people, and in 2010 the Serbian parliament approved a law apologizing for the massacre in Srebrenica and for not doing enough to prevent it; however, it fell short of calling it genocide. A similar formula had been used earlier by the President of Republika Srpska Miroland Dodik when he apologized to the victims. These apologies have brought mixed reactions, with some believing that it is a way to move on, and others questioning how genuine it may be and the motives behind it, especially as Serbia looks towards integration in the European Union.[105] Many in Bosnia have felt insulted by the fact that the word genocide has deliberately been omitted from the apologies, even after the International Court of Justice and the ICTY have both stated clearly that the acts committed in Srebrenica amounted to the crime. The value of these declarations is, in the opinion of this author, limited and it is debatable whether it has a contribution to make to wider reconciliation processes.[106]

Conclusions

This chapter has explored some of the interactions between peacebuilding and transitional justice in the reconstruction process in Bosnia and Herzegovina. The need to end the war and the compromises acquired during the peace negotiations resulted in a constitutional and institutional framework that has made both peacebuilding and transitional justice particularly challenging. From a peacebuilding perspective a superficial analysis shows initial success. Bosnia has not regressed to violence, half of those displaced have now returned and taken their properties back, there is one single army and one single police force, national institutions represent the three constituent peoples, and the political and economic aspirations of EU membership make war seem even further away. From a criminal justice perspective successes are also obvious: 161 of the highest level perpetrators will stand trial at the ICTY and a machinery of national courts is in place to deal with the lower-level ones. However, a closer look at the processes and mechanisms implemented in Bosnia shows a more nuanced picture. As this chapter has argued, the deficiencies in dealing with nationalistic political and power structures, as well as with demobilization and reform of the security sector, impacted on the abilities of the national system to provide accountability. Justice institutions involved in prosecutions have contributed to the process of peacebuilding by generating demand from society for accountability norms and proceedings, and helped pave the way to consolidating a culture of rule of law. However, the fact that justice has been mainly driven by the international community did not contribute to the development of complementary, locally driven processes. The reliance on retributive mechanisms, both internationally and at national level, has also made it more difficult for some of the wider transitional justice goals, those of social restoration through truth and reconciliation, to advance.

The case of Bosnia, as a "laboratory of transitional justice,"[107] provides a number of lessons. Comprehensive DDR and security sector and judicial reform are of paramount importance, not only for the stability and viability of a future democracy, but also for any justice process to take place. Lack of vetting of former war criminals and failure to dismantle old power structures compromises not only security but also justice and, even 15 years after the end of the conflict, social restoration.

The case of Bosnia also shows the difficulties of dealing with victims in a uniform way. In the Bosnia war, veterans and the families of the military fallen and victims of genocide, ethnic cleansing, concentration camps, and mass rapes, and the families of the missing have battled for resources, accountability, and acknowledgement. Equally importantly, they are still battling for their version of the truth. This highlights the necessity of complementary transitional justice mechanisms in order to respond to the needs of all the victims. Criminal trials have played an important role in removing perpetrators from society, punishing those responsible for horrific human rights violations and establishing the facts of the conflict. However, retributive justice can only play a limited role in restoring social peace and relations and, unfortunately, Bosnia is a clear indicator of this.

Notes

1 I would like to acknowledge the support of the British Academy, through a Small Grant (SG100735) for the completion of this chapter. This chapter is based on fieldwork developed by the author in 2009 and 2011 in Bosnia and Herzegovina and 2010 in Serbia and Croatia.

2 As with many conflicts, the figures are only estimates and have been open to manipulation. The latest research by the Research and Documentation Centre in Sarajevo is regarded to have established the most accurate account: RDC, *Population Losses in Bosnia and Herzegovina '92–95*, Sarajevo, 2007.

3 The term Bosniak is used to refer to those who are, in terms of cultural-religious heritage, descendants of Muslim Slavs, regardless of whether or not they practice

Islam. Dina Francesca Haynes, "Introduction," *Deconstructing the Reconstruction. Human Rights and Rule of Law in Postwar Bosnia and Herzegovina* (Aldershot: Ashgate, 2008), p. xv.

4 See, for example, ICTY, *Prosecutor v. Momčilo Krajišnik* (IT-00-39-T), Trial Judgement, 27 September 2006 and *Prosecutor v. Radovan Karadžić* (IT-95-5/18-PT), Third Amended Indictment, 29 February 2009.

5 See Paige Arthur, "How 'Transitions' Reshaped Human Rights: A Conceptual History of Transitional Justice," *Human Rights Law Quarterly*, vol. 31, no. 2, 2009, pp. 321–67; Chandra Lekha Sriram, *Globalizing Justice for Mass Atrocities: A Revolution in Accountability* (London: Routledge, 2005).

6 Haynes, "Introduction," op. cit., p. xviii.

7 Marie-Joelle Zahar, "Foreign Intervention and State Reconstruction: Bosnian Fragility in Comparative Perspective," in Denisa Sostovicova and Vesna Bojicic-Dzelilovic, *Persistent State Weakness in the Global Age* (Farnham: Ashgate, 2009), p. 118.

8 Michael H. Doyle, "Too Little, Too Late? Justice and Security Reform in Bosnia and Herzegovina," in Charles T. Call (ed.), *Constructing Justice and Security After War* (Washington DC: USIP, 2007), p. 232.

9 Communiqué of the Steering Board of the Peace Implementation Council, 25/6/2008 and Council Joint Action 2008/130/CFSP of 18 February 2008, Extending the Mandate of the EUSR in BiH, 19 February 2008.

10 SFOR was replaced by EU forces (EUFOR-ALTHEA) in December 2004.

11 Bonn International Centre for Conversion (BICC), *Turning Soldiers into a Work Force, Demobilization and Reintegration in Post-Dayton Bosnia and Herzegovina*, Brief 27, 2006, p. 9.

12 Ibid.

13 Jessica Alexander *et al.*, *From Barracks to Business. An Evaluation of IOM's Transitional Assistance Program to Former Soldiers in Bosnia and Herzegovina*, Final Report, April 2004, Columbia University Press, pp. 20–21, available at <*www.iom.ba/Downloads/Projects/TADS/Final%20Report%20IOM%20TAFS%20Bosnia%20Columbia.pdf*>, accessed 19 August 2011.

14 Massimo Moratti and Amra Sabic-El-Rayess, *Transitional Justice and DDR: The Case of Bosnia and Herzegovina*, Research Brief, June 2009 (NY: ICTY, 2009), p. 10.

15 World Bank, *Bosnia and Herzegovina, Emergency Demobilization and Reintegration Project*, Report No. T-6947-BI1, Technical Annex, 28 June 1996, available at <*www-wds.worldbank.org/external/default/main?pagePK=64193027&piPK=64187937&theSitePK=523679&menuPK=64187510&searchMenuPK=64187283&theSitePK=523679&entityID=000009265_3961214125242&searchMenuPK=64187283&theSitePK=523679*>, accessed 19 August 2011.

16 BICC, *Turning Soldiers into a Work Force*, op. cit., p. 9.

17 Ibid.

18 IOM, *Transitional Assistance for Former Soldiers Programme* (2003), available at <*www.iom.ba/TADS1.html*>, accessed 19 August 2011, and Alexander *et al.*, *From Barracks to Business*, op. cit.

19 For the process, see Ric Bainter, "The Elephant in the Room: Defense Reform in Bosnia and Herzegovina," in Haynes, *Deconstructing the Reconstruction*, op. cit., pp. 235–57.

20 ICG, *Bosnia's Stalled Police Reform: No Progress, No EU* (Brussels: ICG, 2005), p. 4.

21 Even if the EU criteria were not fulfilled, the EU still signed the SAA; see ICG, *Bosnia's Incomplete Transitions: Between Dayton and Europe* (Brussels: ICG, 2009), p. 11.

22 Moratti and Sabic-El-Rayess, *Transitional Justice and DDR*, op. cit., p. 4.

23 Ibid., p. 1.

24 Thomas Muehlmann, "Police Restructuring in Bosnia-Herzegovina: Problems with Internationally-Led Security Sector Reform," *Journal of Intervention and Statebuilding*, vol. 1, special supplement 1, 2007, pp. 37–65; Gemma Collantes-Celador, "Civil Society and the Bosnian Police Certification Process: Challenging 'the Guardians'," in Vesna Bojicic-Dzelilovic, James Ker-Lindsay, and Denisa Kostovicova (eds), *Civil Society and Transitions in the Western Balkans* (Basingstoke: Palgrave, forthcoming).

25 ICG, *Bosnia's Stalled Police Reform*, op. cit., pp. 2–4.
26 Ibid., p. 29.
27 Vesna Bojicic-Dzelilovic, "Peace on Whose Terms? War Veterans' Associations in Bosnia and Herzegovina," in Edward Newman and Oliver Richmond (eds), *Challenges to Peacebuilding. Managing Spoilers During Conflict Resolution* (New York: United Nations University Press, 2006), pp. 200–18.
28 Ibid.
29 OHR, *Property Law Implementation Plan*, available at <*www.ohr.int/plip*> accessed 19 August 2011 and UNHCR, *Bosnia and Herzegovina*, available at <*www.unhcr.org/pages/49e48d766.html*>, accessed 19 August 2011.
30 Charles Philpott, "Though the Dog is Dead, the Pig Must be Killed: Finishing Property Restitution to Bosnia-Herzegovina's IDPs and Refugees," *Journal of Refugee Studies*, vol. 18, no. 1 (2005), p. 2.
31 ICG, *The Continuing Challenge of Refugee Return in Bosnia and Herzegovina*, Balkan Report no. 137 (Brussels: ICG, 2002), p. 1; Massimo Moratti, "Tackling Obstruction to Property Rights and Return: A Critical Assessment of the Practice of Removing Housing Officials in Bosnia and Herzegovina," in Haynes, *Deconstructing the Reconstruction*, op. cit., pp. 185, 189.
32 Philpott, "Though the Dog is Dead," op. cit., p. 8.
33 Ibid.
34 Ibid., pp. 17–18.
35 Lara Nettelfield, *Courting Democracy in Bosnia and Herzegovina. The Hague Tribunal's Impact in a Postwar State* (Cambridge: Cambridge University Press, 2010), p. 93.
36 Ibid.
37 UNCHR, *Bosnia and Herzegovina*, available at <*www.unhcr.org/pages/49e48d766.html*>, accessed 19 August 2011.
38 UNDP and Oxford Research International (ORI), *The Silent Majority Speaks* (2007), pp. 14–16.
39 See, in general, Diane Orentlicher, *That Someone Guilty Be Punished. The Impact of the ICTY in Bosnia* (New York: OSI and ICTJ, 2010); Eric Stover, *The Witness* (Philadelphia: University of Pennsylvania Press, 2007), p. 110.
40 UN Security Council Resolution 827, UN Doc. S/RES/827, 25 May 1993.
41 Ibid., "Preamble."
42 Payan Akhavan, "Justice in The Hague, Peace in the Former Yugoslavia? A Commentary on the United Nations War Crimes Tribunal," *Human Rights Quarterly*, vol. 20 (1998), pp. 737–816.
43 Laurel E. Fletcher and Harvey M. Weinstein, "'A World unto Itself?' The Application of International Justice in the Former Yugoslavia," in Eric Stover and Harvey Weinstein (eds), *My Neighbour, My Enemy. Justice and Community in the Aftermath of Atrocity* (Cambridge: Cambridge University Press, 2004), p. 34.
44 *Report of the International Tribunal for the Prosecution of Persons Responsible for Serious Violations of International Humanitarian Law Committed in the Territory of the Former Yugoslavia since 1991*, UN Doc. A/49/342-S/1994/1007, II (29 August 1994), para. 16–17; the same view is expressed latter in Antonio Cassese, "Reflections on International Criminal Justice," *The Modern Law Review*, vol. 61, 1998, pp. 1–10.
45 Akhavan, "Justice in The Hague," op. cit., pp. 766–67; Antonio Cassese, "The Role of Internationalized Courts and Tribunals in the Fight Against International Criminality," in Cesare Romano, André Nollkaemper, and Jann Kleffner, *Internationalised Courts. Sierra Leone, East Timor, Kosovo and Cambodia* (Oxford: Oxford University Press, 2004), p. 4.
46 Payan Akhavan, "Beyond Impunity: Can International Criminal Justice Prevent Future Atrocities?" *American Journal of International Law*, vol. 95, no. 7 (2001), p. 2.
47 Orentlicher, *That Someone Guilty Be Punished*, op. cit., p. 79 and Nettelfield, *Courting Democracy*, op. cit., p. 93.

48 See Laurel Fletcher and Harvey M. Weinstein, "Violence and Social Repair: Rethinking the Contribution of Justice to Reconciliation," *Human Rights Quarterly*, vol. 24, 2002, pp. 573–639.

49 See, for example, Mirklos Briro *et al.*, "Attitudes Towards Justice and Social Reconciliation in Bosnia and Herzegovina and Croatia," in Stover and Weinstein, *My Neighbour, My Enemy*, op. cit., pp. 183–206; Jame Meernik, "Justice and Peace? How the International Criminal Tribunal Affects Societal Peace in Bosnia," *Journal of Peace Research*, vol. 42, 2005, pp. 271–89; Janine Natalya Clark, "The Limits of Retributive Justice: Findings of an Empirical Study in Bosnia and Herzegovina," *Journal of International Criminal Justice*, vol. 7, 2009, pp. 463–87; Mirko Klarin, "The Impact of the ICTY Trials on Public Opinion in the Former Yugoslavia," *Journal of International Criminal Justice*, vol. 9 (2009), pp. 89–96; Stephan Parmentier, Marta Valiñas, and Elmar Weitekamp, "How to Repair the Harm After Violent Conflict in Bosnia? Results of a Population-Based Survey," *Netherlands Quarterly of Human Rights*, vol. 21, 2009, pp. 27–44; Sanja Kutnja Ivković and John Hagan, *Reclaiming Justice. The International Tribunal for the Former Yugoslavia and Local Courts* (Oxford: Oxford University Press, 2001); Orentlicher, *That Someone Guilty Be Punished*, op. cit.; and the following UNDP in BiH surveys: *Justice and Truth in BiH: Public Perceptions* (EWS Special Report, 2006), pp. 15–16; *Transitional Justice Guidebook for Bosnia and Herzegovina. Executive Summary* (2009); *Facing the Past and Access to Justice From a Public Perspective* (2011).

50 Janine Natalya Clark, "International War Crimes Tribunals and the Challenge of Outreach," *International Criminal Law Review*, vol. 9 (2009), pp. 99–116. On outreach in general see Clara Ramirez-Barrat, *Making an Impact: Guidelines on Designing and Implementing Outreach Programmes for Transitional Justice* (New York: ICTJ, 2011).

51 Fletcher and Weinstein, "'A World unto Itself?'" op. cit., p. 37; David Tolbert, "The International Criminal Tribunal for the Former Yugoslavia: Unforeseen Successes and Foreseeable Shortcomings," *The Fletcher Forum of World Affairs*, vol. 26, 2002, pp. 5–17.

52 In general on the manipulative discourses in the region see Jelena Subotić, *Hijacked Justice. Dealing with the Past in the Balkans* (Ithaca, NY: Cornell University Press, 2009), and for a focus on Bosnia, see pp. 122–65.

53 Nettelfield, *Courting Democracy*, op. cit., p. 171.

54 UNDP, *Justice and Truth in BiH*, op. cit., pp. 15–16. According to the survey 24.9 percent of those surveyed in the Federation and 20.1 percent in Republika Srpska considered that the ICTY has done a good job and justified its existence, whilst 44.1 percent in the Federation and 25.6 percent in Republika Srpska considered that it has not done a good job, but that it is necessary.

55 Nettelfield, *Courting Democracy*, op. cit., p. 273.

56 Ibid., p. 271.

57 Orentlicher, *That Someone Guilty Be Punished*, op. cit., p. 42. Author's interview with members of Documenta and Humanitarian Law Centre, Zagreb and Belgrade, July 2010.

58 Author's interview with members of Documenta and Humanitarian Law Centre, Zagreb and Belgrade, July 2010.

59 OSCE, *War Crimes Trials before the Domestic Courts in BiH. Progress and Obstacles*, March 2005, p. 4; see, generally, Human Rights Watch, *Justice at Risk: War Crimes Trials in Croatia, Bosnia and Herzegovina and Serbia and Montenegro* (New York: HRW, 2004).

60 OHR, *Jobs and Justice: Our Agenda*, May 2002.

61 Within the State Court, Sections I and II of the Criminal Division (the WCC and the Organised Crimes, Economic Crimes, and Corruption Chamber), the SDWC, and the Special Department for Economic Crimes of the Office of the Prosecutor, the Registry, and the Defence Office, were hybrid. So were the High Judiciary and Prosecutorial Council, the Constitutional Court, and the Human Rights Chamber.

62 UNDP and ORI, *The Silent Majority Speaks*, op. cit., pp. 14–16.

63 For the process, see Dominic Raab, "Evaluating the ICTY and its Completion Strategy. Efforts to Achieve Accountability for War Crimes and Their Tribunals," *Journal of International Criminal Justice*, vol. 3 (2005), pp. 94–95, and Olga Martin-Ortega, "Hybrid Tribunals and the Rule of Law: The War Crimes Chamber in Bosnia and Herzegovina," in H. F. Carey and S. G. Mitchell, *Trials and Tribulations of International Prosecution* (Lexington Books, forthcoming 2011).

64 OHR, *War Crimes Chamber Project, Project Implementation Plan, Registry Progress Report*, 20 October 2004. See Olga Martin-Ortega and Johanna Herman, "The Impact of Hybrid Tribunals: Current Practice in Bosnia and Herzegovina and Cambodia," in M. Reed and A. Lyons (eds), *Contested Transitions: Dilemmas of Transitional Justice in Colombia and Comparative Experience* (Bogota: International Centre for Transitional Justice, 2010).

65 OHR, *Decision Enacting the Law on Amendment to the Law on Court of Bosnia and Herzegovina*, 14 December 2009. For further explanation, see Martin-Ortega and Herman, "The Impact of Hybrid Tribunals," op. cit.

66 State Court's website, <*www.sudbih.gov.ba/?jezik=e*>, accessed 13 September 2011.

67 Janine Natalya Clark, "The State Court of Bosnia and Herzegovina: A Path to Reconciliation?" *Contemporary Justice Review*, vol. 4, 2010, pp. 317–90.

68 UNDP, *Justice and Truth in BiH*, op. cit., p. 16.

69 See, as well, Clark, "The State Court," op. cit., p. 378 on the remarks of president of the Organisation of Missing Serbs in Sarajevo about the State Court being "very much on the side of Muslims."

70 Author's fieldwork notes, Sarajevo, August 2009.

71 Bogdan Ivanešević, *The War Crimes Chamber in Bosnia and Herzegovina: From Hybrid to Domestic Court* (New York: ICTJ, 2008), p. 36.

72 Stephanie Barbour, "Domestic War Crimes Processing in Bosnia and Herzegovina" (Internal Case Study, ICTJ Research Project: Making an Impact: Guidance on Designing Effective Outreach Programs for Transitional Justice, April 2011) (on file with the author), p. 30.

73 Janine Natalya Clark, "Plea Bargaining at the ICTY: Guilty Pleas and Reconciliation," *European Journal of International Law*, vol. 20 (2009), pp. 415–36.

74 OSCE Mission in Bosnia, *Witness Protection and Support in BiH Domestic War Crimes Trials* (Sarajevo: OSCE, 2010); Clark, "The State Court," op. cit., pp. 377–78; Refik Hodžić, "Living the Legacy of Mass Atrocities: Victims' Perspectives on War Crimes Trials," *Journal of International Criminal Justice*, vol. 8, 2010, pp. 113–36; David Schwendiman, "Prosecuting Atrocity Crimes in National Courts: Looking back on 2009 in Bosnia and Herzegovina," *Northwestern Journal of International Human Rights*, vol. 8, issue 3, 2010, pp. 296–99.

75 See Orentlicher, *That Someone Guilty Be Punished*, op. cit.

76 OSCE Mission in Bosnia, *Delivering Justice in Bosnia and Herzegovina. An Overview of War Crimes Processing from 2005 to 2010* (Sarajevo: OSCE, 2011), pp. 62–93; Human Rights Watch, *Still Waiting. Bringing Justice for War Crimes, Crimes against Humanity, and Genocide in Bosnia and Herzegovina's Cantonal and District Courts*, available at <*www.hrw.org/sites/default/files/reports/bosnia0708_1.pdf*>, accessed 13 September 2011.

77 Ibid.

78 The National Prosecution Strategy approved in December 2008 by the Council of Ministers of BiH established as is first objective to prosecute the most complex and top priority war crimes cases within 7 years of the adoption of the strategy and the rest of the cases within 15 years. The National War Crimes Strategy is reproduced in Annex 2 of the Forum for International Criminal and Humanitarian Law, *The Backlog of Core International Crimes Case Files in Bosnia and Herzegovina*, 2009. However, experts consider that only 2,000–3,000 alleged perpetrators could potentially be prosecuted. Author interviews with members of the SDWC, Sarajevo, August–September 2009; and see Iva Vukusic, "An Insider's Account of Domestic Prosecutions in Bosnia-Herzegovina,"

paper presented at the *51st Annual Convention of the International Studies Association*, New Orleans, February 2009.

79 Martin-Ortega and Herman, "The Impact of Hybrid Tribunals," op. cit., and Martin-Ortega, "Hybrid Tribunals and the Rule of Law," op. cit.; Clark, "The State Court," op. cit., p. 383.

80 For some of these, see Huma Haider, "Social Repair in Divided Societies: Integrating a Coexistence Lens into Transitional Justice," *Conflict, Security & Development*, vol. 11, 2011, pp. 175–203; and Johanna Mannergren Selimovic, *Remembering and Forgetting after War. Narratives of Truth, Justice and Reconciliation in a Bosnian Town*, Doctoral Dissertation, Gothenburg: University of Gothenburg, 2010 (under revision for publication).

81 UNDP, *Transitional Justice Guidebook*, op. cit., pp. 26–28; ICTJ, *Bosnia and Herzegovina, Submission to the Universal Periodic Review of the UN Human Rights Council Seventh Session: February 2010* (New York: ICTJ, 2009).

82 In a speech in Sarajevo, in May 2001, the Tribunal's president Claude Jorda noted that a truth and reconciliation commission could only "supplement, and if necessary, reinforce the International Tribunal in its mission of reconciliation" but not in any way represent a parallel and potentially rival institution. Speech reproduced at ICTY Press Release, *The ICTY and the Truth and Reconciliation Commission in Bosnia and Herzegovina*, JL/P.I.S/591-e, The Hague, 17 May 2001.

83 Ibid.

84 On the concerns over amnesties with regard to truth commissions, see UNDP reports: *Transitional Justice Guidebook*, op. cit., p. 28; *Justice and Truth in BiH*, op. cit., p. 12; *Facing the Past*, op. cit., p. 24.

85 Jasna Dragović-Soso and Eric Gordy, "Coming to Terms with the Past: Transitional Justice and Reconciliation in the Post-Yugoslav Lands," in James Ker-Lindsay and Dejan Djokic (eds), *New Perspectives on Yugoslavia: Key Issues and Controversies* (London: Routledge, 2010).

86 Human Rights Chamber, *Freida Selimović and Others v. Republika Srpska*, 7 March 2003.

87 See UNDP, *Transitional Justice Guidebook*, op. cit., p. 29.

88 Ibid., pp. 29–30.

89 Available at <*www.idc.org.ba*>, accessed 14 September 2011.

90 As summed up by the following Coalition for RECOM reports: *Report about the Consultation Process on Instruments of Truth-Seeking About War Crimes and Other Serious Violations of Human Rights in Post-Yugoslav Countries. Review of Opinions, Suggestions and Recommendations Report*, May 2006–June 2009; *Regional debate on the Mandate of RECOM, Sixth Regional Forum on Transitional Justice*, Novi Sad, Vojvodina, Serbia, May–December 2009; *Consultation Process on the RECOM Initiative. An Overview of Thoughts, Suggestions and Recommendations*, July–December 2009 (on file with the author).

91 See Coalition for RECOM, *Development Progress Report*, May 2006–July 2011, available at <*www.zarekom.org/documents/index.en.html*>, accessed 14 September 2011. The coalition has also organized a series of Regional Forums on Transitional Justice. The coalition per se was officially created at the Fourth Forum (Prishtina, 28–29 October 2008), attended by some 1,000 NGOs and victims' organizations; for the process see Natasa Kandič, "The RECOM Initiative: From a Non-Governmental Challenge to a State Project," in Denisa Kostovicova (ed.), *The European Union and Transitional Justice: From Retributive to Restorative Justice in the Western Balkans* (IHLC, 2009), p. 107.

92 Coalition for RECOM reports.

93 Articles 2 and 4 of the *Proposed Statute of the Regional Commission for Establishing the Facts About War Crimes and other Gross Violations of Human Rights Committed on the Territory of the Former Yugoslavia*, 26 March 2011 (Coalition for RECOM), available at <*www.zarekom.org/documents/index.en.html*>, accessed 14 September 2011.

94 Author interviews with members of the Humanitarian Law Centre and Documenta, Belgrade and Zagreb, July 2010.

95 See Youth Initiative for Human Rights in Serbia and in Croatia, *Report on 1 Million Signatures for RECOM Campaign*, available at <*www.zarekom.org/documents/index.en.html*>, accessed 14 September 2011.
96 Jemima García-Godos, "Victim Reparations in Transitional Justice—What is at Stake and Why," *Nordic Journal of Human Rights*, vol. 26, 2008, p. 122.
97 Ibid.
98 UNDP, *Transitional Justice Guidebook*, op. cit., pp. 33–47; UNDP, *Facing the Past*, op. cit., p. 32.
99 Ibid.
100 UNDP, *Facing the Past*, op. cit., pp. 32–33.
101 Ibid., p. 29.
102 Stephan Parmentier, Marta Valiñas, and Elmar Weitekamp, "How to Repair the Harm After Violent Conflict in Bosnia? Results of a Population-Based Survey," *Netherlands Quarterly of Human Rights*, vol. 21, 2009, pp. 27–44.
103 Human Rights Chamber, *Alija Ibisevic and 1804 Others v. Republika Srpska*, 3 June 2003.
104 OHR, *Decision Establishing and Registering the Foundation of the Srebrenica-Potocari Memorial and Cemetery*, 10 May 2001.
105 See, for example, *The New York Times*, "Serbia's Honest Apology," <*www.nytimes.com/2010/04/02/opinion/02judah.html*>, accessed 20 October 2011.
106 On the contrary, see Stephan Parmentier, Marta Valiñas, and Elmar Weitekamp, "How to Repair the Harm After Violent Conflict in Bosnia? Results of a Population-Based Survey," *Netherlands Quarterly of Human Rights*, vol. 21, 2009, pp. 27–44.
107 Dragović-Soso and Gordy, "Coming to Terms with the Past," op. cit., p. 193.

9 Victim-centered justice and DDR in Sierra Leone

Chandra Lekha Sriram

Introduction

At the end of many civil conflicts, the twin demands of peace and justice compete for domestic and international resources and attention. This was no less the case in Sierra Leone than elsewhere. Historically, discussions about the place, if any, of accountability in peacebuilding processes have focused on a wide range of state and internationally sponsored mechanisms to respond to past atrocities and on reform/rebuilding of rule of law.[1] They have only to a lesser degree dealt with two often-competing imperatives—concerns for both victims' rights and disarmament, demobilization, and reintegration of ex-combatants (DDR)—in accountability and peacebuilding processes. In Sierra Leone, accountability mechanisms were most notably the Special Court for Sierra Leone (SCSL) and the internationally mandated Truth and Reconciliation Commission (TRC). This chapter will discuss the impact of these institutions for peacebuilding in the country, considering whether, as its proponents would have it, the court made direct contributions to the immediate demands of peacebuilding, or whether it undermined peacebuilding. Specifically, it will consider the tribunal's relationship to victims' needs and demands, and to the concerns of and need to reintegrate ex-combatants. While these are far from the only elements of concern, they constitute often-competing poles in transitional justice and peacebuilding processes, and ones which are often not considered together.

Hybrid tribunals and truth commissions are seldom the only mechanisms for accountability, dealing with demands of victims, or engaging with ex-combatants. Peace agreements and other documents increasingly acknowledge the importance of traditional mechanisms of conflict resolution and justice, but the literature on transitional justice and peacebuilding has yet to examine the impact of such mechanisms alongside victims' rights and DDR. These mechanisms have flaws, and should not be uncritically accepted, but may indeed have peace-promoting capacities that more familiar transitional justice mechanisms may not. Indeed, in some instances, the use of traditional "cleansing ceremonies" facilitated the reintegration of former child combatants. This is by no means to suggest that these should supplant other mechanisms, but rather that it could be useful to consider how they might complement other transitional justice mechanisms.

Sierra Leone provides an ideal situation in which to examine such complementarities, and the role of a range of transitional justice mechanisms in peacebuilding, as it has established a hybrid tribunal and a truth and reconciliation mechanism, and has used traditional mechanisms for conflict resolution generally and the reintegration of former combatants into communities specifically. Each of these has its own contribution to make to, and tensions with, peacemaking and peacebuilding, and each is also potentially in tension with or complementary to the others.

In this chapter, I first describe very briefly the history of the conflict in Sierra Leone and international peacebuilding efforts, as well as the creation of the SCSL. I then explain the emphasis on victims' rights and DDR as part of a larger assessment of peacebuilding and transitional justice. I explain the expected effects of hybrid tribunals, as well as the growing role played (or expected to be played) by traditional justice and conflict resolution processes in countries emerging from conflict. Then I consider the interaction of victims' rights and DDR in the context of the hybrid tribunal, commission of inquiry, and traditional justice processes. Finally, I conclude with lessons learned for processes not only in Sierra Leone but in other conflict-affected countries.

Methodology

This chapter is based upon fieldwork over several years in Sierra Leone, with visits in 2004, 2008, and 2011. The research builds upon the extensive secondary research now available on peacemaking and peacebuilding in Sierra Leone as well as on the SCSL and the role and operation of traditional justice and conflict resolution processes. The fieldwork entailed semi-structured interviews with a wide range of national and international actors, including national civil society actors promoting human rights, good governance, victims' rights, and the concerns of ex-combatants; officials of the United Nations; other international organizations; bilateral donors; international NGOs; and Sierra Leonean state officials; as well as providers of legal assistance for individuals facing formal court proceedings; and non-state justice and security providers. Interviewees are cited where agreed; otherwise anonymity of respondents is respected.

Conflict, peacebuilding, and justice in Sierra Leone

I will only provide a brief account of the conflict in Sierra Leone here as it has been discussed in detail elsewhere.[2] Conflict between the government and the Revolutionary United Front (RUF) began in 1991 and continued for over a decade, resulting in some 50,000 deaths and widespread atrocities including mutilation and sexual violence. As is well known, forcible recruitment of child soldiers, often through the use of abductions and drugging, was widespread during the conflict, particularly but not only by the RUF, which often compelled these children to commit atrocities against family members and neighbors in an attempt to ensure that they had no place to which they could return.[3]

Negotiations in 1999 led to the Lomé Peace Agreement, and the UN Security Council mandated a peacekeeping force, UNAMSIL.[4] The Lomé agreement was condemned by many for including a blanket amnesty for all crimes committed during the conflict. The United Nations, which acted as a "moral guarantor" of the agreement, issued a reservation indicating that it did not consider the amnesty provision to cover international crimes. Despite the agreement, fighting and atrocities continued, along with attacks on UNAMSIL.

The peacebuilding process saw demands for justice for victims and prosecution of perpetrators, alongside the need to stabilize the country and pacify armed groups, in the first instance through DDR. In May of 2000, the notorious RUF leader Foday Sankoh was captured, provoking discussions of the possibility of an international or other tribunal to prosecute him and other war criminals. As I will discuss later, both a commission of inquiry and a hybrid tribunal were created to address accountability for past abuses. Despite these internationally supported efforts at justice, the reconstruction of the justice sector was slow, making extensive domestic trials unlikely, and the reparations process did not begin until 2009.[5] DDR efforts, which ran in fits and starts from 1998, operated more effectively once a strong peacekeeping force was in place and were completed in 2004. Sierra Leone, now a decade out of conflict, continues to be of significant interest as one of the first two countries of operation of the United Nations Peacebuilding Commission, and indeed it is the related UN Peacebuilding Fund (UN PBF) that has offered the majority of support for reparations in the country, along with a range of other measures.

Why victims' rights and DDR?

While, in practice, as we shall see, it is impossible to treat victim-centered approaches to justice separately from DDR processes, the justifications for each in peacebuilding situations where there are also demands for transitional justice are often articulated separately, by different actors and as though there isn't a connection, or as though there is simply conflict, between the two. Yet, increasingly such processes draw on and modify similar mechanisms, in particular invoking concepts such as restorative justice, traditional justice and conflict resolution, reconciliation, and reintegration. This approach, I will argue, is deeply problematic, failing as it does to recognize the purposes and limitations of such concepts and the ways in which they may have been altered through the course of conflicts. Further, there is a risk that peacebuilding and transitional justice processes which link, intentionally or otherwise, victim-centered justice and DDR, may coerce victims to engage with and "forgive" perpetrators for the purposes of short-term reconciliation processes in ways which do not promote longer-term acceptance and coexistence.[6]

Victim-centered and restorative justice

While restorative justice is far from the same thing as victim-centered justice, as victim-centered justice may involve greater participation by victims in retributive processes as well as a range of other measures, much current practice in transitional justice has emphasized victim-centered justice as restorative justice, further promoting it as contributing to reconciliation.[7] While some advocates and parts of the literature have for a long time argued for a victim-centered, rather than solely retributive, justice, or communally rather than individually focused accountability, practical measures to incorporate victims into traditional justice processes have increased in recent years. This is evidenced by the creation of a victims' trust fund at the International Criminal Court (ICC), the provision for participation by victims in proceedings in such institutions as the ICC and the Extraordinary Chambers in the Courts of Cambodia (ECCC), the expectation that truth and reconciliation commissions provide specific benefits (moral and material) to victims, and the growth of reparations programs as well as UN guidance and principles pertaining to restorative justice.[8]

Advocates and scholars of restorative justice argue that it is not merely an alternative mode of doing justice, or a second-best option when criminal justice is not viable, but rather that it is based in an "alternative vision of justice."[9] On this conception, human beings are relational, which means that conceptions of justice need to recognize that they are connected and that any response to harm must address not just the harm to direct individual victims but a wider set of related actors. Justice on this account seeks the restoration of relationships, not necessarily to the *status quo ante*, but to a peaceful and constructive relationship.[10] This conception is, according to one proponent, forward-looking and focused on reintegration over isolation, and must not only involve victims, wrongdoers, and communities, but focus on restoring relations among all of these.[11]

There are several types of arguments that might be adduced in favor of victim-centered approaches to justice, either instead of, as part of, or as a complement to retributive justice: some practical and some normative. Practical arguments include the need, in post-conflict societies, for victims to accept the return of former perpetrators into their communities, or as normalized members of society at large; to ensure that new conflicts are not stoked by the desire of victims for vengeance; and to reintegrate victims into society who may have been excluded because of their status as "victims." In general, the practical goal is to ensure that victims (and offenders) who may have been alienated from the community at large are reintegrated and that grievances are dealt with through civil, legal means. It is the restoration of a limited degree of trust amongst victims, perpetrators, and the wider community, which is not the same as a deeper sense of reconciliation, about which there is much debate.[12] Normative arguments for victim-centered justice emphasize the harm done to victims and the need to repair relationships. From this perspective, because victims have suffered a harm, attempts should be made to restore them; and because perpetrators have caused that harm, they have the responsibility to attempt to repair the harm. In so doing, on this logic, it becomes possible for offenders to reintegrate into the community and for wider social trust to be restored.[13]

Of course, victim-centered approaches to justice are not an obviously unqualified good—just who the victims are is contested within and across communities, just as who is a genuine perpetrator may be contested. In Sierra Leone, more than one interviewee noted that in some sense everyone who lived in the country during the war is a victim.[14] As is commonly noted in the context of child soldiers, individuals may be both victims and perpetrators. Further, there is a danger of reification of the concept of victim and in particular of overly individualizing the experience of mass atrocity, where many of the harms will have been collective—to direct victims, to their families and immediate communities, and to wider communities.[15]

There is also the risk that victims are used to serve the purposes of reintegration of perpetrators, and are coerced into "reconciling." Or, there is the risk that processes simply coerce participation of victims in the name of restorative justice, which is itself contradictory.[16]

DDR and transitional justice

As I and a colleague have argued elsewhere, DDR and transitional justice processes often operate contemporaneously in countries emerging from conflict, yet are often designed by different actors, without significant consideration of the impact that each process might have on the other.[17] Processes of DDR are designed not only to disarm former combatants, but to promote their turn to a peaceful civilian life in their own former communities or new communities, or their integration into new and reformed state security forces. As such, they usually entail a mixture of training and education, and in some cases cash payments, to induce the transformation of former combatants and in some cases to make their return more attractive to communities. And in some instances, as discussed further below, DDR processes adopt, transform, and co-opt so-called traditional justice and conflict resolution processes such as cleansing ceremonies. At the same time, a range of transitional justice processes seek to address past abuses, many of which will have been committed by former combatants during the conflict. Prosecutions in domestic courts, commissions of inquiry, and traditional justice processes, some or all of which may include reparations, are just a few of the commonly used mechanisms. These are often expected to address the needs of victims, as well as promote reconciliation, in addition to their technical functions.

Clearly, there are risks of competition and conflict between each set of processes. Any DDR process that provides material benefits to former combatants may be criticized by victims, particularly where reparations processes are limited or non-existent. Former combatants may be conflated with perpetrators, notwithstanding the fact that many may not have engaged in abuse of civilians and the fact that many, particularly child soldiers, may have been victims themselves. At the same time, accountability processes may undermine the incentives of former combatants to return to civilian life, if they fear imprisonment or shunning, or the prospect of making reparations from scarce resources. And in some cases, formal processes may be somewhat culturally foreign, with localized preference for, or at least recognition of, traditional processes. Here, DDR and transitional justice activities may converge, but without much reflection on that fact by practitioners of each until relatively recently.[18] In other circumstances, DDR may be implemented more clearly in the "terrain" of transitional justice, as in Colombia where reparations processes and DDR take place simultaneously.[19] And as the theory and practice of DDR and transitional justice have each developed, there is a greater mutual recognition, not least through guidance documents such as the United Nations' *Integrated Disarmament, Demobilization, and Reintegration Standards*. Perhaps notably, there is a recognition that DDR measures must also garner the support of communities and the utility of community development incentives to accept ex-combatants, in the 2006 version of the standards, and a transitional justice module was added to the guidance subsequently.[20] Nonetheless, as Theidon's research in Colombia demonstrates, while there is an official linkage between DDR and reconciliation, demobilized members of the paramilitary not only do not recognize it, but are unaware that it is declared; at the same time community members do not appear to have been consulted about the reintegration of ex-combatants in their regions.[21]

The convergence of transitional justice and DDR processes is perhaps most evident in the context of child soldiers, not least because they are both victims and perpetrators and because they may be in greater need of reintegration into their former communities and family structures, given that they may still be minors. There is also a clear legal proscription of child recruitment: while there are discrepancies with regard to the appropriate age threshold, child recruitment is a crime in international law.[22] And it is with the reintegration of former child soldiers that cleansing ceremonies are often used, in Sierra Leone but also elsewhere in Africa. I discuss these below in the Sierra Leonean context.

Hybrid tribunals, commissions of inquiry, and traditional justice in countries emerging from conflict

Why hybrid tribunals?

Internationalized criminal justice can be pursued through a range of processes, ranging from the ICC, to the soon-closing *ad hoc* tribunals for the former Yugoslavia and Rwanda, to the exercise of universal jurisdiction. Regardless of the form, there are increasing demands that processes imposing criminal accountability on individual perpetrators also serve needs of victims, rather than purely retributive justice. Some advocates argue that trials already do provide important goods for victims, in that they offer them a sense of vindication.[23] They are also often expected to have wider pedagogic impact for affected societies, and assist in the reconstruction of divided societies, although critics suggest they may have the opposite effect, creating divisions between guilty and innocent, and scapegoating some.[24] Nonetheless, demands for prosecutions continue, and increasingly international trials are expected not only to prosecute the accused and punish the guilty but also to take account of the needs of victims.

Hybrid tribunals are but one form of internationalized criminal courts, but one often advocated as having more relevance to victims and societies at large. Specifically, where international criminal justice has often been criticized for not communicating with affected societies, in part because of distance and in part because of the difficulty engaging, there is an increasing demand that trials serve not only a retributive or a deterrent function, but also an expressive one, with meaning for societies.[25] In the absence of such an expressive function, some scholars argue, criminal justice processes in the wake of mass atrocity may lack traction and legitimacy, and the norms they seek to convey and enforce will not be properly internalized. Instead, processes may simply reinforce an elite pact about how to proceed after conflict.[26] In particular, such processes may not be accepted by perpetrators, making it difficult to rebuild social norms proscribing mass violence and atrocity.[27]

Hybrid tribunals, operating as they ordinarily do on the territory of an affected society, are expected to be more accessible to the society and to victims, and thus to serve this expressive function, and serve the needs of victims specifically.[28]

Why commissions of inquiry?

Commissions of inquiry, and particularly so-called truth and reconciliation commissions, are often expected to provide restorative justice—the South African Truth and Reconciliation Commission is frequently cited as the prime example. There have been more than 35 truth commissions since 1974. Such bodies are often expected to give victims a voice and the opportunity to share their experiences, to provide official acknowledgment of their suffering, to provide an account of "the truth," to advocate reparations and various reform measures, and of course to involve not only victims but also perpetrators, as givers of testimony and seekers of reconciliation.[29] As Humphrey puts it, they are expected to "morally reconnect" victims with the wider society.[30] Specifically, such processes are expected to provide a forum for victims to share their experiences, and to receive acknowledgement, but, more than that, to engage all parties involved, including victims, perpetrators, communities that have been harmed, and wider affected communities.[31] The "unearthing" of truth itself is expected to contribute to reconciliation.[32]

Why traditional justice / conflict resolution?

Traditional justice practices are often utilized in the wake of intercommunal conflict to address past harms. These are a diverse set of practices, with some oriented towards conflict resolution, some emphasizing retribution, some emphasizing cleansing, some forgiveness, and many various combinations amongst these. In Sierra Leone, where it is estimated 80 percent of the population does not access the formal justice sector, which may be small, damaged, and concentrated in urban areas, they are an unavoidable presence.[33] Nearly all, however, were designed to address relatively small transgressions, rather than mass violence and grave crimes. Further, many have been transformed in order to address large-scale crimes, losing much of their "traditional" character, as has been the case arguably with *gacaca* in Rwanda.

Nonetheless, such processes are often deployed with a concept of restorative justice in mind, seeking to address the needs of victims, while yet seeking to reconcile victims and perpetrators.[34] And indeed, in some instances, they are deployed specifically to reintegrate former combatants into communities, particularly former child combatants. Advocates of the use of traditional practices would argue that they are more locally owned and legitimate, that they help to promote "reintegrative shaming," and that they can promote reconciliation both between victim and community and offender and community, as well as between victim and offender.[35]

Yet there has been relatively little reflection about the impact of both transforming such traditional processes to deal with serious human rights abuses and efforts to use them to address needs of victims as well as to reintegrate former combatants. Further, as discussed above, such an account of traditional mechanisms fails to take account of the risk that they will be used coercively. Further, in countries such as Sierra Leone, it is essential to acknowledge the degree to which traditional processes may be inconsistent with international human rights standards, or have previously been used in an abusive manner, or have lost legitimacy or relevance over the course of conflict as communities have been shattered or displaced.[36]

Victims' rights, communities, and DDR in Sierra Leone

The challenge of DDR in Sierra Leone was vast. While initially it was estimated that some 45,000 combatants were to be processed, the ultimate figure was much higher, about 73,000.[37] The disarmament stage of DDR involved the collection and destruction of ammunition and weapons turned over by ex-combatants. Ex-combatants were placed in demobilization centers, where they stayed between three days and three weeks, and were given medical and psychological care and information on reintegration support. They were also given subsistence allowances of about US $150; this use of cash incentives was and continues to be the subject of some criticism.[38]

A number of measures were developed during the demobilization phase to promote reintegration of both children and adults into communities. DDR packages were designed to allow former combatants to earn livelihoods in the future and make their return or integration more likely to be welcomed. Adults received a mixture of cash and training; children received training or education. Training included formal education, agricultural training and vocational training, particularly in carpentry, masonry, tailoring, hairdressing, and computers. Formal DDR was completed in 2004 and was considered by many to be a success. However, while significant numbers of former combatants passed through DDR programs, many chose to reintegrate either in the areas where they demobilized, or to areas which were not their original communities, choosing often the anonymity of urban areas.

However, there has been some criticism that the training given may have raised expectations and that there were often insufficient jobs available.[39] There was also a sense that the training was too limited to impart sufficient skills, and indeed the informal epithet heard in relation to what is perceived as an unskilled worker or as poor work product is "DDR-driver" or "DDR-construction," to use two examples. Many who passed through training programs appear to have recognized this and simply sold their starter kits upon, or even prior to, completion of training.[40] Many former combatants used these funds along with DDR Transitional Support Assistance to help in getting started in taxi-driving or motorbike businesses (*okada*). These businesses, while filling a niche in the market and providing a livelihood for many ex-combatants, also meant that they were more likely to remain in urban centers and not return to their former or new villages. As one interviewee suggested to me, while the fact that so many former combatants are gainfully employed in legal jobs might be seen as a success of DDR, the shift to employment which was not part of the DDR training suggests a failing in the DDR program.[41]

The DDR program was far from a complete success. In particular, women and girls had less access to the formal program, because they often did not have weapons to submit, having been accompaniers of fighting forces as porters and bush wives, or because commanders did not permit them to retain weapons which might be turned in. There was, further, a stigma attached to their role as fighters, so some chose not to seek to participate in the process.[42]

The DDR process was also subject to the criticism that it was unfair. Civilians clearly observed that ex-combatants generally received assistance through DDR packages in a process which ended in 2004, leaving former combatants who may also have been perpetrators better off than they might have been, and able to start their own businesses.[43] Meanwhile, affected communities and victims, including amputees and victims of sexual and gender-based violence, waited for development assistance and, until 2009, for a limited reparations program.[44] As one observer put it, return of ex-combatants was made more difficult by the perception that they were being paid for killing and destroying villages.[45]

This did not, however, necessarily preclude acceptance of return of ex-combatants. Indeed, community members in Sierra Leone have told researchers that they would forgive ex-combatants who had committed abuses if they returned and were useful to the community, say through the provision of skills such as carpentry. However, the conception of forgiveness appears to be a thin one—that of not taking revenge, rather than the expression of actual trust.[46]

The challenge of former child soldiers

Reintegration of former child combatants in Sierra Leone brought the tensions between victim-centered approaches to justice and DDR to the fore, not least because many efforts at reintegration of former child combatants utilized cleansing and community-based processes. The reintegration of child soldiers poses particular challenges, because of their relative youth, and the likelihood that children may have had little or no education prior to the conflict, and thus have relatively little to contribute to the economy of a village, and have been compelled to engage in abuses that might make their return to villages unwelcome. Many former child soldiers faced the stigma of being "rebels." Former Civil Defence Forces (CDF) fighters faced far less stigma but were also often excluded from the formal DDR process.[47] Children received training or education rather than cash reintegration packages, out of concern that former commanders would simply take the money.[48] They passed through Interim Care Centers prior to attempts to return them to communities and families. Sport, particularly football, was utilized in some of those centers as part of the transition of youth from fighting forces to return.[49] On the surface, at least, the process was successful—some 98 percent of demobilized children were returned to a parent or relative initially.[50]

Of critical importance, according to some commentators, was community sensitization designed to facilitate acceptance among communities who had been harmed and might understandably prefer that former child soldiers who had abused them never return. Community-based mechanisms, led by local leaders, traditional leaders, and others, emphasizing the children's own victim status, may have facilitated some reintegration.[51] Child welfare or protection committees were created within many villages to address new misbehavior by returning child solders, which mediated between the children and those they harmed; these were partly traditional elders, but also other members of the community and even the police.[52] The emphasis was on mediation as a form of restorative justice, both for those that were wronged and to seek to reform wrongdoers and encourage them to become constructive members of the community.

"Traditional" justice processes as mechanisms of reintegration

In some instances, so-called traditional mechanisms such as cleansing ceremonies have been used to promote reintegration of former child combatants into communities where they may have harmed others; such practices are not unique to Sierra Leone.[53] In Sierra Leone, unlike in northern Uganda, such ceremonies do not appear to have entailed admission of guilt or provision of reparations. Cleansing ceremonies and healing rituals appear to have been part of the reintegration of significant numbers of former child combatants or accompanying personnel, although the numbers are difficult to determine.[54] As with aspects of formal DDR, such social reintegration processes were often gender-biased. Girls fighting in armed groups or accompanying them as porters or bush wives were often excluded from such processes, meaning they had less to offer communities; their status as victims of sexual abuse often further hampered reintegration.[55]

Local Sierra Leonean NGO Fambul Tok, established jointly by Forum of Conscience (Sierra Leone) and Catalyst for Peace (USA), has initiated community-based ceremonies, mixing traditional conciliation practices, narratives of victims, and apologies and requests for forgiveness by victims and perpetrators.[56] The purpose, according to its founder, is societal reconciliation, but not specifically focused on reintegrating former combatants and/or perpetrators.[57] Researchers observing these ceremonies have reached contradictory views about their efficacy, with some interpreting apologies and forgiveness as quite genuine, and others viewing them as either not genuine, or decided upon prior to any ceremony.[58]

However, as Stovel and Valiñas argue, there is a genuine risk that restorative justice uses victims to rehabilitate and reintegrate offenders, which may take insufficient note of the impact on victims and the possibility that they are coerced into "reconciliation."[59] Restorative justice may be coercive of perpetrators as well as victims. As the TRC report recognized, a relatively small number of perpetrators sampled were prepared to apologize for their actions, much less help reconstruct communities, and none sampled were willing to pay reparations to victims.[60] Thus, some form of coercion would be needed to compel them to engage in restorative acts—either threats of prosecution by the state or the prospect of exclusion by communities.

Of course, ritual processes are largely directed by traditional chiefs, who in some cases may have lost legitimacy because of their own pre-war abuses, their own victimization or perpetration of harms during the conflict, social disruptions, and abusive or illegal conduct of traditional processes after the conflict.[61] As Fanthorpe notes, chiefs were targeted alongside other authority figures during the conflict, and chieftaincy has been the subject of struggles for political control in the country for far longer.[62] Abuses by chiefs are frequently cited as generating grievances that helped to stoke the conflict.[63]

As Stovel and others have observed, restorative justice treats humans as relational beings, which means that what is needed is to restore relationships in the wake of conflict, between and amongst victims, perpetrators, and communities.[64] However, and this is the case in many conflict-affected countries, DDR programs in Sierra Leone were not able, and did not seek, to restore social relations as part of reintegration processes. Reintegration is often the least developed part of DDR programs, and Sierra Leone was no exception. Thus while disarmament and demobilization proceeded quickly, reintegration was more complex and arguably less successful.

So, what of mechanisms that are often expected to be specifically oriented towards the needs of victims? I turn now to the TRC, the SCSL, and the reparations program.

The Truth and Reconciliation Commission

The TRC was expected to have served a restorative function and to have been particularly victim-oriented, an expectation placed on many such commissions. It was originally mandated by the 1999 Lomé Peace Agreement and created in 2002, issuing its report in 2004. It took statements across the country, and its final report was ambitious, outlining the domestic and regional causes of the conflict, naming alleged perpetrators, and issuing a series of recommendations regarding legislative and constitutional reform, and it recommended traditional justice mechanisms as well as a reparations program.[65]

However, the commission had a mixed reception in the country. This may have been to do with its fit, or lack of, with Sierra Leonean political and social culture, in part because of its relatively formal structure.[66] Some anthropologists who have long studied Sierra Leone, as well as more recent commentators on the proceedings at the commission, have suggested that the type of truth-telling entailed in such processes may have been culturally a poor fit. They have claimed that Sierra Leoneans do not generally engage in the type of public confession that such commissions provide the space for and that they prefer not to discuss past violence but rather take a "forgive and forget" approach. Instead, it is argued, people rely on ritual processes which may include sacrifice and healing processes.[67] One scholar scrutinizing the proceedings of the TRC in Tonkolili, expecting them to have a cathartic effect on participants that paved the way for reconciliation, found quite the opposite. Many of my interviewees questioned the utility of the commission, often asking whether people who testified were either honest about what they had done or genuine in their apologies.[68] Kelsall similarly found that participants often did not tell the truth before the commission, because such processes are not strong in Sierra Leonean culture. He argues further that the only successful element of proceedings was when rituals were utilized, rather than truth-telling, and suggests that one should abandon the idea that truth can enable reconciliation.[69] The limited improvements in the conditions of victims and communities may also hinder reconciliation.[70]

The Special Court for Sierra Leone

No international or internationalized trials were originally envisioned for Sierra Leone. However, following the capture of Foday Sankoh, the government of Sierra Leone requested that the United Nations create an *ad hoc* tribunal of the type in existence for the former Yugoslavia and Rwanda to try him and other RUF leaders. What was created instead was a hybrid tribunal, of mixed national and international character, called for first by UN Security Council Resolution 1315 in August 2000 and created by bilateral agreement between the UN and the government of Sierra Leone. The court's statute, completed in January 2002, gives it the power to prosecute persons who bear the greatest responsibility for serious violations of national and international humanitarian law since 30 November 1996.[71] The creation and operation of the court have come under criticism, as driven by the preferences of either then-President Kabbah or Western powers, particularly the USA and the United Kingdom, and as dominated by foreigners.[72]

However, the more relevant criticisms for the purposes of this inquiry have been that the court has not had significant relevance for Sierra Leonean society at large, or for specific groups of victims.[73] While the court was sited in Freetown to make it more accessible to society, the severe poverty of the country has meant that few have the luxury of taking time to observe court proceedings; severe illiteracy means that it is difficult for the majority of Sierra Leoneans to follow proceedings through print media.[74] The outreach unit of the court has sought to disseminate the activities of the court throughout the country, with a degree of success.[75] Nonetheless, there remains, even among human rights advocates, a sense that the court has relatively little to do with the demands of average Sierra Leoneans for justice; in particular the characterization of those prosecuted as "most responsible" does not resonate with many who see immediate perpetrators "still strolling around" in their villages.[76] Indeed, some have observed that the disparity between the expenditure on the court, estimated to be some US $250 million, and that spent on reparations, to date about $4.5 million, was seen as an indication of the priorities of the international community.[77]

Others have compared the relatively luxurious conditions of imprisonment of those convicted by the court to the squalid living conditions of many victims and the larger population, and to the appalling conditions in many Sierra Leonean prisons. Justice, on the account of such advocates, should address the needs of victims as well as (but, notably in the views of many, not instead of) prosecuting a few perpetrators.[78] Others suggest that the court did not deal with the real concern of most Sierra Leoneans, poverty, and that true justice would have to address these needs.[79] Indeed some suggest that the court should have provided reparations, a task that was not in its mandate. It is to the reparations which were implemented that I now turn.

The reparations program

The final report of the TRC recommended the provision of reparations to victims of the conflict, among other measures. The Human Rights Commission of Sierra Leone was tasked with the oversight of the implementation of the report; however, it was the National Commission for Social Action (NaCSA) that was given specific responsibility for reparations under legislation passed in 2009.[80] The United Nations provided US $3 million to the reparations fund in December 2008, via the UN PBF, which was to be administered with the oversight of the International Organization for Migration (IOM). This was to build the capacity of NaCSA to administer reparations and for the creation of a register of victims. The program, called the Year One program, created that database, and gave health assistance to victims, particularly amputees and women who had suffered serious injuries as a result of sexual and gender-based violence. It also provided micro-grants to victims. Of nearly 30,000 registered victims, about 20,000 have received such grants, the equivalent of about $100, and there have also been some educational grants.[81]

However, there have been a number of shortcomings with the program. The Year One phase was almost entirely reliant on international support. The War Victims Trust Fund announced by the president of Sierra Leone at the end of 2009 has received limited donations and there is no regular budget line in the national budget for reparations.[82] A smaller follow-on fund of US $450,000 has been provided by the UN PBFund; in addition Unifem (now UN Women) allocated another $1 million (of which half has been released at the time of writing) to provide skills training and micro-grants to victims of sexual violence.[83] As noted by one IOM official, in the absence of follow-on programs, however, there is a risk of injustice, as not all of those who have registered will even receive the small initial micro-grant of about $100.[84] A persistent concern raised by interviewees was about the timing of the reparations—some seven years after the initiation of DDR programming—as well as the disparity in expenditures between the two programs.[85]

Implications

Sierra Leone's experiences with DDR and victim-centered justice are by no means unique, and are illustrative. Rather typically, DDR took place long before reparations were initiated. Transitional justice mechanisms which in part purported to address the needs of victims and society at large, specifically the SCSL and the TRC, continue to be viewed by many, even advocates who see inherent merit in them, as not particularly relevant to society at large or to victims specifically. A persistent claim that I encountered in interviews was that true justice would not address a very small number of perpetrators presented as high level, but rather the perpetrators who remained visible, and in many cases beneficiaries of DDR packages, on a daily basis. Restorative justice processes, specifically variations on ritual cleansing, have been used in a few instances, but questions remain about the impact, in the short or long term, on victims, communities, and perpetrators, as well as about the risk that victims will be used for these processes in ways that do not address their needs and may be somewhat coercive. Advocates in the Campaign for Good Governance suggested that what is needed is a long-term process with more holistic packages, dealing with DDR and reparations as part of longer planning; the head of Timap for Justice similarly suggested an umbrella program that dealt with both DDR and reparations, albeit treating them separately.[86] These might be options worth exploring, although several caveats are noteworthy. First, as Lars Waldorf emphasizes in his chapter in this volume, there is evidence that integrated approaches do not work; nonetheless coordinated approaches might be appropriate. Second, limited resources and the urgency of addressing security may mean that DDR processes are always sequenced not just first, but well before any justice or restorative processes. Nonetheless, more research and creative programming of the type advocated by these Sierra Leonean practitioners might well be needed.

Notes

1 Jennifer J. Llewellyn, "Restorative justice and peacebuilding in post-conflict societies," paper presented at the annual conference of the International Studies Association (San Francisco, CA, 26–29 March 2008), p. 2.

2 See generally John Hirsch, *Sierra Leone: Diamonds and the struggle for democracy* (Boulder, CO: Lynne Rienner, 2001); Comfort Ero and Jonathan Temin, "Sources of conflict in

West Africa," in Chandra Lekha Sriram and Zoe Nielsen, eds, *Exploring Subregional Conflict: Opportunities for conflict prevention* (Boulder, CO: Lynne Rienner, 2004).

3 Special Court for Sierra Leone, *Prosecutor v Issa Hassan Sesay, Morris Kallon and Augustine Gbao*, Case No. SCSL-04-15-T (2 March 2009) and Case No. SCSL-04-15-A (26 October 2009); Valerie Oosterveld, casenotes for these cases, *American Journal of International Law*, vol. 104 (2010), pp. 73–81.

4 *Peace Agreement between the Government of Sierra Leone and the Revolutionary United Front of Sierra Leone*, UN Doc S/1999/777; for the mandate of the United Nations Mission in Sierra Leone (UNAMSIL), UN Security Council Resolution 1270, UN Doc. S/RES/1270 (1999).

5 Chandra Lekha Sriram, "(Re)building the rule of law in Sierra Leone: Beyond the formal sector?" in Chandra Lekha Sriram, Olga Martin-Ortega, and Johanna Herman, eds, *Peacebuilding and Rule of Law in Africa: Just peace?* (London: Routledge, 2010), pp. 127–41.

6 See, e.g., Laura Stovel and Marta Valiñas, "Restorative justice after mass violence: Opportunities and risks for children and youth," *Innocenti Working Paper IWP 2010–15* (Florence: UNICEF Innocenti Research Centre, June 2010), p. vi.

7 For a critique, see Michael Humphrey, "From victim to victimhood: Truth commissions and trials as rituals of political transition and individual healing," *The Australian Journal of Anthropology*, vol. 14, no. 2 (2003), pp. 171–87.

8 See generally United Nations Economic and Social Council, "Basic principles on the use of restorative justice programmes in criminal matters," UN Doc. E/CN.15/2002/5/Add.1; United Nations Office on Drugs and Crime, *Handbook on Restorative Justice Programmes* (Vienna: United Nations, 2006); Matthew Gillett, "Victim participation at the International Criminal Court," *Australian International Law Journal*, vol. 16 (2009), pp. 29–46; Jemima García-Godos, "Victim reparations in the Peruvian Truth Commission and the challenge of historical interpretation," *International Journal of Transitional Justice*, vol. 2 (2008), pp. 63–82; Nneoma V. Nwogu, "When and why it started: Deconstructing victim-centered truth commissions in the context of ethnicity-based conflict," *International Journal of Transitional Justice*, vol. 4 (2010), pp. 275–89; Mark Findlay, "Activating a victim constituency in international criminal justice," *International Journal of Transitional Justice*, vol. 3 (2009), pp. 183–206; Ruth Rubio-Marín and Pablo de Greiff, "Women and reparations,"*International Journal of Transitional Justice*, vol. 1 (2007), pp. 318–37; Conor McCarthy, "Reparations under the Rome Statute of the International Criminal Court and reparative justice theory," *International Journal of Transitional Justice*, vol. 3 (2009), pp. 250–71; Simon Robins, "Towards victim-centred transitional justice: Understanding the needs of families of the disappeared in postconflict Nepal," *International Journal of Transitional Justice*, vol. 5 (2011), pp. 75–98.

9 Llewellyn, "Restorative justice and peacebuilding in post-conflict societies," op. cit., p. 4.

10 Ibid., pp. 5–6.

11 Ibid., pp. 7, 11. See also Ruti G. Teitel, *Transitional Justice* (Oxford: Oxford University Press, 2000).

12 Stovel and Valiñas, "Restorative justice after mass violence," op. cit., pp. 2–4; Chandra Lekha Sriram, *Globalizing Justice for Mass Atrocities: A revolution in accountability* (London: Routledge, 2005), pp. 55–56. Compare Christopher Bennett, "Taking the sincerity out of saying sorry: Restorative justice as ritual," *Journal of Applied Philosophy*, vol. 23, no. 2 (2006), pp. 127–43.

13 Stovel and Valiñas, "Restorative justice after mass violence," op. cit., pp. 4–7, both explicate and critique this perspective.

14 Interview with anonymous Sierra Leonean official, 13 July 2011.

15 See generally Humphrey, "From victim to victimhood," op. cit.

16 Stovel and Valiñas, "Restorative justice after mass violence," op. cit., p. 15; Susan Thomson, "Reeducation for reconciliation," in Scott Straus and Lars Waldorf, eds,

Remaking Rwanda: State building and human rights after mass violence (Madison: University of Wisconsin Press, 2011), pp. 331–39.

17 Chandra Lekha Sriram and Johanna Herman, "DDR and transitional justice: Bridging the divide?" *Journal of Conflict, Security, and Development*, vol. 9, no. 4 (December 2009), pp. 455–74.

18 Ibid., pp. 465–66.

19 Kimberly Theidon, "Transitional subjects: The disarmament, demobilization, and reintegration of former combatants in Colombia," *International Journal of Transitional Justice*, vol. 1 (2007), pp. 66–90, 73.

20 United Nations, *Integrated Disarmament, Demobilization, and Reintegration Standards* (2006), module 6.20, available at <*www.unddr.org/iddrs/06/20.php*>, accessed 19 August 2011.

21 Theidon, "Transitional subjects," op.cit., pp. 79–80, 83.

22 Janet McKnight, "Child soldiers in Africa: A global approach to human rights protection, enforcement, and post-conflict reintegration," *African Journal of International and Comparative Law*, vol. 18 (2010), pp. 113–42; Susan McKay, "Reconstructing fragile lives: Girls' social reintegration in northern Uganda and Sierra Leone," *Gender and Development*, vol. 12, no. 3 (2004), pp. 19–30.

23 Martha Minow, *Between Vengeance and Forgiveness: Facing history after genocide and mass atrocity* (Boston: Beacon Press, 1998); Adam Kochanski, "Transitional justice as liberal peacebuilding: Panacea or false promise?" in Carla Suarez, ed., *Security and Conflict: Evolving theory and practice* (Halifax: Centre for Foreign Policy Studies, 2011).

24 Compare Mark Osiel, *Mass Atrocity, Collective Memory, and the Law* (New Brunswick, NJ: Transaction Books, 1999); Jaime Malamud-Goti, *Game Without End: State terror and the politics of justice* (Norman, OK: University of Oklahoma Press, 1996); Humphrey, "From victim to victimhood," op. cit., p. 181.

25 For a discussion of the problem of externalization of justice, see Chandra Lekha Sriram and Brad R. Roth, "Externalization of justice: What does it mean and what is at stake?" and Sriram, "Universal jurisdiction: Problems and prospects of externalizing justice," both in *Finnish Yearbook of International Law*, vol. XII (2001), pp. 3–6 and 47–70. On the need for international criminal justice to serve expressive functions, and its shortcomings in this regard, see Jaya Ramji-Nogales, "Designing bespoke transitional justice: A pluralist process approach," *Michigan Journal of International Law*, vol. 32 (2010–11), pp. 8–11.

26 Theidon, "Transitional subjects," op. cit., pp. 89–90.

27 Ramji-Nogales, "Designing bespoke transitional justice," op. cit., pp. 13–18.

28 Beth Dougherty, "Right-sizing international criminal justice: The hybrid experiment at the Special Court for Sierra Leone," *International Affairs*, vol. 80, no. 1 (2004), pp. 311–28; compare Chandra Lekha Sriram, "Wrong-sizing international justice? The hybrid tribunal in Sierra Leone," *Fordham International Law Journal*, vol. 29, no. 3 (2006), pp. 472–506.

29 Priscilla Hayner, *Unspeakable Truths: Confronting state terror and atrocity* (London: Routledge 2001); Kochanski, "Transitional justice as liberal peacebuilding," op. cit., p. 12.

30 Humphrey, "From victim to victimhood," op. cit., p. 176; Stovel and Valiñas, "Restorative justice after mass violence," op. cit., p. 14; on the inherent tensions in the range of goals ascribed to transitional justice institutions, see Bronwyn Anne Leebaw, "The irreconcilable goals of transitional justice," *Human Rights Quarterly*, vol. 30, no. 1 (2008), pp. 95–118.

31 Llewellyn, "Restorative justice and peacebuilding in post-conflict societies," op. cit., pp. 13–15.

32 Proscovia Svärd, "The international community and post-war reconciliation in Africa: A case study of the Sierra Leone Truth and Reconciliation Commission" (no date), p. 37, available at <*www.ajol.info/index.php/ajcr/article/viewFile/59306/47604*>.

33 Sriram, "(Re)building the rule of law in Sierra Leone" op. cit.; interview with Peter Viner, Programme Manager, Justice Sector Development Programme, Freetown, 18 July

2011; interview with Simeon M. K. Koroma, Director, Timap for Justice, 20 July 2011.

34 Mark A. Drumbl, *Atrocity, Punishment, and International Law* (Cambridge: Cambridge University Press, 2007), pp. 94–97.

35 Stovel and Valiñas, "Restorative justice after mass violence," op. cit., p. 31. Reintegrative shaming is said to be effective in more "traditional" communitarian societies. See John Braithwaite, *Crime, Shame, and Reintegration* (New York: Cambridge University Press, 1989).

36 Sriram, "(Re)building the rule of law in Sierra Leone," op. cit.

37 "Sierra Leone" in the country programs database, in the UN DDR Resource Centre, available at <*www.unddr.org*>.

38 Interview with Ambrose James, Search for Common Ground, 21 July 2011. Numerous interviews not for attribution, Freetown, July 2011.

39 Williamson, "The disarmament, demobilization, and reintegration of child soldiers: Social and psychological transformation in Sierra Leone," *Intervention*, vol. 4, no. 3 (2006), p. 198.

40 Interview with Alfred Carew, National Forum for Human Rights, 9 July 2011; interview with Professor Ibrahim Abdullah, Fourah Bay College, University of Sierra Leone, 13 July 2011; interview with James; interview with Ibrahim Tommy, Executive Director, Centre for Accountability and Rule of Law, 13 July 2011; interview with King; author's interview with anonymous NGO expert, 18 July 2011.

41 Interview with Abdullah.

42 Megan MacKenzie, "Securitization and desecuritization: Female soldiers and the reconstruction of women in post-conflict Sierra Leone," *Security Studies*, vol. 18, no. 2 (2009), pp. 241–61; interview with Aisha Fofana Ibrahim, Director, Institute for Gender Research, Fourah Bay College, University of Sierra Leone, 21 July 2011.

43 Author's interview with Valnora Edwin and Bernadette French, Campaign for Good Governance (14 July 2011); both noted that DDR grants were paid right at the time of demobilization, allowing former combatants to start small businesses, while victims, many of whom lost homes, breadwinners for the family, or the physical capacity for many jobs, waited to receive reparations.

44 Danny Hoffman, "The civilian target in Sierra Leone and Liberia: Political power, military strategy, and humanitarian intervention," *African Affairs*, vol. 103, no. 411 (2004), pp. 211–26.

45 Interview with Simeon Koroma.

46 Stovel and Valiñas, "Restorative justice after mass violence," op. cit., p. 17; Laura Stovel, "Two faces of reconciliation: The case of post-war Sierra Leone" (2006), p. 1, available at <*www.global.wisc.edu/reconciliation/*>.

47 John Williamson, "The disarmament, demobilization, and reintegration of child soldiers," op. cit., pp. 185–205, 190.

48 Williamson, "The disarmament, demobilization, and reintegration of child soldiers," op. cit., p. 188.

49 Christopher B. Dyck, "Football and post-war reintegration: Exploring the role of sport in DDR processes in Sierra Leone," *Third World Quarterly*, vol. 32, no. 3 (2011), pp. 395–415.

50 Ibid., p. 189.

51 Ibid., pp. 192–93.

52 Ibid., p. 195; Stovel and Valiñas, "Restorative justice after mass violence," op. cit., pp. 8–11.

53 Stovel and Valiñas, "Restorative justice after mass violence," op. cit., pp. 17–18; Erin K. Baines, "The haunting of Alice: Local approaches to justice and reconciliation in Northern Uganda," *The International Journal of Transitional Justice*, vol. 1, no. 1 (2007), pp. 91–114; Victor Igreja, "The politics of peace, justice, and healing in post-war Mozambique: 'Practices of rupture' by *Magamba* spirits and healers in Gorongosa," in

Chandra Lekha Sriram and Suren Pillay, eds, *Peace Versus Justice: The dilemma of transitional justice in Africa* (Durban: University of KwaZulu Natal Press, 2009 and Oxford: James Currey, 2010), pp. 277–300.

54 See Williamson, "The disarmament, demobilization, and reintegration of child soldiers," op. cit., p. 196; Christian Children's Fund claims to have reintegrated 1,000 former girl soldiers through such processes.

55 McKay, "Reconstructing fragile lives," op. cit., p. 23.

56 *Fambul Tok: Community healing in Sierra Leone. Our first year* and *Fambul Tok International: Community healing in Sierra Leone and the world. Our second year* (reports from 2009 and 2010, on file with author).

57 Interview with John Caulker, Fambul Tok, 14 July 2011.

58 Interview with Tommy. Stovel and Valiñas, "Restorative justice after mass violence," op. cit., p. 17; compare Elisabeth Hoffman, "Reconciliation in Sierra Leone: Local processes yield global lessons," *Fletcher Forum of World Affairs*, vol. 32 (2008), pp. 129–41.

59 Stovel and Valiñas, "Restorative justice after mass violence," op. cit., pp. 12, 15.

60 Sierra Leone Truth and Reconciliation Commission, *Witness to Truth* (2004), vol. 3B, chapter 7, para. 62; Stovel and Valiñas, "Restorative justice after mass violence," op. cit., p. 18.

61 Joe A. D. Alie, "Reconciliation and traditional justice: Tradition-based practices of the Kpaa Mende in Sierra Leone," in Luc Huyse and Mark Salter, eds, *Traditional Justice and Reconciliation after Violent Conflict: Learning from African experiences* (Stockholm: International Idea, 2008). See also Paul Richards, Khadija Bah, and James Vincent, "Social capital and survival: Prospects for community-driven development in post-conflict Sierra Leone," *Social Development Papers*, No. 12 (World Bank, April 2004). Interviews in Freetown, not for attribution, July 2011.

62 Richard Fanthorpe, "On the limits of liberal peace: Chiefs and democratic decentralization in post-war Sierra Leone," *African Affairs*, vol. 105, no. 418 (2005), pp. 27–49.

63 Sierra Leone Truth and Reconciliation Commission, *Witness to Truth* (2004). Interview with Bockarie Enssah, Civitan International, 12 July 2011.

64 Stovel, "Two faces of reconciliation," op. cit., p. 3.

65 Sierra Leone Truth and Reconciliation Commission, *Witness to Truth* (2004), available at <*www.sierra-leone.org/TRCDocuments.html*>, accessed 8 August 2011.

66 Interview with Ibrahim Tommy.

67 Ramji-Nogales, "Designing bespoke transitional justice," op. cit., p. 52. See also Rosalind Shaw, "Rethinking truth and reconciliation commissions: Lessons from Sierra Leone," *United States Institute of Peace Special Report*, No. 130 (February 2005), available at <*www.usip.org*>.

68 Interviews in Freetown, not for attribution.

69 Tim Kelsall, "Truth, lies, ritual: Preliminary reflections on the Truth and Reconciliation Commission in Sierra Leone," *Human Rights Quarterly*, vol. 27 (2005), pp. 361–91.

70 Svärd, "The international community and post-war reconciliation in Africa," op. cit., p. 48.

71 Special Court Agreement, 2002, Ratification Act, 2002 Supplement to *Sierra Leone Gazette*, vol. CXXX, No. II (7 March 2002); United Nations Security Council Resolution 1315, UN Doc. S/RES/1315 (2000). See generally Abdul Tejan-Cole, "The Special Court for Sierra Leone: Conceptual concerns and alternatives," *African Human Rights Law Journal*, vol. 1 (2001), pp. 107–26.

72 Sriram, *Globalizing Justice for Mass Atrocities*, op. cit., pp. 94–110; interview with Ambrose James, Search for Common Ground, 21 July 2011; interview with King.

73 A notable exception would be a specific group of victims—those who also passed through the court's Victims and Witnesses Section—who received medical and psychological assistance, protection, and in some cases resettlement in the country,

region, or elsewhere in the world. Interview with Saleem Vahidy, Chief of Witnesses and Victims Section, Special Court for Sierra Leone, 14 July 2011.

74 Sriram, "Wrong-sizing international justice?" op. cit.

75 Jessica Lincoln, *Transitional Justice, Peace and Accountability: Outreach and the role of international courts after conflict* (London: Routledge, 2011).

76 Interview with Edwin and French. Simeon Koroma makes a similar point.

77 Interview with Heike Niebergall, International Organization for Migration, 7 July 2011; interview with Amadou Bangura, NaCSA Reparations Program Officer, 15 July 2011. Estimates vary. See Charles Chernor Jalloh, "Special Court for Sierra Leone: Achieving justice?" *Michigan Journal of International Law*, vol. 32 (Spring 2011), pp. 395–460.

78 Interview with Edwin and French. King noted the perspective of victims that, at the court, the focus was on the perpetrators.

79 Interview with Aisha Ibrahim.

80 See generally, Human Rights Council of Sierra Leone, "State of human rights in Sierra Leone—2009" (Freetown: Human Rights Commission of Sierra Leone, 2009, on file with author). Off the record, several civil society leaders expressed concern about the lack of transparency of NaCSA, which stopped convening the oversight body, which included civil society representatives, without explanation.

81 Interview with Heike Niebergall, International Organization for Migration (IOM), by phone, 7 July 2011; interview with Sanusi Savage, Officer in Charge, IOM, Freetown, 12 July 2011; interview with Amadou Bangura, NaCSA Reparations Program Officer, 15 July 2011. United Nations Peacebuilding Fund, *Support to the Implementation of the Reparations Programme as part of the Recommendations of the Truth and Reconciliation Commission* project document (2008), available at <*www.unpbf.org/sierraleone/sierraleone-projects.shtml*> (accessed 8 August 2011); Mohamad Suma and Cristián Correa, "Report and proposals for the implementation of reparations in Sierra Leone" (New York: International Center for Transitional Justice, December 2009).

82 Interview with anonymous Sierra Leonean official, 13 July 2011.

83 Interview with Niebergall. Suma and Correa note that the government of Sierra Leone provided US $246,000 to Year One. See "Report and proposals," op. cit., p. 14.

84 Interview with Niebergall.

85 Interview with Bangura.

86 Interview with Edwin and French, who also suggest the need for a link of best practice between national and international justice processes. James, Simeon Koroma and Tommy made a similar point.

10 Tempering great expectations: Peacebuilding and transitional justice in Liberia

Rosalind Raddatz

Introduction

Against the odds, Liberia is at peace. In the eight years since the Comprehensive Peace Accord (CPA) was signed, the Liberian government and the international community have made significant progress in peacebuilding, particularly in security sector reform with the restructuring of armed and police forces, the disarmament and demobilization of ex-combatants (DDR), and the steady (albeit slow) rebuilding of the criminal justice system. Nevertheless, each of these undertakings still faces many challenges. There are few trained lawyers, and rural Liberians have virtually no access to the formal justice system. The reintegration and rehabilitation of adult former belligerents remains problematic, with a chronic lack of employment opportunities and active militias in the regions luring many back to battle in neighboring Guinea and Côte d'Ivoire or into the illegal exploitation of natural resources. The limited capacities of the judicial system means that the prosecutions called for by the Truth and Reconciliation Commission (TRC) are unlikely to occur any time soon. These caveats do not undermine the very real achievements that have been made so far in peacebuilding and transitional justice in Liberia, but they do urge a tempering of great expectations.

This chapter addresses the simultaneous peacebuilding and transitional justice activities undertaken in Liberia since 2003, when the civil war ended with a ratified peace agreement. It will argue that, while genuine efforts have been made in both respects, Liberia's peace remains fragile, and demands for expeditious justice are unlikely to be met in the near future.

There are a variety of mechanisms that aim to address the impact of human rights violations in a post-conflict society. Some, such as security sector reform, as well as disarmament, demobilization, and reintegration, are deemed to fall under the rubric of peacebuilding, whereas others are considered as belonging to the realm of transitional justice, namely legal accountability, truth and reconciliation commissions, reparation, and memorialization. Each of these has been tried in Liberia, and while major peacebuilding efforts are highlighted, much of the following explores Liberia's approach to transitional justice to date and what this means for long-term peace and accountability.

Concurrent with institutional peacebuilding, the TRC attempted to provide Liberians with a forum for truth-telling regarding the heinous crimes that took place during the conflict. Beset with ongoing difficulties, including a lack of unanimity among the commissioners, the TRC was innovative in several ways, including its documentation of testimonies from nearly 2,000 Liberian expatriates, its detailing of violations against women and children as well as economic crimes, and its suggestions for customary forms of accountability and truth-telling. Most of the TRC's recommendations have yet to be implemented, in part because of the political controversy around the call for lustration, but also because the state structure lacks the necessary capacity and resources. As a result, many Liberians are looking to customary justice mechanisms in their pursuit for justice. Previous experience suggests that they should harbor modest hopes, lest they be disappointed.

Peacebuilding: "we've come so far, but we know how far there is to go"

When the Liberian war ended with the 2003 Accra CPA, the country was a failed state. The nation's physical infrastructure, including courts and detention centers, was completely destroyed; there was no provision of public services, widespread corruption within the government, virtually no lawful economy, and no government control over the legitimate use of force. Most legal professionals had left the country. Indeed, the nation's entire security system was in disarray. Recognizing that the state apparatus was in tatters, the CPA requested the United Nations to deploy a peacekeeping force to support the transitional government with the implementation of the peace agreement. This peacekeeping force, the United Nations Mission in Liberia (UNMIL), was mandated to work with the government to develop and implement a DDR strategy.

UNMIL's first attempt at DDR, which began two months after the CPA was signed, was an utter failure. Troops were ill-prepared, only one of three containment camps was ready, and there was no guarantee of camp security.[1] In December 2003, after nine people were killed by riots that began when ex-combatants at a cantonment site near Monrovia did not receive immediate cash for their weapons, the program was suspended. DDR resumed four months later after the program had been overhauled.[2] In addition to catering to former belligerents from all armed groups, the revamped program lowered entry requirements[3] to 150 rounds of ammunition or a weapon. In exchange, ex-combatants received a DDR identification card and two cash payments of US $150, and were entitled to "reintegration programming."[4] Despite the shaky start, by November 2004 DDR was deemed officially complete, with 101,496 combatants disarmed and demobilized, and an estimated 90,000 of these having participated in rehabilitation and reintegration.[5]

At a glance, DDR in Liberia appears a success, but the high number of disarmed ex-combatants is evidence of one of the program's significant failings.[6] Prior to DDR, the International Crisis Group (ICG) estimated Liberia had between 48,000 and 58,000 ex-combatants. However, by the time the program ended, more than double the ICG's initial estimates of purported combatants had been processed. Most troubling was the modest number of arms collected—approximately 27,800 guns and six million rounds of ammunition, or an average of one gun per four ex-combatants.[7] The large number of DDR participants was not due to UNMIL's effectiveness, but because people cheated to access its benefits. Since the program paid for only one weapon or 150 rounds per person, opportunistic ex-combatants possessing multiple firearms applied repeatedly at various collection sites. Numerous non-combatants sought to enroll in DDR programs in order to receive assistance they felt they ought to be entitled to.[8] Ultimately, widespread fraud and corruption meant that demands on the system exceeded its capacity.[9]

Nonetheless, as youths no longer terrorize the country with semi-automatic weapons, few dispute the efficacy of the demobilization of ex-combatants. Nonetheless, with countless young men idle and unemployed, congregating on the streets and in the drinking establishments of Monrovia, there is considerable doubt about the effectiveness of the rehabilitation and, particularly, the reintegration of former soldiers.[10] The low number of weapons collected during the program leads skeptics to question whether Liberia was truly disarmed. Many Liberians thus question the fragility of their nation's security.

While some DDR recipients describe the program as "free benefits for the willing," other deserving individuals were not able to avail themselves due to disability, inability to travel, or disinclination to register.[11] The DDR process largely failed to address the needs of many girls and women who were formally associated with the fighting forces because it did not consider their particular wartime experiences.[12] While the total number of female Liberian ex-combatants is unknown, 22,080 women and 2,517 girls officially participated in DDR.[13] It was typically easier for girls to access these programs, since former child soldiers could enter without submitting a weapon or ammunition.[14] The adult program denied access to women not bearing arms; however, many women involved in the war were not exclusively fighters, but also "bush wives" or "camp followers," and as such they did not all carry or own weapons. According to Specht, the majority of young women (aged 18–24) did not participate in DDR.[15] Since individuals who did not formally enroll in DDR were ineligible for skills training or formal education reintegration packages, many women were affected and thus had limited prospects for employment.

Women were further disadvantaged in the aftermath of the war since the majority had suffered gender-based violence.[16] Frequently, girls and women remained in relationships with the men who had sexually assaulted them and, at war's end when asked about their experiences, many could not say whether their relationships were voluntary or forced.[17] Numerous young women were unable to receive special care. While former child combatants were assisted by child protection agencies under UNICEF, girls over the age of 18 who were victims of gender-based violence did not receive protective assistance under adult DDR programs.[18]

There were no formal links between DDR and transitional justice processes in Liberia. By the time the Truth and Reconciliation Commission officially began its work in 2008, DDR was long over. According to Jaye and the International Center for Transitional Justice, it was preferable to sequence DDR and transitional justice, with DDR implemented first.[19]

In the aftermath of the CPA, the transitional government's primary concern was to prevent a return to conflict, which meant that immediate attention went to improving the fledgling state's security rather than pursuing transitional justice.[20] In addition to DDR, security sector reform sought to address the legacy of corruption and human rights violations that were endemic in the police, the army, and the Special Security Services (SSS) that protect the President. The goal is to vet and train Liberia's various security forces into respected, reliable, and autonomous institutions that will outlast the UN's presence. The Liberia National Police (LNP) will become Liberia's primary security provider, whereas the Armed Forces of Liberia (AFL) will be a smaller organization providing external defense.[21] The challenges are many; the country has little experience with effective and accountable policing. Charles Taylor's regime co-opted the country's fragmented police forces to serve its political ends. Consequently, it is not surprising that many Liberians remain skeptical of the LNP's capacity to ensure security.

Nevertheless, since 2004, members of UN Police (UNPOL) have worked alongside the LNP, trying to restore law and order, while struggling to restructure, retrain, and re-equip the Liberian police service. While it was mandated but not funded to do so, UNMIL has trained over 3,500 new police officers along with the Liberian government.[22] Some police forces have been deployed in rural areas, but outside of the capital policing remains inadequate and UNPOL continues to be the country's most visible and reliable police force. In large part, the LNP's limited effectiveness is due to resource constraints; the force faces challenges in infrastructure, logistics (including basics like office supplies and gas), and budgetary constraints, not simply because the national government is strapped, but because many UNMIL donors have delayed and reneged on promised assistance.

The CPA mandated the USA to reform the AFL and dissolve the old army while vetting and retraining a new one using two private security agencies. Recruitment and training has been prolonged because of a rigorous vetting process to prevent former corrupt and abusive members of the forces to enlist anew.[23] As of 2011, Liberia's army numbers approximately 2,000 soldiers, compared with the 9,400 UNMIL military troops and 1,300 police who remain stationed throughout the country.[24] Neither the LNP nor the AFL has reached their 20 percent target for women, although there has been some progress. In the year after the first all-female UN contingent (comprised of 103 Indian police women) was stationed in Liberia in 2007, the number of female applicants to the LNP tripled.[25] According to UNMIL, as of early 2011 more than 400 women have been recruited and trained for duty in the police force.[26]

The nation's security improved immeasurably in the first several years under UNMIL. Even in the politically charged year of the first post-conflict elections, in a 2006 survey of 800 Liberians, 90 percent stated that UNMIL had done a good or very good job at implementing the CPA.[27]

UNMIL, the USA, and international consultants are also active in reforming Liberia's judicial system. Through the Legal and Judicial System Support Division established in 2003, UNMIL's mandate "is to develop and implement pragmatic solutions for the myriad problems and challenges facing Liberia's justice system with the ultimate aim of re-establishing the supremacy of the rule of law in post-conflict Liberia."[28] This is a tall order for an institution that was shattered by the war—even prior to the civil conflict, it lacked credibility. For the most part, judicial reform was overlooked in favor of immediate security and DDR, and it took a full five years after the CPA for Liberia to develop a strategy for the rule of law.[29]

Many Liberians believe that the peaceful future of their nation depends on a functional legal system. "We will never be able to have peace and justice if we don't fully overhaul the justice system. This is vital," says a leading Monrovian cleric.

> Much has been done, but we still have a long way to go. Even for investors, without judicial reform, they're reluctant to come. All people need to feel that there is a system they can appeal to for redress. Until this happens Liberia will not be at peace.[30]

The lack of an effective judicial system fuels impunity, and contributes to the insecurity that Liberians continue to feel despite officially being at peace for eight years.

Additionally, Liberia's dual legal system of formal and customary laws creates complications as well as opportunities for those seeking reform and redress. This dual system was first outlined in the 1943 Rules and Regulations Governing the Hinterland of Liberia ("Rules of the Hinterland"); formal laws governed settlers and missionaries (mostly located in more urban areas), while the majority indigenous African population (nearly all rural dwellers) were governed by customary laws.[31] Locally elected chiefs have their own courts which preside over matters of customary law, including civil matters pertaining to marital status and debt, while criminal matters are supposed to be overseen by formal courts, although petty theft is often addressed by the customary system. Customary disputes are typically resolved in non-punitive, reconciliatory ways, although there are exceptions.[32] There is no clear formula that determines when a case is pursued by the customary or formal systems. Individuals can avail themselves of both systems, which means that some people become judicial opportunists; the loser in one can take her case to the other. However, where there is a conflict between formal and customary law, the formal system prevails.

The oversight of the customary and formal legal systems is disjointed. The Hinterland Regulations (and customary courts) are under the jurisdiction of the Ministry of Internal Affairs and thus are not part of the national court system under the justice ministry.[33] Liberia may have a dual judicial system, but that does not mean two separate ministries should oversee it.

Although customary law is widely practiced in Liberia, it is not well understood by most international legal experts, and to date nearly all of Liberia's judicial reform has focused on the formal system. Despite a shared international and domestic commitment to reform and reconstruction, Liberia's formal justice system remains greatly constrained by limited capacities. What little infrastructure there is resides in Monrovia; some counties have not had functioning courts since before the wars. Only ten of approximately 300 magistrates have a law degree although this is a requirement for the position and between 50 and 75 percent of Justices of the Peace are illiterate.[34] While prosecution staff is mostly in place, in most courts there are no defense lawyers. Prisons are overcrowded, and more than 90 percent of inmates have yet to be tried. Juveniles are particularly vulnerable to extended pre-trial detention since there is only one juvenile court in the country.[35] These limitations are the backdrop to the Liberian Truth and Reconciliation Commission, its call for legal prosecution and censure, and some of the arguments favoring a reconsideration of traditional justice mechanisms.

Origins of the much-hyped and much-maligned TRC

A common transitional justice mechanism is the truth commission. The Liberian Truth and Reconciliation Commission does not have the cachet of previous commissions undertaken in South Africa or Chile, but since its inception it has maintained a high profile domestically, and most Liberians can expound at length on its work.

According to Ntsebeza, truth commissions are only credible and socially significant "when their mandates and composition were determined on the basis of a broad consultative process."[36] Many members of civil society groups were present at the peace negotiations leading up to the 2003 CPA, and while few held sway among the belligerents, all sought some form of accountability mechanism in the peace settlement. The mediators, on the other hand, were most concerned with persuading warring factions to lay down their weapons. In the words of a senior advisor to UNMIL:

> The signatories, even as they participated, were somnambulating. They were there, but there was no criticism of what was going on; the mightiest minds were there, including the then Minister of Justice, the ex-Chief Justice. But really, who were they to stand up to the three warring parties?[37]

During the talks, belligerents gave no consideration to criminal prosecutions or trials, with parties claiming that they would rather fight than agree to a criminal tribunal; instead they pressed for a truth commission.[38] "In the parlance that developed between negotiators, 'truth commission' was considered shorthand for 'amnesty,' or, at any rate, for '*not* a tribunal.'"[39] Even so, guarantees for amnesty were not included in the agreement to establish a truth commission. Some observers noted that the warlords seemed impervious to the threat of prosecution, and that they assumed that amnesty was part of the peace agreement.[40]

After the CPA was ratified, initial attempts by the interim government to establish a truth commission failed. Subsequently, several civil society groups, along with UNMIL, the United Nations Development Programme (UNDP), and the Economic Community of West African States (ECOWAS) carried out public consultations, which led to the 2005 Act to Establish the Truth and Reconciliation Commission of Liberia (TRC Act). When the TRC Act was finally passed, not only was the TRC forbidden from granting amnesty, it was granted the authority to recommend prosecutions and censure.[41] Nonetheless, while Charles Taylor was indicted for war crimes that he allegedly committed in Sierra Leone, many of his former associates continued to hold influential positions in business and government, as did many other perpetrators of the conflict.[42]

The goal of the Commission was to "deal with the root causes of the crises in Liberia, including human rights violations" and to "recommend measures to be taken for the rehabilitation of victims" (TRC Act). The Commission's inquiry ran from 1979 to October 2003, when the transitional government was inaugurated.[43] Under Liberian law, officials of national organizations are required to be Liberian citizens, which meant that none of the nine commissioners had any experience with truth commissions or similar organizations.[44]

As the TRC began work, whatever fears perpetrators may have had likely faded. The TRC lacked stature and resources. Few of its nine commissioners were publicly known, and in a society that venerates its elders, many were surprised at the choice of 35-year-old human rights lawyer, Jerome Verdier, as chairman. Although several commissioners were lawyers, Amnesty International claimed that the TRC "did not have the necessary expertise to make sophisticated legal evaluations," citing the lack of an in-house legal team.[45]

The problems of the Liberian TRC were not unique: truth commissions often promise to achieve more than the allocated time and resources allow. Liberian law gave the TRC "a full smorgasbord of goals: 'national peace, unity, and reconciliation', 'genuine healing,'"[46] as well as a broad mandate to investigate decades of events, but it did not provide the means, time, or expertise for the Commission to achieve its aims. Over time, the Commission did not improve its weak reputation. "The Liberian way of doing things took over," says one observer. "Infighting, mistrust across the board, among committee members, between they and the government, they and the UN, they and members of the international community. It was a multi-headed weapon shooting in all directions including onto itself."[47] To this day, several members remain at odds, and are not on speaking terms.

Initially, the TRC sought to collect statements from 1 percent of the country's population, or approximately 35,000 people. By the end of 2007, despite serious capacity constraints, the Commission had collected and processed over 17,000 statements. This is a significant achievement in its own right; in South Africa, a country with 14 times the population of Liberia, approximately 21,000 statements were taken for its TRC.[48] With the assistance of a team of volunteers, the

Liberian TRC also gathered statements from more than 1,600 members of the Liberian diaspora, residing in Ghana, the UK, and the USA.[49] This was the first time that a TRC had systematically considered and included a diaspora population in its work.[50]

A number of these individuals had valuable information about the political situation prior to the civil wars. For instance, many former members of the Tolbert government (the last Americo-Liberian regime) now reside in the USA. They were able to testify about events that led to the 1980 coup by Samuel Doe, as well as the rise of Charles Taylor as a former Tolbert government minister.[51] The diaspora's role in the conflict was also revealed through these testimonies.[52]

In spite of its innovations, the Liberian TRC remained fraught with challenges and infighting, so much so that two of the nine commissioners refused to endorse the final report. While no one denies that the Liberian TRC was a worthwhile undertaking, few have unilaterally positive assessments of its final report. A more generous appraisal notes how the TRC has shaped the political landscape:

> The issues and recommendations coming out of the TRC will continue to dominate the national agenda. Still, there are real problems around the report and its findings. We hold dearly to the issues of due process and transparency and these were sorely lacking.[53]

While ostensibly upholding the Constitution, the Commission essentially worked as a law unto itself, offering no explanations as to how it came to its conclusions and recommendations. During the process, many victims were disappointed that they were not able to interact as much as they wanted with alleged perpetrators. "One concern that we had was that perpetrators were supposed to be given the chance to interact with their victims, and there was only one county where that took place," says Rev. Benjamin Lartey. "The hearings were more of an environment where people made scholarly presentations. Victims didn't have a chance to meet perpetrators. And all the accused came and said, 'they're lying, who said I did that.'"[54] The fact that many accused appeared to be less than forthcoming and remorseful undermined the integrity of the proceedings to victims.

In all, many observers provide cautious endorsement of the TRC, contending it was a worthwhile, albeit flawed, body.

> In the history of Liberia, this is as much as has ever been said about Liberia and Liberians. Despite my misgivings, and the fact that it wasn't written by Confucius, it is still better than anything stated before. I don't like it when people expect a South African-like report; the capacities just were not there. When the best were not available, we settled with the best available. Therefore, we need to be careful about saying what is the success and failure of the TRC; it is analogous to the capacity of the nation.[55]

Not all reviews are as forgiving or as diplomatic. Steinberg writes, "The substance of the Final Report is something of a mess. Its recommendations stand little chance of surviving judicial review for they do not stand up to the flimsiest definition of the rule of law."[56] It is to the TRC's recommendations for prosecution that we now turn.

Formal accountability: prosecution and lustration

While the exact numbers remain contested, up to 200,000 people were killed (one in every 17 civilians) and nearly a million displaced during the Liberian civil wars.[57] Up to 21,000 child soldiers were forcibly conscripted to torture, sexually assault, and kill; between 60 and 70 percent of women experienced sexual violence; and at least 25 massacres in which a minimum of 100 people were killed are known of.[58] Nearly a decade later, fully 78 percent of the population consider themselves to be victims of the war.[59] For these reasons, many argue that the truth-telling mechanism of the TRC alone is insufficient and that perpetrators need to be held legally accountable for their actions.

The most controversial parts of the Liberian TRC report are its call for the establishment of an Extraordinary Criminal Tribunal and naming of individuals, corporations, and institutions recommended for prosecution or for further investigation. More than 100 people are named for prosecution of gross human rights violations.[60] An additional 49 individuals are recommended for public sanctions in the form of lustration, preventing them from holding public office for 30 years, for having aided, abetted, and otherwise supported perpetuators of the conflict.[61] Number 11 on the list is current President Ellen Johnson Sirleaf.

Most troubling, the report does not outline the criteria it used to determine who should be prosecuted or sanctioned, which means that these recommendations come across as somewhat arbitrary. Many individuals are referred to nowhere else in the report, and as such it is difficult to ascertain what evidence exists to warrant their prosecution and censure. According to a transitional justice expert, "There is a disconnect between the due process and transparency the TRC was mandated to uphold. It is not sufficient to say, we are going to prosecute and sanction, because we are the TRC and we say so."[62]

The TRC's methodology was flawed. For example, the TRC allowed unlimited anonymous testimony, which was subsequently used to build cases against those accused—although how this was done is undocumented. Former commissioner Sheikh Kafumba Konneh argues that the report is unconstitutional, stating:

> The Liberian Supreme Court holds that the language of a statute that is used to describe a crime committed must carry enough information that will give the accused the opportunity to know why he or she is being charged. The Constitution also says that the accused person must be confronted by witnesses and accusers.[63]

Both Konneh and fellow dissenting commissioner Pearl Brown Bull note that individuals who are named for prosecution and censure have no means to defend themselves against the report's claims, something that all accused should be afforded. "If we want our country to develop, to not have a repeat of past conflict, we must protect the rights of people, alleged criminals included."[64]

In a recent landmark decision, the Supreme Court of Liberia ruled part of the TRC Act and the TRC final report to be "unconstitutional and unenforceable," meaning that individuals cited for lustration cannot be prevented from holding office.[65] Archie Williams, a businessman named on the list, brought the case, claiming that, although "he was never served with notification written or oral, from the TRC charging him with any crime" and no witness was ever brought forward to testify as to his alleged wrongdoings,

> the TRC released its [final report] in which, amongst others, it recommended and directed that petitioner, along with certain other Liberians, be barred from holding public office for thirty years, for what the Commission termed as petitioner's major role in the Liberian conflict.[66]

In its ruling, the Supreme Court said the TRC's claim that it is mandatory for the President to implement its recommendations is unconstitutional because any such implementation by the President would be in violation of Williams's constitutional right to due process. The Court's decision notes that TRC's recommendation to ban a number of people from holding public office, including President Johnson Sirleaf, without first upholding their right to due process in keeping with law, is a clear violation of the Liberian Constitution.

There is no doubt that some people on the TRC's "most wanted" list have committed war crimes, and Liberians unquestionably want the war's perpetrators to be held accountable for their actions. However, Liberians also want a strong legal system that holds the right people accountable for their actions.

> If structures are to work, and people are to work and live together, we need accountability. Those who did wrong should be accountable for their wrongdoings, but good accountability depends on being specific. In terms of prosecution, this means that a person has to be found guilty through due process.[67]

At this time, it would be difficult to assure a Liberian accused of any crime, let alone gross human rights violations, that they would be afforded due process.

Despite the inroads that have been made in judicial reform, Liberia's domestic judicial system remains severely constrained. According to Campbell-Nelson, the legal system will not have the capacity to try alleged perpetrators for at least a decade.[68] Thus, even before the TRC tabled its final report, some Liberian human rights activists thought it premature to contemplate legal prosecutions.[69] As part of its statement-taking, the TRC included questions on the theme of reconciliation. In ten out of Liberia's 15 counties, the majority of those questioned wanted to "forgive and forget" and in the remaining counties almost half shared this opinion.[70] As a result, some peace activists found the rush to prosecute to be counter-intuitive:

> The draft report, using these figures, noted that people wanted to move on with reconciliation. This was left out of the final report. What were the reasons for suppressing this? Even the issue of reconciliation and healing was downplayed in the final report.[71]

For those who believe that victims want to see justice in the form of prosecutions, recall that nearly all Liberians see themselves as victims of the war. At this time, only a small proportion of Liberians believe victims will be helped by trials and the punishment of perpetrators.[72]

Even the most ardent supporter of prosecutions, Jerome Verdier, publicly acknowledges that the deficiencies of Liberia's formal legal system are so profound that the TRC's recommendations for legal accountability cannot be pursued domestically, at least for the time being. "The judiciary in Africa is unreliable, corrupt and by no means transparent," he said. "Because of inherent mistrust of the judicial institutions in Liberia, justice is not the first interest of victims of war and conflicts."[73] In the absence of a well-functioning Liberian legal system, Verdier is pinning his hopes on the International Criminal Court (ICC) as an "appropriate strategy for delivering justice to local populations."[74] So far, the ICC has not indicated any interest in undertaking the prosecution of alleged Liberian war criminals. In the meantime, Liberians are hoping that customary justice will give them what formal justice has not.

Customary accountability and conflict resolution: the Palava Hut

Even if the legal system were fully reformed, the sheer number of people who are alleged to have committed crimes would overwhelm the criminal courts and prevent them from hearing any other cases for years to come. For this reason, I argue that many Liberians are warming to the idea of using existing customary justice mechanisms to provide resolution for "lesser" war crimes.[75] Up until and throughout the war, the customary system had proved to be more durable than the formal system in providing Liberians with a forum in which to resolve their disputes. Although the social upheaval of the war has diminished the role of chiefs and elders somewhat, customary mechanisms are widely perceived as having some legitimacy.

With its focus on consensus building and reconciliation, several members of the TRC were particularly predisposed towards customary justice. "In our travels for the TRC, I became convinced that the Liberian people were ready for peace," says former TRC commissioner Sheikh Kafumba Konneh. "In some areas, perpetrators and victims live together and eat together. In places where there has been experimentation regarding transitional justice, victims have publicly forgiven perpetrators."[76]

Most Liberians residing outside of the capital had little recourse to the formal legal system and sought redress through customary dispute mechanisms, including the *Palava Hut* process and *sassywood*. The Palava Hut process (hereafter Palava Hut) is perceived as a non-punitive and reconciliatory process, while the aim of sassywood is to establish guilt and punish the wrongdoer through "trial by ordeal." The practice involves variations of a ritual where alleged wrongdoers are exposed to extreme pain. A person's guilt depends on their reaction; if there is little injury or if they recover well, the accused is considered innocent. Although still common in rural areas, the use of sassywood is illegal. Palava Hut is convened by the elders of a community, nearly always men who are over the age of 45. They typically settle land disputes, divorce, debt, and extramarital affairs, although occasionally they are called upon to decide on cases of theft and murder.[77] There is no one way to practice Palava Hut in Liberia, although it is widely practiced by the Kwa and the Mende ethnic and linguistic groups.

Among the Kwa, the process "seeks a confession of the wrongful act, an apology for the wrong that has been done and forgiveness from the victim."[78] Often, the family of the perpetrator will initiate the process, and the family is involved throughout the process. Cleansing rituals are held, with elders offering advice and warnings to the wrongdoer. Sometimes, especially in cases of theft, the offender or his family is required to make restitution to the victim. In cases of murder, the perpetrator must make public restitution through a public apology and may be banished from the community, to give the family time to grieve for the death of their loved one.

The family is less important in the Mende practice of Palava Hut. Local chiefs and leaders lead the process, which may take place publicly in a palava hut, a round structure with a thatched roof, or privately in a sequestered area where only initiates may participate. The aim is an admission of guilt by the perpetrator, after which "restitution is required in the form of a fine."[79] In cases of violence, the wrongdoer must submit to a cleansing ceremony, which usually includes the sacrifice of an animal. In cases of murder, the process is held privately, with the elders determining whether the crime was premeditated or accidental. The cleansing process is integral, after which families of the victims and perpetrator share a meal as a means to seal reconciliation.

It is important to note that, while the customary legal system is entrenched in Liberia, and Palava Hut is common among some tribes, it is not universally used throughout Liberia. Nonetheless, the concept has gained tremendous traction among civil society groups, who propose it as a means to resolve the harm caused by the country's civil wars, as a way either to address issues brought up by the TRC or to achieve reconciliation. One human rights activist comments:

> The policy of the TRC was to make it victim-oriented. Some came with a sense of arrogance and no remorse. Others came and tried to show remorse, and while they didn't atone for their sins, at least they spoke with their victims. My impression was Liberia had much more testimony than Sierra Leone, but there wasn't much confrontation between victims and

> perpetrators. You need some interaction between the two. When you have an opportunity to talk to that person who has done you harm, it doesn't heal, but it sets the process to heal. When that meeting takes place, confidence and trust building can start.[80]

The TRC was initially seen as the forum where victims could achieve some form of reconciliation. Prior to the TRC's hearings, between 50 and 70 percent of the population claimed to want to meet with the perpetrator who caused their suffering, but few actually had the opportunity to do so.[81] Nonetheless, this suggests that there remains widespread support for reconciliation initiatives.

As a result, some see Palava Hut as an expedient and achievable form of justice, at least in the short-term. In Rev. Lartey's pragmatic view of justice:

> We have to look at the short, medium, and long term. The government can't do it all. It is too expensive to try to undertake prosecutions right now. This doesn't mean that the church doesn't believe in holding people accountable, but we cannot pursue the vigilante approach ... We feel that many things stand in the way of actual prosecution. This is not a process that takes one or two days. Healing and reconciliation is something that we can do right now, supported by the government, and Palava Hut.[82]

This view is echoed by Joe Hindovei Pemagbi:

> Accountability is more than just prosecution. The downside of prosecution is that prosecution isn't necessarily going to heal the wounds; it is not going to build relationships and cohesion in communities. It will just satisfy a certain portion of people. How do we make sure that justice trickles down?[83]

A number of the TRC's recommendations make direct reference to the use of Palava Hut.

For instance, the TRC report names 36 people as perpetrators of the war but recommends them for pardon from criminal prosecution, "without prejudice to the Palava Hut process," because they admitted to their crimes, expressed remorse, and cooperated with the TRC.[84] There are also arguments for limited accountability.

> Regarding perpetrator accountability, those who did wrong should be accountable for their wrongdoings. It's easy to see the big guys, but there are others who need to be held accountable. The big guys should be held accountable for their actions because they could have done differently. Others, less high up, should also have thought of other ways out.[85]

Those "less high up" are mentioned later, in Appendix XII of the final report, where the TRC provides a list of 7,600 people who are recommended to submit to a "justice and accountability mechanism with traditional orientation to foster national healing and reconciliation at the community and grass roots levels creating the opportunity for dialogue and peacebuilding."[86]

Palava Hut is not without its drawbacks, first of which is its lack of universality. There is no guarantee that all Liberians will endorse the process as a means for reconciliation. Even among those communities who use it, Palava Hut is not uniformly practiced, leading some to question how the process would be harmonized into a single national program.[87] Additionally, it has only been used to resolve intra-community conflict, and has not been used as a forum to address violent crimes, including sexual assault. The nation may have elected the first African female president, but Liberia remains a very male-dominated society. The elders who administer the process are nearly always men, many of whom still subscribe to traditional practices in which victims of sexual assault are blamed and shunned; the Women in Peacebuilding Network (WIPNET) has advocated the establishment of female led "peace huts" that respect the spirit of Palava Hut while making it more beneficial to victims. However positive the peace huts are for women, their very existence underscores divisions in Liberian society.

Traditional or customary justice mechanisms are not a panacea, nor are they a guarantee for human rights, which leads even their most avid proponents to call for their systematic institutionalization. "I endorse the mechanism, but it should be contextualized; not everything should go to the Palava Hut," says one human rights activist. "Preconditions are required. Tribal disputes, such as differences between families, or specific violations, can work in Palava Hut. Gross violations, such as massacres, should not go to the Palava Hut."[88] If Liberians are committed to implementing certain TRC recommendations through this process, system designers will have to define its scope, parameters, and powers, while acknowledging the tensions between traditional justice programs and the statutory judicial system.[89]

For all its challenges, many Liberians trust Palava Hut and believe this form of customary justice could provide perpetrators with accountability while achieving some reconciliation. Former TRC commissioner Pearl Brown Bull, whose teenaged son was murdered during the war, states:

> The Palava Hut is the right situation for Liberia: It will condemn wrongdoings. It is the best way forward. We are a religious country. Everyone believes in the hereafter, and we all want to be on the right path for the hereafter. To get forgiveness, through cleansing, they really have to mean what they say. We do not have capacities in jail, and why put people up for human rights violations when they can contribute to society?[90]

Here we see the hope and pragmatism of Liberians who have been victimized by the war. They acknowledge the inherent failings of the TRC but remain hopeful that high-profile and ordinary perpetrators alike will eventually account for their actions during the war and make public amends.

Reconciliation through reparations

Many suggest Liberians' war-weariness is partly what keeps the country at peace, but numerous Liberians are tiring of the unsuccessful pursuit of formal justice.

Some are seeking to move beyond prosecutions altogether: "I'm focused on the long-term perspective, how the non-controversial recommendations will be implemented. I don't want to be looking at prosecution and lustration right now, perhaps never."[91] In this respect, a number of Liberian peace and transitional justice activists believe that the emphasis placed on the Liberian TRC's "naming of names" for prosecution and lustration is not only problematic, but it serves as a detriment to other parts of the report. Beyond the TRC, there are other measures that can also work towards reconciling a nation so long divided.

The TRC's recommendations for reparations and memorialization have been glossed over in favor of the drama surrounding prosecutions and censure. While not eschewing formal legal measures, pragmatic Liberians see these options as less likely to encounter political opposition while still reaching out to the victims of the conflict. "Prosecution and reparations are not in tension and these are not weak alternatives," says Aaron Weah. "They are true victim-centered approaches. They are weak alternatives when they are used to buy silence, but if they evolve from society and victims' groups, and have political buy-in, then these are not weak at all."

The statute creating the TRC mandates it to make recommendations regarding reparations (TRC Act, art. 4, sec. 26). The final report recommends a Reparations Trust Fund of US $500 million over 30 years. According to the TRC, monies for the Fund are to be generated through the nationalization of a Monrovia office building that was initially built with tax money, as well as the nationalization of the J.J. Roberts scholarship fund. The proceeds of the scholarship fund will be earmarked for educating "the children of Liberia."[92] The most casual reader will find it difficult to imagine how the nationalization of a single building, which has since been taken over by the government for public use, could ever generate the hundreds of millions of dollars required to deliver the kinds of reparations that the TRC envisions. Even members of the Independent Human Rights Commission, the Liberian body established to administer reparations, express doubts about where their funding will come from, and their ability to work autonomously. "If you want to remain independent you can't be beholden financially, otherwise you are under government control," says commissioner Thomas Bureh. "We need to be independent, so we need external support."[93] The commissioners do not acknowledge that external donors might also infringe on the Commission's autonomy and, although no donors have yet committed any kind of funding, they remain optimistic—some would say naïve—about the Commission's financial prospects. "We've got to take people at their words that they are going to be supportive," says commissioner Boakai Dukuly.[94]

The reparations proposal is well-intentioned, but woefully incomplete, and subject to much disagreement. For example, within the first five years, that is to say until 2014, "all direct victim support programs must be implemented including memorials, victim support and the process of prosecution."[95] However, the Commission gives little clue as to who should receive reparations, although victims may be individuals or collectives, and women are highlighted as "absolute priorities." As far as the form that reparations should take, the TRC enumerates a range of health, educational, economic, and infrastructural services.[96]

"The whole idea of caring for victims is new to Liberia, which is why they are so important," notes Aaron Weah. "During the war and the peace agreements, more attention was given to appeasing the perpetrators, the warlords and the combatants than in dealing with the victims." Again, in intent, the TRC report seeks redress for victims, but in practice it fails them. Unlike the Ghanaian TRC report, which created a list of victims, the Liberian report provides no preliminary list of potential victims who could or should benefit from reparations. Additionally, and possibly more importantly, the reparations programs that the TRC recommends require massive resources that Liberia simply does not possess. In the laundry list of Liberia's urgent needs, it is unlikely that reparations will become the preferred project of an international community that is tiring of the nation's ongoing demands.

Nonetheless, some believe that reparations are a real means to demonstrate a government's commitment to respecting the rights and needs of the victims.

> All reparations, individual and collective, provide healing. This shows a link between peacebuilding and transitional justice—they are mutually reinforcing, and you cannot have one without the other in post-war Liberia. For instance, if the TRC recommendations consider identity, which they appear to, then there is an issue of memorialization … Any efforts along these lines will go towards stopping a return to war.[97]

However, this view is rather optimistic. The reality is that widespread reparations in Liberia are as improbable as domestic prosecutions of alleged war criminals. Even if the means existed—which they certainly do not—there is no guarantee that the Independent National Commission on Human Rights (INCHR) could administer the funds in an equitable fashion. In fact, any misappropriation or evidence of favoritism would only serve to exacerbate ongoing societal divisions.

A large majority of Liberians are willing to accept community-level measures or symbolic measures as a form of compensation for their suffering.[98] Many communities are pursing memorialization projects to help communities remember and honor those who died in massacres during the civil war. Some forms of memorialization are contentious, but nearly all Liberians can embrace others. Indeed, memorialization efforts such as a national remembrance day, cleansing ceremonies, issuing death certificates to the war dead, and making public apologies to the people of Liberia appear to be quite feasible, as few require many resources.[99]

While most Liberians express some disappointment about the country's pace of peacebuilding and the transitional justice process to date, all claim to be hopeful about the future. "I am optimistic because when you see Liberia, you see resilience," says peace activist Lindora Howard Diawara.

> We don't want to go back to war, we are committed to wanting peace. But peacebuilding is a process, it doesn't just happen. We can see how far we've come since the war, and now we can see how far we need to go.[100]

However far Liberians must go, all remain committed to peace. Justice, though, remains elusive.

Until now, peacebuilding and transitional justice in Liberia has been an eight-year roller coaster ride of great expectations and dashed hopes. After 14 years of war, and as many breached peace agreements, Liberians were desperate for peace, but many were disappointed by DDR cash payouts that appeared to reward combatants for perpetuating war. Liberians then looked to security sector reform and the TRC for justice, only to feel let down by the emphasis on prosecutions that cannot be pursued within the country's limited legal system. Some now see Palava Hut and the International Criminal Court (ICC) as providing the potential for some closure. So far, the ICC prosecutor has not indicated that he will pursue criminal prosecutions in Liberia, and the Palava Hut process, although widely supported, has yet to be tried and proven. Whatever transitional justice processes they embrace, it is improbable that all Liberians will get all that they want. Perhaps eventually they will get what they need.

Acknowledgements

I am particularly grateful to Aaron Weah for his invaluable research assistance. I also thank Jim Dube for his legal insight, Stephen Brown for his comments, and the many Liberians working in transitional justice who kindly shared their observations and experiences with me. I am appreciative of the Social Sciences Research Council of Canada and the Trudeau Foundation for financial support.

Notes

1 Refugees International, "DDRR in Liberia: Do it Quickly—But Do It Right," 3 December 2003, available at: <*http://reliefweb.int/sites/reliefweb.int/files/reliefweb_pdf/node-138701.pdf*> (accessed 27 June 2011).
2 Kathleen M. Jennings, "The Struggle to Satisfy: DDR Through the Eyes of Ex-combatants in Liberia," *International Peacekeeping*, Vol. 14, No. 2 (April 2007), p. 208.
3 Ibid. Jennings speculates that entry requirements might have been lowered to ensure the inclusion of "camp followers": women who were bush wives or fighters or both.
4 Reintegration programming consisted of formal education and vocational or public works training, with the DDR program paying tuition for up to three years and giving participants in registered activities a monthly stipend (between US $15 to 30 per month).
5 UNSC, Fifteenth Progress Report of the Secretary-General on the United Nations Mission in Liberia. UN Doc. S/2007/479, p. 7.
6 Jennings, "The Struggle to Satisfy," op. cit., p. 208.
7 Ibid., p. 209.

8 It is common in post-conflict situations that civilian non-combatants (many of whom are victims) perceive programs such as DDR as rewarding belligerents for perpetuating war, but the need for incentives to induce combatants to lay down arms is clear.

9 Frequently, participants in training programs received their monthly stipend late, and often noted that, by the time they received it, a portion had been taken by the school principal or program fund administrator. See Jennings, "The Struggle to Satisfy," op. cit., p. 210.

10 According to UNDP, 55 percent of Liberia's population is under the age of 20. Although the Liberian government does not track employment rates, NGOs estimate national unemployment at 65–70 percent. Nearly all who work labor at subsistence wages. See Samwar S. Fallah, "Peace Under Threat," *D+C*, No. 07/08 2010, Vol. 51, July/August 2010, available at: <*www.inwent.org/ez/articles/176375/index.en.shtml*> (accessed 27 June 2011).

11 Jennings, "The Struggle to Satisfy," op. cit., p. 212.

12 Helen Liebling-Kalifani *et al.*, "Women War Survivors of the 1989–2003 Conflict in Liberia: The Impact of Sexual and Gender-Based Violence," *Journal of International Women's Studies*, Vol. 12, No. 1 (2009), p. 14, available at: <*www.bridgew.edu/soas/jiws/vol12_no1/pdfs/1_Liebling-Kalifani.pdf*> (accessed 2 April 2011). According to Amnesty International (2008), women and girls represented 30–40 percent of fighting forces, or approximately 25,000–30,000 people. No female combatants negotiated the Accra peace agreement, nor are any presently serving in positions of government authority.

13 National Commission on Disarmament, Demobilization, Rehabilitation and Reintegration (NCDDRR), "Joint Implementation Unit DDRR Consolidated Report (Status of Disarmament and Demobilization Activities as at 11/24/2004)," available at: <*www.humanitarianinfo.org/liberia/coordination/sectoral/DDR/doc/Forthnightly%20Report_24 112004.pdf*> (website is currently unavailable as it is in the process of being archived).

14 Irma Specht (ed.), *Red Shoes: Experiences of Girl Combatants in Liberia* (Geneva: Programme of Crisis Response and Reconstruction, International Labour Office, 2006), available at: <*www.humansecuritygateway.com/documents/ILO_ExperiencesofGirlCombatantsLiberia.pdf*> (accessed 27 June 2011).

15 Ibid., p. 82.

16 Amnesty International, "Liberia: No Impunity for Rape, A Crime Against Humanity and a War Crime" (December 2004), available at: <*www.amnesty.org/en/library/asset/AFR34/017/2004/en/c3b9d317-f7a6–11dd-8fd7-f57af21896e1/afr340172004en.pdf*> (accessed 03 August 2011). Men and boys were also victims of gender-based violence, but women were the majority of victims.

17 Specht, *Red Shoes*, op. cit., p. 106.

18 Specht, *Red Shoes*, op. cit., p. 107.

19 Thomas Jaye, *Transitional Justice and DDR: The Case of Liberia* (Research Brief, International Center for Transitional Justice (ICTJ), 2009), p. 4; interview with Aaron Weah, Program Associate, International Center for Transitional Justice (ICTJ), 23 February 2011, Monrovia.

20 Jaye, *Transitional Justice and DDR*, op. cit.

21 David C. Gompert *et al.*, Oversight of the Liberian National Police (Santa Monica, CA: RAND National Defense Research Institute, 2009), available at: <*www.rand.org/content/dam/rand/pubs/occasional_papers/2009/RAND_OP230.sum.pdf*> (accessed 29 June 2011).

22 Thomas Jaye, "Parliamentary Oversight and Lessons Learned from Internationalized Security Sector Reform" (NYU Center on International Cooperation, 2009), available at: <*www.cic.nyu.edu/peacebuilding/docs/Liberia_SSR.pdf*> (accessed 29 June 2011).

23 Some 75 percent of AFL's new candidates were rejected, compared to the 10 percent that were turned down by the LNP.

24 Number of UNMIL personnel in Liberia as of February 2011. See <*www.un.org/en/peacekeeping/missions/unmil/facts.shtml*> (accessed 20 April 2011).
25 J. M. Guéhenno, Statement to the UN Security Council, Debate on Women, Peace and Security. UN document S/PV.5766, 23 October 2007, p. 5.
26 See "United Nations Police in Liberia," available at: <*http://unmil.org/2content.asp?sub=7& main=20& pgt=2*> (accessed 6 July 2011).
27 Jean Krasno, *Public Opinion Survey of UNMIL's Work in Liberia* (Monrovia: UNDPKO, 2006).
28 See <*http://unmil.org/1content.asp?ccat=ljss& zdoc=1*> (accessed 21 April 2011).
29 See Republic of Liberia, *Poverty Reduction Strategy*, April 2008, available at: <*www.supportliberia.com/assets/95/chapter8.pdf*> (accessed 6 July 2011).
30 Interview with Reverend Benjamin Lartey, Secretary General, Liberia Council of Churches, 23 February 2011, Monrovia.
31 Olga Martin-Ortega and Johanna Herman, "Narrowing Gaps in Justice: Rule of Law Programming in Liberia," in Chandra Lekha Sriram, Olga Martin-Ortega, and Johanna Herman (eds), *Peacebuilding and Rule of Law in Africa: Just Peace?* (London: Routledge, 2010).
32 Where the Liberian Penal Code has been violated, the customary system does not have legitimate jurisdiction, but that does not prevent chiefs, particularly in rural areas, from taking on such cases and meting out punishment in the form of "trial by ordeal." Some of the customary ways of resolving conflict, including punitive processes, are addressed later.
33 In case of abuse, the customary system is accountable to the Ministry of Justice as well as the Supreme Court.
34 American Bar Association Rule of Law Initiative—Liberia, "ABA ROLI Helping to Launch the First Training Center for Judges in Liberia"(April 2008), see <*www.abanet.org/rol/news/news_liberia_new_judicial_training_institute.shtml*> (last accessed 3 August 2011). International Crisis Group, "Liberia: Resurrecting the Justice System," Africa Report No. 107, April 2006, see <*www.crisisgroup.org/~/media/Files/africa/west-africa/liberia/Liberia%20Resurrecting%20the%20Justice%20System.pdf*> (last accessed 3 August 2011).
35 Jaye, *Transitional Justice and DDR*, op. cit.
36 Dumisa Buhle Ntsebeza, "Can Truth Commissions in Africa Deliver Justice?" in Anton Bösl and Joseph Diescho (eds), *Human Rights in Africa: Legal Perspectives on Their Protection and Promotion* (Namibia: Konrad-Adenauer-Stiftung, 2009), p. 387.
37 Interview with a senior transitional justice advisor to UNMIL, 18 February 2011, Monrovia.
38 Priscilla Hayner, *Negotiating Peace in Liberia: Preserving the Possibility for Justice* (Geneva: Henry Dunant Centre for Humanitarian Dialogue, 2007).
39 Jonny Steinberg, "A Truth Commission Goes Abroad: Liberian Transitional Justice in New York," *African Affairs*, Vol. 110, No. 438 (2010), p. 138.
40 Hayner, *Negotiating Peace in Liberia*, op. cit., p. 16.
41 Government of Liberia, "An Act to Establish the Truth and Reconciliation Commission for Liberia" (hereafter, TRC Act), 12 May 2005, Monrovia, available at: <*www.ictj.org/static/Africa/Liberia/liberiatrcact.eng.pdf*> (accessed 17 April 2011), Article IV, Section 4.
42 Jonny Steinberg, "Liberia's Experiment with Transitional Justice," *African Affairs*, Vol. 109, No. 434 (2009), pp. 135–44.
43 Article IV of the TRC Act notes that the TRC could look at "any period preceding 1979." Liberia was colonized in 1847 by a small number of former American slaves who ruled the country to the detriment of most of the nation's aboriginal population until 1979.
44 Lansana Gberie, "Truth and Justice on Trial in Liberia," *African Affairs*, Vol. 107, No. 428 (2008), p. 457.

45 Amnesty International, Liberia: Toward the Final Phase of the Truth and Reconciliation Commission (London, July 2008), p. 29.
46 Steinberg, "A Truth Commission Goes Abroad," op. cit., p. 39.
47 Interview with a senior transitional justice advisor to UNMIL, 18 February 2011, in Monrovia.
48 Kristen Cibelli, Jule Krüger, and Amelia Hoover, *Descriptive Statistics from Statements to the Liberian Truth and Reconciliation Commission. A Report by the Human Rights Data Analysis Group at Benetech and Annex to the Final Report of the Truth and Reconciliation Commission of Liberia*, (2009), available at: <*http://trcofliberia.org/resources/reports/final/descriptive-statistics-from-statements-to-the-liberian-trc-benetech.pdf*> (accessed 5 April 2011).
49 Commissioners created the LTRC Diaspora Project, which partnered with The Advocates for Human Rights (The Advocates), an American human rights organization based in Minneapolis, MN. Laura Young and Rosalyn Park, "Engaging Diasporas in Truth Commissions: Lessons from the Liberian Truth and Reconciliation Commission Diaspora Project," *International Journal of Transitional Justice*, Vol. 3 (2009), pp. 341–61.
50 Young and Park, "Engaging Diasporas in Truth Commissions," op. cit. Other truth commissions, such as those in Haiti, Timor-Leste, and Sierra Leone, have sought the input of diaspora communities, less comprehensively.
51 Ibid., p. 353.
52 Ibid., p. 353.
53 Interview with Aaron Weah, Program Associate, International Center for Transitional Justice (ICTJ), 23 February 2011, Monrovia.
54 Interview with Reverend Benjamin Lartey, Secretary General, Liberia Council of Churches, 23 February 2011, Monrovia.
55 Interview with a senior transitional justice advisor to UNMIL.
56 Steinberg, "Liberia's Experiment with Transitional Justice," op. cit., p. 141.
57 There is no consensus on the total numbers of casualties and displaced persons from the Liberian civil wars. Record keeping during the war was virtually impossible, and various belligerents inflated or diminished numbers for political gain.
58 Amnesty International, "Liberia: Truth, Justice, Reparation for Liberia's Victims," 15 February 2007, available at: <*www.amnesty.org/en/library/info/AFR34/001/2007*> (accessed 17 April 2010).
59 Patrick Vink *et al.*, *Talking Peace: A Population-based Survey on Attitudes about Security, Dispute Resolution and Post-conflict Reconstruction in Liberia* (Berkeley: Human Rights Center, University of California Berkeley, June 2011), available at: <*www.law.berkeley.edu/HRCweb/pdfs/Talking-Peace-Liberia-2011.pdf*> (accessed 5 July 2011).
60 LTRC, *Final Report*, Sec. 12.3, p. 349.
61 LTRC, *Final Report*, Sec. 14.3, p. 361.
62 Interview with Aaron Weah, Program Associate, International Center for Transitional Justice (ICTJ), 23 February 2011, Monrovia.
63 Interview with Sheikh Kafumba Konneh, Muslim clergyman, peace activist, and dissenting TRC commissioner, 17 February 2011, Monrovia.
64 Interview with Councillor Pearl Brown Bull, lawyer, peace activist, and former dissenting TRC commissioner, 16 February 2011, Monrovia.
65 Archie Williams *vs* Christiana Tah (Minister of Justice and Attorney General), the Independent Human Rights Commission, and the Government of Liberia, 21 January 2011. Article 48 of the TRC Act mandates the TRC to recommend to the President the implementation of recommendations coming from the TRC, while Section 14.3 of the TRC report lists and recommends that a number of Liberians be banned from holding public office for 30 years.
66 Ibid., p. 2.
67 Interview with Lindora Howard Diawara, Coordinator, Women in Peacebuilding Network (WIPNET), 20 February 2011, Monrovia.

68 Karen Campbell-Nelson, *Liberia is Not Just a Man Thing: Transitional Justice Lessons for Women, Peace and Security* (Brussels: Initiative for Peacebuilding, 2008).
69 Hayner, *Negotiating Peace in Liberia*, op. cit.
70 Kristen Cibelli, Amelia Hoover, and Jule Kruger, *Descriptive Statistics from Statements to the Liberian Truth and Reconciliation Commission*, 2009, available at: <*http://trcofliberia.org/resources/reports/final*>, p. 43.
71 Interview with Reverend Benjamin Lartey, Secretary General, Liberia Council of Churches, 23 February 2011, Monrovia.
72 Patrick Vink *et al.*, *Talking Peace*, op. cit., p. 67. The report states, "Holding trials to punish perpetrators of violence was proposed by less than 10% of the respondents as an acceptable measure to address the needs of victims" (p. 69).
73 Jerome Verdier, "Post Conflict Justice, Local Ownership and Interventions of the ICC," speech presented to the Public Forum of the Center for Multi Party Democracy, Nairobi, Kenya, 1 April 2011, available at: <*http://alciso-diaspora.org/verdier%20speech.pdf* (accessed 29 June 2011).
74 Ibid.
75 By this I mean crimes committed by rank and file combatants during the course of the civil war. While most of the Liberians I spoke to hoped to see the uncontested key perpetrators of war crimes and crimes against humanity formally prosecuted and tried, they were more optimistic about their chances of seeing lesser perpetrators experience informal justice, such as Palava Hut. Most supported this approach and saw it as a potential vehicle of reconciliation.
76 Interview with Sheikh Kafumba Konneh, Muslim clergyman, peace activist, and dissenting TRC commissioner, 17 February 2011, Monrovia.
77 Ezekiel Pajibo, "Civil Society and Transitional Justice in Liberia: A Practitioner's Reflection from the Field," *International Journal of Transitional Justice*, Vol. 1, No. 2 (2007), pp. 287–96.
78 Ezikiel Pajibo, *Traditional Justice Mechanisms: The Liberian Case* (Sweden: International IDEA, 2008), p. 18.
79 Ibid., p. 21.
80 Interview with Joe Hindovei Pemagbi, Liberia Country Coordinator, Open Society Institute, 18 February 2011, Monrovia.
81 Cibelli *et al.*, *Descriptive Statistics from Statements to the Liberian Truth and Reconciliation Commission*, op. cit., p. 40.
82 Interview with Reverend Benjamin Lartey, Secretary General, Liberia Council of Churches, 23 February 2011, Monrovia.
83 Interview with Joe Hindovei Pemagbi, Liberia Country Coordinator, Open Society Institute, 18 February 2011, Monrovia.
84 TRC, *Final Report*, Sec. 12.3, p. 349.
85 Interview with Lindora Howard Diawara, Coordinator, Women in Peacebuilding Network (WIPNET), 20 February 2011, Monrovia.
86 TRC, *Final Report*, Sec. 15.0, p. 365.
87 Paul James-Allen, Aaron Weah, and Lizzie Goodfriend, *Beyond the Truth and Reconciliation Commission: Transitional Justice Options in Liberia* (New York and Monrovia: International Center for Transitional Justice (ICTJ), 2010), p. 22.
88 Interview with Pindarous Allison, Program Coordinator, Transitional Justice Working Group, 16 February 2011, Monrovia.
89 James-Allen *et al.*, *Beyond the Truth and Reconciliation Commission*, p. 22.
90 Interview with Pearl Brown Bull, lawyer, peacebuilding activist, and former dissenting TRC commissioner, 16 February 2011, Monrovia.
91 Interview with Edward (Eddy) Mulbah, Sr. Technical Advisor, Liberia Peacebuilding Office, 22 February 2011, Monrovia.
92 LTRC, *Final Report*, Sec. 17.2, pp. 378–79.
93 Interview with Thomas Bureh, commissioner, Independent Human Rights Commission, 21 February 2011, Monrovia.

94 Interview with Boakai Dukuly, commissioner, Independent Human Rights Commission, 21 February 2011, Monrovia.

95 LTRC, *Final Report*, Sec. 17.2, pp. 378–79.

96 James-Allen *et al.*, *Beyond the Truth and Reconciliation Commission*, p. 23. See also the TRC *Consolidated Final Report*, sections 17 and 18.5 on reparations, as well as the recommendations in Vol. 3, Titles I and II of the *Final Report.*

97 Interview with Edward (Eddy) Mulbah, Sr. Technical Advisor, Liberia Peacebuilding Office, 22 February 2011, Monrovia.

98 Patrick Vink *et al.*, *Talking Peace*, op. cit., p. 67.

99 The TRC's *Final Report* enumerates a number of possible memorialization measures in Section 17. I have highlighted those that are least contentious and most affordable.

100 Interview with Lindora Howard Diawara, Coordinator, Women in Peacebuilding Network (WIPNET), 20 February 2011, Monrovia.

11 The supposed accountability/peacebuilding dilemma in Uganda

Joanna R. Quinn

Introduction

The literature on transitional justice and peacebuilding has tended to assert two competing claims: either that attempting to promote accountability would undermine peacebuilding efforts, or that accountability is essential to peacebuilding. In Uganda, transitional justice and peacebuilding have been intricately linked and carried out contemporaneously—largely, to the detriment of both. While the Government of Uganda (GOU) does not appear to distinguish between peacebuilding and transitional justice, these goals are not differentiated either from those of development and poverty eradication. In fact, peacebuilding and transitional justice are incorporated in national development policies. This chapter examines key development policies and programs established by the GOU, in order to identify and assess specific activities carried out in support of transitional justice and peacebuilding.

The peacebuilding and transitional justice policies of the GOU are considerably affected by a number of factors that render them less effective. A first element is the necessity of and presence of international donors and NGOs, which do a lot of the "heavy lifting" in the country. The GOU has abdicated much of the responsibility for programming in these areas, and other agencies have stepped in to provide such services. For example, the international donor community provided 36 percent of the budget of the Uganda Human Rights Commission in 2008, which was used to fund "core activities" of the Commission.[1] Although not uncommon in war-affected countries, the government's own *Peace Recovery and Development Plan for Northern Uganda* (*PRDP*) acknowledges that "Northern Uganda has a large number of national and international actors providing humanitarian, recovery and development support to war-affected communities."[2] The document further specifies that humanitarian agencies have been responsible for "life-saving support and relief."[3]

The second exacerbating element is the uncoordinated approach pursued by the GOU with regards to policy implementation. The Government admits that:

> [a] major shortcoming in the current institutional arrangement has been the lack of an agreed framework, strategy and targets for coordinating

> interventions in the North by the various stakeholders. This has made it difficult for Government to assess the amount of resources that have been utilized to address humanitarian and development needs and the impact derived thereof. The situation has been further complicated by the plethora of initiatives and implementation committees that are operating simultaneously but in parallel within the same region organized along geographical, sectoral and functional lines.[4]

While this is common in nearly every sector, it seems particularly striking in policies surrounding transitional justice and peacebuilding. Various agencies at both the national and local levels have taken up portions of the work, including the Ministry of Disaster Preparedness, the Uganda People's Defence Force (UPDF), and the National Security Council.[5]

The third condition exacerbating efforts at peacebuilding and transitional justice is that the GOU is trying to serve many masters. The International Monetary Fund (IMF), for example, holds the GOU captive to its Poverty Reduction and Growth Facility—pushing for particular goals and objectives to be sought and reached, and neglecting other important areas of concern.[6] Uganda's complex relationship with the International Criminal Court (ICC), too, has caused it to pursue accountability in clearly contradictory ways, including the GOU's referral of the situation in Northern Uganda to the ICC in December 2003, which contravened the Amnesty Act proclaimed in 2000.[7]

Fourth, for several reasons, the GOU's strategies have been largely ineffective. This is in part because development needs are astounding; indeed, the problems in Northern Uganda have been disaggregated from development policies in the rest of the country.[8] The conflict in Northern Uganda has not yet technically stopped and agreements on cessation of hostilities have not been signed, although, at the time of writing, the Lord's Resistance Army (LRA) has moved on to wage war and commit abuses in the Democratic Republic of Congo and Central African Republic. And the GOU continues to exaggerate some problems, while underestimating others to its political advantage; for example, the *Poverty Eradication Action Plan* (*PEAP*) says that "5 percent of the population has been displaced,"[9] while that number in Northern Uganda alone represents 80 percent of the population.[10] The GOU's ineffectiveness in this area is a purposeful miscalculation, designed so that by downplaying the severity of the issues, it can expend far less effort. This has been to the detriment of the people of Northern Uganda, where a "negative peace" has emerged.

Fifth, and perhaps most obvious, is the serious nature of underdevelopment in Uganda, as it intersects with long-standing conflicts throughout the country. Technically, Uganda is not yet a country in transition; as Robinson has suggested, it is a country in the "pre-transition" phase.[11] The socio-economic conditions surrounding transitional justice efforts have posed myriad difficulties.

These five factors intensify the problems with peacebuilding and transitional justice strategies in Uganda. They are, however, also important when considering how the GOU has responded to the goals and objectives of both the *PRDP* and the *PEAP*.

Background and history of conflict in Uganda

Extolled as the "pearl of Africa" by explorer Henry Stanley, Uganda is a country whose beauty belies a modern history filled with conflict and violence. Its relatively peaceful colonization by the British in 1894 was soon followed by bloodshed and war among the 56 different ethnic groups that co-exist within the country's boundaries. The ongoing conflict in Northern Uganda is yet another in a series of conflicts drawn loosely along ethnic and geographic lines.

The country achieved independence from the British in 1962, under Prime Minister Milton Obote. Obote's first term in power was characterized by significant numbers of riots and armed attacks.[12] In 1971, his army commander, General Idi Amin Dada, overthrew Obote and seized power. He then began a reign of terror, systematically murdering and torturing those he considered to stand in his way.[13] He targeted those who were seen to have supported Obote, especially people of Acholi and Langi descent, many of whom had tended to dominate the military. In 1972, Amin expelled more than 70,000 Asians living in Uganda, confiscating their property and businesses. During this time, soldiers and police conducted brutal campaigns of torture.[14] The number of people who were killed during this period is estimated at between 300,000[15] and 500,000,[16] earning Amin the nickname, "the butcher."

After a bitter conflict involving Tanzanian government forces, Amin's forces were defeated in 1979. Interim governments were declared in 1979 and 1980. As the result of rigged elections in 1980, Obote returned to power. The country was once again the target of extreme violence and abuse, this time far worse than anything experienced during Obote's first term in office. The paramilitary apparatus of the state again began its practice of routinely violating human rights, by means of rape, torture, looting, and destruction of property.[17] The scale of repression and abuse was roughly the same as it had been under Amin, only this time with a heightened and reinvigorated fury. Conservative estimates again place the number of those killed during this period at approximately 300,000[18] to 500,000.[19] Obote remained in office until July 1985 when he was overthrown, again by a faction of the Ugandan military. From July 1985, a military council governed for six months, until it, too, was overthrown.

At the head of the victorious National Resistance Movement (NRM, formerly the National Resistance Army—NRA) was Yoweri Museveni. When he seized power in 1986, he abolished all political parties except his own. He and his troops had been fighting against the regimes of Amin and Obote, as well as the transitional regimes, in Uganda since 1971. In 2006, Museveni remained in power after several controversial changes of the country's constitution and contentious elections.[20]

As with his predecessors, Museveni has continued to face considerable opposition from many of the 56 different ethnic groups throughout the country. Between 1986 and 2006, Museveni faced more than 20 armed insurgencies.[21] One of the longest lasting, and most devastating, conflicts is the one in Northern

Uganda. "The conflict in Acholiland began soon after Uganda's last regime change in January 1986. It was triggered [in part] by the NRM's methods for consolidating control over the northern parts of the country."[22] Joseph Kony, leader of the LRA, abducted children to conscript into his rebel forces, the boys to act as soldiers, and the girls to be used by him and his fellow rebels as their "wives,"[23] as well as carriers of supplies and even soldiers. He and his troops perpetrated brutal abuses against the people of Northern Uganda. Abducted child soldiers themselves are often forced to commit the most heinous of acts, and often against their own families.[24] In one community, for example, 79 percent of people reported having witnessed torture, 40 percent had witnessed killing, and 5 percent had been forced to physically harm another.[25]

Northern Uganda has been decimated by this conflict, which "has over the years spread across the entire northern region and parts of the east."[26] Those who are now 20 years old or younger have never known anything but the conditions of war and insecurity. Between 30,000 and 45,000 children have been abducted by the LRA.[27] In the early 2000s, children began the phenomenon of "night commuting," wherein an estimated 25,000 children living in these areas walked for miles each night to sleep in the relative safety of centers guarded by the Ugandan military, to avoid being abducted.[28]

At the height of the conflict, in 2004, it was estimated that 80 percent of the region's population were internally displaced persons within the region and living in camps for the internally displaced.[29] These camps are an "integral part of the Ugandan government's anti-insurgency policy. In some places, anyone who refused to move from their rural homes was forcibly displaced."[30] Effectively, the people were "herded into camps where they [were forced to] survive on relief aid."[31] Reports estimated that 1,000 people died each week as a result of the deplorable conditions within the camps.[32] A clear disconnect continues to exist between Northern Uganda and the rest of the country. As one human rights activist said, "We … have two countries in one—the north and the south. This is true politically and economically."[33] Although many have begun to return home, it has become increasingly apparent that the people of Northern Uganda now living in camps may never be able to return to their homes because many have lost their land, and many others may simply prefer to stay.[34] This could further hamper the process of ending the war and is likely to have a direct impact on the economic sustainability of the region.[35]

Although Kony and the LRA have moved on to other countries, including the Democratic Republic of Congo and the Central African Republic, in reality the war in Northern Uganda is far from over. It is not known precisely how many rebel soldiers remain in the bush with the LRA; estimates range from 200 to 20,000.[36] But a succession of peace talks held over the years have broken down, including the Juba talks initiated in 2006 between the LRA and the Government of Uganda. Although five separate agreements were signed during those talks, no comprehensive peace agreement was ever finalized.

Strategies and programs of the GOU

The Government of Uganda has implemented a number of policies and procedures to deal with peacebuilding and transitional justice—although neither one is as traditionally understood in the scholarly literature. Peacebuilding and transitional justice are sometimes presented as part of larger policies that deal with overall development and poverty eradication—although the GOU does acknowledge the inappropriateness of a development framework for dealing with conflict-related problems.[37] Nonetheless, many of the detailed policies surrounding peacebuilding and transitional justice are contained in the *Poverty Eradication Action Plan* and the *Peace, Recovery and Development Plan for Northern Uganda.* Beyond that, peacebuilding and transitional justice policies are presented in a sometimes random array of documents that have been implemented on an *ad hoc* and often-contradictory basis over a period of years. These policies are discussed below.

Peace, Recovery and Development Plan for Northern Uganda

> The PRDP has been prepared on the basis of lessons that have been learnt from the implementation of a plethora of programmes in the North by various actors. In light of these lessons the PRDP has been launched to address a number of key issues [including] conflict, growth and prosperity … [and] political, security and development links.[38]

These are attributed to "a 14-point strategy set out by H.E. President for the recovery of the North."[39] The document is intended to be in force during 2007–10.

The *PRDP* lays out four strategic objectives, including the following:

- consolidation of state authority;
- rebuilding and empowering communities;
- revitalization of the economy; and
- peacebuilding and reconciliation.[40]

Each of these objectives addresses some of the many elements involved in peacebuilding and transitional justice, and there are overlaps among objectives. For the purposes of this chapter, two of the strategic objectives have the most relevance: the consolidation of state authority, and peacebuilding and reconciliation.

The first strategic objective, the consolidation of state authority, seeks to expand police, judicial, and prison services, and strengthen local administration. This includes key activities of peacebuilding and transitional justice, including the facilitation of peace agreement provisions and the enhancement of police, judicial services, prisons, auxiliary forces, and local government. This includes gradual demilitarization and greater or lesser deployment of the Uganda People's Defence Force in various sub-regions.

The second, peacebuilding and reconciliation, seeks to address conflicts and build trust and reconciliation in the community through the improvement of local governance. Peacebuilding and transitional justice activities include public information, education, and communication and counseling programs, and programs for the demobilization and re-integration of ex-combatants. The *PRDP* promises a special focus on what it calls conflict management capacity, rebuilding social capital, and post-conflict stabilization. Reconciliation is assumed to have a natural fit with peacebuilding strategies, with no question asked as to the inclusion of what might otherwise be the programmatic purview of transitional justice policies.

Poverty Eradication Action Plan

The *Poverty Eradication Action Plan* is Uganda's IMF-mandated Poverty Reduction Strategy Paper, and was prepared:

> in broad consultation with stakeholders and development partners, including the staffs of the World Bank and the IMF. Updated every three years with annual progress reports, [it] describe[s] the country's macroeconomic, structural, and social policies in support of growth and poverty reduction, as well as associated external financing needs and major sources of financing.[41]

The plan states that the remaining challenges facing Uganda include the consolidation of national security, dealing with the consequences of conflict, and improving regional equity; restoring sustainable growth in the incomes of the poor; building strong social and economic infrastructure; enhancing human development; and using public resources more efficiently.[42] It is important, here, to note the IMF- and World Bank-friendly language as opposed to the language regularly used by Museveni and others in articulating the challenges faced by the country, because it reveals what these outside bodies and their technocrats expect Museveni will do—versus what has actually been done.[43] For example, Museveni often claimed that nothing needs to be done in Northern Uganda because "[S]ecurity in northern Uganda ha[s] been restored."[44] Yet both the *PEAP* and *PRDP*, written during the same period, acknowledged that it has not.

The goals of the *PEAP* are arranged in five pillars:

- economic management;
- production, competitiveness, and incomes;
- security, conflict-resolution, and disaster-management;
- good governance; and
- human development.[45]

As with the *PRDP*, many of the objectives and goals seem to flow from one pillar to another. For the purposes of this chapter, two pillars have the most relevance: security, conflict-resolution, and disaster-management; and good governance.

The first of these, security, conflict-resolution, and disaster-management, takes an "everything but the kitchen sink" approach, with goals including addressing rebel insurgency, cattle rustling, and prostitution[46]—suggesting that the GOU (or its master, the IMF) has no intention of addressing the underlying complexities of the problems. These aims are clearly disparate and ought to be addressed by different strategies and under different arms of government to be properly attended to.

The second, good governance, includes democracy, human rights, and what is called "political governance," as well as justice, law and order, and public accountability and transparency. Its key areas of focus include democratization, constitutional review, electoral politics, political governance, international conventions, and national governance, and only scant attention is paid to access to justice, its quality, efficiency, and effectiveness.

Amnesty Act

In November 1999, the Government of Uganda passed the Amnesty Act, which was enacted in January 2000. The Act reads as follows:

> An amnesty is declared in respect of any Ugandan who has at any time since the 26th day of January, 1986 engaged in or is engaging in war or armed rebellion against the government of the Republic of Uganda by:
>
> (a) actual participation in combat;
> (b) collaborating with the perpetrators of the war or armed rebellion;
> (c) committing any other crime in the furtherance of war or armed rebellion; or
> (d) assisting or aiding the conduct or prosecution of the war or armed rebellion.[47]

By July 2008, the Amnesty Commission had granted amnesty to 22,107 ex-combatants, called "reporters."[48]

The amnesty "was conceived as a tool for ending conflict … a significant step towards ending the conflict in the north and working towards a process of national reconciliation."[49] The Government of Uganda, however, is largely seen to have, at the very best, ambiguous support for the amnesty process, and has not presented a consistent position on the Amnesty Act since its enactment. Numerous informants questioned whether or not the government was really serious about the amnesty. One elderly man in Kitgum articulated a commonly held view: "Parliament said [the Amnesty Act] was ok, but the president himself didn't want it. This is no secret."[50]

This conception of amnesty is substantially different from amnesties that have been implemented in other situations of transitional justice. The self-amnesty granted in Chile, for example, was granted to military personnel in the early years of the military dictatorship, and in *blanket* form, to keep them from being prosecuted in the future. The amnesty granted in South Africa as part of the Truth and Reconciliation Commission process was granted on an *ad hoc* basis in exchange for testimony. The amnesty in Uganda was established *before* the end of the conflict. While people in Uganda appear to perceive of the amnesty as having been very much a tool to end the war, there is less clarity over the consequences it might have afterward. Even Parliament has vacillated over the potential applicability of the Amnesty Act to the "big fish" of the LRA, including Joseph Kony.[51]

Juba Agreements

The Government of Uganda and the Lord's Resistance Army have met several times in a series of failed peace talks including the Pece Stadium Accord (1988), the Addis Ababa Accord (1990), a series of peace talks (1994), and another set negotiated by Betty Bigombe (2005).[52] The latest round of peace talks began in August 2006 and petered out by May 2008. These were held in Juba, South Sudan. The Juba talks were brokered by the new Government of South Sudan, which "ha[d] a clear interest in ending the threat to regional security the northern Uganda conflict poses."[53] The involvement of the Government of South Sudan began in May 2006, when the LRA contacted South Sudanese Vice President Riek Machar and asked him to approach the GOU about commencing peace talks. The GOU and LRA were able to agree on the inclusion of five agenda items for the talks: cessation of hostilities; finding long-term solutions to conflict; accountability and reconciliation; ceasefire; and demobilization, disarmament, reintegration, and resettlement.[54]

The "Agreement on Accountability and Reconciliation" and the subsequent "Annexure to the Agreement on Accountability and Reconciliation"[55] are reasonably broad in their commitments to justice. None of the several references to traditional justice in any way define (nor, contrarily, do they limit) the form that such mechanisms might take, how they would be implemented, or who would have ultimate jurisdiction over them. At the same time, however, they are specific with regard to the kinds of institutions that are to be established to bring about this kind of justice.

The "Agreement on Accountability and Reconciliation" and the "Annexure" address what might be considered traditional transitional justice concerns. The "Annexure" commits the Government to "expeditiously prepare and develop the necessary legislation and modalities for implementing" all that the two "Accountability Agreements" contain.[56] Indeed, the Government is now obligated to undertake a range of activities related to justice. These include the enactment of legislation required to provide for the institutions to be created,[57] the adaptation of the existing legal framework to incorporate the terms of the agreements,[58] the creation of an investigations unit,[59] the provision of fair, speedy, and public hearings,[60] and the amendment of the Uganda Human Rights Commission or the Amnesty Act.[61] In addition, the Government has guaranteed that it will make arrangements for victim reparations[62] and to determine[63] and promote[64] the appropriate roles of traditional mechanisms.

The other four agreements include the kinds of activities normally sought through peacebuilding processes. These include cessation of hostilities and a permanent ceasefire. They also include, under the heading "comprehensive solutions," some preliminary power-sharing arrangements, as well as disarmament, demobilization, and reintegration of ex-combatants (DDR), economic development needs, the recognition of vulnerable groups, and important references to property rights and compensation including land and cattle. The fifth agreement explicitly includes DDR specifications with particular reference to children, youth, women, and those with special needs. In the absence of any kind of actual, sustained peacebuilding process, these agreements are considered to be "peacebuilding."

International Criminal Court Act, 2010

Subsequent to the referral by the government of the situation in Northern Uganda[65] to the Prosecutor of the International Criminal Court in 2003, Uganda began the process of amending its national legislation to allow its own national courts to proceed with prosecutions for genocide, crimes against humanity, and war crimes and to allow Uganda to fully cooperate with the ICC. The War Crimes Division of the High Court will be eligible to try any crimes committed from 1987, which the GOU considers the beginning of the conflict with the LRA. After nearly six years of study and debate, the bill was passed into law on 10 March 2010, to the wide protest of many from Northern Uganda who perceived the ICC as malicious and biased against those from Northern Uganda.

Not content to rely on the ICC alone, the GOU has also established a War Crimes Division of the High Court that will be suitable for these kinds of cases. Justices of international stature and with experience in international criminal courts have been appointed,[66] and a roster of staff, including a registry office with a Registrar, an office of the prosecutor, and office of the defense counsel, awaits a case to try.[67] The Government of Uganda, through its Justice, Law and Order Sector Transitional Justice Working Group, was trying to determine the modalities of the inclusion of customary law within the War Crimes Division of the High Court and elsewhere, as well as financial and workload considerations.[68]

The policies laid out above are important because, collectively, they prescribe the GOU's course of action on peacebuilding and transitional justice. As noted at the outset of this chapter, far from presenting any kind of dilemma, peacebuilding and transitional justice in Uganda have been addressed together, although the solutions are often contradictory or work to weaken both. In fact, both form a central part of Uganda's plan for national development.

Peacebuilding and transitional justice activities

While the policies presented above tell a story of goodwill and institutional practices intent on remedying the situation in Uganda—and in Northern Uganda, in particular—the Government's actions are far less promising. In programming on accountability, security-sector reform, DDR, development of the rule of law, land claims, displacement, and cattle-rustling, the Government's record tells a different story. As we shall see, there is a considerable gap between programming and policy for each of these activities.

Accountability

While the GOU has laid what appears to be a strong foundation for accountability in the country, it is the case that its record of holding to account those who are alleged to have committed criminal acts is, in fact, abysmal. Little or nothing has been done in this regard.

The Lord's Resistance Army has fought against Museveni almost from the moment that Museveni assumed power. For the most part, however, he has done little to quash their rebellion. One MP speculated openly about the reasons why Museveni has done little to end the conflict:

> First, he wants to leave the door open for the inflow of international funds, and so fuels the conflict. Second, Museveni knows that the North is full of opposition; if they were pacified, they would mount serious political opposition, so it's better to keep them disconnected and devastated politically, socially, and economically. Third, ideologically, Museveni believes that an impoverished society is easier to manage, so it's better to keep the situation in the north in turmoil.[69]

Aside from brutal campaigns waged by the UPDF, such as Operation Iron Fist (2002), Museveni seems to have been reluctant to do anything to halt the conflict with the LRA, or to bring them to justice. Throughout all of their interactions, the UPDF has failed to capture the members of the LRA against whom warrants have been issued. There is wide speculation that Museveni simply lacks the heart for their capture.

Even if he could catch them, Museveni has, in fact, backed away from at least two mechanisms of justice and accountability which he put into place. The first is the Amnesty Act (2000), discussed above. As an indication of his unhappiness with the Amnesty process, Museveni formally requested that the ICC investigate the actions of the LRA in December 2003.[70] This meant that the future of the Amnesty process was put in doubt. Yet his subsequent indecision regarding the ICC, the establishment of the War Crimes Division of the High Court, and the mounting speculation that Uganda will appeal to the Pre-Trial Chamber of the Court under the "complementarity" clause of the Rome Statute, or the "admissibility" clause, seems to indicate that Museveni has backed away from the ICC referral as well.[71]

It should be noted that ordinary national courts exist for the hearing of lesser cases in this regard—although these are rather dismally understaffed, "inadequate, vandalised and in some places non-existent."[72] Very few of those cases have, however, ever been heard in any of the available courts. Indeed, the amnesty has removed much of the need for this, since ex-combatants, once granted amnesty, may not be tried for the same crimes.

While it is the case that, during the height of the conflict, the community in Northern Uganda claimed to want "Peace First, Justice Later,"[73] this has now changed. The people of Northern Uganda *do* want accountability, but they are also sensitive to the extreme needs of their community, including what to do with ex-combatants who were abducted; how to deal with those who aided and abetted LRA soldiers, mostly their own young children; and how best they can resume their lives after conflict.

It is particularly interesting to juxtapose the strong and strident outrage that emerged from within communities across Uganda to the perceived imposition of the ICC against the relative silence from those same groups on the emergence of a War Crimes Division of the High Court at the national level, since both bodies are essentially aiming at the same outcome: the prosecution of senior LRA officials. While there has certainly been debate, many from within the international community have been part of the dialogue and have provided technical expertise surrounding the development of the War Crimes Division, now called the International Crimes Division (ICD), including scholars and the diplomatic and donor sector. Likewise, while many voices in Northern Uganda and elsewhere can be heard lamenting the fact that the Court will try suspects in Kampala and that they will not be tried via traditional justice mechanisms, such as *mato oput*, these voices are considerably more muted than on the ICC question.[74] This silence is due, in part, to the complexity of the situation, in which many people who have committed crimes have done so because they were forced, through abduction, for example. It is also due to an uncertainty about how the ICC will interact with those measures already in place in Uganda.

Security-sector reform

Questions related to the implementation and consolidation of transitional justice are clearly linked to peacebuilding—both in the programmatic and the policy decisions that are being made. One of the most important is the issue of security sector reform (SSR), which is pledged in any number of ways in the documents examined above. For example, the *PRDP* discusses military operations by the UPDF, demobilization of rebel forces, and disarmament of the Karamojong and others[75] and pledges to address these and other issues through its "consolidation of state authority" objective.[76] It speaks more specifically to reform of the Uganda Police Force,[77] the Uganda Prisons Service,[78] and the UPDF.[79] The *PEAP*, too, notes the critical nature of security needs.[80]

Yet SSR remains hung up on development-related problems. Further, security force and local defense unit members were involved in killings and extreme torture. Prison conditions were severe. And "the UPDF continued to be constrained by limited resources, including low pay and lack of vehicles, equipment, and training."[81] What ought to be an important facet of any successful peacebuilding or transitional justice strategy is stalled. As such, SSR is not currently being used to strengthen any of the proposed, existing, or non-existent peacebuilding or transitional justice programming.

DDR

Indeed, questions of disarmament, demobilization, and reintegration are also central to both peacebuilding and transitional justice. Yet "DDR" as understood in Uganda is not DDR as understood in the scholarly literature on the topic. Although Uganda has "no formal demobilization process for captured, escaped or rescued LRA child soldiers,"[82] the Amnesty Commission is involved in a limited fashion in demobilization and resettlement through a series of satellite teams, called Demobilization and Resettlement Teams (DRT), which operate in districts around Uganda. These teams are responsible to "decommission arms, demobilize, resettle and reintegrate reporters."[83] However, these responsibilities are largely left to other agencies to carry out, and the government plays a fairly minor role overall. "There are six DRT offices around the country ... all of which rely heavily on other government agencies, civil society organizations, the community and donors for successful implementation."[84]

Non-governmental actors working in Northern Uganda on programs for formerly abducted child soldiers provide the majority of assistance, including psychosocial reintegration and rehabilitation, along with physical treatment. At the height of the conflict, 13 reception centers were in operation in Northern Uganda.[85] There is mounting evidence to suggest that a number of ex-combatants failed to pass through the reception centers, although firm numbers are not available.[86] Other agencies have also been involved in the rehabilitation of ex-combatants, though outside of the formal reception center model.[87]

Another form of DDR in Uganda is child recruitment by the Uganda People's Defence Force (UPDF)—although this is not legitimately DDR, by any definition. When ex-combatant children are captured by the UPDF, they are typically handed over to Child Protection Units for debriefing and medical care, and then transferred to reception centers, discussed further below. There are reports indicating that that some children are being absorbed directly into the UPDF without being sent into the rehabilitation programs.[88] There is a long record of ex-combatants being absorbed directly into the ranks of the UPDF; many ex-combatants report being strongly coerced to join.[89] Some children, further, report harassment, beatings, and other forms of mistreatment there.[90]

> [T]here is a policy of actively recruiting younger men into local defence forces or into the UPDF, allegedly with a degree of compulsion. A special battalion of the UPDF, the 105th, has been established specifically for this purpose. By the end of 2004, almost eight hundred had been integrated in this way (to the considerable unease of UNICEF and other agencies, because many had participated in atrocities and some were thought to be under-age for recruitment).[91]

This recruitment or absorption is seen as something of a third option for viable DDR by many in Uganda, along with giving ex-combatants the opportunity to pursue further education, and offering vocational training, although this is certainly not the perspective of the United Nations and other agencies.[92]

Traditional leaders have also played a strong role in the rehabilitation of formerly abducted children. Simultaneously, and in collaboration with the work of the rehabilitation centers, the Acholi traditional leaders, *Ker Kwaro Acholi*, have taken an active role in reintegrating children back into the community. *Ker Kwaro Acholi* routinely assist returnees to carry out traditional cleansing ceremonies. One is a ceremony called *mato oput* (drinking the bitter herb), and another is called *nyono tong gweno* (a welcome ceremony in which an egg is stepped on over an *opobo* twig). Overall, the ceremonies allow the Acholi to acknowledge that this person has been accepted back into the community, and that the community is pleased to have them back.[93] In many cases, these ceremonies appear to have more cultural relevance than other initiatives.[94] However, some of the literature has been quite critical of these.[95]

Rule of law

The GOU recognizes the "[d]eterioration of law and order … certain districts, particularly in North Eastern Uganda, are affected by continued lawlessness, weak state authority and inter-ethnic clashes";[96] "Law and order … remains weak."[97] As such, the *PRDP* proposes to establish law and order and enhance the functionality of judicial and legal services under its objective to "consolidate state authority."

While the GOU has pledged to spend approximately US $6,89 million on judicial reform,[98] this amounts to just over 1 percent of the total *PRDP* spending—and is roughly one-tenth of what will be spent on areas such as "Woodcover and Community Forestry." More is budgeted than what the GOU has pledged. The balance of spending in this sector is expected to be picked up, presumably, by international donors.

It is certainly clear that a compelling argument could and should be made concerning the link between rule of law programming and the successful carrying out of transitional justice policies. The consolidation of law and order throughout the country and the rebuilding of the judicial infrastructure would provide a basis for understanding the kinds of accountability measures that might be put in place, as well as prevent more abuses from occurring. Unfortunately, this kind of nuanced argument is completely missing.

Combining peacebuilding and transitional justice: together, but not integrated

In Uganda, processes of peacebuilding and transitional justice are not being run side by side; they are being programmed together. Yet, as demonstrated above, the GOU's intertwining of peacebuilding and transitional justice, and, further, with broader development goals, has not managed to improve the promotion of either one. The peacebuilding and transitional justice activities spelled out in the documents outlined above have only partially been achieved. Many have failed outright, or have never been given the chance to succeed.

Given the two competing claims prominent in the literature, that attempting to promote accountability would undermine peacebuilding efforts, or that accountability is essential to peacebuilding, one might expect that the intricate linkages between the two would result in stronger programs on both sides of the equation. In Uganda, quite the opposite is true; accountability and peacebuilding programming is weak throughout the country, and particularly in Northern Uganda. Coupled as it is with development policies and plans, peacebuilding and transitional justice appear to get lost in the jumble of ideas that are thrown around in post-conflict settings. In the end, very little of either one is actually carried out.

Transitional justice has failed in Uganda; peacebuilding has not succeeded either. Rather than finding evidence of any clear will to carry out either one, many of the ideas presented in the national plans and discussed here amount to no more than a "wish list." While transitional justice and peacebuilding efforts certainly need to be funded to a much higher degree, and taken more seriously than has been done until now, this is only part of the story. The coordination of actors and programs in both peacebuilding and transitional justice also requires a significant level of care that is missing at the present time.

Uganda is a country in which "transitional justice" is being applied before any kind of actual transition has taken place. If the use of transitional justice in Uganda is premature, it might only be natural for problems endemic to pre-transitional situations to abound. The expected outcomes in this case cannot be the same as for truly transitional societies, and expectations will have to be adjusted. It is, however, difficult to tell whether accountability measures already in place in Uganda actually affect the overall peacebuilding process.[99]

The GOU has been forced to deal with questions of accountability—or, at least, to make it look as though it is doing so—not least because of the presence of the ICC and the situation under review by the Court. To be sure, the referral of the situation in Northern Uganda to the Office of the Prosecutor of the ICC in many ways triggered a series of inventions and interventions which remain, still, to be clarified. The legitimacy of those who negotiated the Juba Agreements and the outcome of these agreements are also unclear.

There is a dilemma, to be sure, but it is not between peacebuilding and transitional justice. It is between development and peacebuilding/transitional justice. At stake is what qualifies as legitimate country programming, in meeting the real needs of the people of Uganda, and what is taken seriously. The case of Uganda warns us against the incorporation of peacebuilding and transitional justice efforts into development programming. At the very least, development plans that entail such activities need to accord them more respect and support.

Notes

1 Uganda Human Rights Commission, *11th Annual Report of the Uganda Human Rights Commission to the Parliament of the Republic of Uganda* (Kampala: UHRC, 2008), pp. 148–51. The Uganda Human Rights Commission is a government body whose chairperson and other members are appointed directly by the President. See Republic of Uganda, Cap.24, *The Uganda Human Rights Act (2000).*

2 Republic of Uganda, *Peace, Recovery and Development Plan for Northern Uganda (PRDP) 2007–2010* (Kampala: Government of Uganda, September 2007), p. 28.

3 Republic of Uganda, *PRDP*, op. cit., p. 20.

4 Republic of Uganda, *PRDP*, op. cit., p. 103.

5 Republic of Uganda, *PRDP*, op. cit., pp. 103–05.

6 International Monetary Fund, "Press Release No. 06/14: IMF Executive Board Completes Final Review of Uganda's PRGF Arrangement and Approves 16-month Policy Support Instrument," 24 January 2006 (press release online); available from <www.imf.org/external/np/sec/pr/2006/pr0614.htm> (accessed 6 February 2010).

7 Museveni officially referred the situation to the ICC in December 2003. It has been commonly assumed that Museveni approached the Court first. Information has surfaced that the Chief Prosecutor actually approached Museveni to ask him to refer the situation. See Nicholas Waddell and Phil Clark, eds, *Courting Conflict? Justice, Peace and the ICC in Africa* (London: Royal African Society, March 2008), p. 43. There is a great deal of debate about what this discrepancy means.

8 Republic of Uganda, *PRDP*, op. cit., p. 103.

9 Ministry of Finance, Planning and Economic Development, Government of Uganda, *Poverty Eradication Action Plan (PEAP) (2004/5–2007/8)*, IMF Country Report No. 05/307 (Washington, DC: IMF, August 2005), p. 99.

10 Geresome Latim, Secretary to the Paramount Chief of Acholi, interview by author, 22 November 2004, Gulu town, Uganda; also World Vision, *Pawns of Politics: Children, Conflict and Peace in Northern Uganda* (Kampala: World Vision, 2004), p. 4.

11 Darryl Robinson, presentation at the conference, "Cross-Purposes? International Law and Political Settlements," held by the Nationalism and Ethnic Conflict Research Group, The University of Western Ontario, 9 June 2007.

12 Dirk Berg-Schlosser and Rainer Siegler, *Political Stability and Development: A Comparative Analysis of Kenya, Tanzania and Uganda* (Boulder, CO: Lynne Rienner Publishers, 1990), p. 196.

13 Nancy G. Wright, "Uganda: History From 1971," *Encyclopedia of Africa South of the Sahara*, ed. John Middleton (New York: Charles Scribner's Sons, 1996), p. 306.

14 Berg-Schlosser and Siegler, op. cit., p. 199; Edward Khiddu-Makubuya, "Paramilitarism and Human Rights," in *Conflict Resolution in Uganda*, ed. Kumar Rupesinghe (Oslo: International Peace Research Institute, 1989), pp. 141–57.

15 Philip Briggs, *Uganda* (Old Saybrook, CT: The Globe Pequot Press, 1998), p. 23.

16 Yoweri Kaguta Museveni, *Sowing the Mustard Seed* (London: Macmillan, 1997), p. 41.

17 Berg-Schlosser and Siegler, op. cit., p. 199; Khiddu-Makubuya, "Paramilitarism," op. cit., p. 153.

18 *Uganda* (Brooklyn, NY: Interlink Books, 1998), p. 53; Thomas P. Ofcansky, *Uganda: Tarnished Pearl of Africa* (Boulder, CO: Westview, 1996), p. 55.

19 Abdul Nadduli, LC5 District Chairman, interview with author, 17 November 2004, Luweero town, Uganda.

20 Museveni was returned to power in the first multi-party elections since his accession to power, on 23 February 2006, reportedly with 59 percent of the vote.

21 These include rebellions by the Action Restore Peace, Allied Democratic Forces, Apac rebellion, Citizen Army for Multiparty Politics, Force Obote Back, Former Uganda National Army, Holy Spirit Movement, the Lord's Army, Lord's Resistance Army, National Federal Army, National Union for the Liberation of Uganda, Ninth October

Movement, People's Redemption Army, Uganda Christian Democratic Army, Uganda Federal Democratic Front, Uganda Freedom Movement, Ugandan National Democratic Army, Uganda National Federal Army, Ugandan National Liberation Front, Ugandan National Rescue Fronts I and II, Ugandan People's Army, Ugandan People's Democratic Army, Uganda Salvation Army, and the West Nile Bank Front. Compiled from Lucy Hovil and Zachary Lomo, *Working Paper 11: Behind the Violence: Causes, Consequences and the Search for Solutions to the War in Northern Uganda* (Kampala: Refugee Law Project, February 2004), p. 4; and Lucy Hovil and Zachary Lomo, *Working Paper 15: Whose Justice? Perceptions of Uganda's Amnesty Act 2000: The Potential for Conflict Resolution and Long-Term Reconciliation* (Kampala: Refugee Law Project, February 2005), p. 6.

22 Catherine Barnes and Okello Lucima, "Introduction," *Accord* (2002) 11, p. 1.

23 This is a common euphemism for a sex slave.

24 Lucy Hovil and Joanna Quinn, *Working Paper 17: Peace First, Justice Later* (Kampala: Refugee Law Project, July 2005), p. 3.

25 Tim Allen, *War and Justice in Northern Uganda: An Assessment of the International Criminal Court's Intervention* (London: Crisis States Research Centre, Development Studies Institute, London School of Economics, February 2005), p. 24.

26 UN Office for the Coordination of Humanitarian Affairs, "Uganda: War-ravaged North Rues Museveni Win," IRINnews.org (1 March 2006); available from <www.irinnews.org/print.asp?ReportID=51960> (accessed 10 March 2006).

27 Tim Allen points out that "the scale of abduction is a matter of speculation" due to insufficient monitoring. See Allen, *War and Justice in Northern Uganda*, op. cit., p. iii.

28 *"When the Sun Sets, We Start To Worry … ": An Account of Life in Northern Uganda*, OCHA/IRIN, November 2003, p. 8.

29 Geresome Latim, Secretary to the Paramount Chief of Acholi, interview by author, 22 November 2004, Gulu town, Uganda; also World Vision, *Pawns of Politics*, op. cit., p. 4.

30 Allen, *War and Justice in Northern Uganda*, op. cit., p. 23.

31 Moses Odokonyero, "Acholi's Political 'Elephant Breed' Fails," *The Monitor* (Kampala), 10 March 2006.

32 Betty Bigombe and John Prendergast, "Stop the Crisis in Northern Uganda," *The Philadelphia Inquirer*, 21 February 2006.

33 James Otto quoted in UN Office for the Coordination of Humanitarian Affairs, "Uganda: War-ravaged North Rues Museveni Win," op. cit.

34 "UNDMT Technical Group Status Report: Preparatory Planning for Displaced Persons" as cited in Chris Dolan, "Understanding War and Its Continuation: The Case of Northern Uganda" (PhD diss., University of London, 2005), p. 167.

35 Hovil and Quinn, *Peace First, Justice Later*, op. cit., p. 9.

36 The exact number of abductees in the conflict is unknown. One study estimates that "the LRA abducted 54,000 to 75,000 people, including 25,000 to 38,000 children, into their ranks between 1986 and 2006." Phong N. Pham, Patrick Vinck, and Eric Stover, "The Lord's Resistance Army and Forced Conscription in Northern Uganda," *Human Rights Quarterly*, 30.2 (May 2008), p. 404. "The scale of abduction is a matter of speculation" due to insufficient monitoring. Allen, *War and Justice in Northern Uganda*, op. cit., p. iii. Forced conscription has been reported in many of the conflicts that have taken place since 1962, into both Government of Uganda and rebel ranks. Dennis Pain, *The Bending of Spears: Producing Consensus for Peace and Development in Northern Uganda* (London: International Alert, 1997), p. 29.

37 Republic of Uganda, *PRDP*, op. cit., p. 20.

38 Ibid., p. vi.

39 Museveni's 14 points are the following: "1. elimination of the terrorist threat to stability; 2. building of security and access roads; 3. provision of water; 4. revival and re-enhancement of education; 5. provision of emergency relief; 6. health, immunisation and educational outreach, including an all-out war against HIV/AIDS;

7. farming with oxen and ploughs for food security and income generation among the poor; 8. provision of light processing facilities such as rice hurlers and maize millers; 9. enhanced micro-finance for micro-business by ex-LRA; 10. re-education and re-orientation of the minds and hearts of the population towards peace and development rather than war, and psychosocial counselling for children and others rescued from LRA fighting ranks; 11. vocational/skills training, especially for young people; 12. outreach to the local population; 13. beginning with industrialisation in Northern Uganda by, for instance, helping the sugar industry … and a biofuel industry … and a fruit processing factory … ; 14. hydro-power development … "; Republic of Uganda, *PRDP*, op. cit., pp. 18–19.

40 Republic of Uganda, *PRDP*, op. cit., pp. vii–viii.

41 Ministry of Finance, *PEAP*, op. cit., p. i.

42 Ministry of Finance, *PEAP*, op. cit., p. ii.

43 Republic of Uganda, *PRDP*, op. cit., pp. 16–17.

44 Agness Nandutu, "Museveni Blames Donors Over Funds," *The Monitor* (Kampala), 10 March 2006.

45 Ministry of Finance, *PEAP*, op. cit., p. xv.

46 As discussed below, extensive cattle rustling has affected many parts of Northern and North-Eastern Uganda, particularly in areas including Karamoja, but also across the Greater North. It is symptomatic of endemic problems including widespread famine, the proliferation of small arms, modernization, and the disappearance of traditional modes of livelihood.

47 The Republic of Uganda, *Amnesty Act 2000*, Part II.3(1).

48 Moses Draku, Principal Public Relations Officer, Amnesty Commission, interview by author, 7 July 2008, Kampala, Uganda.

49 Hovil and Lomo, *Working Paper 15: Whose Justice? Perceptions of Uganda's Amnesty Act 2000*, op. cit., p. 6.

50 Hovil and Lomo, *Working Paper 15: Whose Justice? Perceptions of Uganda's Amnesty Act 2000*, op. cit., p. 18.

51 In April 2010, the Minister of State for Internal Affairs, Matia Kasaija, requested that Parliament agree not to grant amnesty to Kony, Dominic Ongwen, Okot Odhiambo, and Thomas Kwoyelo, and then withdrew his request. See Parliament of Uganda, *Parliament of Uganda eNewsletter* 3.35 (April 12–16, 2010), p. 1.

52 *Listen to the People: Peace and Reconciliation in Northern Uganda* (Kampala: HURIPEC, 3 May 2004), pp. 92–93.

53 Refugees International, *Bulletin: Uganda: Challenges of Peace and Justice* (Washington: Refugees International, 19 February 2008), p. 1.

54 The agreements were as follows: *Agreement on Cessation of Hostilities* (26 August 2006); *Agreement on Comprehensive Solutions* (2 May 2007); *Agreement on Accountability and Reconciliation* (29 June 2007) and the subsequent *Annexure to the Agreement on Accountability and Reconciliation* (19 February 2008); *Agreement on a Permanent Ceasefire* (23 February 2008); *Agreement on Disarmament, Demobilisation and Reintegration* (29 February 2008); *Agreement on Implementing and Monitoring Mechanisms* (29 February 2008).

55 In this chapter, these two agreements are hereafter referred to as the "Principal Agreement" and the "Annexure," respectively. Together, they are referred to as the "Accountability Agreements."

56 Government of Uganda and Lord's Resistance Army/Movement, "Annexure to the Agreement on Accountability and Reconciliation" (Juba, 19 February 2008), Art. 2.0.

57 Government of Uganda and Lord's Resistance Army/Movement, "Annexure," Art. 4.0.

58 Government of Uganda and Lord's Resistance Army/Movement, "Agreement on Accountability and Reconciliation" (Juba, 29 June 2007), Art. 4.4.

59 Government of Uganda and Lord's Resistance Army/Movement, "Annexure," Art. 10.0.

60 Government of Uganda and Lord's Resistance Army/Movement, "Principal Agreement," Art. 3.2.
61 Government of Uganda and Lord's Resistance Army/Movement, "Principal Agreement," Art. 14.4.
62 Government of Uganda and Lord's Resistance Army/Movement, "Annexure," Art. 16.0.
63 Government of Uganda and Lord's Resistance Army/Movement, "Annexure," Art. 20.0.
64 Government of Uganda and Lord's Resistance Army/Movement, "Principal Agreement," Art. 3.1.
65 See note 7, above.
66 Appointed by Principal Jus. James Ogoola, these are Jus. Dan Akiiki-Kiiza, Head Justice, who served at Sierra Leone's Special Court for Sierra Leone (2004–06), Jus. Eldad Mwangusya, Deputy Head, and Justice Faith Ibanda Nahamya, who also served at Sierra Leone's SCSL. See also Bill Oketch, "Uganda Set for First War Crimes Trial," *IWPR Institute for War and Peace Reporting*, 14 July 2010; available from <http://iwpr.net/print/report-news/uganda-set-first-war-crimes-trial>; accessed 29 November 2010.
67 Hillary Nsamba, "Ogoola Names Judges on Anti-Corruption, War Crimes Court," *The New Vision*, 1 October 2008; available from <www.newvision.co.ug/D/8/12/629897/war%20crimes%20court%20Akiiki-%20kiiza>; accessed 30 September 2008.
68 Christopher Gashirabake, Ministry of Justice and Constitutional Affairs, interview by author, 4 July 2008, Kampala, Uganda and Hon. Jus. James Ogoola, Principal Justice, High Court and Chairman, Transitional Justice Working Group, interview by author, 25 September 2008, Kampala, Uganda.
69 Author's interview with MP from northern municipality who requested anonymity, 3 November 2004, Kampala, Uganda.
70 See note 8, above.
71 In fact, complementarity is a subset of the question of admissibility.
72 Republic of Uganda, *PRDP*, op. cit., p. 45.
73 See Hovil and Quinn, *Working Paper 17: Peace First, Justice Later*, op. cit.
74 See, for example, Tim Allen, *Trial Justice* (London: Zed Books, 2006).
75 Republic of Uganda, *PRDP*, op. cit., p. 27.
76 Republic of Uganda, *PRDP*, op. cit., p. 38.
77 Republic of Uganda, *PRDP*, op. cit., p. 42.
78 Republic of Uganda, *PRDP*, op. cit., p. 48.
79 Republic of Uganda, *PRDP*, op. cit., p. 51.
80 Ministry of Finance, *PEAP*, op. cit., p. 113.
81 US Department of State, "Uganda: Country Report on Human Rights Practices 2008," 25 February 2009; available from <www.state.gov/g/drl/rls/hrrpt/2008/af/119030.htm> (accessed 7 February 2010).
82 The Coalition to Stop the Use of Child Soldiers, *Child Soldiers Global Report 2004* (report online); available from <www.child-soldiers.org/document_get.php?id=801> (accessed 28 April 2007).
83 *Amnesty Act 2000*, op. cit., S.12.
84 Hovil and Lomo, *Working Paper 15: Whose Justice? Perceptions of Uganda's Amnesty Act 2000*, op. cit., p. 7.
85 Erin Baines, Eric Stover, and Marieke Wierda, *War-Affected Children and Youth in Northern Uganda: Toward a Brighter Future: An Assessment Report* (Chicago: John D. and Catherine T. MacArthur Foundation, 2006), p. 33.
86 Tim Allen, "A Review of Lessons Learned by Reception Centres on Effective Interventions for Former Abductees in Northern Uganda: A Preliminary Study, UNICEF and USAID, October 2005," in *War-Affected Children and Youth in Northern Uganda: Toward a Brighter Future: An Assessment Report*, eds Erin Baines, Eric Stover, and Marieke Wierda (Chicago: John D. and Catherine T. MacArthur Foundation, 2006), p. 18.

87 Edward Sembidde, Save the Children in Uganda, interview by author, 26 November 2004, Kampala, Uganda.

88 Stephen Charchuk, "An Assessment of the Current Community-Wide System for Rehabilitation and Reintegration of Child Soldiers in Northern Uganda" (MA thesis, Royal Roads University, 2007), p. 39.

89 Refugees International, "Northern Uganda: Child Mothers and Returnees Require Special Care," 7 November 2002; available from <www.refugeesinternational.org/content/article/detail/827> (accessed 22 April 2007).

90 Ibid.

91 Tim Allen, *Trial Justice* (London: Zed Books, 2006), pp. 77–78.

92 United Nations High Commission on Human Rights, *Report of the United Nations High Commissioner for Human Rights on the Mission Undertaken by Her Office, Pursuant to Commission Resolution 2000/60, To Assess the Situation on the Ground with Regard to the Abduction of Children from Northern Uganda*, 9 November 2001, E/CN.4/2002/86.

93 Hovil and Quinn, *Peace First, Justice Later*, op. cit., p. 24.

94 Joanna R. Quinn, "Comparing Formal and Informal Mechanisms of Acknowledgement in Uganda," a paper prepared for presentation on the panel, "Africa as a Subject of International Justice," at the International Studies Association Annual Meeting, San Diego, CA, 23 March 2006, pp. 23–27.

95 George Kegoro, "The Place of Informal Justice Mechanisms in Post Conflict Peace and Justice Issues," a paper prepared for presentation at the Headline Seminar on the Rule of Law in Fragile and Conflict-Affected Countries, at the World Bank, Washington, DC, 21 July 2009. See also Nagy's chapter in this volume.

96 Republic of Uganda, *PRDP*, op. cit., p. 23.

97 Republic of Uganda, *PRDP*, op. cit., p. 24.

98 Republic of Uganda, *PRDP*, op. cit., p. 137.

99 There are interesting parallels to be made, in this regard, with Par Engstrom's chapter in this volume.

12 Colombia: Accountability and DDR in the pursuit of peace?

Jemima García-Godos

Introduction

Can transitional justice be applied before the end of conflict? Can it be applied in the absence of political transitions? In Colombia, the explicit inclusion of accountability measures in the negotiations with the paramilitaries, and the subsequent institutionalization of specific transitional justice mechanisms, illustrate one way in which transitional justice can relate to peacebuilding processes. In 2002, peace talks between the Colombian government and paramilitary armed forces led to the demobilization of the umbrella organization *Autodefensas Unidas de Colombia* (AUC). In July 2005, Law 975 (known as the "Law of Justice and Peace") was passed, with the purpose "to facilitate the peace processes, as well as the individual or collective reincorporation of the members of the illegal armed group back into civilian life, protecting the right to truth, justice and reparation of the victims."[1] Soon after, the government created specialized bodies, including the National Commission on Reparation and Reconciliation (*Comisión Nacional de Reparación y Reconciliación*—CNRR) and the National Unit for Justice and Peace (*Unidad Nacional de Fiscalías para la Justicia y la Paz*—UNFJP), at the Prosecutor General's Office, to implement the various tasks envisaged by the law.[2] A complex institutional apparatus has been put in place to implement this legislation. The conflict with the guerrillas, however, continues, and the negotiations with the paramilitaries and the implementation of the Law of Justice and Peace occurred during the two administrations of democratically elected president Álvaro Uribe. In other words, no obvious political transition has occurred. Based on the empirical evidence, the answer to the two opening questions seems to be affirmative. Thus, a third question arises from the Colombia experience: Can accountability and disarmament, demobilization, and reintegration of ex-combatants (DDR) be applied at the same time in pursuit of peace?

The ongoing Colombian experience with transitional justice presents a puzzle for political observers, academics, and human rights activists alike. The Colombian process involves a clear link between the demobilization of illegal armed groups and attending to the rights of the victims. Indeed, the process involves both the demobilization of illegal armed groups *and* the implementation of victims' rights—at the same time and through the same legal instrument.[3] As part of the process, a complex scheme of measures has been developed encompassing retributive justice, truth-seeking, and individual and collective victim reparations. While the protection and promotion of victims' rights to truth, justice, and reparation are the main demands of victims' organizations and many other voices from civil society, the process has been overshadowed by reports of the limited effect of demobilization by the paramilitaries and their reorganization under new structures. The progress achieved by specific transitional justice measures varies greatly indeed, but it is not insignificant. As the Colombian process moves on to a new phase with the approval of the "Victims' Law,"[4] I will seek to assess the results so far of this particular combination of DDR with transitional justice mechanisms, and specifically to evaluate the effects that these measures may have on the overall objectives of accountability and peacebuilding in Colombia. In this chapter I argue that engaging in transitional justice and DDR at the same time is a challenging task mainly because the success of the process depends on its legitimacy. Legitimacy in turn, depends on the effective implementation of the components of both processes. Once established, the instruments of transitional justice and DDR develop their own dynamics, capable of moving the process forward—or backwards. For all its limitations, the Justice and Peace process marks a milestone in the quest for justice and accountability in Colombia.

The chapter begins with a brief history of the Colombian armed conflict, followed by an account of the transitional justice processes in the country and their current structure and implementation. The process involves various institutional actors, making inter-institutional coordination both a necessity and a challenge. I then briefly discuss the DDR policies implemented parallel to the transitional justice process, seeking to identify points of complementarity and contradiction between these two fields. I conclude with lessons learned concerning the combination of accountability with DDR measures in the Colombian experience.

The Colombian armed conflict

Armed conflict has been a feature of Colombian history since its independence in 1810, although the intensity, the locations, and the actors involved have changed over time. Before and during the nationwide civil war known as *La Violencia* (1948–57) the antagonists were the two economic, social, and political elites organized under the Liberal and Conservative parties. In 1957 they reached a peace agreement whereby power was to be shared equally between the parties for 16 years. The political regime thus changed from a two-party system to a consociational regime called the National Front.[5] However, the inter-elite war was soon replaced by an anti-regime insurgency waged by various guerrilla groups; this conflict continues until this day.[6] The human cost of this conflict has been considerable. It is estimated that 94,000 people (51,500 civilians) died as a consequence of the armed conflict in the period 1964–2007.[7] Close to 7,700 were forcibly disappeared, 51,500 were kidnapped, and at least 11,000 were tortured. About 4,500 massacres were carried out, and between 3 and 4.6 million people were forcibly displaced.[8]

According to the CNRR, the current conflict can be traced back to 1964, when the first of the communist guerrillas, FARC-EP (*Fuerzas Armadas Revolucionarias de Colombia—Ejército del Pueblo*), the ELN (*Ejército de Liberación Nacional*), and EPL (*Ejército Popular de Liberación*) were established.[9] In the 1970s these groups were joined by a "second wave of guerrillas," most of which demobilized by 1989–90. The establishment of paramilitary groups coincided with the formation of the first communist guerrillas. The origin of paramilitary groups can be linked to the laws enabling and/or encouraging the existence of pro-systemic forces, in 1965.[10] This meant legalizing the formation of private self-defense or paramilitary groups, a measure later endorsed by Congress.[11] This legal framework remained in place until 1989, when it was eliminated during peace negotiations with the "second wave" of guerrillas.[12] As the FARC and ELN regained ground in the early 1990s, a new legal framework created self-defense groups, known as *Convivir*.[13] The differences between these and traditional paramilitaries were more a matter of definition than practice.[14] From these groups developed the modern paramilitaries, one of the most violent actors in the armed conflict, which were later organized under the banner *Autodefensas Unidas de Colombia*.[15]

The AUC evolved from the regionally based *Autodefensas Campesinas de Córdoba y Urabá* (ACCU), founded in 1986. By 2005 the AUC had some 30,000 members.[16] Over time, the paramilitaries consolidated control and started to engage and displace the guerrillas. The numerous local and regional self-defense groups enjoyed great support from the national army and their founders in local government, as well as from the drugs and rural elites. In the 1990s the balance of power within these fragmented groups shifted from the original leadership asserted by rural elites to military commanders. The paramilitaries took over areas controlled by drug-lords and guerrillas, co-opting and expelling cartels and rural elites, and eventually controlled a large percentage of the drug trade.[17]

The military expansion of the paramilitary forces ran parallel with their incursion into politics. The areas under their control became strictly regulated, and the official decentralization process of the 1990s had the unintended effect of tightening their grip on local and regional political institutions. By controlling local constituencies, the paramilitaries were also given access to national politics. In 2002 they claimed to control 35 percent of the Colombian national Congress, and one-third of Colombia's municipalities.[18] In December 2002 the AUC declared a unilateral ceasefire, a government precondition for talks with any of the armed groups. Negotiations were formalized on 15 July 2003 with the Pact of Santa Fé de Ralito, whereby AUC leaders agreed to fully demobilize by the end of 2005.[19] Starting in 2003—even before the negotiations had concluded—by 2006 some 37 AUC groups had demobilized.[20]

A legal framework for peace negotiations and accountability: the introduction of transitional justice in Colombia

The main legal instrument regulating the Colombian process, the 2005 Law of Justice and Peace (Law 975), clearly links the demobilization of illegal armed groups and the rights of the victims. Its origins lie in several previous legislative attempts to end the armed conflict.[21] A law passed in 2002 gave the government the legal mandate to initiate a process of negotiation with one of the "armed groups at the margins of the law," the paramilitaries.[22] This law established the legal framework to enable peace negotiations and to initiate the codification of victims' rights, the regulation of demobilization, and the reinsertion of former paramilitaries into society.[23] These instruments were strongly criticized and seen by many as legal tools guaranteeing impunity instead of punishment for AUC members, while granting them benefits that few in Colombia enjoyed.[24]

Congressional legislation was necessary to finalize the negotiation process. The first bill presented by the government (known as the "Alternative Penalties Law") proposed to guarantee amnesty for all demobilized armed actors, based on a restorative concept suggesting that criminal punishment would not contribute to reconciliation.[25] The bill was heavily criticized by national and international human rights organizations, victims' organizations, and some political groups, and was rejected by the Congress.[26] A new bill was drafted by the allies of the executive in Congress and was passed on 25 July 2005 as Law 975, the "Law of Justice and Peace." The law utilizes the discourse of transitional justice, acknowledging the need for retributive justice and recognizing the role of the victims and their rights in the peace process. By the time the law was approved, the AUC had already begun to demobilize in great numbers, and continued to do so even after the terms set for demobilization in 2003 had changed.

Shortly after the approval of Law 975, a case was filed at the Colombian Constitutional Court, questioning its constitutionality. Ruling C-370 of 2006 by the court found the overall law to be constitutional, while finding particular aspects of it unconstitutional and in need of different interpretation and implementation.[27] Supplementary decrees have amended the legislation further.[28] The legal content of the law is thus now significantly different from what the paramilitary leaders agreed to when they began dismantling their organizations in 2003, and, as a consequence, some paramilitaries withdrew from the process.[29] The process of demobilization continued and by 2007 president Uribe proclaimed that the paramilitaries no longer existed in Colombia.[30]

The other beneficiaries of the Peace and Justice process: victims of the Colombian armed conflict

Law 975 addresses two very different types of actors: members of illegal armed groups willing to demobilize and the victims of the Colombian armed conflict. It is necessary here to emphasize that the overall label of "victims" encompasses a very large and extremely heterogeneous group of people, in terms of composition, background, organization, outlook, and interests. Common to all victims is that they have experienced at least one form of human rights violation, yet their ways of dealing with their victimization vary. Not all victims join or are organized in specific groups or associations, although there is a large number of victims' organizations at the national, regional, and local levels. They are usually based on geographical distinctions or specific characteristics of the victim group, such as the type of violation suffered; some also have a broader base in terms of composition and the ways in which violations can be addressed.[31] Victims' organizations face many challenges, both institutionally and in terms of security. Their leaders are often under threat by the illegal armed groups still operating, and several have been killed.[32] These organizations have tense relations with government institutions and express various degrees of mistrust for the transitional justice process.[33]

The work of victims' organizations is supplemented by organizations that work with or on behalf of the plight of victims, and which are themselves not necessarily composed of victims themselves, such as human rights organizations, academic institutions, and a range of other non-governmental organizations.[34] As with victims' organizations, these are very diverse in terms of mission, strategy, operations, and ideology. Some provide specific services, such as legal or mental health counseling.

Although approved by Congress and sanctioned by the Constitutional Court, Law 975 was (and still is) questioned by civil society actors, including victims' organizations, on various grounds. For some observers, it seemed paradoxical that the government would engage in a peace process with the paramilitaries, who were considered to be pro-government forces. It was argued that the framework served particular economic interests, impunity, and potential political gain.[35] Victims' organizations and related organizations have continuously denounced the law as one of impunity, designed to consolidate existing power relations.[36] Similarly, the Colombian Commission of Jurists does not believe that the process contributes to the solution of the conflict or the fulfillment of victims' rights.[37] The application of transitional justice mechanisms when no obvious transition has taken place has also been questioned and there have been serious doubts about the plausibility of aiming for peace with all "organised armed groups at the margins of the law" through the same legal framework.[38] A further concern has been the security of victims, who might be put at risk by the very procedures established for the Justice and Peace process. Law 975 was implemented in a highly contested environment.

Transitional justice in practice

The objective of the Law of Justice and Peace is, as Article 1 clearly states, to facilitate the peace process and the reintegration of demobilized paramilitaries or guerrillas, while securing the rights of victims to truth, justice, and reparations.[39] The transitional justice scheme set up to implement the law involves the participation of a number of specialized public agencies, some newly created, others granted new mandates, and most of them within the justice and social sectors. The scheme is complex, and the relation between the different agencies develops in intricate ways. I next discuss various components of the Colombian transitional justice process as they are currently applied to fulfill victims' rights to justice, truth, and reparation.

Retributive justice and partial conditioned amnesties: the right to justice

According to official numbers, a total of 31,671 members of paramilitary groups had demobilized by August 2006, mostly through collective demobilization.[40] Only a fraction of the demobilized (2,716) entered into the Justice and Peace process: those who at the moment of demobilization had criminal charges or judicial procedures pending against them, or had admitted to conducting criminal acts. They are referred to as *postulados*, and by entering the process they commit to contribute to the clarification of the truth, refrain from illegal and criminal acts, and declare and surrender all economic resources and assets to sustain proper victim reparations. The remaining demobilized combatants were granted a conditioned amnesty and joined reintegration programs organized by the government.

Law 975 applies to both paramilitary and guerrilla members who can demobilize either collectively or individually. According to government figures, the total number of demobilized personnel by October 2010 was 54,297, of which 58 percent had demobilized collectively (31,472) and 42 percent on an individual basis (22,825).[41] With the increase in demobilized former paramilitaries and guerrillas came an increase in the number of *postulados*: 4,779 people by October 2010, 88 percent from paramilitary groups, the rest from five guerrilla groups.[42]

The *postulados*' participation in the Justice and Peace process involves several quasi-judicial and judicial steps which seek to gather information about criminal acts committed by the individual *postulado* and his group, enabling judicial and police investigation, and the opening of new cases requiring criminal investigation.[43] Victims, their families, and their representatives can participate directly or indirectly in the proceedings, which for the most part are led and organized by the UNFJP, at the Prosecutor General's Office, with offices in Bogotá, Barranquilla, and Medellín. Possibly the most publicized phase in this process is the one known as *versiones libres*, or "free accounts," during which individual *postulados* discuss the crimes committed by themselves and their groups, and provide information about specific cases. Free accounts sessions are announced widely, to ensure the participation of victims. The hearings are also broadcasted directly to other cities and local communities, to ensure the spread of information. Once this part of the process is completed, formal charges which initiate judicial proceedings are to be raised by the Prosecutor. Once a sentence has been reached, this will be reduced according to the Justice and Peace process to periods between five to eight years. At the end of the process a special hearing/session will take place to establish the reparations to be provided by the individual *postulado* to his victim(s).

The retributive justice component of the Peace and Justice process has been time-consuming, and its effectiveness with regard to victims' rights has been questioned. According to official figures, 2,424 free accounts have been initiated since the start of the process in 2005, while roughly 2,300 *postulados* are still waiting to engage in free accounts; 1,317 free versions have concluded. From those concluded, 468 *postulados* have reached the judicial proceedings, but only two had reached a sentence by mid-2010 and only three reparations hearings had taken place.[44] The amount of information brought to light during the free versions stage has been enormous and, for each criminal act declared, new victims are identified and new cases are established. The number of possible criminal charges is beyond what was envisaged when the process was designed. For example, the 129 *postulados* at the stage of formulation of charges by October 2010 will be charged with 11,746 acts of criminal conduct.[45]

The process faces serious administrative and logistical challenges, and is particularly vulnerable to political manipulation. In May 2008, the Colombian government extradited 13 top paramilitary leaders to the USA for drugs-related charges at the request of the US government. The Colombian government argued that the paramilitary leaders had not complied with the obligations set forth by Law 975 and had violated the terms of the agreement and were no longer protected from extradition to the USA.[46] This sudden and unexpected measure has been linked to what is known in Colombia as the *parapolitica scandal*, in reference to the influence that paramilitary forces exercised over political institutions in the country. The claim previously made by the AUC leaders, that 30 percent of Congress representatives had been elected with their assistance, had been substantiated in an academic paper studying voting patterns in regions where the AUC exerted *de facto* control.[47] Through the *versiones libres*, however, sensitive information linking the paramilitaries to political leaders and public officials at the highest level was presented by the paramilitary leaders themselves.[48] Victims' and human rights organizations have denounced the extradition as a strategy to impede investigations.[49] The extradition of paramilitary members in 2008 was a serious blow that undermined the public's view of the legitimacy of the process. The Government has insisted that the extraditions have not affected the victims' right to truth, as most of the seconds-in-command are still in Colombia and are actively disclosing information about the crimes committed and AUC activities.[50]

Judicial and historical truth: the right to truth

According to Article 7 of Law 975, victims have the right to know the truth about the crimes committed by illegal groups and the whereabouts of kidnapped persons and those forcefully disappeared. The law considers the judicial process of the Justice and Peace framework as a source of truth.[51] The law also dictated that one of the many functions of the CNRR was to deliver a report on the reasons behind the emergence and evolution of illegal armed groups. Based on this mandate, the CNRR established the Group for Historical Memory (GHM) to develop an overall history of the Colombian armed conflict, focusing not only on its structural origins and dynamics, but also on the many voices, local histories, and experiences of the conflict, and in particular to elaborate a victim-oriented perspective. The GHM has undertaken research on emblematic cases of the armed conflict, each resulting in a published volume, broadly disseminated through different media. Although it has some similarities to truth commissions in the region, the GHM considers its mandate as different and, at most, preliminary to that of a truth commission.

Judicial and administrative reparations: victims' right to reparation

The explicit recognition of victims' rights is possibly one of the most salient features of the Law of Justice and Peace, in which the right to reparation for crimes committed by demobilized members of illegal armed groups has been the cornerstone for promoting and protecting the rights of victims. The principle of "integral reparations" (*reparación integral*) guides these efforts, seeking to provide victims with both material and symbolic forms of reparations, as well as satisfaction and guarantees of non-repetition.

The law envisaged provision of reparations resulting from each judicial process. The process starts with the registration by individual victims of human rights violations and criminal acts to which they or their closest relatives have been exposed.[52] In the registration, the victim is asked to identify the individual victimizer or at least the group he belonged to, in order to establish a procedural link between victim and victimizer. By October 2010, 309,920 claims were registered, about half of them by the General Prosecutor's Office (to which UNFJP belongs), the rest by other public agencies such as the National Registrar, or the CNRR.[53] Reparations to the victims are to be provided by the relevant victimizer after a guilty sentence has been reached. If a victim is unable to identify his or her victimizer, then reparations will be provided from the Reparations Fund, which includes the assets provided by the *postulados* when joining the Justice and Peace process. The form and size of reparations will be decided through a special hearing known as *incidente de reparación*, in which victims put forward reparations claims that will be decided upon by the judge. By October 2010, only three cases had reached this stage. The judicial path to reparations is a very lengthy process and has being heavily criticized by victims' organizations, human rights organizations, and civil society organizations alike.

Partly in response to criticism with respect to its commitment to victims' rights, the government established an administrative reparations program in April 2008 (*Programa de Reparación Individual por Vía Administrativa*).[54] While the judicial path demands a high level of evidence of victimization, the administrative path has a lower threshold of evidence, and is more favorable for those who cannot identify or are afraid to confront their victimizers, those who do not have the financial resources to bring their claim before the special courts, and those who were victims of organizations other than the paramilitaries. In this program, the state assumes the task of compensating the victims based on a principle of solidarity with the victims, and not out of responsibility for the crimes committed. The principle guiding the "solidarity compensation" (*indemnización solidaria*) is strongly defended by the state and challenged by victims' organizations and CSOs.[55]

Administrative reparations only provide monetary compensation for crimes committed against individuals; they do not include damage to property.[56] Compensation amounts vary depending on the nature of victimization, ranging from 27 to 40 basic monthly salaries, to be paid as a lump sum. *Acción Social*, in charge of the Reparations Fund, is mandated to establish and implement the administrative reparations program. Registration in this program did not exclude victims from the possibility of obtaining reparations from their victimizers through the judicial process. The original registration period for this program was two years, from April 2008 until April 2010. According to official figures, 331,604 applications had been registered by the closing of registration. The majority of applications concerned death and arbitrary killings; 78 percent were for homicides and 10 percent for enforced disappearance. The remaining 12 percent of applications referred to other crimes such as kidnapping, injuries, torture, rape and sexual violence, and recruitment of child soldiers. By October 2010, 20,837 families had received monetary compensation from the administrative reparations program.[57]

Victim reparations included the development of collective reparation initiatives, with the aim of restoring citizens' rights and rule of law, particularly in those areas most affected by the armed conflict. Eight pilot projects of collective reparations have been implemented since 2007 by the CNRR, serving as the baseline for the current development of the Institutional Program on Collective Reparations. The often slippery issue of reconciliation has been addressed via the linkage of trust, democracy, and co-existence. In cooperation with relevant institutional partners, such as the High Commissioner for Reintegration and the Ministry of Education, the Reconciliation Unit at the CNRR aims to raise national awareness about reconciliation promoting it at the policy level.[58]

The CNRR has sought to promote victims' rights and a victim-oriented perspective in the various components of the Colombian transitional justice scheme. Through its extensive regional networks and in cooperation with public institutions at the regional and local levels, the CNRR succeeded in putting the rights of victims on the national public agenda. The CNRR has developed a nation-wide outreach program, organizing advisory and counseling sessions for victims (known as *Jornadas de Atención a Víctimas*), preparing user-oriented information including audio-visual material, in-depth analysis, and reports, and participating in the public debate and more.[59]

Inter-institutional coordination in the Justice and Peace framework

The implementation of Law 975 requires the participation of several public agencies and institutional actors, most notably, the Special Unit for Justice and Peace at the Office of the Prosecutor General (UNFJP), the CNNR, and *Acción Social*, each of them with their own departments and units, fulfilling various tasks either independently or in collaboration with other institutions. There are also several cross-cutting, inter-agency coordinating bodies that have been created with representatives from these and other public institutions. While Law 975 introduced a transitional justice approach to the demobilization of illegal armed groups and the resolution of the armed conflict, transitional justice as a specific area of public policy was not formally established before 2008, when the Ministry of Interior and Justice was reorganized and the Department for Transitional Justice (DTJ) was created in November to formulate, coordinate, and promote a public national policy on transitional justice.[60] The department is mandated to oversee the inter-institutional coordination regarding the implementation of Law 975 and the various laws regulating demobilization and reintegration and also functions as the Technical Secretariat for the Inter-institutional Committee for Justice and Peace, led by the Minister of Interior and Justice. Several functions of this department are similar to those of the CNRR; however, the scope of the DTJ is more oriented towards policymaking and monitoring,[61] while the CNRR has a more operational and advisory role. Given the complexity, the variety of components, and plurality of actors involved in the Justice and Peace process, it is likely that the DTJ, placed as it is within a government ministry, will play a key role in the future development of the process.

Internal displacement and restitution of land and property

One of the most notable features of the Colombian armed conflict is the massive numbers of internally displaced persons (IDPs). Figures vary, but the number of IDPs is nevertheless in the millions. Official figures by *Acción Social* indicate 3.3 million IDPs, while non-governmental organization and coordinator of the follow-up commission on internal displacement, CODHES, suggests that 5.1 million people were displaced in Colombia in the period 1985–2010, roughly 11 percent of the entire Colombian population.[62] This phenomenon is so extensive that any attempt to secure the rights of victims in Colombia will need to take into account the rights of the largest group of victims in the country: victims of forced or arbitrary displacement.

The attention of the Colombian state to the victims of internal displacement precedes the Justice and Peace process and can formally be traced back to 1997.[63] The protection of the rights of IDPs, however, did not improve, and in 2004 the Constitutional Court described "an unconstitutional state of affairs" with regard to Colombian IDPs.[64] A civil society initiative called the "Follow-up Commission on Public Policy regarding Internal Displacement" was established in November 2005 and has played an active role in the development of indicators and recommendations on internal displacement ever since. Since 2007, the Follow-up Commission has undertaken several studies and reports at the request of the Constitutional Court to monitor the situation of IDPs and progress concerning their rights. Several mechanisms have been implemented, mostly coordinated by *Acción Social* through the National System for the Attention of Displaced Population (*Sistema Nacional de Atención Integral de Población Desplazada*—SNAIPD).[65]

While Law 975 does not mention forced displacement directly, it does create an institutional mechanism for restitution of land and property via Regional Commissions for the Restitution of Property, while giving the CNRR the mandate to coordinate the activities of the regional commissions.[66] Land and property restitution is an extremely complex issue in Colombia, both in terms of the technical and administrative challenges it poses and in regards to the strong economic and political interests involved. Land and property restitution as a form of victim reparations would have to deal with, for example, the co-existence of several forms of property and tenure, incomplete cadastral records, the existence of parallel registration systems, multiple registrations and claims over the same property (both simultaneously and over time), coercive practices of land expropriation and usurpation (often legalized through formal and judicial channels), and the presence of strong economic actors and activities in disputed lands.[67] While the CNRR advanced an agenda concerning restitution of land and property, and implemented a number of pilot projects to test different modalities for restitution, progress in this area has been relatively limited.[68] Security challenges for both the returning populations and community leaders leading restitution claims jeopardize the few advances made.[69]

Forced or arbitrary displacement is explicitly identified as a crime under the individual administrative reparations program. Benefits for IDPs under this program are provided by family unit through housing support. IDP families already registered under the SNAIPD have automatic access to the administrative reparations program, although double benefits are not allowed.[70] This could explain the relatively "low" number of people registered in the administrative reparations program compared to the millions of Colombian IDPs. While housing support schemes may alleviate some of the immediate and short-term needs of displaced families, displaced families appear to aspire to return and restitution.

The Victims' Law of 2011: strengthening victims' rights

As discussed above, components of the Justice and Peace process have developed at different speeds and there have been limitations. The design and implementation of a comprehensive victim reparations program that goes beyond monetary compensation is still pending. The first proposal focusing on victims' rights and reparation was presented to Congress in 2008 and dismissed the following year.[71] Six weeks after assuming power in August 2010, president Juan Manuel Santos presented a proposal to the national Congress promising to address "the pending debt" that the country owed the victims of the armed conflict, which became known as the "Victims' Law." Shortly after, separate proposed legislation on land restitution was merged with the victims' legislation, placing the issue of internal displacement and land restitution at the center of a national program for victim reparations. Outreach activities by the CNRR and civil society organizations, congressional debates, and wide media coverage promoted public discussion of the legislation, which was approved by Congress on 1 June and signed on 10 June 2011 as Law 1448 of 2011. The legislation has been welcomed by broad sectors of

Colombian society, including victims' organizations, for seeking to address victims' rights, particularly land and property restitution.[72] The law includes victims of both illegal armed groups such as paramilitaries and guerrillas, and members of the Colombian police and armed forces. Victim reparations can be claimed for harm since 1985, while land and property restitution applies to acts since 1991. The law establishes new institutions, including the creation of a national victims' registry, a national system for victims' reparations, and a national network for victim reparations served by a specialized administrative unit, a national registry for usurped lands, a specialized unit for land restitution, and a center for historical memory. The main task of these institutions is to develop and implement a national reparations program that includes compensation, restitution, rehabilitation, and guarantees of non-repetition for the victims; the threshold of proof has been significantly reduced in favor of the victim. Since late 2011, the government has passed the regulations needed to implement Law 1448.[73] The law transformed *Acción Social* into an administrative department, the Department for Social Prosperity,[74] which will encompass some of the new units. Others, such as the Land Restitution Unit, are based in the Ministry of Agriculture, which is in the process of opening 21 offices across the country.[75] The law does not affect the judicial processes implemented under Law 975.

DDR completed?

The Colombian process brings together the demobilization of armed actors with the rights of victims. A point of departure for the process has been the collective and progressive demobilization of paramilitaries from 2002–06, followed by the gradual and individual demobilization of guerrilla soldiers since 2002. According to official numbers, by 5 November 2010 22,704 members of illegal armed groups had demobilized individually, two-thirds of these FARC guerrillas.[76]

While Law 975 explicitly deals with the legal benefits to which demobilized personnel are entitled under the Justice and Peace scheme, Law 782 of 2002 regulates procedures of demobilization and reintegration.[77] Several regulatory decrees were issued from 2003 to 2007, establishing, among other things, the creation in 2006 of the High Advisory on Reintegration (*Alta Consejería para la Reintegración*, ACR), a unit strategically placed at the Office of the President with a mandate to develop, implement, and evaluate a national policy on the social and economic reintegration of demobilized paramilitaries and guerrillas, in coordination with the Ministry of Defense (MD), the Ministry of Interior and Justice, and the (now closed) Office of the High Commissioner for Peace.[78]

Since its creation, the ACR has developed a number of programs, providing social and educational services, health services, occupational training, and support for income-generative activities, and psychosocial counseling for the demobilized and their families. In December 2008, the ACR succeeded in establishing a public national policy on reintegration.[79] Institutional development in reintegration was parallel to developments in transitional justice. Operationally regulated by two different bodies of law and developed from two different institutions, the goals and strategies are converging in practice. One example is the work done by the CNRR's Area on Reconciliation, which has identified the ACR as a strategic partner for its project implementation. The ACR recognizes the important role that the effective reintegration of the demobilized into civilian life in local communities has in breaking the cycle of violence and is seeking to coordinate with other public agencies.[80]

Unfortunately, while a large number of paramilitaries and guerrillas have been demobilized, there are continuous reports of the presence of illegal armed groups in various parts of the country, operating with similar modalities to that of former paramilitaries.[81] In its first report on DDR, the CNRR confirmed the emergence and/or reorganization of illegal armed groups and called for decisive action to dismantle possible new paramilitary structures.[82] The report identified three types of illegal armed groups: dissidents (those belonging to demobilized AUC, who refuse to demobilize), rearmed groups (those who took up arms again after having demobilized), and emergent groups (new groups forming after the demobilization process).[83] In a second report on DDR, the CNRR examined the nature and dynamics of operations of these illegal armed groups, exploring the negative effects these have on the reintegration part of the DDR process.[84] While the illegal armed groups show diversity in form, structure, membership, and operations, they do share some common features: links to illegal and criminal activities such as narco-trafficking, the use of extortion and violence, and abuse of power. There is also evidence that these groups often operate with the direct or indirect support of local public officials and members of the police and armed forces.[85]

The presence of illegal armed groups is a reminder that effective territorial control by state forces and public institution is yet to be achieved in Colombia. The demobilized population is not only a target of new recruitment by these groups, but they and their families are also targets of threats and violence by groups active at regional and local levels. The existence of illegal armed groups also represents a threat to the security of victims participating in the Justice and Peace process. This situation is particularly acute in areas affected by internal displacement. On average, ten victims of internal displacement have been killed every year since 2007 in various parts of the country.[86]

In spite of their many advances, both the DDR and the Justice and Peace processes are still vulnerable to sudden changes and/or socio-political turmoil. In 2010, a challenge was brought before the constitutional court regarding the application of the "principle of opportunity" under Law 1312 of 2009 to exempt demobilized personnel from investigation and prosecution. In November 2010, the Court declared Law 1312 unconstitutional, on the grounds that the principle of opportunity had been designed to apply to regular criminal acts, and not as part of a political process such as demobilization and peacebuilding.[87] The court held that the duty of the prosecutor to investigate all acts of criminal conduct could not be removed by the principle of opportunity, and that doing so would go against basic principles of Colombian and international human rights law. As a direct consequence of this decision, more than 31,000 demobilized former paramilitary members could face arrest orders for having been part of illegal armed groups; the partial and conditional amnesty granted by Law 975 would cease, creating an uncertainty which could affect the reintegration process. In an unprecedented effort by several public institutions, including the ACR and DTJ, a new law was passed by Congress in December 2010, making explicit reference to the demobilized personnel and their obligations regarding the fulfillment of victims' rights.[88]

Conclusions

In introducing this chapter, I asked whether accountability and DDR could be applied at the same time in pursuit of peace. While the experience of Colombia demonstrates that it is possible to implement transitional justice mechanisms before a full ceasefire with all armed actors is in place, it also demonstrates that benefits such as partial and conditional amnesties, reduced sentences, and reintegration programs are effective incentives for the demobilization of armed actors. The rights of victims can effectively be incorporated in legal tools that are designed to move forward with conflict resolution, peacebuilding, and transitional justice. The effective implementation of such policies, however, faces a number of challenges.

The institutional challenge is perhaps the most visible one. Institutional developments have proceeded in transitional justice and DDR in parallel, with relatively little interaction with each other until recently. Even within transitional justice, several public agencies are involved, not always in tune with the activities and objectives of others. Implementing a transitional justice process alongside a demobilization process is not only a very demanding administrative project, but it also involves a process of institution-building that governments may not be aware of or prepared for. New institutions will have to be developed and interagency coordination reinforced or established. Countries emerging from armed conflict may not have the capacity and resources to manage such complex institutional challenges. In Colombia, new institutions have been created, developed, and expanded, and have carved a space for themselves, their mandates, and agendas in national policy. These processes are not just bureaucratic ones, but have a direct impact on the lives of victims and demobilized paramilitary and guerrilla fighters.

The Colombian process demonstrates the limits of maximalist ideals of retributive justice. The judicial path to reparations has proven slow and limited despite significant efforts. The slowness of the process creates the perception that justice is simply dragging on rather than addressing victims' rights to justice and reparations. The scope of the issues and measures developed as a result of the Justice and Peace process has expanded exponentially. The challenge, therefore, is how to make the process manageable without giving away the goals of justice, peace, and reparations for the victims.

The new Victims' Law opens the way for the establishment of an extensive administrative reparations program, similar to other processes on the continent, where administrative programs are predominant. The use of selective prosecutions may be a way to address the significant number of cases blocking the system. This would entail proceeding with prosecutions with a few selected charges that can guarantee an indictment for the victimizers, without having to wait for the investigation of all cases. This is a common approach in both national and international tribunals dealing with human rights violations and core international crimes. Engaging in transitional justice and DDR at the same time is challenging. From a basis of the imperfect but much-needed implementation of the Law of Justice and Peace, Colombia now enters a new phase for the implementation of victims' rights.

Notes

1 Law 975 of 2005. *Por la cual se dictan disposiciones para la reincorporación de miembros de grupos armados organizados al margen de la ley, que contribuyan de manera efectiva a la consecución de la paz nacional y se dictan otras disposiciones para acuerdos humanitarios*, Congress of the Republic of Colombia (CRC).
2 The CNRR is an independent body created by Law 975 for a period of eight years, composed of 11 commissioners from different public sectors and representatives from victims' organizations and civil society.
3 Jemima García-Godos and Knut Andreas Orgland Lid, "Transitional Justice and Victims' Rights before the End of a Conflict: The Unusual Case of Colombia," *Journal of Latin American Studies*, vol. 42 (2010), pp. 487–516.
4 Law 1448 of 2010. *Por la cual se dictan medidas de atención, asistencia y reparación integral a la víctimas del conflicto armado interno y se dictan otras disposiciones*, CRC. Approved and ratified on 10 June 2011. This law was designed to address victims' rights directly, in particular, victims' right to restitution of land and property.
5 Jonathan Hartlyn, *La política del régimen de coalición; La experiencia del Frente Nacional en Colombia* (Bogotá, 1993); Robert H. Dix, "Consociational Democracy: The Case of Colombia," *Comparative Politics*, vol. 12, no. 3 (1980), pp. 303–21.
6 Colombian scholars debate whether the current conflict is simply the continuation of the bipartisan violence, or if it is governed by different dynamics. See Francisco Gutiérrez, María Emma Wills, and Gonzalo Sánchez (eds), *Nuestra guerra sin nombre. Transformaciones del conflicto en Colombia* (Bogotá, 2006); Andrés Dávila, *El juego del poder: Historia, armas y votos* (Bogotá, 1998); Fabio Sánchez, Ana María Díaz, and Michel Formisano, "Conflicto, Crimen Violento y Actividad Criminal en Colombia: Un Análisis Espacial," *Documentos CEDE* (Bogotá, 2003).
7 All figures are from Diego Otero, *Experiencias de investigación: Las cifras del conflicto colombiano*, (Bogotá, 2008), available at <http://www.setianworks.net/indepazHome/attachments/191_cifras%201964%20–2007.pdf>.
8 Internal Displacement Monitory Centre (IDMC), available at <www.internal-displacement.org/idmc/website/countries.nsf/(httpEnvelopes)/A7E1B7BD7528B329C12575E500525165?OpenDocument#expand>; accessed 22 September 2009.
9 Norman Offstein, "An Historical Review and Analysis of Colombian Guerrilla Movements: FARC, ELN and EPL," *Revista Desarrollo y Sociedad*, no. 52 (September 2003), pp. 99–142; Ricardo Peñaranda, Javier Guerrero *et al.* (eds), *De las armas a la política* (Bogotá, 1999).
10 Decree 3398 of 1965. *Por el cual se organiza la defensa nacional*, Presidency of the Republic of Colombia (PRC).
11 Law 48 of 1968. *Por la cual se adoptan como legislación permanente algunos decretos*, CRC.
12 Decree 1194 of 1989. *Por el cual se adiciona el decreto legislativo 0180 de 1988, para sancionar nuevas modalidades delictivas, por requerirlo el restablecimiento del orden público*, PRC.

13 Decree 356 of 1994. *Por el cual se expide el estatuto de vigilancia y seguridad privada*, PRC.
14 In his biography, former paramilitary leader Carlos Castaño considered the decree to have favored self-defense groups closely aligned to the drugs trade. Current president Alvaro Uribe used this decree actively while holding the position of governor in the state of Antioquia. See Mauricio Aranguren, *Mi confesión* (Bogotá, 2001). See also Fabio Sánchez and Mario Chacón, "Conflict, State and Decentralisation. From Social Progress to Armed Dispute for Local Control 1974–2002," *Crisis States Programme, Working Paper No. 70* (2005).
15 Yamile Salinas, Darío Gonzáles, and Eliza González, *Tierra, oro y conflictos* (Bogotá, 2008).
16 Nazih Richani, "The Political Economy of Violence: The War System in Colombia," *Journal of Interamerican Studies and World Affairs*, vol. 39, no 2 (1997), pp. 27–81.
17 Gustavo Duncan, *Los señores de la guerra. De paramilitares, mafiosos y autodefensas en Colombia* (Bogotá, 2006).
18 "Congreso, En La Mira Para," *El Tiempo* (17 March 2002). This was subsequently substantiated by Colombian researchers and information provided by former paramilitary leaders during the Justice and Peace hearings. These events are known today as "the *parapolítica* scandal." See Mauricio Romero (ed.), *Parapolítica. La ruta de la expansión paramilitar y los acuerdos políticos* (Bogotá, 2007).
19 *Acuerdo de Santa Fé de Ralito para Contribuir a la Paz en Colombia* (2003).
20 *Proceso de Paz con las Autodefensas: Informe Ejecutivo* (Bogotá: Alto Comisionado para la Paz, 2006).
21 Law 418 of 1997. *Por lo cual se consagran unos instrumentos para la búsqueda de la convivencia*, CRC. Law 548 of 1999. *Por medio de la cual se prorroga la vigencia de la ley 418 del 26 de Diciembre 1997*, CRC.
22 Law 782 of 2002. *Por medio de la cual se prorroga la vigencia de la ley 418 del 26 de Diciembre 1997, prorrogada y modificada por la ley 548 de 1999 y se modifican algunas de sus disposiciones*, CRC.
23 Other issues regulated by Law 782 include witness protection and the surrender of military equipment and material goods possessed by illegal armed groups (Articles 50–82).
24 Amnesty International, *Colombia. Los paramilitares en Medellín: ¿Desmovilización o legalización?* (London, 2005); CIDH, *Informe sobre la implementación de la Ley de Justicia y Paz: Etapas iniciales del proceso de desmovilización de las AUC y primeras diligencias judiciales* (San José, 2007).
25 Legislative Bill 85, 2003, *Ley de Alternatividad Penal.*
26 María Paula Saffon and Rodrigo Uprimny, "Uses and Abuses of Transitional Justice in Colombia," in Morten Bergsmo and Pablo Kalmanovitz (eds), *Law in Peace Negotiations* (Oslo: Torkel Opsahl Electronic Publisher, 2009).
27 Sentence C-370 of 2006 issued by the Constitutional Court of Colombia (Bogotá, 2006) <www.corteconstitucional.gov.co/relatoria/2006/C-370–06.htm>.
28 Decree 3391 of 2006, *Por el cual se reglamenta parcialmente la ley 975 de 2005*, PRC; Decree 4436 of 2006, *Por la cual se reglamenta parcialmente la ley 782 de 1997*, PRC.
29 An annotated law text including the Corte Constitucional (CC) decisions and specific considerations can be found in <www.fiscalia.gov.co/justiciapaz/Documentos/LEY_975_concordada.pdf>. Vicente Castaño Gil, one of the three AUC founders, withdrew from the process in 2006, as did others.
30 Sergio de León, "El presidente Uribe asegura que en Colombia 'hoy no hay paramilitarismo,'" *Revista Semana* (Bogotá, 20 July 2007).
31 The diverse range of organizations includes the *Asociación Caminos de Esperanza de las Madres de la Candelaria* (<www.madresdelacandelaria.org>) and *La Ruta Pacífica de las Mujeres* (<www.rutapacifica.org.co>), both geographically based inter-regional groups addressing the needs of women victims of the armed conflict. *Organización Nacional de Indígenas de Colombia* (ONIC; <www.onic.org.co>) and *Unidad Indígena del Pueblo Awa* represent indigenous groups, at the national and local level respectively. Others, such as the *Asociación de Familiares de Detenidos Desaparecidos* (ASFADDES;

<www.asfaddes.info/node>), work for the rights of the disappeared, regardless of the ethnicity or sex of the individual. Groups such as *País Libre* (<www.paislibre.org>) work with victims of kidnapping. At national level, *Movimiento Nacional de Víctimas de Crímenes de Estado* (MOVICE; <www.movimientodevictimas.org>), an umbrella organization comprising 200 victims' associations and groups, plays an active role in the national debate concerning the Colombian process.

32 Following the murder of peasant leader Benigno Gil Valencia on 22 November 2008, the CNRR called for the protection of peasant leaders and victim representatives putting forward claims for land restitution. Gil Valencia was spokesman for the *Mesa Nacional de Trabajo Campesina para el Programa de Recuperación de Tierras* in Mutatá (*CNRR Comunicado*, 24 November 2008, available at <www.cnrr.org.co>).

33 Victims' organizations were skeptical toward the process from the beginning. MOVICE, the largest and most vocal organization, did not participate in the institutional framework established to oversee the initial process of consultation led by CNRR. Victims' organizations were originally represented at the CNRR by ONIC and *País Libre.*

34 See, for example, DeJusticia <www.dejusticia.org>, CINEP (*Centro de Investigación y Educación Popular*), available at <www.cinep.org.co>, and particularly CODHES (*Consultoría para los Derechos Humanos y el Desplazamiento*), available at <www.codhes.org>.

35 A more thorough discussion of other motives is beyond the scope of this chapter.

36 This is clearly expressed in the Act of Constitution of the largest victims' organization in Colombia, MOVICE (*Movimiento Nacional de Víctimas de Crímenes de Estado*), created on 25 June 2005, available at <www.movimientodevictimas.org/index.php?option=com_content&task=view&id=14&Itemid=61>. MOVICE has remained firm in its opposition to Law 975.

37 See Ana María Díaz (ed.), *Colombia: El espejismo de la justicia y la paz. Balance sobre la aplicación de la ley 975 de 2005* (Bogotá, 2008).

38 Rafael Pardo, *Fin del paramilitarismo ¿Es posible su desmonte?* (Bogotá, 2007). Rodrigo Uprimny and María Paula Saffon, *Desplazamiento forzado y justicia transicional en Colombia. Estudio sectorial* (Bogotá, 2007); Saffon and Uprimny, "Uses and Abuses," op. cit.; Gustavo Gallón, Michael Reed, and Catalina Lleras (eds), *Anotaciones sobre la ley de justicia y paz. Una mirada desde los derechos de las víctimas* (Bogotá, 2007).

39 Law 975 of 2005, Art. 1. For a more detailed discussion of each transitional justice mechanism, see García-Godos and Lid, "The Unusual Case of Colombia," op. cit.

40 Proceso de Paz Informe Ejecutivo.

41 Seguimiento Matriz de Justicia y Paz—Comité de Coordinación Interinstitucional de Justicia y Paz, *Quinto Bimestre 2010*, (Bogotá: October 2010), *Desmovilizados* (ACR, MD), available at <www.mij.gov.co/econtent/library/documents/DocNewsNo1799DocumentNo6358.PDF>; last accessed 5 April 2011.

42 Ibid.

43 Chapter IV, Law of Justice and Peace.

44 Seguimiento Matriz, Proceso (Concejo Supremo de Justicia—CSJ).

45 Seguimiento Matriz, Proceso (CSJ).

46 "Paras Extraditados Seguían Delinquiendo e Incumplían Compromisos de Ley de Justicia y Paz: Uribe," *El Tiempo* (13 May 2008).

47 Mauricio Romero, *Parapolítica. La ruta de la expansión paramilitar y los acuerdos políticos* (Bogotá: Corporación Nuevo Arco Iris, 2007), available at <www.nuevoarcoiris.org.co/sac/?q=node/80>.

48 "Conmigo Extraditaron la Verdad': Salvatore Mancuso en Entrevista Exclusiva," *Revista Cambio* (28 May 2009), available at <http://justiciaypazcolombia.com/Conmigo-extraditaron-la-verdad>; accessed 2 September 2010.

49 Corporación Nuevo Arco Iris (2009) *Denuncian ante CIDH a Colombia por extradición de 'paras' y parapolítica*, 23 March 2009, Observatorio del Conflicto, available at <www.nuevoarcoiris.org.co/sac/?q=node/325>.

50 Eduardo Pizarro "La Extradición y las Víctimas," *Semana* (19 May 2008), available at <www.eltiempo.com/opinion/columnistas/eduardopizarroleongmez/ARTICULO-WEB-PLANTILLA_NOTA_INTERIOR-4199074.html>.

51 García-Godos and Lid, "Unusual case of Colombia," op. cit., p. 506.

52 This is done by filling up the form "*Hechos atribuibles a grupos organizados al margen de la ley*," developed by UNFPJ. It needs to be accompanied with documentation supporting the claim. See <www.fiscalia.gov.co/justiciapaz/Documentos/Formato_Victimas.pdf>.

53 Seguimiento Matriz, Registro (Fondo Nacional de Garantias—FNG).

54 Decree 1290 of 2008. *Por el cual se crea el programa de reparación individual por vía administrativa para las víctimas de los grupos armados organizados al margen de la ley*, Colombian Ministry of Interior and Justice.

55 On the difference between solidarity and responsibility as the basis for victim reparations, see Nelson Camilo Sánchez, "¿Perder es Ganar un Poco? Avances y Frustraciones de la Discusión del Estatuto de Víctimas en Colombia," in Catalina Díaz, Nelson Camilo Sánchez, and Rodrigo Uprimny (eds), *Reparar en Colombia: Los dilemas en contexto de conflicto, pobreza y exclusión* (Bogotá: ICTJ—DeJusticia, 2009), pp. 623–718.

56 Law 975 concerns all types of criminal acts penalized in the national penal code, without mentioning any specific type of crime. Damage to property is indirectly addressed by way of restitution, identified in the law as a form of victim reparations. The administrative reparations decree, on the contrary, does make explicit reference to the types of crimes considered for monetary compensation, including internal displacement. See Art. 5, Decree 1290/2108.

57 The number of individual applications processed and approved for compensation payments is not available, and the only indicator made public is the number of families receiving compensation, along with the amount of money disbursed. See "Pagos Reparación Individual vía Administrativa," Subdirección de Atención a Víctimas de la Violencia, Acción Social (Bogotá, October 2010).

58 Author's interview with CNNR Coordinator on Reconciliation, María Angélica Bueno (Bogotá 25 November 2011); "CNRR Proyecta Trabajo en Reconciliación para los Próximos Tres Años," (15 December 2010), available at <www.cnrr.org.co/contenido/09e/spip.php?article3874>.

59 The relative success of the CNRR is partly due to the leadership and commitment of its first president, Eduardo Pizarro Leóngomez, replaced in December 2010 by current Vice-President Angelino Garzón.

60 Decree 4530 of 2008. *Por el cual se modifica la estructura del Ministerio del Interior y Justicia y se dictan otras disposiciones*, Ministry of Interior and Justice, Colombia.

61 Author's interview with Andrea León López, Advisor at the Department of Transitional Justice, Ministry of Interior and Justice (Bogotá, November 2010).

62 "¿Consolidación de Qué? Informe Sobre Desplazamiento, Conflicto Armado y Derechos Humanos en Colombia en 2010," *CODHES Informa*, No. 77 (Bogotá, 15 February 2010), p. 8, available at <www.codhes.org/images/stories/pdf/bolet%C3%ADn%2077.pdf>; accessed 17 April 2011.

63 Law 387 of 1997. *Por la cual se adoptan medidas para la prevención del desplazamiento forzado; la atención, protección, consolidación y estabilización socioeconómica de los desplazados internos por la violencia en la República de Colombia*, CRC.

64 Colombian Constitutional Court. Sentence T-025, 22 January 2004.

65 See <www.accionsocial.gov.co/contenido/contenido.aspx?catID=295&conID=1933>.

66 Law 975/2005, Art. 52.

67 See Francisco Gutiérrez Sanín, "Land and Property Rights in Colombia—Change and Continuity," *Nordic Journal of Human Rights*, vol. 28, no. 2 (2010), pp. 230–61; and Knut Andreas Orgland Lid and Jemima García-Godos, "Land Restitution in the Colombian Transitional Justice Process," *Nordic Journal of Human Rights*, vol. 28, no. 2 (2010), pp. 262–88.

68 For a detailed discussion of the CNRR activities on land restitution, see Lid and García-Godos, "Land Restitution," op. cit.

69 Several community leaders have been killed during ongoing restitution processes or after the returns have been completed. CODHES, "¿Consolidación de Qué?," op. cit., p. 12.

70 In the instructions regarding registration to the administrative reparations program it is clearly stated that IDPs already registered with the SNAIPD did not need to register their victimization for internal displacement, only for other criminal acts. See <www.accionsocial.gov.co/contenido/contenido.aspx?catID=297&conID=1736&pagID=5326>.

71 This initiative was known as "Estatuto de Víctimas" (Law proposal 044/08, Senate, 157/08). For a discussion of this proposal, see Nelson Camilo Sánchez, "Perder es Ganar un Poco? Avances y Frustraciones de la Discusión del Estatuto de Víctimas en Colombia," in Catalina Díaz, N. C. Sánchez, and Rodrigo Uprimny (eds), *Reparar en Colombia: Los dilemas en contextos de conflicto, pobreza y exclusión* (Bogotá: ICTJ—DeJusticia), pp. 623–718.

72 "Ley de Víctimas: un paso histórico," *Semana*, Issue 1517, 28 May 2011, available at <www.semana.com/nacion/ley-victimas-paso-historico/157521-23.aspx>.

73 An updated list of decrees regulating Law 1448 can be found in in its own website, created by the Ministry of Justice and the Law, available at <www.leydevictimas.gov.co/#!-reglamentacion>; last accessed 28 March 2012.

74 Departamento para la Prosperidad Social: La Entidad—Antecedentes, available at <www.dps.gov.co/contenido/contenido.aspx?catID=3&conID=544&pagID=823>; last accessed 28 March 2012.

75 Ministry of Agriculture and Rural Development, Boletín de Prensa No. 077, 15 March 2012, available at <www.minagricultura.gov.co/archivos/_bol_077-2012reclamaciones_de_los_despojados_ya_supera_las_700_mil_hectareas.pdf>; last accessed 28 March 2012.

76 "Reintegración en Colombia. Hechos y Datos" (Bogotá: Alta Consejería para la Reintegración, Presidencia de la República, 2010).

77 Law 782 of 2002. *Por la cual se prorroga la vigencia de la Ley 418 de 1997, prorrogada y modificada por la Ley 548 de 1999 y se modifican algunas de sus disposiciones*, CRC. This law was renewed and extended by Law 1106 of 2006.

78 These are Decrees 128 of 2003, 3043 of 2006, and 395 of 2007.

79 CONPES, "Política Nacional de Reintegración Social y Económica para Personas y Grupos Armados Ilegales," *Documento CONPES* 3554 (Bogotá: Consejo Nacional de Política Económica y Social, 2008).

80 Author's interview with Joshua Mitrotti, General Manager, High Advisory for Reintegration (1 December 2010, Bogotá).

81 *Décimo Cuarto Informe Trimestral de la MAPP OEA* (28 April 2010).

82 CNRR, "Disidentes, Rearmados y Emergentes: Bandas Criminales o Tercera Generación Paramilitar?" (Área de DDR, CNRR, Bogotá 2007).

83 Ibid., p. 58.

84 CNRR, "La Reintegración. Logros en Medio de Reames y Dificultades no Resueltas" (Área de DDR, CNRR, Bogotá, 2010).

85 Ibid., p. 145.

86 CODHES, "Líderes y Personas en Situación de Desplazamiento Asesinadas del 1 de Marzo 2002 a Marzo 23 2011" (Bogotá, 2010), available at <www.codhes.org/images/stories/pdf/cld%20asesinados%20marzo%2025%202011.pdf>.

87 Constitutional Court, Comunicado No. 59 (23 November 2010).

88 MAPP-OEA, "OEA Celebra Radicación de Proyecto de Ley que Favorece la Justicia Transicional y Da Sostenibilidad al Proceso de Reintegración," *Comunicado*, 30 November 2010, available at <www.es.emailbrain.com/new/viewnewsletter2.aspx?SiteID=19053&sid=34&NewsletterID=171102>; Law 1424 of 2010, *Por la cual se dictan disposiciones de justicia transicional que garanticen verdad, justicia y reparación a las víctimas de desmovilizados de grupos organizados al margen de la ley, se conceden beneficios jurídico y se dictan otras disposiciones*, CRC.

13 The national accord, impunity, and the fragile peace in Kenya

Stephen Brown

Introduction

Kenya's presidential elections on 27 December 2007 ended in a photo-finish. Amidst a very tense atmosphere and after 24 hours of counting and tabulations *in camera*, the Electoral Commission declared on 30 December that incumbent president Mwai Kibaki was the victor. At the eleventh hour, Raila Odinga, his main rival, lost the significant lead he had held in most opinion polls during the campaign and in the partial returns during the counting process.[1] Odinga and supporters of his party, the Orange Democratic Movement (ODM), cried foul and refused to accept the results. Demonstrations quickly sprung up in ODM strongholds, especially in Nyanza province, home to Odinga and the majority of his fellow Luo.[2]

In the days that followed, ODM supporters in Nyanza and Rift Valley provinces, as well as in Nairobi, perpetrated attacks, sometimes deadly, on Kikuyu and members of other ethnic groups that generally supported Kibaki and his Party of National Unity (PNU). Members of the Kikuyu and allied ethnicities responded with similarly violent reprisals against Luo, Kalenjin, and others assumed to support the ODM. The police, during this period, used lethal violence against peaceful demonstrators and are widely believed to have received shoot-to-kill orders from the highest level.[3]

The violence spread and caused at least 1,100 deaths, while displacing 500,000 or more Kenyans from their home, land, and businesses. It ended two months after the elections, when Kibaki and Odinga signed a power-sharing agreement, known as the National Accord. More broadly, the National Dialogue and Reconciliation process set in motion the creation of a series of institutions and activities that would, it was hoped, document what had happened and prevent future outbreaks of large-scale violence. These included a number of mechanisms that fall under the rubric of transitional justice, such as establishing a record on the institutional failures that occurred in the election process and appropriate measures to strengthen the Electoral Commission, determining the causes of the post-election violence and suggesting means to prevent its recurrence, obtaining accountability for the crimes committed, and promoting reconciliation.

This was not Kenya's first experience of large-scale political violence. In fact, immediately before and after the 1992 and 1997 general elections, a similar total number of people were killed and displaced. Those "ethnic clashes" in the 1990s, as they are usually called, were mainly instances of state-induced violence against members of ethnic groups who generally supported multi-partyism and challengers to the rule of authoritarian president Daniel arap Moi, but lived in zones dominated by Moi's party, the Kenya African National Union (KANU). The latter had ruled the country from independence in 1963 until Kibaki's election in 2002, after Moi retired. Despite systematic and credible documentation on which senior officials incited, organized, and financed the violence in the 1990s, the government never charged any of them. Thus, prior to the 2007–08 election violence, a history of complete impunity prevailed.

Although I use the term "transitional justice" in order to highlight links between processes discussed in this study and in the others in this volume, as well as in the broader literature, Kenya is not a typical example. For one, the transition to a new political order is only partial, lacking the solid break with the past that has occurred in such places as Bosnia and Herzegovina or Sierra Leone, both discussed in this volume. The former single party that had ruled Kenya since independence is no longer in power, but many of its officials—some of whom played an important role in many gross human rights violations in the past—still sit in Parliament and Cabinet. For that reason, it would be more accurate to refer to "post-conflict" or "post-atrocity" justice than transitional justice. I also discuss peace and peacebuilding in a somewhat different way from most, since Kenya experienced only intermittent violent conflict and no civil war, unlike the other countries analyzed in this book. The agreement signed to end the violence is not a typical peace agreement, though it contains many common elements, such as provisions for temporary governance structures, including power sharing, and new institutions. As no formal military combatants were involved, there has, however, been no discussion of disarmament, demobilization, and reintegration (DDR) in Kenya—though, as I shall argue, the continued existence of armed militias poses a serious threat to future stability.

This chapter assesses the performance to date of the National Dialogue and Reconciliation mechanisms of 2008 and how well they can be expected to function in the near future. In particular, it examines the contributions of the National Dialogue and Reconciliation process to transitional justice and peacebuilding in the Kenyan context—and the relationship between justice and peace. Goals discussed include holding perpetrators accountable, attending to victims' needs and the restitution of the assets they lost, establishing a broadly accepted account of what had occurred and why, and preventing recurrence. It draws on fieldwork conducted in Nairobi in December 2008 and January 2010, during which time I interviewed officials from embassies, aid missions, international organizations, Kenyan civil society organizations, and the government. Important local initiatives across the country, such as district peace committees, and reconciliation at the interpersonal level, unfortunately lie beyond the scope of this study.[4]

I argue that, though the agreements ended the widespread violence, it would be premature to assert that they re-established "positive peace," i.e. based on good inter-group relations, rather than merely a "negative peace," with a potentially fragile absence of generalized inter-group violence. While a few of the transitional justice mechanisms have attained some of their particular goals, the majority have not. As a result of the lacunae in transitional justice, perpetrators go unpunished (with the possible exception of a handful of individuals whom the International Criminal Court will try) and victims' needs are generally ignored (resulting in the general absence of victim-centered approaches to peacebuilding). Paradoxically, the lack of implementation and sometimes active sabotage of key initiatives included in crucial National Accord–related initiatives have helped keep the peace agreement in place. Powerful PNU and ODM political elites have joined forces to prevent, as best they can, measures that are not in their shared interest, notably accountability for the crimes committed—since several high-placed officials of both parties are alleged to be among those who bear the greatest responsibility for planning and financing the violence. The debates on the concrete trade-offs between or complementarity of transitional justice and peacebuilding apply with difficulty to Kenya: several years after the Accord was signed, it has produced no justice and only a tenuous peace.

The remainder of this chapter is organized as follows: first, I examine the concrete measures agreed to in the National Dialogue and Reconciliation process and the direct institutional outcomes, namely the appointment of several commissions and the adoption of a new constitution. Second, I analyze the indirect institutional outcomes, with a focus on the efforts to set up a special hybrid tribunal and the involvement of the International Criminal Court. Third, I examine key National Accord issues that remain insufficiently addressed or left off the agenda. The conclusion attempts to tease out the complex relationship between transitional justice and peacebuilding in Kenya and what lessons it might suggest for other countries.

Kenya's peace agreement: the Kenya National Dialogue and Reconciliation process

The international community responded rapidly to the post-election crisis in Kenya. The African Union appointed a Panel of Eminent African Personalities to mediate talks between the PNU and ODM, headed by former UN Secretary-General Kofi Annan and strongly supported by Western aid donors.[5] Early in the process, the two sides agreed on a four-point agenda: 1) ending the violence and restoring fundamental rights and liberties; 2) addressing the humanitarian crisis, as well as promoting reconciliation, healing, and restoration; 3) overcoming the political crisis; and 4) working on long-term issues and solutions.[6] The National Dialogue and Reconciliation process, as it became known, produced a series of joint ODM and PNU statements and agreements between February and May 2008. The foremost of these was the National Accord and Reconciliation Act, signed by Kibaki and Odinga on 28 February 2008, which instituted a power-sharing coalition government and basically ended the ongoing violence—thus resolving agenda items 1 and 3. The various agreements led to a number of other concrete measures, with both direct and indirect results, but also some significant gaps, all examined below.

Direct institutional outcomes

The agreements led directly to the creation of a number of commissions and other institutional reforms, including constitutional and electoral.

Commission of Inquiry into the Post-Election Violence

One of the most important commissions that the National Dialogue created was the Commission of Inquiry into the Post-Election Violence (CIPEV), also known as the Waki Commission, named after its chair, Kenyan Justice Philip Waki.[7] In June 2008, the chair and the other two CIPEV Commissioners, a human rights lawyer from the Democratic Republic of Congo and a senior police official from New Zealand, were sworn in. The appointment of international members was designed to enhance the commission's impartiality and legitimacy.

The Waki Report is an invaluable account of the violent acts that took place across the country in the two months that followed the December 2007 elections. Released in October 2008, it documents a broad range of atrocities and determined that the three sets of actors—ODM supporters and PNU supporters, as well as the police—shared responsibility for about one-third of the deaths each.[8] The data from the report not only helped establish a credible account of the nature of the violence, they also provided powerful evidence against self-serving and divisive claims that one "side" was responsible for the majority of the violence or that the majority of victims were from one particular ethnic group.

A key recommendation of the Waki Commission was the creation of a Special Tribunal for Kenya, a hybrid national/international tribunal discussed below, that would prosecute a hundred or perhaps several hundred suspected perpetrators. To help ensure that the coalition government followed up on its promise to implement the recommendation, the commission gave it 105 days from the report's publication date to create the tribunal. To avoid the report being ignored, a common fate of such documents in Kenya, the commissioners included a "Trojan horse" that vastly improved the odds of implementation.[9] Justice Waki sent Kofi Annan a sealed envelope that contained a list of names of people whom the commission believed to bear the greatest responsibility for organizing and financing the violence, accompanied by multiple boxes of evidence. Were the coalition government to fail to set up a credible tribunal by the deadline, 30 January 2009, Kofi Annan was to forward the documents to the prosecutor of the International Criminal Court (ICC), Luis Moreno-Ocampo, and request that he seek to open an investigation.[10] The results of this initiative are discussed below, under the rubric of indirect outcomes.

Truth, Justice and Reconciliation Commission

The idea of a truth commission was resurrected during the National Dialogue and Reconciliation process. The Kibaki government had in fact previously considered setting up a truth commission after it first came to power in January 2003.

Soon after, it appointed a task force on the issue, but then ignored its recommendations for setting up a truth commission.[11] Though the actual reason is unknown, a plausible explanation is that the Kibaki government was in fact a loose and last-minute alliance of parties and powerful individuals (National Rainbow Coalition, NARC) that had joined together shortly before the December 2002 general elections to defeat KANU, the incumbent party, and its presidential candidate, Uhuru Kenyatta. NARC included in its ranks a number of high-level former KANU politicians who themselves are widely believed to be deeply involved in many of the abuses during the rule of Daniel arap Moi (1978–2002), including massive corruption schemes and the organization and financing of widespread state-induced violence against opposition supporters in the 1990s, mentioned above. The Kibaki government relied on those individuals and their followers to govern and therefore had a strong incentive against investigating and prosecuting the main perpetrators—that is an important reason why one cannot say that Kenya has had a meaningful break with the past.

Within a week of signing the National Accord, PNU and ODM representatives reached an agreement that spelled out the parameters, principles, and composition of a Truth, Justice and Reconciliation Commission (TJRC) and committed the parties to create the commission expeditiously.[12] After a series of delays, the commission did not begin hearings until April 2011. The delays can be attributed mainly to the coalition government's foot-dragging, including the withholding of financial support, as well as the controversial appointment of Bethuel Kiplagat as commission chairperson, whom many Kenyans—and a few reports of previous commissions of inquiry—associate with the abuses committed under Moi's rule, including some that the TJRC would be investigating. As a result, the TJRC will be hard pressed to finalize its report before the next elections, due to be held by March 2013—thereby increasing the likelihood of its politicization during the electoral campaign, potentially fomenting more violence.

The TJRC's internal divisions and slow pace are not the only factors hampering the commission's work. The TJRC Act gave the commission an extremely broad mandate: to investigate human and economic rights abuses in Kenya between independence in December 1963 and the signing of the National Accord in February 2008. Among other reservations to the legislation, Kenyan and international human rights organizations criticized the insufficient independence granted to the commission and the government's central role in determining whether to prosecute or grant an amnesty. Many also believed that the provisions for witness protection and reparations were insufficient or left too vague.[13]

Though in theory a truth commission can promote reconciliation by allowing individuals to tell their stories, establishing an accurate historical account of abuses, restoring dignity to victims, and providing symbolic recognition and material reparations, Kenya's TJRC faces many challenges before it is able to achieve any of those outcomes. Making public the crimes of high-profile perpetrators and then granting them amnesties could make victims feel revictimized and even increase tensions.[14] The airing of an official "truth," especially when highly contested, does not *ipso facto* lead to reconciliation—it can in fact exacerbate local tensions and put witnesses at risk, as the experience of local *gacaca* courts in Rwanda demonstrates.[15] Given that the government has withheld payments of the TJRC's budget, it will probably be even more reluctant to provide victims with compensation. Foreign aid donors are highly unlikely to underwrite payments to individuals.[16]

Other processes and promises

The National Accord commits the coalition government to carrying out a number of other activities, the two most prominent of which are constitutional reform and the review of the 2007 presidential elections. Constitutional reform had been high on the public agenda for at least two decades. It completely dominated the political scene in 2004–05, culminating in a rejection of the proposed draft in a plebiscite in 2005.[17] The promulgation of a new constitution in August 2010, after 70 percent of Kenyan voters expressed their support in a referendum, is arguably the most important concrete achievement to date of the National Dialogue and Reconciliation process. The new constitution has the potential to catalyze widespread institutional reforms. The longer-term impact of the new constitution will depend heavily on the government's respect for constitutionalism and the rule of law, which in turn is subject to its political will.[18] Worrisome in that respect was Kibaki's attempt to appoint a new Attorney-General, Chief Justice, and Director of Public Prosecutions without consulting the prime minister, as the law requires. However, he eventually acquiesced to national and international pressure. A key undertaking will be the overhaul of the judiciary (widely perceived as very corrupt) and the police (responsible for extrajudicial killings with impunity, accord to a UN report), to which the government's commitment is tepid, at best.[19]

An important element of the National Accord was the commitment to determine what had gone wrong with the electoral process—thus establishing a definitive account of the spark that ignited the violence—and how to prevent recurrence. The ODM and PNU negotiation teams signed an agreement, on 4 March 2008, on the establishment of an Independent Review Committee, "mandated to investigate all aspects of the 2007 Presidential Election and make findings [sic] and recommendations to improve the electoral process."[20] The commission's report, issued in September 2008, offered a comprehensive review of procedures and numerous technical recommendations. Among other things, it led to the disbandment of the Electoral Commission of Kenya and the appointment of an interim new one, as well as to electoral reforms, such as redrawing district boundaries. As for its investigations into alleged irregularities in the presidential elections, the commission did not identify any clear patterns of fraudulent practices that would suggest that the incumbent government had systematically acted to steal the elections. This passive endorsement of Kibaki's victory disappointed many Kenyans and outside observers, including foreign diplomats, who felt that the report did not go far enough when it attributed irregularities to incompetence rather than intent.[21] Though the commission kick-started the reform of electoral procedures and institutions, it did not identify the legitimate winner of the 2007 presidential elections. The commission thus did not contribute to an indirect outcome of reconciliation based on a shared understanding of events. In fact, a finding in favor of either Kibaki or Odinga would likely have reignited conflict, rather than contribute to peacebuilding. The reform of electoral institutions that resulted from the commission will, however, improve the odds of future elections not only being free and fair, but also widely perceived to be so, reducing the odds of large-scale violence.

The National Dialogue and Reconciliation process also included commitments to a number of other longer-term issues, notably in a specific agreement signed by PNU and ODM representatives on 23 March 2008. The statement of principles listed a number of areas of reform that would contribute to sustainable peace over the longer term (agenda item 4), including constitutional and legal reform, land reform, poverty reduction, reduction of regional disparities, employment creation, especially for youth, and the creation of a National Ethnic and Race Relations Commission.[22] Of these areas, the coalition government has made good on its commitment to constitutional reform and the appointment of an Ethnic and Race Relations Commission, and has slowly begun judicial reform, which can all be considered direct outcomes of the National Dialogue and Reconciliation process. The remaining issues, however, are tremendous undertakings, some of which—such as job creation and the reduction of poverty levels—have been on the government's agenda since independence. Their presence in the statement of principles is unlikely in and of itself to lead to much progress, which is unfortunate from a peacebuilding perspective, because those seeking to recruit and mobilize individuals to carry out election-related violence often capitalize on underlying tensions and inequalities (whether perceived or real), as well as the ready availability of people (mainly young men) who could be easily mobilized.

Indirect institutional outcomes

The coalition government's concrete measures described above set in motion a number of other mechanisms and activities that indirectly resulted from the National Dialogue and Reconciliation process. The two most important ones, from the point of view of peace and justice, involve accountability for the atrocities committed, to be obtained locally at a special tribunal or by the ICC in The Hague. Holding perpetrators accountable via retributive justice may be of succor to victims and, at least in theory, be restorative as well. However, convictions would not automatically provide victims with pressing material needs, such as restitution or compensation.

Hybrid tribunal

After the Waki Commission published its report, the coalition government announced that it accepted the findings and would implement all of its recommendations. The most prominent of these was the proposal to create a Special

Tribunal for Kenya, mentioned above. Two of the tribunal's three judges and the special prosecutor were to be from other Commonwealth countries. Similar to the Waki Commission that proposed it, the special tribunal's international personnel would help guarantee its independence and fairness.

Despite three versions of legislation being drafted, the coalition government never actually created the hybrid tribunal. Many MPs opposed the first bill for differing and even opposing reasons. Some were concerned that the legislation contained loopholes that would make it ineffective in the struggle against impunity. A presidential pardon, for instance, could prevent a convicted perpetrator from serving his sentence. Those MPs preferred justice in The Hague, since the accused would be unlikely to unduly influence the ICC process, as they feared would be the case in a Kenya-based tribunal, despite the proposed safeguards of international staff.[23] Other MPs opposed the legislation because they feared that the hybrid tribunal *would* be effective and might pursue them or their allies, while the ICC seemed like a distant threat that could be dealt with later. Still others voted against the legislation because they felt the government had not consulted widely enough or allowed sufficient time to debate the bill.[24]

Despite promises to reintroduce improved legislation to establish a hybrid tribunal, the government never did. When Kofi Annan tired of the Kenyan government's recalcitrance and prevarications in July 2009, he forwarded the Waki envelope and evidence to Moreno-Ocampo. In response to the government's inaction, a backbench MP introduced a private member's bill on the establishment of a special tribunal. A sufficient number of MPs boycotted its reading in Parliament to prevent it from ever achieving the required quorum for debate.[25] Despite Parliament's and Cabinet's overwhelming expressions of support in public, they privately ensured that the Special Tribunal for Kenya would never be created—keeping in place the tradition of complete impunity for massive crimes.

Still, the public debates on accountability issues, the ultimately unsuccessful struggle to establish a special tribunal, and the evident hypocrisy of elected officials all combined to constitute unparalleled civic education among Kenyans of all walks of life on domestic and international accountability mechanisms and create a sustained demand for accountability.[26] They also promoted trust in and calls for the ICC to pursue those bearing the greatest responsibility for the post-election violence.

International Criminal Court

The ICC's *raison d'être* is to pursue grave transgressions of international criminal law in instances where the national government is unable or unwilling to pursue credible local trials, as is the case in Kenya. However, the Kenyan government and the ICC have been dancing an intricate *pas de deux*. Were it not for the Waki envelope and the specter of ICC involvement, it is highly unlikely that the Kenyan government would have embraced the recommendation of establishing a Special Tribunal for Kenya, including the introduction of legislation to do so. In fact, many Kenyan politicians' support for the hybrid tribunal mirrored the likelihood of ICC involvement. The higher the probability of ICC action, the more strongly some prominent politicians voiced support for the tribunal—in order to forestall ICC involvement. When the ICC "threat" seemed more distant, the special tribunal seemed less urgent.[27]

ICC Prosecutor Moreno-Ocampo obtained permission from the pre-trial chamber to open an investigation into the situation in Kenya in March 2010. At his request, the chamber issued summonses to appear to six high-level Kenyan officials. The three suspects in the first case were associated with the ODM (Cabinet ministers William Ruto and Henry Kosgey, as well as radio executive Joshua arap Sang, accused of fanning ethnic hatred). In the second case, all three suspects were linked to the PNU (Uhuru Kenyatta, deputy prime minister and minister of finance; Francis Muthaura, head of the civil service and secretary to the Cabinet; and former head of the police Hussein Ali, subsequently demoted to the position of Postmaster General). The ODM–PNU symmetry is generally understood to be the prosecutor's attempt to "balance" the accusations in order to show no bias, thus avoiding being accused of a witch-hunt and ensuring a high level of legitimacy for the ICC judicial process, as well decreasing the potential for further upheaval. Nevertheless, some Kalenjin politicians have tried to make political capital out of the fact that Moreno-Ocampo's three ODM-associated suspects are all ethnic Kalenjin from the Rift Valley, whereas no Luo was accused.

The ICC prosecutor's public naming of the suspects quickly set in motion a number of efforts to avoid them going to trial in The Hague, mostly conducted while publicly insisting on the government's complete support for and cooperation with the ICC. Three strategies soon emerged, some concurrently. The first involved the resurrection of the plan to set up a local tribunal (though purely national, not hybrid) that would be able to try the ICC suspects, among others, and thus obviate the need for ICC involvement. This strategy was unlikely to make a difference to the ICC judges, as once the investigations were authorized, the chamber would not normally reverse course. Even if it were possible for the ICC to accept a local tribunal as a substitute for its own proceedings, the tribunal would have to try the same six suspects for the same crimes, and the process would have to be credible, which is a highly improbable scenario. Local trials would depend on the prior reform of the Kenyan judiciary and police—no small or quick task. Credible proceedings would be unlikely, since the politicians' goal in setting up a local tribunal appears to be evading accountability, not just bringing the process to Kenyan soil.

The second strategy involved a Kenyan withdrawal from the ICC, preferably as part of a mass walkout of African countries dissatisfied with the ICC's alleged anti-Africa bias. Immediately after Moreno-Ocampo named the six suspects in December 2010, the Kenyan parliament unanimously passed a (non-binding) motion to withdraw from the ICC. The initiative found an ally in Sudanese president al-Bashir and Kenyan officials won African Union support for ignoring any forthcoming ICC summonses to appear or arrest warrants. However, Kenyan officials abruptly dropped the campaign for departure *en masse*, perhaps because they realized that their formal withdrawal would be effective only one year after official notification and that the ICC would retain jurisdiction over grave crimes committed on Kenyan soil while the country was still a member.

The third strategy was a concerted but ultimately unsuccessful effort to persuade members of the UN Security Council, especially the five permanent members who wield veto power, to pass a resolution instructing the ICC to suspend its involvement for one year, based on the argument that the current ICC process posed a risk to international peace and security. This is the only permissible reason to forestall, albeit temporarily, the ICC. Credible domestic trials alone are insufficient grounds for the Security Council to suspend proceedings.

Despite the Kenyan government's multiple attempts to prevent ICC involvement, the ICC confirmed charges against four of the six accused (Kenyatta, Ruto, Muthaura, and Sang) in January 2012. At best, the ICC could find four perpetrators guilty of crimes against humanity committed during the two-month period that followed Kenya's 2007 general elections. This would constitute a remarkable break with the complete impunity of the past and be very important symbolically for victims. However, the lower-level perpetrators that victims identified as responsible for their personal plight would remain unaffected. Barring any credible Kenyan tribunal, the hundreds and perhaps thousands of other perpetrators will not be held accountable for their actions.[28] This scenario does not provide much hope for deterring future outbreaks of mass violence, for instance in conjunction with the general elections due to be held by March 2013. For one, future perpetrators would make sure to not leave a clear trail of evidence, which did not matter in the past. They might also ensure that they are not among the half-dozen of those most responsible for the violence, as the ICC is unlikely to prosecute more than a handful in any future case of election violence.

Some Kenyan government officials have, in fact, begun to recast the role of the ICC and international criminal justice as antithetical to peace and national reconciliation, as well as national sovereignty. To discredit international accountability mechanisms, a few officials have publicly suggested that Justice Waki committed treason when he handed over the evidence to a foreigner and that Kofi Annan, previously trumpeted as the savior of Kenya for his role in the National Accord mediations, was actually a puppet of the West. Some uninformed outside observers have rather naïvely accepted the politicians' self-serving framing of the ICC as a new threat to the country's well-being, forgetting that the lack of accountability for previous serious crimes, including the killings and forced displacement associated with the 1992 and 1997 elections, facilitated the 2007–08 post-election violence. For instance, a well-intentioned December 2010 *Washington Post* editorial endorses continued impunity, warning of the risk that prosecution "will drag Kenya back toward civil war" and concluding that "Justice for human rights crimes is important; but Kenya's continued peace and democratic process is of greater value than another endless prosecution in The Hague."[29] ICC trials could indeed serve as a pretext for the accused and their allies to foment further violence in protest of the supposedly unfair charges and alleged unwarranted targeting of specific communities, especially if convictions fall disproportionately on one side. However, these are likely to be of short duration and remain localized.[30] Thus, accountability might pose a minor threat to the negative peace in the short term, but continued impunity poses a much bigger threat to negative peace in the medium and long term. Each bout of inter-ethnic violence renders more difficult the path to an eventual positive peace.

Opinion polls suggest that self-serving politicians failed to persuade ordinary Kenyans. A poll released in February 2011 found that over 60 percent of those polled opposed withdrawal from the ICC, a position supported by 36 percent.[31] An April 2011 poll revealed that 61 percent of respondents felt that those responsible for the violence should face ICC trials, while only 32 percent preferred either a hybrid national/international tribunal (24 percent) or local courts (8 percent).[32]

Unfinished business

The Kenyan government has achieved a lot more on some agenda items than others. As mentioned above, the National Accord quickly put an end to the violence (item 1) and the political crisis (item 3). Results remain far more elusive, however, on addressing the humanitarian crisis, promoting reconciliation, healing, and restoration (item 2), and working on long-term issues and solutions (item 4).

With regards to item 2, the most important remnants of the humanitarian crisis are the internally displaced persons (IDPs), the main (surviving) victims of the post-election chaos. As mentioned above, the violence displaced more than 500,000 people. Though the political crisis was resolved in 2008, the following year 60 percent or more of IDPs were still unable to return home and most were living in deplorable conditions, while few received sufficient compensation or assistance for resettlement.[33] About 350,000 found refuge in one of more than 100 tented camps for IDPs, where they joined a similar number of people displaced by state-induced violence in the 1990s who had never been relocated. Despite the coalition government's public commitment to resettle all IDPs by the end of 2010, at least 300,000 of the 2007–08 IDPs remained in camps in February 2011, three years after the crisis ended.[34]

Item 2's other objectives—reconciliation, healing, and restoration—are also elusive and complex. Though most may not see themselves that way, members of several communities are both perpetrators and victims, a fact that would immensely complicate any discussion of reparations or compensation, with a potential for renewed animosity. Likewise, what might bring about healing for one community, for instance the conviction of a high-level organizer of the violence against its members, could—if seen as unjust or imbalanced—fuel further resentment among the perpetrator's ethnoregional group. Moreover, the restitution of property could provoke renewed antagonism, especially if its legal ownership is contested or perceived as unjust.[35]

As explained earlier, the main institutional response in this area is the Truth, Justice and Reconciliation Commission, which only began to hold hearings in

April 2011, after many delays and widespread criticism. Moreover, though they are at the core of peacebuilding and transitional justice efforts, the outcomes of healing and reconciliation are extremely difficult to measure.[36] Still, there appear to be few signs that inter-ethnic relations have substantially improved, especially at the local level, though more research is required to make a more definitive statement. Though a few new alliances have formed across the 2007 electoral divide, it is mainly limited to the elite level and the "coalition of the accused," who share interests in evading accountability, yet sometimes still rally support via ethnic nationalist discourse.[37] Ethnic partisanry was clearly a major factor in responses to the ICC prosecutor's charges against the "Ocampo Six." Once ICC trials begin, arguments and revelations regarding crimes committed, as well as the identities of those most responsible, could also stoke tensions along ethnic lines, for instance if Kikuyu suspects portray Kikuyu-perpetrated violence as justified self-defense against prior Kalenjin attacks.

The coalition government has already dealt effectively with some of the components of agenda item 4—longer-term issues. Its main achievement is the drafting, approval by plebiscite, and promulgation of a new constitution. It has also initiated the reform of other institutions, notably the electoral ones, but very little has been done on reforming the judiciary, the police, and the civil service. Likewise, there has been scant progress, if any, on the other item 4 issues: land reform; poverty, inequity and regional imbalances; unemployment, particularly among the youth; consolidation of national cohesion and unity; and transparency, accountability, and impunity. Though constitutional and institutional reform may have positive effects in the future, in the short-to-medium term, it is unlikely to have an impact on justice or peacebuilding.

Off the agenda

Peace agreements usually contain provisions on the demobilization, disarmament, and reintegration (DDR) of armed groups. The National Dialogue and Reconciliation agenda, however, contained no mention of DDR. Though the armed groups in Kenya differ greatly from the parties that negotiate the end to civil wars—typically a country's armed forces and one or more rebel groups—the issue remains extremely salient. Much of the violence around the 1992, 1997, and 2007 elections was perpetrated by organized militias (often known by the Kiswahili word *jeshi*). Some *jeshis* are beholden to a specific political figure, who funds them and has them do his bidding. Others are fundamentally "guns for hire." The most famous irregular armed group is Mungiki, an officially banned, large, Kikuyu-based organization that is part religious cult, part criminal gang, and part *jeshi*. During the 2008 post-election violence, PNU officials are alleged to have paid Mungiki to carry out brutal attacks on ODM supporters in Naivasha and Nakuru.[38] The failure of the National Accord to address what to do about the various militias is one of its biggest flaws. The coalition government's lack of any serious attempts to disarm the *jeshis* is one of the greatest threats to peace in future elections. In fact, various communities have been arming themselves in anticipation of future attacks, notably in the Rift Valley, the main location of political violence since the 1990s. In a new arms race, they are purchasing sophisticated weapons, such as AK-47 machine guns, from illegal arms dealers.[39]

The other major area of concern left out of the National Accord regards the protection of victims, in particular those who have served or could serve as witnesses for various official investigations. The Kenyan press and NGOs have already noted with alarm that a significant number of those who testified before the Waki Commission have been threatened, injured, or even killed, possibly by members of *jeshis*. Some have already recanted their testimony. The ICC will protect and relocate any witnesses who testify in The Hague. However, those who spoke to ICC pre-trial investigators in Kenya will get no support. The coalition government, under pressure from NGOs and aid donors, strengthened its witness protection program in 2010, but critics claim it still cannot provide adequate protection. The insufficiencies of the program and the protection of witnesses more generally will be serious impediments if there are prosecutions held in Kenya. In a related concern, Deputy Prime Minister Uhuru Kenyatta, one of the "Ocampo Six" named in December 2010, remained on the Witness Protection Agency advisory board until he bowed to ICC pressure and resigned in March 2011—and may have had access to witnesses' confidential information.[40]

Conclusion: no justice, fragile peace

Ideally, transitional justice measures not only promote accountability and fight impunity in relation to past violence, they also act as an incentive for peace and deter future abuses. In Kenya, however, the coalition government formed in response to the post-election violence in 2007–08 had only an insincere commitment to transitional justice, especially to the matter of accountability for the gross abuses. In particular, it expected that the report of the Commission of Inquiry into the Post-Election Violence would merely gather dust. It was caught off guard by the Waki Report's leverage, using Kofi Annan and the secret envelope, but it still managed to scuttle the proposed hybrid tribunal to try suspected perpetrators of the violence. The government also established a Truth, Justice and Reconciliation Commission—a staple of transitional justice mechanisms meant to contribute directly to peacebuilding—but gave it a feeble mandate and sabotaged its work sufficiently to remove any significant threat of negative repercussions on the political class. It has raised the prospect of a national tribunal, mainly in an attempt to forestall ICC trials, but has taken little action, including in the necessary concomitant major reform of the discredited judiciary and police—though the appointment of a well-respected human rights scholar and former activist as Chief Justice of the Supreme Court may set in motion a positive process. Victims of past violence remain vulnerable, especially if they are able to provide testimony against perpetrators and the government does not provide sufficient witness protection. This will make prosecutions more difficult, at least in Kenya. Only the ICC in The Hague could escape its grasp, but its work will be slow and distant from Kenyans' everyday activities and, moreover, will not try more than four suspects.

The reason Kenyan transitional justice mechanisms will have such limited outcomes is relatively simple: There has not been a meaningful transition or break with the past, as a number of perpetrators remain in positions of power and there have been no high-level prosecutions for any of the crimes of the authoritarian past. The National Accord put in place a power-sharing coalition government in which prominent members of the political elite on both sides shared a common interest in avoiding accountability for the atrocities that their members helped organize and finance. The lack of accountability has in fact helped keep the peace agreement going. It is the "politics of collusion" that bring together the various party leaders and ethnoregional political barons and has made it possible to manipulate important components of the Kenya Dialogue and Reconciliation process according to their own needs.[41] The National Accord has nonetheless achieved more than a mere ceasefire. It has created significant momentum for constitutional reform and the strengthening of election-related institutions. Some judicial reform and other measures might follow. Even after several years, however, it has failed to compensate or relocate hundreds of thousands of victims of the 2007–08 violence, many of whom still languish in IDP camps. Two key issues were left off the National Dialogue and Reconciliation agenda—the disarmament of militias and the protection of witnesses—which will cause greater insecurity at the local level and facilitate future outbreaks of widespread, organized political violence, including in conjunction with the next general elections, to be held by March 2013.

An analysis of Kenya's National Accord cannot test the hypothesis that transitional justice contributes to peace. It does, however, suggest that the lack of transitional justice, especially accountability for past atrocities, may temporarily keep the "negative" peace, but it might make future conflict more likely. Continued impunity compounds the shared understanding that violence is a useful political tool. Accountability mechanisms, on the other hand, may put some victims and witnesses at risk in the short term, but they also could facilitate a more positive peace in the future. They are unlikely, in practice, to meet victims' material needs and we still do not know enough to predict how they might affect reconciliation, healing, and restoration.

For the time being, there is no real trade-off in Kenya between peace and justice, but rather a substantial lack of both. The National Accord has permitted negative peace to prevail, with few signs of positive peace. Tensions will mount again once the ICC trials begin and the 2012–13 campaign and general elections will no doubt exacerbate the situation, raising the risk of broader violence—especially as armed militias are allowed to continue to operate. Government promises of justice, premised on prior judicial and police reform, to be followed by credible trials of numerous perpetrators of the 2007–08 atrocities appear unrealistic, especially in the short-to-medium term, mainly due to lack of will. The only measure that can escape the government's control and shatter Kenya's record of complete impunity is to be found at the international level. The ICC might condemn and sentence some of those most responsible for Kenya's latest bout of large-scale, election-related violence, but even in the best case scenario it will apply only to a small number of individuals and is unlikely to deter in and of itself future violence.

Kenya also serves as a cautionary tale for other countries at risk of conflict, including with regard to: 1) the application of transitional justice mechanisms in situations where no significant transition has taken place; 2) the potential for anti-accountability alliances to sabotage domestic justice mechanisms, especially under power-sharing coalition governments; 3) the importance of DDR, even in agreements that end conflicts that are not really civil wars; and 4) the needs and vulnerability of victims and their central role as witnesses in achieving accountability.

Acknowledgements

The author gratefully acknowledges funding from the Social Sciences and Humanities Research Council of Canada.

Notes

1 David Throup, "The Count," *Journal of Eastern African Studies*, vol. 2 (2008), pp. 290–304.

2 The Kenyan government does not publish census data on ethnicity. However, common estimates for the main ethnic groups in Kenya are the Kikuyu (21–24%), Luhya and Luo (13–14% each), Kalenjin (11–13%), Kamba (11%), Kisii (6%), and Meru (5–6%). Electoral alliances between ethnic "power brokers" vary widely from election to election. In 2007, most Kikuyu, Kamba, and Meru supported the incumbent Mwai Kibaki and his Party of National Unity. The main support for the main presidential challenger, Raila Odinga, and his Orange Democratic Movement came from the Kalenjin and Luo.

3 The International Criminal Court (discussed below) did not, however, confirm charges against the head of police Mohammed Hussein Ali for his alleged role in the post-election violence.

4 For analysis of local peacebuilding in one Kenyan community, see Jacqueline M. Klopp, Patrick Githinji, and Keffa Karuoya, "Internal Displacement and Local Peacebuilding in Kenya: Challenges and Innovations," Special Report 251 (Washington, DC: United States Institute of Peace, September 2010).

5 For more on the talks and international contributions, see Stephen Brown, "Donor Responses to the 2008 Kenyan Crisis: Finally Getting it Right?" *Journal of Contemporary African Studies*, vol. 27 (2009), pp. 389–406; Monica Kathina Juma, "African Mediation of the Kenyan Post-2007 Election Crisis," *Journal of Contemporary African Studies*, vol. 27 (2009), pp. 407–30; and Gilbert M. Khadiagala, "Regionalism and Conflict Resolution: Lessons from the Kenyan Crisis," *Journal of Contemporary African Studies*, vol. 27 (2009), pp. 431–44.

6 Kenyan National Dialogue and Reconciliation, "Annotated Agenda and Timetable," 1 February 2008.

7 The commission's mandate, according to an agreement signed on 4 March 2008 by the PNU and ODM negotiating teams, was "(i) to investigate the facts and surrounding circumstances related to acts of violence that followed the 2007 Presidential Election, (ii) investigate the actions or omissions of State security agencies during the

course of the violence, and make recommendation [sic] as necessary, and (iii) to recommend measures of a legal, political or administrative nature, as appropriate, including measures with regard to bringing to justice those persons responsible for criminal acts" (p. 2).

8 Waki Commission, *Report of the Commission of Inquiry into Post-Election Violence*, Nairobi (October 2008).

9 The expression was used by Mugambi Kiai, Open Society Institute, interviewed by Stephen Brown and Chandra Lekha Sriram, Nairobi, Kenya, 15 January 2010. The best example of a similar report being ignored in the past is the report of the Judicial Commission Appointed to Inquire into Tribal Clashes in Kenya, known as the Akiwumi Commission, presented to President Daniel arap Moi in 1999, but released publicly only in 2002. It contained serious allegations against many high-level government and ruling party officials, but the government undertook no investigations or prosecutions.

10 Waki Commission, *Report of the Commission of Inquiry*, op. cit., p. 473.

11 Task Force on the Establishment of a Truth, Justice and Reconciliation Commission, "Report of the Task Force on the Establishment of a Truth, Justice and Reconciliation Commission" (Nairobi: Government Printer, 2003).

12 Kenyan National Dialogue and Reconciliation, "Truth, Justice and Reconciliation Commission," 4 March 2008.

13 See discussion in Stephen Brown, "Kenya," in Lavinia Stan and Nadya Nedelsky (eds), *Encyclopedia of Transitional Justice* (Cambridge University Press, in press).

14 European ambassador, interviewed by Stephen Brown, Nairobi, Kenya, December 2008.

15 Jennie E. Burnet, "The Injustice of Local Justice: Truth, Reconciliation, and Revenge in Rwanda," *Genocide Studies and Prevention*, vol. 3 (2008), pp. 173–93; Max Rettig, "Gacaca: Truth, Justice, and Reconciliation in Postconflict Rwanda?" *African Studies Review*, vol. 51 (2008), pp. 25–50.

16 Western official, interviewed by Stephen Brown and Chandra Lekha Sriram, Nairobi, Kenya, January 2010.

17 For further information, see Beth Elise Whitaker and Jason Giersch, "Voting on a Constitution: Implications for Democracy in Kenya," *Journal of Contemporary African Studies*, vol. 27 (2009), pp. 1–20.

18 See discussion in Stephen Brown, "Lessons Learned and Forgotten: The International Community and Electoral Conflict Management in Kenya," in David Gillies (ed.), *Elections in Dangerous Places: Democracy and the Paradoxes of Peacebuilding* (Montreal: McGill-Queen's University Press, 2011), pp. 127–43; Susanne D. Mueller, "Dying to Win: Elections, Political Violence, and Institutional Decay in Kenya," *Journal of Contemporary African Studies*, vol. 29 (2011), pp. 99–117.

19 On the judiciary, see International Bar Association and International Legal Assistance Consortium, "Restoring Integrity: An Assessment of the Needs of the Justice System in the Republic of Kenya" (February 2010). On police impunity, see Philip Alston, "Report of the Special Rapporteur on Extrajudicial, Summary or Arbitrary Executions," UN Doc. A/HRC/11/2/Add.6, 26 May 2009.

20 National Dialogue and Reconciliation, "Independent Review Committee," 4 March 2008.

21 Two Western embassy officials and one Western ambassador, interviewed by Stephen Brown, Nairobi, Kenya, December 2008.

22 Kenya National Dialogue and Reconciliation, "Statement of Principles on Long-Term Issues and Solutions," 23 May 2008.

23 Even if the judges were impartial, many feared that perpetrators would be able to tamper with evidence, silence or threaten witnesses, or otherwise prevent a guilty verdict.

24 Godfrey M. Musila, "Options for Transitional Justice in Kenya: Autonomy and the Challenge of External Prescriptions," *International Journal of Transitional Justice*, vol. 3 (2009), p. 452.

25 A more detailed account of the various attempts to create a hybrid tribunal is available in Stephen Brown with Chandra Lekha Sriram, "The Big Fish Won't Fry Themselves: Criminal Accountability for Post-Election Violence in Kenya," *African Affairs*, vol. 111 (2012), pp. 244–60.

26 Mugambi Kiai, Programme Officer, Open Society Initiative for East Africa, interviewed by Stephen Brown and Chandra Lekha Sriram, Nairobi, Kenya, 15 January 2010.

27 See Brown with Sriram, "The Big Fish Won't Fry Themselves," op. cit.

28 Human Rights Watch identified only six convictions of low-level individuals, with three other local cases in progress as of December 2011, almost four years after the violence ended. Its report also noted a marked anti-ODM bias in the selection of cases. See Human Rights Watch, "*'Turning pebbles': Evading Accountability for Post-Election Violence in Kenya*" (New York: Human Rights Watch, 2011), pp. 39–44.

29 "Justice for Kenya," *Washington Post*, p. A14, 30 December 2010.

30 Several unattributable interviews conducted by Stephen Brown and Chandra Lekha Sriram in Nairobi, Kenya, January 2010.

31 *The Standard* (Nairobi), 10 February 2011.

32 Synovate, "Kenyans' Perception towards the ICC Process," 6 April 2011, available at <*http://www.synovate.co.ke/spr/index.php/site/poll/kenyans_perception_towards_the_icc_process_6th_april_2011*>, accessed 10 July 2011.

33 Jacqueline M. Klopp, "Kenya's Unfinished Agendas," *Journal of International Affairs*, vol. 62 (2009), p. 148. See also Prisca Kamungi and Jacqueline M. Klopp, "Failure to Protect: Lessons from Kenya's IDP Network," *Forced Migration Review*, vol. 28 (2007), pp. 52–53.

34 Victoria Mwirichia and Jeniffer Katusya Barako Elema, "How Far is Home For Kenya's Internally Displaced Persons?" (Nairobi: Institute for Security Studies), 24 February 2011, available at <*http://www.issafrica.org/iss_today.php?ID=1238*>, accessed 17 April 2011.

35 On this and other challenges to peacebuilding posed by internal displacement, see Klopp *et al.*, "Internal Displacement and Local Peacebuilding in Kenya," op. cit., pp. 3–4.

36 See Colleen Duggan, "Editorial Note," *International Journal of Transitional Justice*, vol. 4 (2010), pp. 315–28 (special issue on "Transitional Justice on Trial: Evaluating Its Impact").

37 For instance, former rivals Uhuru Kenyatta (PNU) and William Ruto (ODM) have joined forces to try to avoid being tried by the ICC. There are rumors that they might run on the same ticket during the 2013 elections. However, their alliance might be short lived: after ICC trials begin, they are likely to incriminate each other's side, presenting themselves and their communities as victims.

38 Waki Commission, *Report of the Commission of Inquiry*, op. cit.

39 "Kenyans 'Rearming for 2012 Poll,'" BBC News online, 7 October 2009, available at <*http://news.bbc.co.uk/2/hi/8293745.stm*>, accessed 17 April 2011.

40 "Lack of a Credible Witness Protection Unit a Major Setback," *The Standard* (Nairobi), 9 April 2011.

41 Nic Cheeseman and Blessing-Miles Tendi, "Power-Sharing in Comparative Perspective: The Dynamics of 'Unity Government' in Kenya and Zimbabwe," *Journal of Modern African Studies*, vol. 48 (2010), pp. 203–29.

14 Conclusions and considerations for practitioners

Chandra Lekha Sriram and Jemima García-Godos

Introduction

Summing up the findings of an edited volume of detailed analytic and country chapters is a challenge. We have chosen here to focus upon a few of the numerous issues and lessons developed in this book, and to identify lessons which might be of utility for policymakers engaged in peacebuilding and transitional justice activities. First, in light of the impact of such activities on development, the developmental context that enables or constrains such activities, and the reality that development actors remain in country long after international peacebuilding and transitional justice practitioners have left, we consider the opportunities for closer linkages between the transitional justice activities and development in a peacebuilding context. Second, we consider the opportunities and risks of developing disarmament, demobilization, and reintegration of ex-combatants (DDR) and victim-centered justice activities in tandem, either in broad cooperation or in a more tightly integrated fashion, in light of the fact that such activities often overlap in time and space, in terms of the (largely international) policymaking entities, and in that the subjects of each are generally expected to coexist in fairly close proximity in the long term. Finally, we consider options for timing and sequencing of DDR and victim-oriented transitional justice processes, recognizing that the timing of DDR processes may be relatively inflexible and dictated by the demands of peace agreements and the need to stabilize a situation. We identify the risks and, where possible, opportunities of choices in all three areas, and offer not prescriptions, but guidance regarding key issues and challenges for practitioners to map and examine before pursuing these activities.

Development and transitional justice in peacebuilding contexts

Although transitional justice and development activities have not historically been officially linked, they inevitably affect one another. Scholars and practitioners of transitional justice have increasingly scrutinized this connection.[1] They do so not least because transitional justice activities, like the conflicts they often follow or accompany, frequently occur in countries with significant development needs and external development involvement. According to the Human Development Index for 2011, which ranks 187 countries and territories, four of the countries examined in this volume are among those with "low human development" (Kenya, Uganda, Sierra Leone, Liberia), that is, countries with low rankings in terms of basic aspects of human development: health, knowledge, and income.[2] Taking inequality into account, Colombia joins Cambodia in the medium human development category, while Lebanon and Bosnia and Herzegovina are ranked among countries with high levels of human development.[3] A common feature of most of the countries studied in this volume is the poverty and deprivation that a great majority of the population experiences in their everyday lives. When people struggle to meet their most basic needs, often aggravated by previous or current situations of armed conflict, displacement, and discrimination, the pursuit of public policies on transitional justice and peacebuilding may seem, for many, naive or idealistic. How can transitional justice and peacebuilding objectives and programs take into account the multifaceted challenges of poverty and inequality in which they so often have to be implemented?

In the introduction to this volume, we discussed the need for practitioners to be aware of the national and local contexts in which accountability mechanisms are to be applied and to recognize the relationship between transitional justice goals and national development objectives and policies. We also called for caution regarding the limits of transitional justice mechanisms, which are designed primarily to address past human rights violations, and which may not necessarily be either sufficient or appropriate to address structural inequalities. However, there may yet be some opportunities to constructively link development, transitional justice, and peacebuilding.

Opportunities

The participation of civil society in decision-making processes affecting the lives of local populations is of vital importance for rights-based development.[4] The implementation of transitional justice mechanisms and peacebuilding measures may raise awareness about accountability and victims' rights in general, providing civil society actors and victims' organizations with the necessary tools (discursive, juridical, administrative) to frame demands and assert rights. These processes can be observed in a great variety of settings and take different forms. In Colombia, the largest victims' movement developed in response to the Justice and Peace Law of 2005. In Cambodia, the establishment of the Extraordinary Chambers in the Courts of Cambodia (ECCC) and the inclusion of victims in the proceedings were accompanied by the creation of a Victims Support Section which is tasked to develop non-judicial measures that can be awarded as moral and collective reparations. These measures are to be developed in cooperation with civil society organizations and victims' groups, who seized this opportunity to frame victims' rights.

Linking development policies to transitional justice and peacebuilding activities may allow for more efficient use of scarce resources. In post-conflict societies, limited pools of trained staff, infrastructure, and funds may be strained by the creation of new and often parallel institutions specifically designed for transitional justice and/or peacebuilding activities. Using existing institutions to pursue transitional justice activities could alleviate the pressure on resources and might also contribute to the sensitization of officials in state bureaucracies regarding accountability and victims' rights. In Colombia, the national development agency *Acción Social* was tasked with providing assistance to the internally displaced people through the National System for the Attention of Displaced Population. *Acción Social* is a national institution operating across the country with professional staff, infrastructure, and partnerships with other national and local institutions. It is also well known among civil society actors and local populations, and thus recognizable among beneficiary groups such as victims' organizations and representatives. While it was originally obliged to provide this assistance following a sentence by the Colombian Constitutional Court declaring the situation of the internally displaced as "an unconstitutional state of affairs,"[5] *Acción Social* was well-placed, based on this experience, to support the establishment of the national victim reparations program envisaged by the new Victims' Law of 2011. The government has thus transformed it into the Department for Social Prosperity to assume the new task. In a more limited example, in Sierra Leone, the National Commission for Social Action (NaCSA) was tasked with delivering victim reparations which were provided by the international community; international actors provided funds to build the capacity of NaCSA to develop the victims' registry as well.

Low- and middle-income countries use national development plans and poverty reduction strategies as a central policymaking tool. Such plans and strategies may, and in some cases do, include transitional justice and peacebuilding activities. Such activities, which include accountability for past human rights violations and the reintegration of former combatants, are expected by some programmers and analysts to promote the consolidation of the rule of law, the (re)establishment of civic trust, and the reinforcement of public security. National development strategies might be designed with these concerns in mind, promoting mechanisms that facilitate access to justice, reform of security policies, or coordination between public services and victim reparations programs. Unfortunately, while it is possible to identify potential synergies, good practices in this area are still scarce. As Quinn discusses in the context of Uganda and as discussed below, the inclusion of transitional justice and peacebuilding measures in development policies may not produce positive results.

Risks

Uganda's attempt to combine a range of activities through comprehensive development policies seems to be more a response to pressures from international donors than a serious attempt to consider the implications and requirements of each area: transitional justice, peacebuilding, poverty, and development. States may find it challenging to meet the demands of donors and international organizations to address development needs, accountability, and peacebuilding simultaneously. This may heighten the challenges that national implementing agencies often have with complex reporting procedures and benchmarks. In Uganda, limited capacity combines with limited political commitment to address the needs of the people in Northern Uganda, in which a situation of armed conflict persists. Uganda's incorporation of transitional justice and peacebuilding in national development plans watered down both transitional justice and peacebuilding activities, according to Quinn. However, it may be the case that development goals should take priority over accountability or peacebuilding measures.

Accountability for past atrocities can strain development activities, including the promotion of the ordinary rule of law, particularly where the national judicial system is tasked with prosecution of mass human rights violations or war crimes. In Bosnia, significant resources have been provided to the state-level War Crimes Chamber. However, local courts (at entity level) also have jurisdiction over war crimes. Some argue that police, prosecutorial resources, and court time have been diverted from the investigation and adjudication of ordinary crimes.

Possibly the most serious risk regarding the implementation of transitional justice and peacebuilding mechanisms is not so much what is done; the gap is, rather, between what governments and donors promise and what victims expect, and what is delivered. As Raddatz argues with respect to the experience of Liberia, it is necessary to temper great expectations. Practitioners create expectations for, and victims often demand, a range of outcomes, from truth to criminal accountability, to memorials, to reparations, to reconciliation. In practice, however, practitioners must make pragmatic decisions regarding resources, including allocation of reparations and provision of other, non-monetary compensation.

Transitional justice is not a panacea for all of the social problems that societies in transition might experience. While transitional justice practitioners must be aware of wider demands for distributive justice, particularly given that maldistribution of wealth and land may have been the cause and/or the consequence of earlier conflict and abuse, the tools of transitional justice are not necessarily suited to address structural inequalities. Structural inequalities might be addressed through agrarian reform or redistribution, often the recommendations of commissions of inquiry, but these proposals are seldom implemented. They may nonetheless raise expectations, and processes that do not deliver on such expectations may weaken the delicate links of trust between local populations and victims' groups, and governments.

What should transitional justice and peacebuilding practitioners consider when addressing development-related issues?

Committed as we are to accountability, justice, and peace, it may be difficult for academics, practitioners, and human rights advocates to recognize that victims may not prioritize criminal accountability or a truth commission report. Victims may instead prioritize finding a job, securing food and healthcare, or taking care of a disabled relative. Thus it is essential to be clear about who the victims of past human rights violations are, what types of victimhood they have experienced, and what their current needs are. The situation of amputees in Sierra Leone illustrates this clearly. The loss of a limb (or more) creates a permanent disability affecting a person's quality of life for the duration of her life, affecting her ability to perform private functions such as personal hygiene, to take care of children, to cook, or to secure and perform a paying job. In such a situation, lump-sum cash payments, such as the US $100 reparations grant provided in Sierra Leone, are ill-suited for individuals with long-term needs, not only amputees but also victims of debilitating trauma. Such victims are likely to require longer-term, sustained support, and indeed one-off payments may falsely raise hopes among victims that they will receive regular payments. The sense of abandonment that victim communities often already experience might be increased by unfounded expectations, risking a kind of double victimization.

Victim reparations provide acknowledgement of violations, and there are many forms of reparation. While certain groups of victims may need monetary compensation, many transitional societies facing poverty and development challenges will only be able to provide limited reparations. A combination of individual reparations and collective reparations in the form of services might provide a variety of measures that may at least partly fulfill the needs and interests of victims and might be compatible with development-oriented policies and programs. Specific groups of victims can be provided services such as health and educational programs, housing support, access to justice, restoration of personal documents, and legal support. Collective reparations could be provided either in material and symbolic forms, such as support for a community house, or in the creation of sites of memory and commemoration. Educational curricula and civic education processes can promote understanding and memory of the past, and institutional reforms can help to guarantee non-repetition of abuses. Collective reparations can have an impact on victims beyond those that have taken part in an accountability process, and may be particularly important in countries with a large number of victims. National agencies frequently implement such programs, although the sources of funding may be national, as in Colombia, or largely international, as in Sierra Leone.

Coordination and integration

Discussions of coordination and integration in the context of peacebuilding and transitional justice often turn upon coordination of international and bilateral actors, who frequently bring different priorities or agendas to the work, or do not seek to coordinate efforts, taxing local absorptive capacities. Here, however, we have been concerned with a different order of coordination—between or amongst the various activities of peacebuilding and transitional justice themselves, with a particular eye on measures that seek to address needs and demands of victims, and measures that seek immediate DDR and longer-term reintegration of former combatants. Some chapters also considered whether, beyond simple coordination, these activities can or should be more tightly integrated with one another.

However, the chapters in this volume illuminate a range of challenges for any coordination or integration of DDR processes with victim-centered justice. There are evident tensions between victim-centered justice and DDR. Nonetheless, such processes often operate in close proximity to one another—they often operate in the same territory, at the same time, and involve some of the same programmers and/or beneficiaries. They may also involve overlapping sets of service providers—state, international, or local. Thus, it is worth asking: Could these activities be coordinated with one another, or even integrated?

In many of the country studies in this volume, justice processes and DDR have clearly not been coordinated, and have often either been in tension with one another or not occurred contemporaneously. For example, in Cambodia, the ECCC process was initiated decades after the original violence, and after relevant peace agreements and peacekeeping/peacebuilding processes under the United Nations Transitional Authority in Cambodia (UNTAC). In Bosnia, the initial accountability processes at the International Criminal Tribunal for the Former Yugoslavia (ICTY) were active alongside peacebuilding in the country temporally, but not geographically; the local hybrid War Crimes Chamber began work significantly later. In Lebanon, DDR activities never disarmed a key fighting and political force, Hezbollah, and the only accountability process currently in place does not address past abuses that took place during the conflict. Kenya did not experience a traditional armed conflict, and no traditional peacebuilding process was put in place. DDR was also not put into place, and militias remain armed; in such a context accountability processes, particularly the involvement of the ICC, appear popular in polls but their deeper impact on victims or the wider society remains to be seen. In Sierra Leone, reparations were initiated many years after the completion of the DDR process, leaving the perception amongst victims that former combatants, many of whom were also perpetrators of serious abuses, were given priority by the international community; at the same time prosecutions at the Special Court of Sierra Leone (SCSL) appeared initially to be an impediment to DDR. In Liberia as well, victims may have gained little from the much-criticized Truth and Reconciliation Commission (TRC), while former combatants received the benefits of DDR training and packages. In all of these situations, processes of victim-centered justice or DDR either were absent or, where both were present, were often in tension or at least were not designed to communicate with one another. So, should DDR and victim-centered approaches to justice be coordinated, or even integrated?

Waldorf observes an increased emphasis at the UN, with the creation of the Integrated Disarmament, Demobilization and Reintegration Standards (IDDRS) in 2006, on integrating DDR programming with wider peacebuilding measures, which increasingly include transitional justice processes, and the subsequent inclusion of a transitional justice module in the IDDRS reinforces this trend. Waldorf argues that the work of Pablo de Greiff has been influential, particularly on the IDDRS, in suggesting that transitional justice and DDR have shared linked goals, of building trust between ex-combatants and society and between victims and society. Sharp discusses the potential role that the UN Peacebuilding Commission may play in promoting integration or at least coordination of these processes. Other scholars have argued for more than coordination, suggesting that processes must be fused, or integrated.[6] While there is scant evidence of such coordination, much less integration, as a matter of deliberate programming in-country to date, it is worth considering the opportunities and risks of a more coordinated or even integrated approach, based on what experience we have witnessed.

Opportunities

Coordinating victim-centered justice and DDR processes could allow for mutual reinforcement, provided appropriate incentive structures could be put in place. This might perhaps mitigate the seemingly zero-sum nature of each activity. How might this work in practice? One incentive, amnesties, is arguably off of the table; the IDDRS rule out amnesties based on their presumed inconsistency with international legal standards.[7] In Colombia, combatants who had not committed crimes and had no criminal charges against them were granted amnesty, and those who were facing criminal charges were offered reduced sentences as incentives for demobilization. While blanket amnesties are inconsistent with international standards, the use of conditional amnesties might in some instances help to promote demobilization.

At the same time, prosecutions are likely to undermine demobilization, but is this always the case? Certainly, some members of armed groups may choose not to disarm out of fear of prosecution, as appears to have initially been the case in Sierra Leone. However, punitive, reintegrative, and reparative processes could be linked, to a degree. Where ex-combatants have engaged in serious abuses, it might be possible to promote acceptance of their return by victims and communities by linking reintegration to traditional justice activities. Truth commissions may provide an opportunity for ex-combatants who were perpetrators of serious abuses to apologize and seek forgiveness. Traditional justice, or what Waldorf terms "local justice," might also enable perpetrators to engage victims and communities. Thus, in Northern Uganda, as Quinn discusses, and in Sierra Leone to a lesser degree, as Sriram discusses, some local communities, in some cases with support of international NGOs, have utilized local cleansing and other ceremonies to promote reintegration by former child combatants in particular. If former combatants provide the material for reparations, this might also enable their reintegration into communities. As the chapter by García-Godos explains, the Justice and Peace process in Colombia has linked demobilization of illegal armed groups to truth-seeking and reparations processes, and to a degree to accountability processes. Demobilized ex-combatants engage first into *versiones libres* to give an accounting of their crimes in relation to specific cases, providing a degree of truth to victims. In the judicial processes that follow, victims can also seek reparations from relevant perpetrators.

Risks

Of course, former combatants and entire armed groups may not accept the linkage of processes. This may be the case because they reject individually, or collectively, the stain of accusations of human rights violations, or because they simply reject the prospect of punishment. This has been the case in Colombia; some paramilitaries withdrew from the DDR process as amendments to the Law of Justice and Peace progressively altered its content, creating tighter linkages between transitional justice and DDR, but also imposing greater obligations upon armed groups.

Victims and victims' groups might also reject the linkages. In Colombia, as García-Godos argues, many victims view the Law of Justice and Peace as one of impunity, designed to assist pro-government forces, and neither contributing to the end of conflict nor addressing victims' rights. While there are arguments in favor of using traditional justice processes to both return former (largely child) combatants to communities and promote community and victim acceptance, there is also the risk that linking DDR, particularly longer-term reintegration, to victims may effectively instrumentalize victims, encouraging or socially coercing their acceptance of the return of some perpetrators for the sake of wider community reconciliation. In Sierra Leone, longer-term acceptance of the return of former combatants has been limited, and indeed the use of traditional mechanisms may merit skepticism, given wider criticisms that the latter have suffered, including their loss of legitimacy, abuses by practitioners, and lack of operation across communities. Integration of processes might also, as discussed above in the section on development, go one step further and include transitional justice, peacebuilding, and development activities in a single strategy. However, as Quinn argues, linking and carrying out transitional justice and peacebuilding processes simultaneously can be to the detriment of both.

With the creation of new institutions comes an increase in institutional complexity, and side-effects of that complexity. These may include delays: in Colombia while there have been many *versiones libres* given, many more have yet to be heard, and there have been few prosecutions or reparations hearings. And while the institutional apparatuses of transitional justice and DDR have grown alongside one another and are authorized by the same legal source in Colombia, according to García-Godos they have not necessarily been coordinated.

As Waldorf and many writing on DDR have observed, DDR programs tend to focus on short-term programs and are not generally successful at long-term reintegration. Indeed, he suggests, in line with other scholars, that reintegration might be better left to communities. This approach might be an opportunity or pose new risks. Development actors, working with governments and a range of peacebuilders, are likely to be engaged in supporting transitional justice activities and wider rule of law reform, support to affected communities, and reconstruction. Adding reintegration to their portfolios may enable the longer-term reintegration that has proven elusive and might allow for more integration between those activities and transitional justice activities. However, there is also a risk that such an approach would generate the perception that there is a zero-sum competition amongst beneficiaries, and possibly for providers, between support to victims and communities and support to former combatants, or create incentives to promote reintegration over concerns of communities and victims.

What should transitional justice and peacebuilding practitioners consider when considering coordination and integration?

Practitioners engaged in DDR and justice processes need to understand one another's goals, tools, and constituents, prior to considering any degree of coordination, much less integration. Experience to date suggests that coordination has been relatively rare, and not necessarily strategic. Given the potential opportunities and risks noted above, those seeking to program these activities might want to assess the situation through a number of queries.

First, they should consider the likely responses of victims, ex-combatants, and affected communities alike to any linked processes. Ex-combatants, particularly those who have not perpetrated atrocities, may well resent and resist the linkage of DDR, and particularly reintegration to formal and informal processes that conflate them with perpetrators of serious crimes. Victims and communities, as well, may resent that their forgiveness is expected to facilitate return, i.e. that linking the two instrumentalizes those most harmed by past abuses.[8]

Second, practitioners considering using traditional or local mechanisms of justice or conflict resolution should carefully scope the appropriateness of these in the eyes of those expected to be involved. If such mechanisms are not appropriate because they and their practitioners have lost respect or legitimacy through the course of the conflict, or because they do not function well across communities, their effects will be limited.

Third, they should consider existing institutional capacity. This is more than simply the financial capacity to engage in DDR processes, particular reintegration, or transitional justice processes including trials, truth commissions, and/or reparations. It also refers to the institutional complexity created by developing such processes in tandem, as can be seen in the complex infrastructure operating in Colombia.

Timing and sequencing

Any discussion of timing and sequencing in peacebuilding or transitional justice is inevitably fraught, as clearly no rigid ordering or timetable can be prescribed for a diverse set of situations. Further, any recommendations are necessarily limited by the fact that DDR will, for pragmatic reasons, generally have temporal and financial priority, even if justice processes are also being undertaken alongside conflict resolution efforts in some countries. At least the disarmament and demobilization (or DD) elements of DDR will usually be undertaken first, given the need to stabilize a country and implement a peace agreement. DDR processes have not been successful at promoting longer-term social reintegration, and

Waldorf may be right that this is best left to transitional justice processes. That said, there are serious temporal considerations that need to be addressed as DDR goes forward and justice processes are initiated. In reviewing the findings of the chapters, we could identify clear risks, but no clear opportunities, regarding timing and sequencing, so we only discuss risks and identify some guidance for practitioners.

Risks

Long delays between DDR and victim-centered justice can have deleterious effects. Clearly, even if DD must have temporal priority, the resentment felt by victims and communities as a result of long delays to reparations programs or truth-telling and justice processes can be limited if such processes are initiated relatively early. While, in Sierra Leone, the TRC and the Special Court began operation within a few years of the end of conflict, there remains skepticism about their effects on, or reception by, victims. The reparations process, by contrast, took place some nine years after the end of conflict. The apparent disparity between the rapid provision of DDR training and packages and delayed reparations can create resentment amongst victims. Further, victims who have suffered serious material harm may suffer further in the meantime, particularly where the harms they have suffered impede gainful employment or basic daily personal tasks.

However, these risks may be unavoidable. As some of the studies, such as those in Bosnia and Herzegovina and Sierra Leone, demonstrate, many victim-centered approaches to justice simply cannot be set up as quickly as DDR programs in the wake of conflict. It takes time to develop a mandate for a commission of inquiry, to appoint commissioners and other staff, and to develop operating procedures, even if sufficient funds are available, which may not be the case. Those seeking to create reparations processes must raise a budget, create a new institution or adapt and empower an existing one, create a victims' registry, and develop procedures for distribution of funds. Programmers and analysts need realistic timeframes for the implementation of transitional justice mechanisms in general and victim-centered justice in particular; these are long-term processes. Processes of implementation may take longer than the usual three-to-five-year programming cycles of donors and international organizations.

What should transitional justice and peacebuilding practitioners consider when considering timing and sequencing?

There is, however, a moral and practical dilemma: if victim-centered justice processes, particularly reparations programs, take significant amounts of time to implement, what can be done in the meantime? Humanitarian, peacebuilding, and development actors may well have to fill the gap with direct assistance. Their activities are unlikely to have a specific justice and/or reparations aspect, but nonetheless may be more timely than oft-delayed victim-centered processes.

However, it is worth noting that it does not appear to be the case that, as the saying goes, "justice delayed is justice denied." Rather, demands for justice in a range of forms—truth-telling, trials, reparations—clearly remain active, even growing, long after the original atrocities occurred, as is evident in Cambodia, Bosnia and Herzegovina, and Lebanon.

Avenues for further research

The eight country studies in this volume represent a range of experiences—in type and duration of conflict or abuses; in geographic location; in international peacemaking, peacebuilding, and transitional justice intervention; and, temporally, in the global evolution of peacebuilding and transitional justice. Taken together, they illustrate the diversity of experiences, of successes and failures, in the pursuit of transitional justice and peacebuilding (and, in some countries, the virtual absence of one or both in any systematic sense, but with elements of each deployed). They are, however, not comprehensive. A number of questions arise from this study that might benefit from further systematic cross-country comparisons.

Transitional justice without transition and "atypical" transitional justice or peacebuilding

If there is such a thing as a "typical" set of peacebuilding and transitional justice processes, our country studies demonstrate how frequently reality deviates from the typical. At least three of our eight country studies cannot be properly characterized as involving peacebuilding, for a range of reasons. Kenya did not experience a violent conflict akin to a civil war, but rather brief and severe election-related violence, albeit with an internationally mediated agreement akin to a power-sharing peace agreement. It has not experienced an international peacebuilding presence, nor have militias involved in the violence been demobilized. It is difficult to argue that it has undergone a political or post-conflict transition. Yet it has had national debate about a range of transitional justice measures and is the subject of four ICC prosecutions. Colombia has undertaken a justice and peace process involving prosecutions, truth-telling, reparations, and DDR, all linked, and yet it is not clearly in a peacebuilding situation, given that conflict with the guerrilla group FARC continues and the demobilization process currently underway is with paramilitaries which were closely aligned with the government. Lebanon's Ta'if accord accompanied the end of the conflict, but lacks common features of a peace agreement and has not been the subject of an international peacebuilding mission, while the major militia and political force Hezbollah was not disarmed. Yet a common tool of transitional justice, the internationalized criminal tribunal, is being deployed to address, not the legacies of the conflict, but several post-conflict assassinations. All of which begs the question: What difference do transitional justice mechanisms make, not only in peacebuilding contexts, but in situations where peacebuilding has not been pursued in the traditional sense? Future research might examine the effects of pursuing transitional justice in the absence of transition and of pursuing transitional justice in the wake of conflict with and without peacebuilding measures.

Defining the subject/actor/agent in transitional justice

The implementation of transitional justice and peacebuilding measures is based on established definitions of actors—individual or collective—who are assigned specific roles in a social landscape in which human rights violations have been committed. As Engstrom notes, as transitional justice mechanisms have become ever more embedded in the peacebuilding landscape, there has also been a judicialization of transitional justice responses. Yet, clearly courts cannot and will not address all accountability needs in a conflict-affected country, nor are they always well-suited to do so. Judicial processes require relatively clear definitions of who constitutes a victim and/or a perpetrator, while in many situations, some of which are discussed in this volume, the same individual might be a victim, an ex-combatant, or a perpetrator, either at the same time or at different points in time. How will a given person be treated in a judicial process, or in a reparations program? What criteria can be applied to delineate boundaries between these—often opposite—roles? And what happens when the majority of the population might be considered victims, as in Liberia, Sierra Leone, or Cambodia? The legal categories and operational definitions that we apply in transitional justice and peacebuilding have serious implications because they affect access to certain benefits or programs, but also because they may shape the ways that past abuse is addressed in a society.

Further, how are these definitions being appropriated and reinterpreted by social actors such as victims' organizations and victims' movements? How do these actors relate to the processes and institutions developed to implement transitional justice, and do they take part in a redefinition of legal and operational categories? Empirical research on the implications of definitions concerning the subjects or actors of transitional justice could illuminate these nuances.

The international reproduction of transitional justice

Transitional justice has become an industry, with institutions and service providers that operate globally and which can shape transitional justice and peacebuilding policy and programming agendas in numerous countries. Has the spread of transitional justice resulted from a learning or demonstration effect across borders, and who are the actors involved? What mechanisms or fora are used to promote transitional justice practices? There is a noticeable increase in numbers of transitional justice experts and advisory services, some more influential than others. Who are these international actors; how might we scrutinize their influence without jeopardizing their quest for accountability? In a field that has grown rapidly in size, political influence, and finance in the past two decades, a serious examination of the differences between analysis and advocacy and the roles of advocates and scholars is necessary. So, too, is an examination of the relationship among local, national, and international transitional justice practitioners.

Traditional justice: practices and appearances

Greater attention has been paid to traditional practices of accountability with the rise of transitional justice globally, and they are increasingly well-documented. However, there is more to be examined regarding the way these practices are applied in practice and the consequences they have for local communities. As the chapter by Nagy in this volume demonstrates, some of these practices may risk cooptation by external actors, whether international actors or the state, or may entail coercion of victims and/or perpetrators. More empirical studies are needed to document the use of traditional practices dealing with accountability, forgiveness, and reintegration at the local level, as well as the relation of these practices to formal systems of justice.

The studies in this volume have examined the interaction between two specific aspects of transitional justice and peacebuilding: the promotion of victim-centered approaches to justice and short-term DDR processes, and longer-term security and reintegration challenges. Our focus was based on the recognition that, while these aspects are often in tension with one another, they also increasingly involve overlapping processes and actors, with programming often developed without significant reflection or planning to deal with these overlaps. The lessons are complex, sometimes contradictory, and demonstrate the need for further research. Our contribution seeks to document the challenges of pursuing justice, particularly victim-centered justice, and disarmament, demobilization, and reintegration simultaneously, but also the pitfalls of failure to consider how these activities interact and affect both victims and ex-combatants.

Notes

1 This is also important given the recent literature advocating more development-sensitive transitional justice activities, such as the 2008 special issue of the *International Journal of Transitional Justice* on development and transitional justice. See also Pablo de Greiff and Roger Duthie, eds, *Transitional Justice and Development: Making connections* (New York: Social Science Research Council, 2009), available at <*www.ssrc.org/workspace/images/crm/new_publication_3/%7B1ed88247-585f-de11-bd80-001cc477ec70%7D.pdf*>.

2 UNDP, *FAQs about the Human Development Index (HDI)* <*http://hdr.undp.org/en/media/FAQs_2011_HDI.pdf*>.

3 The countries addressed in this volume are ranked by the Human Development Index 2011 (with 1 as the highest and 187 the lowest score): Lebanon 71, Bosnia and Herzegovina 74, Colombia 89, Cambodia 139, Kenya 143, Uganda 161, Sierra Leone 180, Liberia 182. *UNDP Human Development Report 2011*, pp. 135–38, available at <*http://hdr.undp.org/en/media/HDR_2011_EN_Table3.pdf*>. Last accessed 1 March 2012.

4 United Nations, *Claiming the Millennium Development Goals: A human rights approach*, (New York and Geneva, OHCHR, 2008), p. 11, available at <*www2.ohchr.org/SPdocs/Claiming_MDGs_en.pdf*>.

5 Colombian Constitutional Court, Sentence T-025, 22 January 2004.

6 Kimberly Theidon, "Transitional subjects: The disarmament, demobilization and reintegration of former combatants in colombia," *International Journal of Transitional Justice*, vol. 1 (2007), pp. 66–90.
7 Waldorf notes that this removes what may be an important peacebuilding tool.
8 Laura Stovel and Marta Valiñas, "Restorative justice after mass violence: Opportunities and risks for children and youth," *Innocenti Working Paper IWP 2010–15* (Florence: UNICEF Innocenti Research Centre, June 2010), p. vi.

Bibliography

Books

Adebajo, Adekeye and Ismail Rashid (eds), *West Africa's Security Challenges: Building Peace in a Troubled Region* (Boulder, CO: Lynne Rienner, 2004).

Alden, Chris, Monika Thakur, and Matthew Arnold, *Militias and the Challenges of Post-Conflict Peace: Silencing the Guns* (London: Zed Books, 2011).

Allen, Tim, *Trial Justice: The International Criminal Court and the Lord's Resistance Army* (London and New York: Zed Books, 2006).

Berg-Schlosser, Dirk and Rainer Siegler, *Political Stability and Development: A Comparative Analysis of Kenya, Tanzania and Uganda* (Boulder, CO: Lynne Rienner, 1990).

Braithwaite, John, *Crime, Shame, and Reintegration* (New York: Cambridge University Press, 1989).

Briggs, Philip, *Uganda* (Old Saybrook, CT: The Globe Pequot Press, 1998).

Broomhall, Bruce, *International Justice and the International Criminal Court: Between Sovereignty and the Rule of Law* (Oxford: Oxford University Press, 2004).

Chandler, David, *A History of Cambodia* (Boulder, CO: Westview, 2008).

Chesterman, Simon, *You, The People: The United Nations, Transitional Administration, and State Building* (Oxford: Oxford University Press, 2004).

Collier, Paul, V. L. Elliott, Havard Hegre, Anke Hoeffler, Marta Reynal-Querol, and Nicholas Sambanis, *Breaking the Conflict Trap: Civil War and Development Policy* (Washington: World Bank, 2003).

Cousens, Elizabeth M. and Chetan Kumar, *Peacebuilding as Politics* (London: Lynne Rienner, 2001).

Dávila, Andrés, *El juego del poder: Historia, armas y votos* (Bogotá, 1998).

de Greiff, Pablo, "Establishing Links between DDR and Reparations," in Ana Cutter Patel, Pablo de Greiff, and Lars Waldorf, *Disarming the Past: Transitional Justice and Ex-Combatants* (New York: SSRC, 2010).

——, (ed.), *The Handbook of Reparations* (Cambridge: Cambridge University Press, 2006).

de Greiff, Pablo and Roger Duthie (eds), *Transitional Justice and Development: Making Connections* (New York: Social Science Research Council, 2009).

Díaz, Ana María (ed.), *Colombia: El espejismo de la justicia y la paz. Balance sobre la aplicación de la ley 975 de 2005* (Bogotá, 2008).

Doyle, Michael W. and Nicholas Sambanis, *Making War and Building Peace* (Princeton, NJ: Princeton University Press, 2006).

Drumbl, Mark A., *Atrocity, Punishment, and International Law* (Cambridge: Cambridge University Press, 2007).

Duncan, Gustavo, *Los señores de la guerra. De paramilitares, mafiosos y autodefensas en Colombia* (Bogotá, 2006).

Fisk, Robert, *Pity the Nation: Lebanon at War* (Oxford: Oxford Paperbacks, 2001).

Freeman, Mark, *Necessary Evils: Amnesties and the Search for Justice* (Cambridge: Cambridge University Press, 2009).

Fujii, Lee Ann, *Killing Neighbors: Webs of Violence in Rwanda* (Ithaca, NY and London: Cornell University Press, 2009).

Gallón, Gustavo, Michael Reed, and Catalina Lleras (eds), *Anotaciones sobre la ley de justicia y paz. Una mirada desde los derechos de las víctimas* (Bogotá, 2007).

Gutiérrez, Francisco, María Emma Wills, and Gonzalo Sánchez (eds), *Nuestra guerra sin nombre. Transformaciones del conflicto en Colombia* (Bogotá, 2006).

Hartlyn, Jonathan, *La política del régimen de coalición: La experiencia del Frente Nacional en Colombia* (Bogotá, 1993).

Hayner, Priscilla, *Unspeakable Truths: Confronting State Terror and Atrocity* (London: Routledge 2001).

Haynes, Dina Francesca (ed.), *Deconstructing the Reconstruction. Human Rights and Rule of Law in Postwar Bosnia and Herzegovina* (Aldershot: Ashgate, 2008).

Hirsch, John, *Sierra Leone: Diamonds and the Struggle for Democracy* (Boulder, CO: Lynne Rienner, 2001).

Holsti, Kal, *The State, War, and the State of War* (Cambridge: Cambridge University Press, 1996).

Howard, Rhoda E., *Human Rights and the Search for Community* (Boulder, CO: Westview, 1995).

International Center for Transitional Justice, *Handbook on the Special Tribunal for Lebanon* (New York: ICTJ, 2008).

Ivković, Sanja Kutnja and John Hagan, *Reclaiming Justice. The International Tribunal for the Former Yugoslavia and Local Courts* (Oxford: Oxford University Press, 2001).

Kaldor, Mary, *New and Old Wars: Organized Violence in a Global Era* (Cambridge: Polity Press, 2002).

Kritz, Neil J. (ed.), *Transitional Justice: How Emerging Democracies Reckon with Former Regimes* (Washington, DC: United States Institute of Peace Press, 1995).

Lincoln, Jessica, *Transitional Justice, Peace and Accountability: Outreach and the Role of International Courts after Conflict* (London: Routledge, 2011).

MacGinty, Roger, *International Peacebuilding and Local Resistance: Hybrid Forms of Peace* (London: Palgrave, 2011).

Mackey, Sandra, *Lebanon: A House Divided* (New York: W.W. Norton, 2006).

Malamud-Goti, Jaime, *Game Without End: State Terror and the Politics of Justice* (Norman, OK: University of Oklahoma Press, 1996).

Mallinder, Louise, *Amnesty, Human Rights and Political Transitions: Bridging the Peace and Justice Divide* (Oxford: Hart, 2008).

Mani, Rama, *Beyond Retribution: Seeking Justice in the Shadows of War* (Cambridge: Polity Press, 2002).

Mannergren Selimovic, Johanna, *Remembering and Forgetting after War. Narratives of Truth, Justice and Reconciliation in a Bosnian Town*, Doctoral dissertation (Gothenburg: University of Gothenburg, 2010, under revision for publication).

Mauricio, Aranguren, *Mi confesión* (Bogotá, 2001).

Minow, Martha, *Between Vengeance and Forgiveness: Facing History after Genocide and Mass Atrocity* (Boston: Beacon Press, 1998).

Museveni, Yoweri Kaguta, *Sowing the Mustard Seed* (London: Macmillan, 1997).

Nettelfield, Lara, *Courting Democracy in Bosnia and Herzegovina. The Hague Tribunal's Impact in a Postwar State* (Cambridge: Cambridge University Press, 2010).

Newman, Edward, Roland Paris, and Oliver P. Richmond (eds), *New Perspectives on Liberal Peacebuilding* (Tokyo: United Nations University, 2010).

Ochola, Robert Lukwiya, *The Acholi Religious Leaders' Peace Initiative in the Battlefield of Northern Uganda: An Example of an Integral, Inculturated and Ecumenical Approach to Pastoral Work in a War Situation*, PhD dissertation (Leopold-Franzens-Universität Innsbruck, June 2006).

Ofcansky, Thomas P., *Uganda: Tarnished Pearl of Africa* (Boulder: Westview, 1996).

Olsen, Tricia D., Leigh A. Payne, and Andrew G. Reiter, *Transitional Justice in Balance: Comparing Processes, Weighing Efficacy* (Washington, DC: United States Institute of Peace, 2010).

Osiel, Mark, *Mass Atrocity, Collective Memory, and the Law* (New Brunswick, NJ: Transaction Books, 1999).

Pain, Dennis. *The Bending of Spears: Producing Consensus for Peace and Development in Northern Uganda* (London: International Alert, 1997).

Pardo, Rafael, *Fin del paramilitarismo ¿Es posible su desmonte?* (Bogotá, 2007).

Paris, Roland, *At War's End: Building Peace after Civil Conflict* (Cambridge: Cambridge University Press, 2004).

Patel, Ana Cutter, Pablo de Greiff, and Lars Waldorf, *Disarming the Past: Transitional Justice and Ex-Combatants* (New York: SSRC, 2010).

Peñaranda, Ricardo and Javier Guerrero (eds), *De las armas a la política* (Bogotá, 1999).

Ponzio, Richard J., *Democratic Peacebuilding: Aiding Afghanistan and Other Fragile States* (Oxford: Oxford University Press, 2011).

Richards, Paul (ed.), *No Peace, No War: An Anthropology of Contemporary Armed Conflicts* (Oxford: James Currey, 2005).

Richmond, Oliver, *The Transformation of Peace* (London: Palgrave, 2005).

Romero, Mauricio (ed.), *Parapolítica. La ruta de la expansión paramilitar y los acuerdos políticos* (Bogotá, 2007).

Salinas, Yamile, Darío Gonzáles, and Eliza González, *Tierra, oro y conflictos* (Bogotá, 2008).

Shaw, Martin, *War and Genocide* (Cambridge: Polity Press, 2003).

Sriram, Chandra Lekha, *Globalizing Justice for Mass Atrocities: A Revolution in Accountability* (London: Routledge, 2005).

——, *Confronting Past Human Rights Violations: Justice Versus Peace in Times of Transition* (London: Frank Cass, 2004).

Sriram, Chandra Lekha and Karin Wermester (eds), *From Promise to Practice: Strengthening UN Capacities for the Prevention of Violent Conflict* (Boulder, CO: Lynne Rienner, 2003).

Sriram, Chandra Lekha, Olga Martin-Ortega, and Johanna Herman (eds), *Peacebuilding and Rule of Law in Africa* (New York: Routledge, 2010).

Stedman, Stephen John, Elizabeth Cousens, and Donald Rothchild, *Ending Civil Wars: The Implementation of Peace Agreements* (Boulder, CO: Lynne Rienner, 2001).

Stover, Eric, *The Witness* (Philadelphia: University of Pennsylvania Press, 2007).

Stover, Eric and Harvey M. Weinstein (eds), *My Neighbor, My Enemy: Justice and Community in the Aftermath of Mass Atrocity* (Cambridge: Cambridge University Press, 2004).

Straus, Scott, *The Order of Genocide* (Ithaca and London: Cornell University Press, 2006).

Straus, Scott and Lars Waldorf (eds), *Remaking Rwanda: State Building and Human Rights after Mass Violence* (Madison: University of Wisconsin Press, 2011).

Subotić, Jelena, *Hijacked Justice. Dealing with the Past in the Balkans* (Ithaca, NY: Cornell University Press, 2009).

Teitel, Ruti G., *Transitional Justice* (New York: Oxford University Press, 2000).

Thomson, Susan M., *Resisting Reconciliation: State Power and Everyday Life in Post-Genocide Rwanda*, Doctoral dissertation (Dalhousie University, 2009).

Traboulsi, Fawwaz, *A History of Modern Lebanon* (London: Pluto Press, 2007).

Uprimny, Rodrigo and María Paula Saffon, *Desplazamiento forzado y justicia transicional en Colombia. Estudio sectorial* (Bogotá, 2007).

Uvin, Peter, *Aiding Violence: The Development Enterprise in Rwanda* (West Hartford, CT: Kumarian Press, 1998).

Weinstein, Jeremy M., *Inside Rebellion: The Politics of Insurgent Violence* (Cambridge: Cambridge University Press, 2007).

Articles, book chapters, and reports

Akhavan, Payam, "Are International Criminal Tribunals a Disincentive to Peace? Reconciling Judicial Romanticism with Political Realism," *Human Rights Quarterly*, vol. 31 (2009), pp. 624–54.

——, "Beyond Impunity: Can International Criminal Justice Prevent Future Atrocities?" *American Journal of International Law*, vol. 95, no. 7 (2001), pp. 7–31.

——, "Justice in The Hague, Peace in the Former Yugoslavia? A Commentary on the United Nations War Crimes Tribunal," *Human Rights Quarterly*, vol. 20 (1998), pp. 737–816.

Alexander, Jessica, Jennifer DePiazza, Augustin Flory, Alan Moseley, Amra Sabic-El-Rayess, Regina Reza, and Samuel Rikkers, *From Barracks to Business. An Evaluation of IOM's Transitional Assistance Program to Former Soldiers in Bosnia and Herzegovina*, Final Report, April 2004, Columbia University Press, pp. 20–21, available at <www.iom.ba/Downloads/Projects/TADS/Final%20Report%20IOM%20TAFS%20Bosnia%20Columbia.pdf>, accessed 19 August 2011.

Alie, Joe A. D., "Reconciliation and Traditional Justice: Tradition-Based Practices of the Kpaa Mende in Sierra Leone," in Luc Huyse and Mark Salter (eds), *Traditional Justice and Reconciliation after Violent Conflict: Learning from African Experiences* (Stockholm: International Idea, 2008).

Allen, Tim, "Ritual (Ab)use? Problems with Traditional Justice in Northern Uganda," in Nicholas Waddell and Phil Clark (eds), *Courting Conflict? Justice, Peace and the ICC in Africa* (London: Royal African Society, 2008), pp. 47–54.

——, "A Review of Lessons Learned by Reception Centres on Effective Interventions for Former Abductees in Northern Uganda: A Preliminary Study, UNICEF and USAID, October 2005," in Erin Baines, Eric Stover, and Marieke Wierda (eds), *War-Affected Children and Youth in Northern Uganda: Toward a Brighter Future: An Assessment Report* (Chicago: John D. and Catherine T. MacArthur Foundation, 2006).

——, *War and Justice in Northern Uganda: An Assessment of the International Criminal Court's Intervention* (London: Crisis States Research Centre, Development Studies Institute, London School of Economics, 2005).

Alto Comisionado para la Paz de Colombia, *Proceso de Paz con las Autodefensas: Informe Ejecutivo* (Bogotá, 2006).

American Bar Association Rule of Law Initiative—Liberia, "ABA ROLI Helping to Launch the First Training Center for Judges in Liberia" (April 2008), available at <www.abanet.org/rol/news/news_liberia_new_judicial_training_institute.shtml>.

Amnesty International, "Never Forgotten: Lebanon's Missing People" (April 2011), available at <www.amnesty.org/en/library/asset/MDE18/001/2011/en/4c0716c2-8825-41d6-b816-c678ef4eeb44/mde180012011en.pdf>.

——, *Colombia. Los paramilitares en Medellín: ¿Desmovilización o legalización?* (London, 2005).

Annan, Jeannie and Ana Cutter Patel, "Critical Issues and Lessons in Social Reintegration: Balancing Justice, Psychological Well Being, and Community Reconciliation" (Bogota: CIDDR, 2009).

Aptel, Cécile, "Some Innovations in the Statute of the Special Tribunal for Lebanon," *Journal of International Criminal Justice*, vol. 5 (2007), pp. 1107–24.

Arab Reform Initiative and Palestinian Center for Policy and Survey Research, "The State of Reform in the Arab World 2009–10" (Arab Reform Initiative, March 2010), available at <www.arab-reform.net>.

Arthur, Paige, "How 'Transitions' Reshaped Human Rights: A Conceptual History of Transitional Justice," *Human Rights Law Quarterly*, vol. 31, no. 2 (2009), pp. 321–67.

Baines, Erin K., "Complex Political Perpetrators: Reflections on Dominic Ongwen," *Journal of Modern African Studies*, vol. 47, no. 2 (2009), pp. 163–91.

——, "The Haunting of Alice: Local Approaches to Justice and Reconciliation in Northern Uganda," *International Journal of Transitional Justice*, vol. 1, no. 1 (2007), pp. 91–114.

Baines, Erin, Eric Stover, and Marieke Wierda, *War-Affected Children and Youth in Northern Uganda: Toward a Brighter Future: An Assessment Report* (Chicago: John D. and Catherine T. MacArthur Foundation, 2006).

Bainter, Ric, "The Elephant in the Room: Defense Reform in Bosnia and Herzegovina," in Dina Francesca Haynes (ed.), *Deconstructing the Reconstruction. Human Rights and Rule of Law in Postwar Bosnia and Herzegovina* (Aldershot: Ashgate, 2008), pp. 235–57.

Ball, Nicole and Luc van de Goor, "Disarmament, Demobilization and Reintegration: Mapping Issues, Dilemmas and Guiding Principles" (The Hague: Netherlands Institute of International Relations, 2006).

Barbour, Stephanie, "Domestic War Crimes Processing in Bosnia and Herzegovina" (Internal Case Study, ICTJ Research Project: Making an Impact: Guidance on Designing Effective Outreach Programs for Transitional Justice, April 2011).

Barnes, Catherine and Okello Lucima, "Introduction," *Accord* (2002) 11, p. 1.

Bartu, Peter and Neil Wilford, "Transitional Justice and DDR: The Case of Cambodia" (New York: ICTJ, 2009).

Bassiouni, M. Cherif, "Searching for Peace and Achieving Justice: The Need for Accountability," *Law and Contemporary Problems*, vol. 59 (1996), pp. 9–28.

Baumgartner, Elisabeth, "Aspects of Victim Participation in the Proceedings of the International Criminal Court," *International Review of the Red Cross*, vol. 90 (2008), no. 870, pp. 409–40.

Bell, Christine, "Transitional Justice, Interdisciplinarity and the State of the 'Field' or 'Non-Field,'" *International Journal of Transitional Justice*, vol. 3, no. 1 (2009), pp. 5–27.

Bennett, Christopher, "Taking the Sincerity out of Saying Sorry: Restorative Justice as Ritual," *Journal of Applied Philosophy*, vol. 23, no. 2 (2006), pp. 127–43.

Beyond Juba Project, "Tradition in Transition" (Kampala: Faculty of Law, Makerere University, the Refugee Law Project and the Human Rights and Peace Centre, 2009).

Blattman, Christopher and Jeannie Annan, "Child Combatants in Northern Uganda: Reintegration Myths and Realities," in Robert Muggah (ed.), *Security and Post-Conflict Reconstruction: Dealing with Fighters in the Aftermath of War* (Abingdon: Routledge, 2009).

Bojicic-Dzlilovic, Vesna, "Peace on Whose Terms? War Veterans' Associations in Bosnia and Herzegovina," in Edward Newman and Oliver Richmond (eds), *Challenges to Peace-building. Managing Spoilers During Conflict Resolution* (New York: United Nations University Press, 2006), pp. 200–18.

Bonn International Centre for Conversion, *Turning Soldiers into a Work Force, Demobilization and Reintegration in Post-Dayton Bosnia and Herzegovina*, Brief 27, 2006.

Borzello, Anna, "The challenge of DDR in Northern Uganda: The Lord's Resistance Army," *Conflict, Security & Development* 7 (2007), pp. 387–415.

Bouta, Tsjeard, "Gender and Disarmament, Demobilization and Reintegration, Building Blocs for Dutch Policy" (The Hague: Netherlands Institute of International Relations "Clingendael," 2005).

Brahm, Eric, "Uncovering the Truth: Examining Truth Commission Success and Impact," *International Studies Perspectives*, vol. 8 (2007), pp. 16–35.

Branch, Adam, "Uganda's Civil War and the Politics of ICC Intervention," *Ethics & International Affairs*, vol. 21, no. 2 (2007) pp. 179–98.

Briro, Mirklos, Dean Ajdukovic, Dinka Corkalo, Din Djipa, Petar Milin, and Harvey Weinstein, "Attitudes Towards Justice and Social Reconciliation in Bosnia and Herzegovina and Croatia," in Eric Stover and Harvey Weinstein (eds), *My Neighbour, My Enemy. Justice and Community in the Aftermath of Atrocity* (Cambridge: Cambridge University Press, 2004), pp. 183–206.

Brown, Stephen, "Kenya," in Lavinia Stan and Nadya Nedelsky (eds), *Encyclopedia of Transitional Justice* (Cambridge: Cambridge University Press, forthcoming).

——, "Justice pénale internationale et violences électorales: Les enjeux de la CPI au Kenya," *Revue Tiers Monde*, no. 205 (2011), pp. 85–102.

——, "Lessons Learned and Forgotten: The International Community and Electoral Conflict Management in Kenya," in David Gillies (ed.), *Elections in Dangerous Places: Democracy and the Paradoxes of Peacebuilding* (Montreal: McGill-Queen's University Press, 2011), pp. 127–45.

——, "Donor Responses to the 2008 Kenyan Crisis: Finally Getting it Right?" *Journal of Contemporary African Studies*, vol. 27 (2009), pp. 389–406.

Buckley-Zistel, Susanne, "'We are Pretending Peace'—Local Memory and the Absence of Social Transformation and Reconciliation in Rwanda," in Phil Clark and Zachary D. Kaufman (eds), *After Genocide: Transitional Justice, Post-conflict Reconstruction and Reconciliation in Rwanda and Beyond* (New York: Columbia University Press, 2009), pp. 125–44.

Burgess, Patrick, "A New Approach to Restorative Justice—East Timor's Community Reconciliation Process," in Naomi Roht-Arriaza and Javier Mariezcurrena (eds), *Transitional Justice in the 21st Century* (Cambridge: Cambridge University Press, 2006), pp. 176–205.

Burnet, Jennie E., "The Injustice of Local Justice: Truth, Reconciliation, and Revenge in Rwanda," *Genocide Studies and Prevention*, vol. 3 (2008), pp. 173–93.

Buyse, Antoine, "Hybrid Human Rights Mechanisms in Post-Conflict Transitions: the Experience of the Bosnian Human Rights Chamber," in Oxford Transitional Justice Research (OTJR) (eds), *Critical Perspectives in Transitional Justice* (Antwerp: Intersentia, 2011).

Carames, Albert, Vicenc Fisas, and Daniel Luz, "Analysis of Disarmament, Demobilization and Reintegration (DDR) Programmes Existing in the World during 2005" (Barcelona: Escola de Cultura de Pau, 2006).

Cassese, Antonio, "The Role of Internationalized Courts and Tribunals in the Fight Against International Criminality," in Cesare Romano, André Nollkaemper, and Jann Kleffner, *Internationalised Courts. Sierra Leone, East Timor, Kosovo and Cambodia* (Oxford: Oxford University Press, 2004), pp. 3–15.

——, "Reflections on International Criminal Justice," *The Modern Law Review*, vol. 61 (1998), pp. 1–10.

Centre for International Cooperation and Security, "Disarmament, Demobilisation and Reintegration (DDR) and Human Security in Cambodia" (University of Bradford: July 2008).

Chakravarty, Anuradha, "Gacaca Courts in Rwanda: Explaining Divisions within the Human Rights Community," *Yale Journal of International Affairs*, vol. 1, no. 2 (2006), pp. 132–45.

Cheeseman, Nic and Blessing-Miles Tendi, "Power-Sharing in Comparative Perspective: The Dynamics of 'Unity Government' in Kenya and Zimbabwe," *Journal of Modern African Studies*, vol. 48 (2010), pp. 203–29.

Christie, Nils, "Conflict as Property," *British Journal of Criminology*, vol. 17 (1977), pp. 1–15.

CIDH, *Informe sobre la implementación de la Ley de Justicia y Paz: Etapas iniciales del proceso de desmovilización de las AUC y primeras diligencias judiciales* (San José, 2007).

Clark, Janine Natalya, "The State Court of Bosnia and Herzegovina: a Path to Reconciliation?" *Contemporary Justice Review*, vol. 4 (2010), pp. 317–90.

——, "International War Crimes Tribunals and the Challenge of Outreach," *International Criminal Law Review*, vol. 9 (2009), pp. 99–116.

——, "Plea Bargaining at the ICTY: Guilty Pleas and Reconciliation," *European Journal of International Law*, vol. 20, (2009), pp. 415–36.

——, "The Limits of Retributive Justice: Findings of an Empirical Study in Bosnia and Herzegovina," *Journal of International Criminal Justice*, vol. 7 (2009), pp. 463–87.

Clark, Phil, "Hybridity, Holism, and 'Traditional' Justice: The Case of the Gacaca Courts in Post-Genocide Rwanda," *George Washington International Law Review*, vol. 39 (2007), pp. 765–837.

Clark, Phil and Nicola Palmer, "Challenging Transitional Justice," in Oxford Transitional Justice Research (OTJR) (eds), *Critical Perspectives in Transitional Justice* (Antwerp: Intersentia, 2011).

Coalition for RECOM, *Development Progress Report*, May 2006–July 2011, available at <www.zarekom.org/documents/index.en.html>, accessed 14 September 2011.

——, Proposed Statute of the Regional Commission for Establishing the Facts About War Crimes and Other Gross Violations of Human Rights Committed on the Territory of the Former Yugoslavia, 26 March 2011, available at <www.zarekom.org/documents/index.en.html>, accessed 14 September 2011.

——, *Consultation Process on the RECOM Initiative. An Overview of Thoughts, Suggestions and Recommendations*, July–December 2009.

——, *Regional Debate on the Mandate of RECOM, Sixth Regional Forum on Transitional Justice*, Novi Sad, Vojvodina, Serbia, May–December 2009.

——, *Report about the Consultation Process on Instruments of Truth-Seeking About War Crimes and Other Serious Violations of Human Rights in Post-Yugoslav Countries. Review of Opinions, Suggestions and Recommendations Report*, May 2006–June 2009.

Cockayne, James, "The Special Tribunal for Lebanon: A Cripple from Birth?" *Journal of International Criminal Justice*, vol. 5 (2007), pp. 1061–64.

Cohen, Ronald L., "Provocations of Restorative Justice," *Social Justice Research*, vol. 14 (2001), pp. 209–32.

Collantes-Celador, Gemma, "Civil Society and the Bosnian Police Certification Process: Challenging 'the Guardians,'" in Vesna Bojicic-Dzelilovic, James Ker-Lindsay, and Denisa Kostovicova (eds), *Civil Society and Transitions in the Western Balkans* (Basingstoke: Palgrave, forthcoming).

Colletta, Nat J. and Robert Muggah, "Context Matters: Interim Stabilization and Second Generation Approaches to Security Promotion," *Conflict, Security & Development*, vol. 9 (2009), pp. 425–53.

Colletta, Nat J., Markus Kostner, and Ingo Wiederhofer, "Disarmament, Demobilization, and Reintegration: Lessons and Liabilities in Reconstruction," in Robert I. Rotberg (ed.), *When States Fail: Causes and Consequences* (Princeton, NJ: Princeton University Press, 2004).

Collier, Paul and Anke Hoeffler, "Military Expenditure in Post-Conflict Societies" (Centre for the Study of African Economies, Oxford University, 8 April 2004).

Coulter, Chris, "Reconciliation or Revenge: Narratives of Fear and Shame among Female Ex-Combatants in Sierra Leone" (Uppsala: Department of Cultural Anthropology and Ethnology, 2006).

de Feyter, Koen, Marc Bossuyt, Paul Lemmens, and Stephan Parmentier (eds), *Out of the Ashes: Reparation for Victims of Gross and Systematic Human Rights Violations* (Antwerp and Oxford: Intersentia, 2005).

de Hemptinne, Jerome, "Challenges Raised by Victims' Participation in the Proceedings at the Special Tribunal for Lebanon," *Journal of International Criminal Justice*, vol. 8 (2010), pp. 165–79.

Diaz, Catalina, "Colombia's Bid for Justice and Peace" (Nuremberg: Working Group on Development and Peace (FriEnt), 2007).

Dietrich Ortega, Luisa Maria, "Transitional Justice and Female Ex-Combatants: Lessons Learned from International Experience," in Ana Cutter Patel, Pablo de Greiff, and Lars Waldorf, *Disarming the Past: Transitional Justice and Ex-Combatants* (New York: SSRC, 2010).

Dix, Robert H., "Consociational Democracy: The Case of Colombia," *Comparative Politics*, vol. 12, no. 3 (1980), pp. 303–21.

Dougherty, Beth, "Right-Sizing International Criminal Justice: The Hybrid Experiment at the Special Court for Sierra Leone," *International Affairs*, vol. 80, no. 1 (2004), pp. 311–28.

Doyle, Michael W., "Too Little, Too Late? Justice and Security Reform in Bosnia and Herzegovina," in Charles T. Call (ed.), *Constructing Justice and Security After War* (Washington DC, USIP, 2007), pp. 231–70.

——, "Peacebuilding in Cambodia: Legitimacy and Power," in Elizabeth M. Cousens and Chetan Kumar (eds), *Peacebuilding As Politics* (Boulder, CO: Lynne Rienner, 2001).

Dragović-Soso, Jasna and Eric Gordy, "Coming to Terms with the Past: Transitional Justice and Reconciliation in the Post-Yugoslav Lands," in James Ker-Lindsay and Dejan Djokic (eds), *New Perspectives on Yugoslavia: Key Issues and Controversies* (London: Routledge, 2010), pp. 193–212.

Duggan, Colleen, "Editorial Note," *International Journal of Transitional Justice*, vol. 4 (2010), pp. 315–28.

Duthie, Roger, "Toward a Development-Sensitive Approach to Transitional Justice," *International Journal of Transitional Justice*, vol. 2 (2008), pp. 292–309.

——, "Transitional Justice and Social Reintegration," in Stockholm Initiative on Disarmament Demobilisation Reintegration, *Background Studies* (Stockholm: Ministry for Foreign Affairs, 2005).

Duthie, Roger and Irma Specht, "DDR, Transitional Justice, and the Reintegration of Former Child Combatants," in Ana Cutter Patel, Pablo de Greiff, and Lars Waldorf, *Disarming the Past: Transitional Justice and Ex-Combatants* (New York: SSRC, 2010).

Ebo, Adedeji, "Security Sector Reform as An Instrument of Sub-Regional Transformation in West Africa," in Alan Bryden and Heiner Hanggi (eds), *Reform and Reconstruction of the Security Sector* (Munster: DCAF/LIT Verlag, 2004) pp. 65–92.

Ero, Comfort and Jonathan Temin, "Sources of Conflict in West Africa," in Chandra Lekha Sriram and Zoe Nielsen (eds), *Exploring Subregional Conflict: Opportunities for Conflict Prevention* (Boulder, CO: Lynne Rienner, 2004).

Fanthorpe, Richard, "On the Limits of Liberal Peace: Chiefs and Democratic Decentralization in Post-War Sierra Leone," *African Affairs*, vol. 105, no. 418 (2005), pp. 27–49.

Findlay, Mark, "Activating a Victim Constituency in International Criminal Justice," *International Journal of Transitional Justice*, vol. 3 (2009), pp. 183–206.

Finnemore, Martha J. and Stephen Toope, "Alternatives to 'Legalization': Richer Views of Law and Politics," *International Organization*, vol. 55 (2001), pp. 744–47.

Finnström, Sverker, "Reconciliation Grown Bitter? War, Retribution, and Ritual Action in Northern Uganda," in Rosalind Shaw and Lars Waldorf (eds), *Localizing Transitional Justice: Interventions and Priorities after Mass Violence* (Stanford, CA: Stanford University Press, 2010), pp. 135–56.

Fletcher, Laurel and Harvey M. Weinstein, "A World Unto Itself? The Application of International Justice in the Former Yugoslavia," in Eric Stover and Harvey Weinstein (eds), *My Neighbour, My Enemy. Justice and Community in the Aftermath of Atrocity* (Cambridge: Cambridge University Press, 2004), pp. 29–49.

——, "Violence and Social Repair: Rethinking the Contribution of Justice to Reconciliation," *Human Rights Quarterly*, vol. 24 (2002), pp. 573–639.

Follath, Erich, "New Evidence Points to Hezbollah in Hariri Murder," *Der Spiegel* (23 May 2009), available at <www.spiegel.de/international/world/0,1518,626412-2,00.html>.

Gaeta, Paola, "To Be (Present) or Not To Be (Present): Trials *In Absentia* before the Special Tribunal for Lebanon," *Journal of International Criminal Justice*, vol. 5 (2007), pp. 1165–74.

Galtung, Johan, "Violence, Peace, and Peace Research," *Journal of Peace Research* 6, no. 3 (1969), pp. 167–91.

García-Godos, Jemima, "Land Restitution in the Colombian Transitional Justice Process," *Nordic Journal of Human Rights*, vol. 28, no. 2 (2010), pp. 262–88.

——, "Victim Reparations in the Peruvian Truth Commission and the Challenge of Historical Interpretation," *International Journal of Transitional Justice*, vol. 2 (2008), pp. 63–82.

——, "Victim Reparations in Transitional Justice: What is at Stake and Why," *Nordic Journal of Human Rights*, vol. 26 (2008), pp. 111–30.

García-Godos, Jemima and Knut Andreas Orgland Lid, "Transitional Justice and Victims' Rights before the End of a Conflict: The Unusual Case of Colombia," *Journal of Latin American Studies*, vol. 42 (2010), pp. 487–516.

Gberie, Lansana, "Truth and Justice on Trial in Liberia," *African Affairs*, vol. 107, no. 428 (2008).

George, Alexander L., "Case Studies and Theory Development: The Method of Structured, Focused Comparison," in P. G. Lauren (ed)., *Diplomacy: New Approaches in History, Theory, and Policy* (New York: Free Press, 1979), pp. 43–68.

Gillett, Matthew, "Victim Participation at the International Criminal Court," *Australian International Law Journal*, vol. 16 (2009), pp. 29–46.

Gompert, David C., Robert C. Davis, and Brooke Stearns Lawson, "Oversight of the Liberian National Police" (Santa Monica, CA: RAND National Defense Research Institute, 2009), available at <www.rand.org/content/dam/rand/pubs/occasional_papers/2009/RAND_OP230.sum.pdf>.

Haider, Huma, "Social Repair in Divided Societies: Integrating a Coexistence Lens into Transitional Justice," *Conflict, Security & Development*, vol. 11 (2011), pp. 175–203.

Hamieh, Christine Sylva and Roger MacGinty, "A Very Political Reconstruction: Governance and Reconstruction in Lebanon after the 2006 War," *Disasters*, vol. 34 (2010), pp. S103–S123.

Hammarberg, Thomas, "Efforts To Establish a Tribunal Against the Khmer Rouge Leaders: Discussions Between the Cambodian Government and the UN," paper presented at a seminar organized by SIDA, Stockholm, 29 May 2001.

Hayner, Priscilla, *Negotiating Justice: Guidance for Mediators* (Geneva: The Centre for Humanitarian Dialogue, 2009).

——, *Negotiating Peace in Liberia: Preserving the Possibility for Justice* (Geneva: Henry Dunant Centre for Humanitarian Dialogue, 2007).

Hendrickson, Dylan, "Cambodia's Security-Sector Reforms: Limits of a Downsizing Strategy," *Conflict, Security & Development*, vol. 1, no. 1 (2001), pp. 67–82.

Henham, Ralph, "International Sentencing as a Force for Achieving Peace Through Justice," in Oxford Transitional Justice Research (OTJR) (eds), *Critical Perspectives in Transitional Justice* (Antwerp: Intersentia, 2011).

——, "Some Reflections on the Role of Victims in the International Criminal Trial Process," *International Review of Victimology*, vol. 11 (2004), pp. 201–24.

Herman, Johanna, "Reaching for Justice: The Participation of Victims at the Extraordinary Chambers in the Courts of Cambodia," Centre on Human Rights in Conflict Policy Paper no. 5, September 2010.

Hodžić, Refik, "Living the Legacy of Mass Atrocities: Victims' Perspectives on War Crimes Trials," *Journal of International Criminal Justice*, vol. 8, 2010, pp. 113–36.

Hoffman, Danny, "The Civilian Target in Sierra Leone and Liberia: Political Power, Military Strategy, and Humanitarian Intervention," *African Affairs*, vol. 103, no. 411 (2004), pp. 211–26.

Hovil, Lucy and Joanna Quinn, *Working Paper 17: Peace First, Justice Later* (Kampala: Refugee Law Project, 2005).

Hovil, Lucy and Zachary Lomo, *Working Paper 15: Whose Justice? Perceptions of Uganda's Amnesty Act 2000: The Potential for Conflict Resolution and Long-Term Reconciliation* (Kampala: Refugee Law Project, 2005).

——, *Working Paper 11: Behind the Violence: Causes, Consequences and the Search for Solutions to the War in Northern Uganda* (Kampala: Refugee Law Project, 2004).

Hoyle, Carolyn, "Can International Justice Be Restorative Justice? The Role of Reparations," in Oxford Transitional Justice Research (OTJR) (eds), *Critical Perspectives in Transitional Justice* (Antwerp: Intersentia, 2011).

Human Rights Watch, "Seductions of 'Sequencing'" (18 March 2011).

——, "Uprooted and Forgotten: Impunity and Human Rights Abuses in Northern Uganda" (Human Rights Watch, 2005).

——, *Justice at Risk: War Crimes Trials in Croatia, Bosnia and Herzegovina and Serbia and Montenegro* (New York: HRW, 2004).

Humphrey, Michael, "From Victim to Victimhood: Truth Commissions and Trials as Rituals of Political Transition and Individual Healing," *The Australian Journal of Anthropology*, vol. 14, no. 2 (2003).

Humphreys, Macartan and Jeremy M. Weinstein, "Demobilization and Reintegration in Sierra Leone: Assessing Progress," in Robert Muggah (ed.), *Security and Post-Conflict Reconstruction: Dealing with Fighters in the Aftermath of War* (Abingdon: Routledge, 2009), pp. 47–69.

——, "Demobilization and Reintegration," *Journal of Conflict Resolution*, vol. 51 (2007), pp. 531–67.

Huyse, Luc, "Conclusions and Recommendations," in Luc Huyse and Marc Salter (eds), *Traditional Justice and Reconciliation after Violent Conflict: Learning from African Experiences* (Stockholm: International IDEA, 2008), pp. 181–98.

——, "Amnesty, Truth or Prosecution," in Luc Reychler and Thania Paffenholz (eds), *Peace-Building, a Field Guide* (Boulder, CO: Lynne Rienner, 2001).

Igreja, Victor, "The Politics of Peace, Justice, and Healing in Post-War Mozambique: 'Practices of Rupture' by *Magamba* Spirits and Healers in Gorongosa," in Chandra Lekha Sriram and Suren Pillay (eds), *Peace Versus Justice: The Dilemma of Transitional Justice in Africa* (Durban: University of KwaZulu Natal Press, 2009 and Oxford: James Currey, 2010), pp. 277–300.

Ingelaere, Bert, "Do We Understand Life after Genocide? Center and Periphery in the Construction of Knowledge in Postgenocide Rwanda," *African Studies Review*, vol. 53, no. 1 (2010).

——, "The Gacaca Courts in Rwanda," in Luc Huyse and Marc Salter (eds), *Traditional Justice and Reconciliation after Violent Conflict: Learning from African Experiences* (Stockholm: International IDEA, 2008), pp. 24–59.

International Bar Association and International Legal Assistance Consortium, *Restoring Integrity: An Assessment of the Needs of the Justice System in the Republic of Kenya* (February 2010).

International Center for Transitional Justice, *Bosnia and Herzegovina, Submission to the Universal Periodic Review of the UN Human Rights Council Seventh Session: February 2010* (New York: ICTJ, 2009).

International Criminal and Humanitarian Law Centre, *The Backlog of Core International Crimes Case Files in Bosnia and Herzegovina*, 2009.

International Crisis Group, "Trial by Fire: The Politics of the Special Tribunal for Lebanon," *Middle East Report No 100* (2 December 2010), p. 37, available at <www.crisisgroup.org/~/media/Files/Middle%20East%20North%20Africa/Iraq%20Syria%20Lebanon/Lebanon/100%20Trial%20by%20Fire%20–%20The%20Politics%20of%20the%20Special%20Tribunal%20for%20Lebanon.ashx>.

——, *Bosnia's Incomplete Transitions: between Dayton and Europe* (Brussels, ICG, 2009).

——, "Liberia: Resurrecting the Justice System," Africa Report No. 107, April 2006, available at <www.crisisgroup.org/~/media/Files/africa/west-africa/liberia/Liberia%20Resurrecting%20the%20Justice%20System.pdf>.

——, *Bosnia's Stalled Police Reform: No Progress, No EU* (Brussels, ICG, 2005).

——, *The Continuing Challenge of Refugee Return in Bosnia and Herzegovina*, Balkan Report no. 137 (Brussels: ICG, 2002).

Ivanešević, Bogdan, *The War Crimes Chamber in Bosnia and Herzegovina: From Hybrid to Domestic Court* (New York: ICTJ, 2008).

Jain, Neha, "Conceptualizing Internationalisation in Hybrid Criminal Courts," *Singapore Year Book of International Law*, vol. 12 (2008), pp. 81–95.

James-Allen, Paul, Aaron Weah, and Lizzie Goodfriend, *Beyond the Truth and Reconciliation Commission: Transitional Justice Options in Liberia* (New York and Monrovia: International Center for Transitional Justice (ICTJ), 2010).

Jaquemet, Iolanda, "Fighting Amnesia: Ways to Uncover the Truth about Lebanon's Missing," *International Journal of Transitional Justice*, vol. 3, no. 1 (2008), pp. 1–18.

Jaramillo, Sergio, Yanet Giha, and Paula Torres, *Disarmament, Demobilization and Reinsertion Amidst the Conflict: The Case of Colombia* (New York: International Center for Transitional Justice, 2009).

Jaye, Thomas, "Parliamentary Oversight and Lessons Learned from Internationalized Security Sector Reform," (NYU Center on International Cooperation, 2009), available at <www.cic.nyu.edu/peacebuilding/docs/Liberia_SSR.pdf>.

——, *Transitional Justice and DDR: The Case of Liberia*, Research Brief (International Center for Transitional Justice (ICTJ), 2009).

Jennings, Kathleen M., "The Political Economy of DDR in Liberia: A Gendered Critique," *Conflict, Security & Development*, vol. 9 (2009), pp. 475–94.

——, "Unclear Ends, Unclear Means: Reintegration in Postwar Societies—The Case of Liberia," *Global Governance*, vol. 14 (2008), pp. 327–45.

——, "The Struggle to Satisfy: DDR Through the Eyes of Ex-Combatants in Liberia," *International Peacekeeping*, vol. 14, no. 2 (April 2007).

Jordash, Wayne and Tim Parker, "Trials *In Absentia* at the Special Tribunal for Lebanon: Incompatibility with International Human Rights Law," *Journal of International Criminal Justice*, vol. 8 (2010), pp. 487–509.

Jubilut, Liliana Lyra, "Towards a New Jus Post Bellum: The United Nations Peacebuilding Commission and the Improvement of Post-Conflict Efforts and Accountability," *Minnesota Journal of International Law*, vol. 9 (2011), pp. 26–64.

Judicial System Monitoring Programme (JSMP), "Unfulfilled Expectations: Community Views on CAVR's Community Reconciliation Process" (Dili: JSMP, 2004).

Juma, Monica Kathina, "African Mediation of the Kenyan Post-2007 Election Crisis," *Journal of Contemporary African Studies*, vol. 27 (2009), pp. 407–30.

Kamungi, Prisca M., "The Politics of Displacement in Multiparty Kenya," *Journal of Contemporary African Studies*, vol. 27 (2009), pp. 345–64.

Kamungi, Prisca M. and Jacqueline M. Klopp, "Failure to Protect: Lessons from Kenya's IDP Network," *Forced Migration Review*, vol. 28 (2007), pp. 52–53.

Kelsall, Tim, "Truth, Lies, Ritual: Preliminary Reflections on the Truth and Reconciliation Commission in Sierra Leone," *Human Rights Quarterly*, 27 (2005), pp. 361–91.

Khadiagala, Gilbert M., "Regionalism and Conflict Resolution: Lessons from the Kenyan Crisis," *Journal of Contemporary African Studies*, vol. 27 (2009), pp. 431–44.

Khiddu-Makubuya, Edward, "Paramilitarism and Human Rights," in Kumar Rupesinghe (ed.), *Conflict Resolution in Uganda* (Oslo: Peace Research Institute of Oslo, 1989).

Kiernan, Ben, "Conflict in Cambodia 1945–2002," *Critical Asian Studies*, vol. 34, no. 4 (2002), pp. 483–95.

Klarin, Mirko, "The Impact of the ICTY Trials on Public Opinion in the Former Yugoslavia," *Journal of International Criminal Justice*, vol. 9 (2009), pp. 89–96.

Klopp, Jacqueline M., "Kenya's Unfinished Agendas," *Journal of International Affairs*, vol. 62 (2009), pp. 143–58.

Klopp, Jacqueline M., Patrick Githinji, and Keffa Karuoya, "Internal Displacement and Local Peacebuilding in Kenya: Challenges and Innovations," Special Report 251, (Washington, DC: United States Institute of Peace, September 2010).

Knight, Mark and Alpaslan Özerdem, "Guns, Camps and Cash: Disarmament, Demobilization and Reinsertion of Former Combatants in Transitions from War to Peace," *Journal of Peace Research*, vol. 41 (2004), pp. 499–516.

Knudsen, Are, "Precarious Peacebuilding: Post-War Lebanon, 1990–2005," CMI Working Paper (Bergen: Chr. Michelsen Institute, 2005).

Kochanski, Adam, "Transitional Justice as Liberal Peacebuilding: Panacea or False Promise?" in Carla Suarez (ed.), *Security and Conflict: Evolving Theory and Practice* (Halifax: Centre for Foreign Policy Studies, 2011).

Kraft, Martin, Muzna Al-Mazri, Heiko Wimmen, and Natascha Zupan, "Walking the Line: Strategic Approaches to Peacebuilding in Lebanon" (Bonn: Working Group on Development and Peace, German Development Service, and Heinrich Böll-Stiftung, December 2008), pp. 15–24.

Lambourne, Wendy, "Transitional Justice and Peacebuilding after Mass Violence," *International Journal of Transitional Justice*, vol. 3 (2009), pp. 28–48.

Latigo, James Ojera, "Northern Uganda: Tradition-Based Practices in the Acholi Region," in Luc Huyse and Marc Salter (eds), *Traditional Justice and Reconciliation after Violent Conflict: Learning from African Experiences* (Stockholm: International IDEA, 2008), pp. 85–120.

Leebaw, Bronwyn Anne, "The Irreconcilable Goals of Transitional Justice," *Human Rights Quarterly*, vol. 30, no. 1 (2008), pp. 95–118.

Le Mon, Christopher, "Rwanda's Troubled Gacaca Courts," *Human Rights Brief*, vol. 14, no. 2, Winter 2007, pp. 16–20.

Leonard, Pamela Blume, "An Introduction to Restorative Justice," in Elisabeth Beck *et al.* (eds), *Social Work and Restorative Justice. Skill for Dialogue, Peacemaking and Reconciliation* (Oxford; Oxford University Press, 2011), pp. 31–63.

Lid, Knut Andreas O. and Jemima García-Godos, "Land Restitution in the Colombian Transitional Justice Process," *Nordic Journal of Human Rights*, vol. 28 (2010), pp. 262–88.

Liebling-Kalifani, Helen, Victoria Mwaka, Ruth Ojiambo-Ochieng, Juliet Were-Oguttu, Eugene Kinyanda, Deddeh Kwekew, Lindora Howard, and Cecilia Danuweli, "Women War Survivors of the 1989–2003 Conflict in Liberia: The Impact of Sexual and Gender-Based Violence," *Journal of International Women's Studies*, vol. 12, no. 1 (2009), available at <www.bridgew.edu/soas/jiws/vol12_no1/pdfs/1_Liebling-Kalifani.pdf>.

Linton, Suzannah, "Putting Cambodia's Extraordinary Chambers into Context," *Singapore Year Book of International Law*, vol. 11 (2007), pp. 195–259.

Longman, Timothy, "An Assessment of Rwanda's *Gacaca* Courts," *Peace Review*, vol. 21, no. 3 (2009), pp. 303–12.

——, "Justice at the Grassroots? Gacaca Trials in Rwanda," in Naomi Roht-Arriaza and Javier Mariezcurrena (eds), *Transitional Justice in the Twenty-First Century* (New York: Cambridge University Press, 2006) pp. 206–28.

MacKenzie, Megan, "Securitization and Desecuritization: Female Soldiers and the Reconstruction of Women in Post-Conflict Sierra Leone," *Security Studies*, vol. 18, no. 2 (2009).

Martin-Ortega, Olga, "Hybrid Tribunals and the Rule of Law: The War Crimes Chamber in Bosnia and Herzegovina," in H. F. Carey and S. G. Mitchell, *Trials and Tribulations of International Prosecution* (Lexington Books, forthcoming, 2012).

Martin-Ortega, Olga and Johanna Herman, "The Impact of Hybrid Tribunals: Current Practice in Bosnia and Herzegovina and Cambodia," in M. Reed and A. Lyons (eds), *Contested Transitions: Dilemmas of Transitional Justice in Colombia and Comparative Experience* (Bogota: International Centre for Transitional Justice, 2010), pp. 230–59.

——, "Narrowing Gaps in Justice: Rule of Law Programming in Liberia," in Chandra Lekha Sriram, Olga Martin-Ortega, and Johanna Herman (eds), *Peacebuilding and Rule of Law in Africa: Just Peace?* (London: Routledge, 2010).

McCandless, Erin, "Lessons from Liberia: Integrated Approaches to Peacebuilding in Transitional Settings," Occasional Paper 160, Institute for Security Studies (2008).

McCarthy, Conor, "Reparations under the Rome Statute of the International Criminal Court and Reparative Justice Theory," *International Journal of Transitional Justice*, vol. 3 (2009), pp. 250–71.

McEvoy, Kieran, "Letting Go Of Legalism: Developing a 'Thicker' Version of Transitional Justice," in Kieran McEvoy and Lorna McGregor (eds), *Transitional Justice From Below: Grassroots Activism and the Struggle for Change* (Oxford and Portland, OR: Hart, 2008), pp. 15–45.

McKay, Susan, "Reconstructing Fragile Lives: Girls' Social Reintegration in Northern Uganda and Sierra Leone," *Gender and Development*, vol. 12, no. 3 (2004), pp. 19–30.

Mearsheimer, John J., "The Gathering Storm: China's Challenge to US Power in Asia," *The Chinese Journal of International Politics*, vol. 3 (2010).

Meernik, James, "Justice and Peace? How the International Criminal Tribunal Affects Societal Peace in Bosnia," *Journal of Peace Research*, vol. 42 (2005), pp. 271–89.

Merry, Sally Engle, "From Law and Colonialism to Law and Globalization," *Law and Social Inquiry*, vol. 28, no. 2 (2003), pp. 569–90.

——, "Legal Pluralism," *Law and Society Review*, vol. 22, no. 5 (1988), pp. 869–96.

Meyerstein, Ariel, "Between Law and Culture: Rwanda's *Gacaca* and Postcolonial Legality," *Law & Social Inquiry*, vol. 32, no. 2 (2007), pp. 467–508.

Milanovich, Marko, "An Odd Couple: Domestic Crimes and International Responsibility in the Special Tribunal for Lebanon," *Journal of International Criminal Justice*, vol. 5 (2007), pp. 1139–52.

Mitton, Keiran, "Engaging Disengagement: The Political Reintegration of Sierra Leone's Revolutionary United Front," *Conflict, Security & Development*, 8 (2008), pp. 193–222.

Moore, Sally Falk, "Law and Social Change: The Semi-Autonomous Social Field as an Appropriate Subject of Study," *Law and Society Review*, vol. 7, no. 4 (1973), pp. 719–46.

Moratti, Massimo, "Tackling Obstruction to Property Rights and Return: A Critical Assessment of the Practice of Removing Housing Officials in Bosnia and Herzegovina," in Dina Francesca Haynes (ed.), *Deconstructing the Reconstruction. Human Rights and Rule of Law in Postwar Bosnia and Herzegovina* (Aldershot: Ashgate, 2008), pp. 176–204.

Moratti, Massimo and Amra Sabic-El-Rayess, *Transitional Justice and DDR: The Case of Bosnia and Herzegovina*, Research Brief, June 2009 (NY: ICTY, 2009).

Moreno Ocampo, Luis, "Transitional Justice in Ongoing Conflicts," *International Journal of Transitional Justice*, vol. 1 (2007) pp. 8–9.

Muehlmann, Thomas, "Police Restructuring in Bosnia-Herzegovina: Problems with Internationally-Led Security Sector Reform," *Journal of Intervention and Statebuilding*, vol. 1, special supplement 1, 2007, pp. 37–65.

Mueller, Susanne D, "Dying To Win: Elections, Political Violence, and Institutional Decay in Kenya," *Journal of Contemporary African Studies*, vol. 29 (2011), pp. 99–117.

Muggah, Robert, "Introduction: The Emperor's Clothes?" in Robert Muggah (ed.), *Security and Post-Conflict Reconstruction: Dealing with Fighters in the Aftermath of War* (Abingdon: Routledge, 2009), pp. 1–29.

——, "No Magic Bullet: A Critical Perspective on Disarmament, Demobilization and Reintegration (DDR) and Weapons Reduction in Post-Conflict Contexts," *Round Table*, vol. 94 (2005), pp. 239–52.

Muggah, Robert, Desmond Molloy, and Maximo Halty, "(Dis)integrating DDR in Sudan and Haiti? Practitioners' Views To Overcoming Integration Inertia," in Robert Muggah (ed.), *Security and Post-Conflict Reconstruction: Dealing with Fighters in the Aftermath of War* (Abingdon: Routledge, 2009).

Muggah, Robert, Mats Berdal and Stina Torjesen, "Conclusions: Enter an Evidence-Based Security Promotion Agenda," in Robert Muggah (ed.), *Security and Post-Conflict Reconstruction: Dealing with Fighters in the Aftermath of War* (Abingdon: Routledge, 2009).

Musila, Godfrey M., "Options for Transitional Justice in Kenya: Autonomy and the Challenge of External Prescriptions," *International Journal of Transitional Justice*, vol. 3 (2009), pp. 445–64.

Mwirichia, Victoria and Jeniffer Katusya Barako Elema, "How Far is Home For Kenya's Internally Displaced Persons?" Nairobi: Institute for Security Studies, 24 February 2011, available at <www.issafrica.org/iss_today.php?ID=1238>, accessed April 2011.

Nagy, Rosemary, "Whose Justice? Gacaca, National Trials and the International Criminal Tribunal for Rwanda," in Joanna R. Quinn (ed.), *Reconciliation(s): Transitional Justice in Post-Conflict Societies* (Kingston: McGill-Queen's University Press, 2009).

Nerguizian, Aram and Anthony Cordesman, "The Lebanese Armed Forces: Challenges and Opportunities in Post-Syria Lebanon" (Washington, DC: Center for Strategic and International Studies, 10 February 2009).

Nino, Carlos, "The Duty to Punish Past Abuses of Human Rights Put into Context: The Case of Argentina," *Yale Law Journal*, vol. 100 (1991), pp. 2619–40.

Ntsebeza, Dumisa Buhle, "Can Truth Commissions in Africa Deliver Justice?" in Anton Bösl and Joseph Diescho (eds), *Human Rights in Africa: Legal Perspectives on Their Protection and Promotion* (Namibia: Konrad-Adenauer-Stiftung, 2009).

Nwogu, Nneoma V., "When and Why It Started: Deconstructing Victim-Centered Truth Commissions in the Context of Ethnicity-Based Conflict," *International Journal of Transitional Justice*, vol. 4 (2010), pp. 275–89.

Offstein, Norman, "An Historical Review and Analysis of Colombian Guerrilla Movements: FARC, ELN and EPL," *Revista Desarrollo y Sociedad*, no. 52 (September 2003), pp. 99–142.

Öjendal, Joakim and Mona Lilja, "Beyond Democracy in Cambodia: Political Reconstruction in a Post-Conflict Society?" in Joakim Öjendal and Mona Lilja (eds), *Beyond Democracy in Cambodia: Political Reconstruction in a Post-Conflict Society?* (Copenhagen: Nias, 2009).

Open Society Justice Initiative, "Recent Developments at the Extraordinary Chambers in the Courts of Cambodia" (Open Society Foundation: June 2011).

Orentlicher, Diane, "'Settling Accounts' Revisited: Reconciling Global Norms with Local Agency," *International Journal of Transitional Justice*, vol. 1 (2007).

——, "Settling Accounts: The Duty to Prosecute Human Rights Violations of a Prior Regime," *Yale Law Journal*, vol. 100 (1991), pp. 2537–261.

Otero, Diego, *Experiencias de investigación: Las cifras del conflicto colombiano* (Bogotá, 2008), available at <http://www.setianworks.net/indepazHome/attachments/191_cifras%201964%20–2007.pdf>.

Pajibo, Ezikiel, *Traditional Justice Mechanisms: The Liberian Case* (Sweden: International IDEA, 2008).

Pajibo, Ezekiel, "Civil Society and Transitional Justice in Liberia: A Practitioner's Reflection from the Field," *International Journal of Transitional Justice*, vol. 1, no. 2 (2007), pp. 287–96.

Parmentier, Stephan, Marta Valiñas, and Elmar Weitekamp, "How to Repair the Harm After Violent Conflict in Bosnia? Results of a Population-Based Survey," *Netherlands Quarterly of Human Rights*, vol. 21 (2009), pp. 27–44.

Patel, Ana Cutter, "Transitional Justice and DDR," in Robert Muggah (ed.), *Security and Post-Conflict Reconstruction: Dealing with Fighters in the Aftermath of War* (Abingdon: Routledge, 2009), pp. 268–84.

Peake, Gordon, "What the Timorese Veterans Say: Unpacking DDR in Timor-Leste," in Robert Muggah (ed.), *Security and Post-Conflict Reconstruction: Dealing with Fighters in the Aftermath of War* (Abingdon: Routledge, 2009), pp. 165–89.

Pham, Phuong N., Patrick Vinck, and Eric Stover, "The Lord's Resistance Army and Forced Conscription in Northern Uganda," *Human Rights Quarterly*, vol 30, issue 2 (2008), pp. 404–11.

Pham, Phuong, Patrick Vinck, Michelle Balthazard, Sokhom Hean and Eric Stover, "So We Will Never Forget: A Population-Based Survey on Attitudes about Social Reconstruction and the Extraordinary Chambers in the Courts of Cambodia" (Berkeley: Human Rights Center, January 2009).

Pham, Phuong, Patrick Vinck, Marieke Wierda, Eric Stover, and Adrian di Giovanni, "Forgotten Voices: A Population-Based Survey of Attitudes About Peace and Justice in Northern Uganda" (New York: International Centre for Transitional Justice, 2007).

Philpott, Charles, "Though the Dog is Dead, the Pig Must be Killed: Finishing Property Restitution to Bosnia-Herzegovina's IDPs and Refugees," *Journal of Refugee Studies*, vol. 18, no. 1 (2005), pp. 1–24.

Pigou, Piers, "The Community Reconciliation Process of the Commission for Reception, Truth and Reconciliation" (Dili: United Nations Development Programme Timor-Leste, 2004).

Pouligny, Beatrice, "The Politics and Anti-Politics of Contemporary 'Disarmament, Demobilization and Reintegration' Programs" (Paris: CERI, 2004).

Prison Reform International, "The Contribution of the Gacaca Jurisdictions to Resolving Cases Arising from the Genocide" (London and Kigali: PRI, 2010).

Pugel, James, "Measuring Reintegration in Liberia: Assessing the Gap between Outputs and Outcomes," in Robert Muggah (ed.), *Security and Post-Conflict Reconstruction: Dealing with Fighters in the Aftermath of War* (Abingdon: Routledge, 2009), pp. 70–102.

Pugh, Michael and Neil Cooper, with Jonathan Goodhand, "Sierra Leone in West Africa," in Pugh, Cooper, and Goodhand (eds), *War Economies in Regional Context* (Boulder, CO: Lynne Rienner, 2004).

Quinn, Joanna R., "Tradition?! Traditional Cultural Institutions on Customary Practices in Uganda," International Studies Association Annual Conference, New York, 16 February 2009.

——, "Accountability and Reconciliation: Traditional Mechanisms of Acknowledgement and the Implications of the Juba Peace Process," in *Reconstructing Northern Uganda* (University of Western Ontario, London, 9 April 2008).

Raab, Dominic, "Evaluating the ICTY and its Completion Strategy. Efforts to Achieve Accountability for War Crimes and Their Tribunals," *Journal of International Criminal Justice*, vol. 3 (2005), pp. 82–102.

Rabil, Robert, "Hezbollah: Lebanon's Power Broker," *The Journal of International Security Affairs*, no. 15 (Fall 2008), available at <www.securityaffairs.org/issues/2008/15/rabil.php>.

Ramirez-Barrat, Clara, *Making an Impact: Guidelines on Designing and Implementing Outreach Programmes for Transitional Justice* (New York: ICTJ, 2011), available at <http://ictj.org/sites/default/files/ICTJ-Global-Making-Impact-2011-English.pdf>, accessed 6 September 2001.

Ramji-Nogales, Jaya, "Designing Bespoke Transitional Justice: A Pluralist Process Approach," *Michigan Journal of International Law*, vol. 32 (2010–11).

Rauschenbach, Mina and Damien Scalia, "Victims and International Criminal Justice: A Vexed Question?" *International Review of the Red Cross*, vol. 90 issue 870, (2008), pp. 441–59.

Refugees International, *Bulletin: Uganda: Challenges of Peace and Justice* (Washington: February 2008).

——, "Northern Uganda: Child Mothers and Returnees Require Special Care" (Washington, 7 November 2002), available at <www.refugeesinternational.org/content/article/detail/827>.

Rettig, Max, "Gacaca: Truth, Justice and Reconciliation in Post-Conflict Rwanda," *African Studies Review*, vol. 51, no. 3 (2008), pp. 22–50.

Reyntjens, Filip, "Post-1994 Politics in Rwanda: Problematising 'Liberation' and 'Democratisation,'" *Third World Quarterly*, vol. 27, no. 6 (2006), pp. 1103–17.

——, "Rwanda, Ten Years On: From Genocide to Dictatorship," *African Affairs*, vol. 103 (2004), pp. 177–210.

Richani, Nazih, "The Political Economy of Violence: The War System in Colombia," *Journal of Interamerican Studies and World Affairs*, vol. 39, no 2 (1997), pp. 27–81.

Richards, Paul, Khadija Bah, and James Vincent, "Social Capital and Survival: Prospects for Community-Driven Development in Post-Conflict Sierra Leone," *Social Development Papers* no. 12 (World Bank, April 2004).

Robins, Simon, "Towards Victim-Centred Transitional Justice: Understanding the Needs of Families of the Disappeared in Postconflict Nepal," *International Journal of Transitional Justice*, vol. 5 (2011), pp. 75–98.

Romano, Cesare P. R., André Nollkaemper, and Jann K. Kleffner (eds), *Internationalized Criminal Courts: Sierra Leone, East Timor, Kosovo, and Cambodia* (Oxford: Oxford University Press, 2004).

Romero, Mauricio, *Parapolítica. La ruta de la expansión paramilitar y los acuerdos políticos* (Bogotá: Corporación Nuevo Arco Iris, 2007), available at <www.nuevoarcoiris.org.co/sac/?q=node/80>.

Ross, Michael, "The Political Economy of the Resource Curse," *World Politics*, vol. 51 (January 1999), pp. 297–322.

Roth, Kenneth, "The Power of Horror in Rwanda," *Los Angeles Times* (11 April 2009), available at <www.hrw.org/en/news/2009/04/11/power-horror-rwanda>.

Roth, Kenneth and Alison Des Forges, "Justice or Therapy?" *Boston Review*, vol. 27, no. 3–4 (2002).

Rubio-Marín, Ruth and Pablo de Greiff, "Women and Reparations," *International Journal of Transitional Justice*, vol. 1 (2007), pp. 318–37.

Sader, Choucri, "A Lebanese Perspective on the Special Tribunal for Lebanon," *Journal of International Criminal Justice*, vol. 5 (2007), pp. 1083–89.

Saffon, Maria Paula and Rodrigo Uprimny, "Uses and Abuses of Transitional Justice in Colombia," in Morten Bergsmo and Pablo Kalmanovitz (eds), *Law in Peace Negotiations* (Oslo: Torkel Opsahl Academic Publisher, 2010), pp. 354–94.

Salem, Paul, "Lebanon's Multiple Crises Risk Escalation" (Carnegie Endowment for International Peace, Carnegie Middle East Center, 12 July 2010), available at <http://carnegie-mec.org>.

Sánchez, Fabio and Mario Chacón, "Conflict, State and Decentralisation. From Social Progress to Armed Dispute for Local Control 1974–2002," *Crisis States Programme*, Working Paper No. 70 (2005).

Sánchez, Fabio, Ana María Díaz, and Michel Formisano, "Conflicto, Crimen Violento y Actividad Criminal en Colombia: Un Análisis Espacial," *Documentos CEDE* (Bogotá, 2003).

Sánchez, Nelson Camilo, "¿Perder es ganar un poco? Avances y frustraciones de la discusión del Estatuto de Víctimas en Colombia," in Catalina Díaz, Nelson Camilo Sánchez, and Sanín, Francisco Gutiérrez, "Land and Property Rights in Colombia—Change and Continuity," *Nordic Journal of Human Rights*, vol. 28, no. 2 (2010), pp. 230–61.

Sayigh, Yezid, "'Fixing Broken Windows': Security Sector Reform in Palestine, Lebanon, and Yemen," *Carnegie Papers*, no. 17 (Beirut: Carnegie Middle East Center, October 2009).

Schwendiman, David, "Prosecuting Atrocity Crimes in National Courts: Looking Back on 2009 in Bosnia and Herzegovina," *Northwestern Journal of International Human Rights*, vol. 8, issue 3, 2010, pp. 270–300.

Seils, Paul and Marieke Wierda, "The International Criminal Court and Conflict Mediation," *International Center for Transitional Justice Occasional Paper Series* (June 2005).

Sesay, Mohamed Gibril and Mohamed Suma, "Transitional Justice and DDR: The Case of Sierra Leone," International Center for Transitional Justice (June 2009).

Shaftari, M. Assad, "Letter from a Militia Leader in Lebanon's Civil War" (2005) <www.caritas.org/activities/peace_reconciliation/Peacebuilding_Slideshow.html?cnt=337> accessed 15 July 2012.

Shaw, Rosalind, "Linking Justice with Reintegration? Ex-Combatants and the Sierra Leone Experiment," in Rosalind Shaw and Lars Waldorf (eds), *Localizing Transitional Justice: Interventions and Priorities after Mass Violence* (Palo Alto, CA: Stanford University Press, 2010), pp. 111–34.

——, "Rethinking Truth and Reconciliation Commissions: Lessons from Sierra Leone," *United States Institute of Peace Special Report*, no. 130 (February 2005), available at <www.usip.org>.

Slye, Ronald C., "The Cambodian Amnesties: Beneficiaries and the Temporal Reach of Amnesties for Gross Violation of Human Rights," *bepress Legal Series*, Working Paper 33 (2003).

Snyder, Jack and Leslie Vinjamuri, "Trials and Errors: Principle and Pragmatism in Strategies of International Justice," *International Security*, vol. 28 (2003/04), pp. 5–44.

Souaré, Issaka K., "The International Criminal Court and African Conflicts: The Case of Uganda," *Review of African Political Economy*, vol. 36, no. 121 (2009), pp. 369–88.

Specht, Irma (ed.), *Red Shoes: Experiences of Girl Combatants in Liberia* (Geneva: Programme of Crisis Response and Reconstruction, International Labour Office, 2006), available at <www.humansecuritygateway.com/documents/ILO_ExperiencesofGirlCombatantsLiberia.pdf>.

Specker, Leontine, "The R-Phase of DDR Processes" (The Hague: Netherlands Institute of International Relations, 2008).

Sriram, Chandra Lekha, "Transitional Justice and the Liberal Peace," in Edward Newman, Roland Paris, and Oliver P. Richmond (eds), *New Perspectives on Liberal Peacebuilding* (Tokyo: United Nations University Press, 2009), pp. 112–30.

Sriram, Chandra Lekha, "Justice as Peace? Liberal Peacebuilding and Strategies of Transitional Justice," *Global Society*, vol. 21 (2007), pp. 579–91.

Sriram, Chandra Lekha, "Wrong-Sizing International Justice? The Hybrid Tribunal in Sierra Leone," *Fordham International Law Journal*, vol. 29, no. 3 (February 2006), pp. 472–506.

Sriram, Chandra Lekha and Johanna Herman, "DDR and Transitional Justice: Bridging the Divide?" *Conflict, Security, and Development*, vol. 9, no. 4 (December 2009), pp. 455–74.

Sriram, Chandra Lekha, Olga Martin-Ortega, and Johanna Herman, "Beyond Justice Versus Peace: Transitional Justice and Peacebuilding Strategies," in Karin Aggestam (ed.), *The Study of Just and Durable Peace* (London: Routledge, forthcoming 2012).

Sriram, Chandra Lekha, Olga Martin-Ortega, and Johanna Herman, "Justice Delayed? Internationalised Criminal Tribunals and Peace-Building in Lebanon, Bosnia and Cambodia," *Conflict, Security, and Development*, vol. 11, no. 3 (July 2011), pp. 335–56.

Sriram, Chandra Lekha, Olga Martin-Ortega, and Johanna Herman, "Evaluating and Comparing Strategies of Peacebuilding and Transitional Justice," *JAD-PbP Working Paper Series* No. 1 (May 2009).

Steinberg, Jonny, "A Truth Commission Goes Abroad: Liberian Transitional Justice in New York," *African Affairs*, vol. 110, no. 438 (2010).

——, "Liberia's Experiment with Transitional Justice," *African Affairs*, vol. 109, no. 434 (2009), pp. 135–44.

Stovel, Laura and Marta Valiñas, "Restorative Justice after Mass Violence: Opportunities and Risks for Children and Youth," Innocenti Working Paper IWP 2010–15 (Florence: UNICEF Innocenti Research Centre, June 2010).

Suma, Mohamad and Cristián Correa, "Report and Proposals for the Implementation of Reparations in Sierra Leone" (New York: International Center for Transitional Justice, December 2009).

Svärd, Proscovia, "The International Community and Post-War Reconciliation in Africa: A Case Study of the Sierra Leone Truth and Reconciliation Commission" (no date), p. 37, available at <www.ajol.info/index.php/ajcr/article/viewFile/59306/47604>.

Synovate, "Kenyans' Perception towards the ICC Process," 6 April 2011, available at <http://www.synovate.co.ke/spr/index.php/site/poll/kenyans_perception_towards_the_icc_process_6th_april_2011>, accessed 10 July 2011.

Tamanaha, Brian Z., "The Folly of the 'Social Scientific' Concept of Legal Pluralism," *Journal of Law and Society*, vol. 20, no. 2 (1993), pp. 192–217.

Task Force on the Establishment of a Truth, Justice and Reconciliation Commission, "Report of the Task Force on the Establishment of a Truth, Justice and Reconciliation Commission" (Nairobi: Government Printer, 2003).

Tejan-Cole, Abdul, "The Special Court for Sierra Leone: Conceptual Concerns and Alternatives," *African Human Rights Law Journal*, vol. 1 (2001), pp. 107–26.

Thallinger, Gerhard, "The UN Peacebuilding Commission and Transitional Justice," *German Law Journal*, vol. 8 (2007), pp. 681–710.

The Coalition to Stop the Use of Child Soldiers, *Child Soldiers Global Report 2004* (2004), available at <www.child-soldiers.org/document_get.php?id=801>, last accessed 15 July 2012.

Theidon, Kimberly, "Reconstructing Masculinities: The Disarmament, Demobilization and Reintegration of Former Combatants in Colombia," *Human Rights Quarterly*, vol. 31 (2009), pp. 1–34.

Theidon, Kimberley, "Transitional Subjects: The Disarmament, Demobilization, and Reintegration of Former Combatants in Columbia," *The International Journal of Transitional Justice*, vol. 1 (2007) pp. 66–90.

Thoms, Oskar N. T., James Ron and Roland Paris, "State-Level Effects of Transitional Justice: What Do We Know?" *International Journal of Transitional Justice*, vol. 4 (2010), pp. 1–26.

——, "The Effects of Transitional Justice Mechanisms: A Summary of Empirical Research Findings and Implications for Analysts and Practitioners," Centre for International Policy Studies Working Paper, April 2008.

Thomson, Susan M. and Rosemary Nagy, "Law, Power and Justice: What Legalism Fails to Address in the Functioning of Rwanda's *Gacaca* Courts," *International Journal of Transitional Justice*, vol. 5, no. 1 (2011), pp. 11–30.

Throup, David, "The Count," *Journal of Eastern African Studies*, vol. 2 (2008), pp. 290–304.

Tolbert, David, "Introductory Note to the Special Tribunal for Lebanon: Orders Regarding the Detention of Persons and Memorandum of Understanding," *International Legal Materials*, vol. 48 (April–June 2009), pp. 1149–51.

——, "The International Criminal Tribunal for the Former Yugoslavia: Unforeseen Successes and Foreseeable Shortcomings," *The Fletcher Forum of World Affairs*, vol. 26 (2002), pp. 5–17.

Tove, Grete Lie, Helga Malmin Binningsbo, and Scott Gates, "Post-Conflict Justice and Sustainable Peace," Post-Conflict Transition Working Paper, World Bank Policy Research Working Paper (April 2007).

Tzanakopoulos, Antonios, "Special Tribunal for Lebanon: The First Orders by the Pre-Trial Judge," *ASIL Insights*, vol. 13, issue 11 (7 August 2009), available at <www.asil.org>.

Un, Kheang, "The Judicial System and Democratization in Post-Conflict Cambodia," in Joakim Öjendal and Mona Lilja (eds), *Beyond Democracy in Cambodia: Political Reconstruction in a Post-Conflict Society* (Copenhagen: NIAS Press, 2009).

——, "Patronage Politics and Hybrid Democracy: Political Change in Cambodia, 1993–2003," *Asian Perspective*, vol. 29, no. 2 (2005), pp. 203–30.

Uprimny, Rodrigo (ed.), *Reparar en Colombia: Los dilemas en contexto de conflicto, pobreza y exclusión* (Bogotá: ICTJ—DeJusticia, 2009), pp. 623–718.

Uvin, Peter, *Ex-Combatants in Burundi: Why They Joined, Why They Left, How They Fared* (Washington, DC: The World Bank/Multi-Country Demobilization and Reintegration Program, 2007).

Vandeginste, Stef and Chandra Lekha Sriram, "Power-Sharing and Transitional Justice: A Clash of Paradigms?" *Global Governance*, vol. 17, no. 4 (October 2011).

Vinjamuri, Leslie and Aaron P. Boesenecker, "Accountability and Peace Agreements: Mapping Trends from 1980 to 2006," *Centre for Humanitarian Dialogue Report*, September 2007.

Vinck, Patrick, Phuong Pham, and Tino Kreutzer, *Talking Peace: A Population Based Survey on Attitudes about Security, Dispute Resolution and Post-Conflict Reconstruction in Liberia* (Berkeley: Human Rights Center, University of California Berkeley, June 2011), available at <www.law.berkeley.edu/HRCweb/pdfs/Talking-Peace-Liberia-2011.pdf>.

Vukusic, Iva, "An Insider's Account of Domestic Prosecutions in Bosnia-Herzegovina," Paper presented at the *51st Annual Convention of the International Studies Association*, New Orleans, February 2009.

Waddell, Nicholas and Phil Clark (eds), *Courting Conflict? Justice, Peace and the ICC in Africa* (London: Royal African Society, March 2008).

Waldorf, Lars, "Ex-Combatants and Truth Commissions," in Ana Cutter Patel, Pablo de Greiff, and Lars Waldorf, *Disarming the Past: Transitional Justice and Ex-Combatants* (New York: SSRC, 2010), pp. 14–35.

——, "Transitional Justice and DDR in Post-Genocide Rwanda" (New York: International Center for Transitional Justice, 2009).

——, "Mass Justice for Mass Atrocity: Rethinking Local Justice as Transitional Justice," *Temple Law Review*, vol. 79 (2006), pp. 1–88.

Welsh, Jennifer, "Implementing 'The Responsibility to Protect': Where Expectations Meet Reality," *Ethics and International Affairs*, vol. 24 (2010).

Wetzel, Jan Erik and Yvonne Mitri, "The Special Tribunal for Lebanon: A Court 'Off the Shelf' for a Divided Country," *The Law and Practice of International Courts and Tribunals* (2008), pp. 81–114.

Whitaker, Beth Elise and Jason Giersch, "Voting on a Constitution: Implications for Democracy in Kenya," *Journal of Contemporary African Studies*, vol. 27 (2009), pp. 1–20.

Wierda, Marieke, Habib Nassar, and Lynn Maalouf, "Early Reflections on Local Perceptions, Legitimacy and Legacy of the Special Tribunal for Lebanon," *Journal of International Criminal Justice*, vol. 5 (2007), pp. 1065–81.

Williamson, John, "The Disarmament, Demobilization, and Reintegration of Child Soldiers: Social and Psychological Transformation in Sierra Leone," *Intervention*, vol. 4, no. 3 (2006), pp. 185–205.

Witte, Eric, "Beyond 'Peace vs Justice': Understanding the Relationship Between DDR Programs and the Prosecution of International Crimes," in Ana Cutter Patel, Pablo de Greiff, and Lars Waldorf, *Disarming the Past: Transitional Justice and Ex-Combatants* (New York: SSRC, 2010), pp. 86–107.

Woodman, Gordon R., "Legal Pluralism and the Search for Justice," *Journal of African Law* 40, no. 2 (1996), pp. 152–67.

World Bank, "Implementation Completion Report," Report no. 36269, 22 May 2006.

World Vision, *Pawns of Politics: Children, Conflict and Peace in Northern Uganda* (Kampala: World Vision, 2004).

Wright, Nancy G., "Uganda: History From 1971," in John Middleton (ed.), *Encyclopedia of Africa South of the Sahara* (New York: Charles Scribner's Sons, 1996).

Young, Laura and Rosalyn Park, "Engaging Diasporas in Truth Commissions: Lessons from the Liberian Truth and Reconciliation Commission Diaspora Project," *International Journal of Transitional Justice*, vol. 3 (2009), pp. 341–61.

Yun, Janice, "Special Tribunal for Lebanon: A Tribunal of International Character Devoid of International Law," *Santa Clara Journal of International Law*, vol. 7 (2009–10), pp. 181–96.

Zahar, Marie-Joelle, "Foreign Intervention and State Reconstruction: Bosnian Fragility in Comparative Perspective," in Denisa Sostovicova and Vesna Bojicic-Dzelilovic, *Persistent State Weakness in the Global Age* (Farnham: Ashgate, 2009), pp. 115–28.

Zorbas, Eugenia, "'Keep Out of Our Affairs': How the Post-Genocide Government in Rwanda Manages Relations with Donors," International Studies Association Annual Conference, Chicago, 2007.

Official documents, legislation, and judicial decisions

Alston, Philip, "Report of the Special Rapporteur on Extrajudicial, Summary or Arbitrary Executions," UN Human Rights Council document A/HRC/11/2/Add.6, 26 May 2009.

Cambodia, *Law on the Establishment of the Extraordinary Chambers*, with inclusion of amendments as promulgated on 27 October 2004. Cambodia, NS/RKM/1004/006, available at <www.eccc.gov.kh/en/documents/legal/law-establishment-extraordinary-chambers-amended>, accessed 16 July 2012.

——, *Law on the Outlawing of the "Democratic Kampuchea" Group* (English translation based on the text published by the *Phnom Penh Post*, vol. 3, no. 14, 15–28 July 1994), available at <www.eccc.gov.kh/en/documents/legal/law-outlaw-democratic-kampuchea-group>, accessed 16 July 2012.

Cibelli, Kristen, Jule Krüger, and Amelia Hoover, Descriptive Statistics from Statements to the Liberian Truth and Reconciliation Commission. A Report by the Human Rights Data Analysis Group at Benetech and Annex to the Final Report of the Truth and Reconciliation Commission of Liberia (2009), available at <http://trcofliberia.org/resources/reports/final/descriptive-statistics-from-statements-to-the-liberian-trc-benetech.pdf>.

Colombian Constitutional Court, Sentence T-025, 22 January 2004.

Congress of the Republic of Colombia, Law 1448 of 2010. *Por la cual se dictan medidas de atención, asistencia y reparación integral a las víctimas del conflicto armado interno y se dictan otras disposiciones.*

——, Law 975 of 2005. *Por la cual se dictan disposiciones para la reincorporación de miembros de grupos armados organizados al margen de la ley, que contribuyan de manera efectiva a la consecución de la paz nacional y se dictan otras disposiciones para acuerdos humanitarios.*

——, Law 782 of 2002. *Por medio de la cual se prorroga la vigencia de la ley 418 del 26 de Diciembre 1997, prorrogada y modificada por la ley 548 de 1999 y se modifican algunas de sus disposiciones.*

——, Law 548 of 1999. *Por medio de la cual se prorroga la vigencia de la ley 418 del 26 de Diciembre 1997.*

——, Law 418 of 1997. *Por lo cual se consagran unos instrumentos para la búsqueda de la convivencia.*

——, Law 48 of 1968. *Por la cual se adoptan como legislación permanente algunos decretos.*

European Union, Council Joint Action 2008/130/CFSP of 18 February 2008, Extending the Mandate of the EUSR in BiH, 19 February 2008.

Extraordinary Chambers in the Courts of Cambodia, Internal Rules, 12 June 2007.

Government of Liberia, "An Act to Establish the Truth and Reconciliation Commission for Liberia" (hereafter, *TRC Act*), 12 May 2005, Monrovia, available at <www.ictj.org/static/Africa/Liberia/liberiatrcact.eng.pdf>.

Government of Uganda, *Peace, Recovery and Development Plan for Northern Uganda (PRDP) 2007–2010* (Kampala, September 2007).

Government of Uganda, *Amnesty Act 2000* (Kampala, 2000)

Government of Uganda and Lord's Resistance Army/Movement, "Annexure to the Agreement on Accountability and Reconciliation" (Juba, 19 February 2008).

Government of Uganda and Lord's Resistance Army/Movement, "Agreement on Accountability and Reconciliation" (Juba, 29 June 2007).

Government of Uganda, Ministry of Finance, Planning and Economic Development, *Poverty Eradication Action Plan (2004/5–2007/8)*, IMF Country Report No. 05/307 (Washington, DC: IMF, August 2005).

International Criminal Tribunal for the Former Yugoslavia, *Prosecutor vs. Radovan Karadžić* (IT-95–5/18-PT), Third Amended Indictment, 29 February 2009.

International Criminal Tribunal for the Former Yugoslavia, *Prosecutor v. Momčilo Krajišnik* (IT-00-39-T), Trial Judgment, 27 September 2006.

International Criminal Tribunal for the Former Yugoslavia, First Report of the International Tribunal for the Prosecution of Persons Responsible for Serious Violations of International Humanitarian Law Committed in the Territory of the former Yugoslavia since 1991, UN Doc. A/49/342-S/1994/1007, II (29 August 1994).

International Organisation for Migrations, *Transitional Assistance for Former Soldiers Programme* (2003), available at <www.iom.ba/TADS1.html>, accessed 19 August 2011.

Kenya National Commission on Human Rights, *On the Brink of the Precipice: A Human Rights Account of Kenya's Post-2007 Election Violence* (Nairobi: KNCHR, 15 August 2008).

Krasno, Jean, *Public Opinion Survey of UNMIL's Work in Liberia* (Monrovia: UNDPKO, 2006).

Michael, Sarah, *Reintegration Assistance for Ex-Combatants: Good Practices and Lessons for the MDRP* (Washington, DC: The World Bank Multi-Country Demobilization and Reintegration Program, 2006).

National Commission on Disarmament, Demobilization, Rehabilitation and Reintegration (NCDDRR), "Joint Implementation Unit DDRR Consolidated Report (Status of Disarmament & Demobilization Activities as at 11/24/2004)," available at <www.humanitarianinfo.org/liberia/coordination/sectoral/DDR/doc/Forthnightly%20Report_24112004.pdf> (2004).

OCHA/IRIN, *"When the Sun Sets, We Start to Worry … ": An Account of Life in Northern Uganda* (OCHA/IRIN, November 2003).

Office of the High Representative, *Decision Enacting the Law on Amendment to the Law on Court of Bosnia and Herzegovina*, 14 December 2009, <www.ohr.int/decisions/judicialrdec/default.asp?content_id=44283>.

——, *War Crimes Chamber Project, Project Implementation Plan, Registry Progress Report*, 20 October 2004, available at <www.ohr.int/ohr-dept/rule-of-law-pillar/pdf/wcc-project-plan-201004-eng.pdf>.

——, *Jobs and Justice: Our Agenda*, May 2002.

——, *Decision Establishing and Registering the Foundation of the Srebrenica-Potocari Memorial and Cemetery*, 10 May 2001.

——, *Property Law Implementation Plan* (no date), available at <www.ohr.int/plip>, accessed 19 August 2011.

Orentlicher, Diane, *That Someone Guilty Be Punished. The Impact of the ICTY in Bosnia* (New York: Open Society Institute and International Centre for Transitional Justice, 2010).

OSCE (Mission in Bosnia), *Delivering Justice in Bosnia and Herzegovina. An Overview of War Crimes Processing from 2005 to 2010* (Sarajevo: OSCE, 2011).

OSCE, *War Crimes Trials before the Domestic Courts in BiH. Progress and Obstacles*, March 2005.

Parliament of Uganda, *Parliament of Uganda eNewsletter*, vol 3, issue 35 (Kampala: 12–16 April 2010).

Presidency of the Republic of Colombia, Decree 1290 of 2008. *Por el cual se crea el programa de reparación individual por vía administrativa para las víctimas de los grupos armados organizados al margen de la ley.*

——, Decree 4530 of 2008. *Por el cual se modifica la estructura del Ministerio del Interior y Justicia y se dictan otras disposiciones.*

——, Decree 4436 of 2006. *Por la cual se reglamenta parcialmente la ley 782 de 1997.*

——, Decree 3391 of 2006. *Por el cual se reglamenta parcialmente la ley 975 de 2005.*

——, Decree 356 of 1994. *Por el cual se expide el estatuto de vigilancia y seguridad privada.*

——, Decree 1194 of 1989. *Por el cual se adiciona el decreto legislativo 0180 de 1988, para sancionar nuevas modalidades delictivas, por requerirlo el restablecimiento del orden público.*

——, Decree 3398 of 1965. *Por el cual se organiza la defensa nacional.*

Republic of Liberia, *Poverty Reduction Strategy*, April 2008, available at <www.supportliberia.com/assets/95/chapter8.pdf>.

Sierra Leone Truth and Reconciliation Commission, *Witness to Truth* (2004) at <www.sierra-leone.org/TRCDocuments.html>.

Special Court Agreement 2002, Ratification Act, 2002 Supplement to *Sierra Leone Gazette*, vol. CXXX, No. II (7 March 2002).

Special Court for Sierra Leone, *Prosecutor v Issa Hassan Sesay, Morris Kallon and Augustine Gbao*, Case No. SCSL-04-15-A (26 October 2009).

——, *Prosecutor v Issa Hassan Sesay, Morris Kallon and Augustine Gbao*, Case No. SCSL-04-15-T (2 March 2009).

Special Tribunal for Lebanon, *Appointment of Defence Counsel. Rule 58 of the Rules of Procedure and Evidence*, Case No. CH/PTJ/2010/01 (26 April 2010).

Special Tribunal for Lebanon, *Order Assigning Matter to Pre-Trial Judge*, Case No. CH/PRES/2010/01 (15 April 2010).

——, *Order Regarding the Detention of Persons Detained in Lebanon in Connection with the Case of the Attack against Prime Minister Rafiq Hariri and Others*, Case No. CH/PTJ/2009/06 (29 April 2009), reproduced in *International Legal Materials*, vol. 48 (April–June 2009), pp. 1152–60.

The Constitution of Lebanon (1926, as amended 1990), available at <www.servat.unibe.ch/icl/le00000_.html#A095>, accessed 12 December 2009.

Uganda Human Rights Commission, "11th Annual Report of the Uganda Human Rights Commission to the Parliament of the Republic of Uganda" (Kampala: UHRC, 2008).

UN Commission on Human Rights, "Study on the Right to the Truth, Report of the Office of the United Nations High Commissioner for Human Rights, 8 February 2006," UN Doc E/CN.4/2006/91.

UN, Report of the Group of Experts for Cambodia Established Pursuant to General Assembly Resolution 52/135, UN Doc. A/53/850, 16 March 1999.

UNDP, *Facing the Past and Access to Justice From a Public Perspective* (UNDP in BiH, Sarajevo, 2011), available at <www.undp.ba/index.aspx?PID=36&rid=127>, accessed 6 September 2011.

——, *Transitional Justice Guidebook for Bosnia and Herzegovina. Executive Summary* (UNDP in BiH, Sarajevo, June 2009), available at <www.undp.ba/index.aspx?PID=36&rid=88>, accessed 6 September 2011.

——, *Justice and Truth in BiH: Public Perceptions* (UNDP in BiH, Sarajevo, 2006), pp. 15–16, available at <www.undp.ba/index.aspx?PID=36&rid=50>, accessed 6 September 2011.

——, *Practice Note: Disarmament, Demobilization and Reintegration of Ex-Combatants* (New York: UNDP, 2005).

UNDP and Oxford Research International, *The Silent Majority Speaks* (2007), available at <www.undp.ba/upload/News/The%20Silent%20Majoriti%20Speaks%20Report.pdf>, accessed 19 August 2011.

United Nations, *The Rule of Law and Transitional Justice in Conflict and Post-Conflict Societies. Report of the Secretary-General*, UN Doc. S/2011/634 (12 October 2011).

——, *Report of the Peacebuilding Commission on its Fourth Session*, UN Doc. A/65/701-S/2011/41 (28 January 2011).

——, *Review of the United Nations Peacebuilding Architecture*, UN Doc. A/64/868-S/2010/393 (21 July 2010).

——, *Guidance Note of the Secretary-General, United Nations Approach to Transitional Justice* (March 2010), available at <www.unrol.org/files/TJ_Guidance_Note_March_2010FINAL.pdf>.

——, *Report of the Secretary-General on Peacebuilding in the Immediate Aftermath of Conflict*, UN Doc. A/63/881-S/2009/304 (New York: UN, 2009).

——, *Review of Progress in the Implementation of the Strategic Framework for Peacebuilding in Burundi*, UN Doc. PBC/2/BDI/10 (9 July 2008).

——, *Fifteenth Progress Report of the Secretary-General on the United Nations Mission in Liberia*, UN Doc. S/2007/479 (20 September 2007).

——, *Strategic Framework for Peacebuilding in Burundi*, UN Doc. PBC/1/BDI/4 (22 June 2007).

——, Security Council Resolution 1757, UN Doc. S/RES/1757 (30 May 2007).

——, *Integrated Disarmament, Demobilization, and Reintegration Standards* (2006), available at <www.unddr.org/iddrs>.

——, *Disarmament, Demobilization and Reintegration: Report of the Secretary General*, UN Doc. A/60/705 (New York: UN, 2006).

——, *United Nations Integrated Disarmament, Demobilization, and Reintegration Standards* (2006), available at <www.unddr.org/iddrs/framework.php>.

——, Security Council Resolution 1664, UN Doc. S/RES/1664 (29 March 2006).

——, General Assembly Resolution 60/180, UN Doc. A/RES/60/180 (30 December 2005).

——, Security Council Resolution 1645, UN Doc. S/RES/1645 (20 December 2005).

——, *2005 World Summit Outcome*, UN Doc. A/Res/61 (24 October 2005).

——, *Report of the International Independent Investigation Commission Established Pursuant to Security Council Resolution 1595*, UN Doc. S/2005/662 (20 October 2005).

——, Security Council Resolution 1595, UN Doc. S/RES/1595 (7 April 2005).

——, *Draft Set of Principles To Combat Impunity* (latest update), UN Doc. E/CN.4/2005/102/Add.1 (8 February 2005).

——, *Report of the High-Level Panel on Threats, Challenges and Change*, UN Doc. A/59/565 (2 December 2004).

——, *The Rule of Law and Transitional Justice in Conflict and Post-Conflict Societies: Report of the Secretary-General*, UN Doc. S/2004/616 (23 August 2004).

——, General Assembly Resolution 52/135, *Situation of Human Rights in Cambodia*, UN Doc. A/RES/52/135 (12 December 1999).

——, Security Council Resolution 1270, UN Doc. S/RES/1270 (22 October 1999).

——, *Peace Agreement Between the Government of Sierra Leone and the Revolutionary United Front of Sierra Leone*, UN Doc S/1999/777.

——, Security Council Resolution 827, UN Doc. S/RES/827 (25 May 1993).

——, *An Agenda for Peace, Preventive Diplomacy, Peacemaking and Peace-Keeping*, UN Doc. A/47/277 – S/24111 (17 June 1992).

United Nations Department of Peacekeeping Operations, *Second Generation Disarmament, Demobilization and Reintegration Practices in Peace Operations* (New York: DPKO, 2010).

United Nations Department of Public Information, *Acuerdo de Santa Fé de Ralito para Contribuir a la Paz en Colombia* (2003). Agreements on a comprehensive political settlement of the Cambodia conflict, Paris, 23 October 1991, January 1992.

United Nations Economic and Social Council, "Basic Principles on the Use of Restorative Justice Programmes in Criminal Matters," UN Doc. E/CN.15/2002/5/Add.1 (2002).

United Nations High Commission on Human Rights, "Report of the United Nations High Commissioner for Human Rights on the Mission Undertaken by Her Office, Pursuant to Commission Resolution 2000/60, To Assess the Situation on the Ground With Regard to the Abduction of Children from Northern Uganda," E/CN.4/2002/86 (Geneva: 9 November 2001).

United Nations Office on Drugs and Crime, *Handbook on Restorative Justice Programmes* (Vienna: United Nations, 2006).

United Nations Peacebuilding Fund, *Support to the Implementation of the Reparations Programme as Part of the Recommendations of the Truth and Reconciliation Commission*, project document (2008), available at <www.unpbf.org/sierraleone/sierraleone-projects.shtml>.

US Department of State, "Uganda: Country Report on Human Rights Practices 2008" (Washington, DC: 25 February 2009), available at <www.state.gov/g/drl/rls/hrrpt/2008/af/119030.htm>, accessed 7 February 2010.

Waki Commission, *Report of the Commission of Inquiry into Post-Election Violence* (Nairobi: October 2008).

World Bank, *Greater Great Lakes Regional Strategy for Demobilization and Reintegration* (Washington, DC: World Bank, 2002).

——, *Bosnia and Herzegovina, Emergency Demobilization and Reintegration Project*, Report No. T-6947-BI1, Technical Annex, 28 June 1996, available at <www-wds.worldbank.org/external/default/main?pagePK=64193027&piPK=64187937&theSitePK=523679&menuPK=64187510&searchMenuPK=64187283&theSitePK=523679&entityID=000009265_3961214125242&searchMenuPK=64187283&theSitePK=523679>, accessed 19 August 2011.

Index

Taylor & Francis

eBooks

FOR LIBRARIES

ORDER YOUR FREE 30 DAY INSTITUTIONAL TRIAL TODAY!

Over 22,000 eBook titles in the Humanities, Social Sciences, STM and Law from some of the world's leading imprints.

Choose from a range of subject packages or create your own!

Benefits for you

- Free MARC records
- COUNTER-compliant usage statistics
- Flexible purchase and pricing options

Benefits for your user

- Off-site, anytime access via Athens or referring URL
- Print or copy pages or chapters
- Full content search
- Bookmark, highlight and annotate text
- Access to thousands of pages of quality research at the click of a button

For more information, pricing enquiries or to order a free trial, contact your local online sales team.

UK and Rest of World: **online.sales@tandf.co.uk**

US, Canada and Latin America:
e-reference@taylorandfrancis.com

www.ebooksubscriptions.com

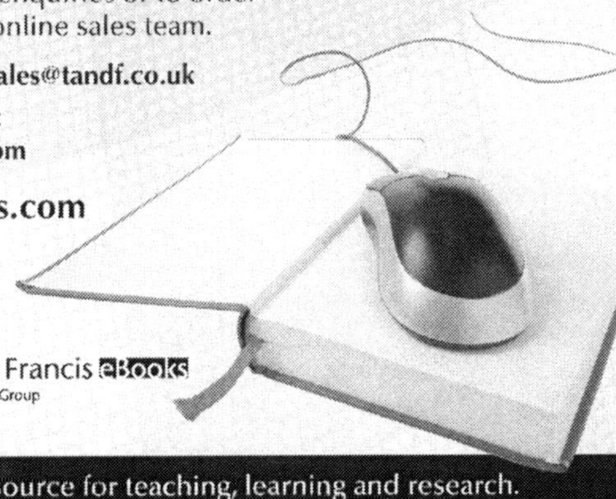

ALPSP Award for BEST eBOOK PUBLISHER 2009 Finalist

Taylor & Francis eBooks
Taylor & Francis Group

A flexible and dynamic resource for teaching, learning and research.